T0276742

IET SECURITY SERIES 01

Information Security

Also available:

Age Factors in Biometric Processing, M.C. Fairhurst (Editor)
978-1-84919-502-7
Iris and Periocular Biometrics, C. Rathgeb, C. Busch (Editors)
978-1-78561-168-1
Engineering Secure Internet of Things Systems, B. Aziz, A. Arenas, B. Crispo
978-1-78561-053-0
Mobile Biometrics, G. Guo, H. Wechsler (Editors)
978-1-78561-095-0
Data Security in Cloud Computing, V. Kumar, R. Ko, S. Chaisiri (Editors)
978-1-78561-220-6
User-Centric Privacy and Security in Biometrics, C. Vielhauer (Editor)
978-1-78561-207-7

Information Security
Foundations, technologies and applications

Edited by
Ali Ismail Awad and Michael Fairhurst

The Institution of Engineering and Technology

Published by The Institution of Engineering and Technology, London, United Kingdom

The Institution of Engineering and Technology is registered as a Charity in England & Wales (no. 211014) and Scotland (no. SC038698).

© The Institution of Engineering and Technology 2018

First published 2018

The Institution of Engineering and Technology
Michael Faraday House
Six Hills Way, Stevenage
Herts, SG1 2AY, United Kingdom

www.theiet.org

British Library Cataloguing in Publication Data
A catalogue record for this product is available from the British Library

ISBN 978-1-84919-974-2 (hardback)
ISBN 978-1-84919-976-6 (PDF)

Typeset in India by MPS Limited

Contents

Part I

Theories and foundations

Chapter 1

Introduction to information security foundations and applications

Ali Ismail Awad[1,2]

1.1 Background

Information security has extended to include several research directions like user authentication and authorization, network security, hardware security, software security, and data cryptography. Information security has become a crucial need for protecting almost all information transaction applications. Security is considered as an important science discipline whose many multifaceted complexities deserve the synergy of the computer science and engineering communities.

Recently, due to the proliferation of Information and Communication Technologies, information security has started to cover emerging topics such as cloud computing security, smart cities' security and privacy, healthcare and telemedicine, the Internet-of-Things (IoT) security [1], the Internet-of-Vehicles security, and several types of wireless sensor networks security [2,3]. In addition, information security has extended further to cover not only technical security problems but also social and organizational security challenges [4,5].

Traditional systems' development approaches were focusing on the system's usability where security was left to the last stage with less priority. However, the new design approaches consider security-in-design process where security is considered at the early phase of the design process. The new designed systems should be well protected against the available security attacks. Having new systems such as IoT or healthcare without enough security may lead to a leakage of sensitive data and, in some cases, life threatening situations.

Taking the social aspect into account, security education is a vital need for both practitioners and system users [6]. Users' misbehaviour due to a lack of security knowledge is the weakest point in the system security chain. The users' misbehaviour is considered as a security vulnerability that may be exploited for launching security attacks. A successful security attack such as distributed denial-of-service attack will impose incident recovery cost in addition to the downtime cost.

[1]Department of Computer Science, Electrical and Space Engineering, Luleå University of Technology, Sweden
[2]Faculty of Engineering, Al Azhar University, Qena, Egypt

These are just some representative examples to illustrate the diversity and importance of a broad understanding of security issues across the wide range of information processing tasks encountered in the modern world. While, naturally, a single book cannot cover every relevant technique and security approach which can be deployed, or present an example of every application for which a detailed security analysis is important in a practical environment, by introducing carefully selected topics and, especially, by inviting key practitioners in the field to present and discuss them, it is possible to provide both a thorough overview of the field and an appreciation of the fundamentals of this increasingly important and influential area.

As the following section will explain, the book is split between a discussion of some principles and fundamentals which underpin the study of information security in all its diversity, and the working out of these principles in practice, giving an insight into practical system implementation in a range of different application domains and deploying a variety of technologies.

1.2   The structure of this book

This book comes in two main sections: Theories and Foundations and Technologies and Applications. The first section offers theoretical foundations to different information security aspects; however, the second section deals with many technologies and applications from a technical perspective. The general philosophy behind the book is to present balanced materials from the theoretical and the technical viewpoints. In the following pages, we shed light on the contents of the book.

1.2.1   Part I: Theories and foundations

This part is mainly dedicated to the foundations and the theoretical concepts of information security in different domains. The part has eight chapters in total, including this chapter, Chapter 1. A brief summary of each chapter in this part is as follows:

Chapter 2, 'Information security foundation, theories and future vision', presents a solid overview on information security theories and foundations with a focus on information security needs and applications. Several information security-related aspects such as information assurance, cybersecurity, and information systems security are highlighted. Information security confidentiality, integrity, and availability and other information security key definitions are described throughout this chapter according to International Organization for Standardization and National Institute of Standards and Technology [7]. Security vulnerabilities and threat protection approaches are also discussed as part of this chapter [8]. An overview of the information security future vision is presented as the last section at the end of the chapter.

Chapter 3, 'Information systems security issues in the context of developing countries', takes information systems security to the developing countries' dimension [9,10]. This review presented throughout this chapter is relevant for understanding the current state of information systems security in the developing countries. The chapter finds security vulnerabilities and risks increase together with the technology prolif-eration. The chapter identifies the reasons behind the lack of information systems security deployments in the developing countries from non-technical perspectives. Issues such as education, legalization, policies, and cultures are discussed to empha-size their impacts on information systems security applications within the developing counties' framework.

Chapter 4, 'Biometric systems, modalities and attacks', focuses on biometrics as science for human identification using some physiological or behavioural char-acteristics [11]. Biometrics is considered as an emerging technology for providing access control for civilian and forensic applications [12,13]. The chapter presents an overview of the biometric system's components and attributes, biometric modalities, and the required features or criteria for selection of biometric modalities. The perfor-mance evaluation parameters for a generic biometric system such as false match rate and false non-match rate are offered [14]. Data fusion techniques and performance evaluation of multi-model biometric systems are described as well [15]. Biometric standardizations are well documented at the end of this chapter.

Chapter 5, 'Foundation of healthcare cybersecurity', studies healthcare as an area where information and cybersecurity play a crucial role due to the sensitivity of hosted or exchanged patients' information [16,17]. The chapter offers a solid foundation of the healthcare security and privacy considerations. Major components of generic healthcare systems and the associated security and privacy requirements are presented within the contents of the chapter. Security threats' landscape and vulnerabilities exploited for healthcare cyberattacks are identified and discussed in addition to several attack types [18]. Tools for defending and mitigating security attacks are discussed and reported at the end of the study [19].

Chapter 6, 'Security challenges and solutions for e-business', connects e-business domain to information security by studying the common security attacks, threats, and countermeasures in e-business [20,21]. The chapter discusses new attacks mitiga-tion approaches as of biometrics authentication [22–24], attacks identification using machine learning and data mining mechanisms, blockchains for peer-to-peer secu-rity accomplishment, security modelling, and security-as-a-service [25]. Apart from the technical concepts, the chapter sheds light on the social dimension by studying the impact of information security education and user involvement on defending the security attacks on e-business [26]. The chapter is also well connected to biometric systems described in Chapter 4.

Chapter 7, 'Recent security issues in Big Data: from past to the future of informa-tion systems', bridges both information security and Big Data by presenting a study on the trendy security issues in Big Data [27,28]. The chapter highlights information security concepts such as privacy, integrity, availability, and confidentiality on the Big Data discipline. Advanced Big-Data-related topics like Cloud Security Alliance, security standards in Big Data, and Information Systems Audit and Control Associ-ation are also described [29]. Finally, the chapter explains a use case on Big-Data security.

Chapter 8, 'Recent advances in unconstrained face recognition', goes a step further in biometric technology by reporting the recent trends and advances in face recognition systems in unconstrained environments [30,31]. In two separate sections, the chapter presents comprehensive information on face representation methods and the available benchmark databases for face recognition [32,33]. The chapter explains the metric learning approaches and pose-invariant face recognition challenges as advanced topics in the face recognition domain. Performance evaluation of face recognition and open issues for future consideration are mentioned at the end of this chapter. The foundation information in this chapter is well connected to the previous chapters such as Chapters 4 and 6.

1.2.2   Part II: Technologies and applications

This part of the book covers specific technologies and applications of information security. A broad scope of technical topics is covered in eight chapters contained in this part. A brief summary of each chapter is explained in the following paragraphs:

Chapter 9, 'Hardware security: side-channel attacks and hardware Trojans', addresses relevant topics related to hardware security with a focus on side-channel attacks [34]. The chapter starts with a good preliminary discussion of the significance of hardware security in comparison to the software one. Several side-channel attacks such as power analysis attack, fault analysis attack, and timing analysis attack are presented [35]. A countermeasure for every mentioned attack is described in this chapter. The chapter also clarifies the hardware design and fabrication processes in connection to the security considerations. A separate section is devoted for malicious hardware Trojans detection, classification, and protection at the end of the study [36].

Chapter 10, 'Cybersecurity: timeline malware analysis and classification', focuses on cybersecurity challenges and tackles the problems associated with the proliferation of malware types as serious threats in information systems security [37,38]. A comprehensive malware analysis and classification are presented as preliminary work. The chapter presents a cumulative timeline analysis approach for malware detection that achieves high accuracy over an extended time period. The chapter offers very rich information on malware collection, analysis, and classification with a great focus on presenting different algorithms and technical explanations [39].

Chapter 11, 'Recent trends in the cryptanalysis of block ciphers', presents cryptanalysis of block ciphers as a challenge in data cryptography research domain. The chapter starts with an interesting overview of cryptography and moves forward to focus on symmetric key cryptographic primitives [40,41]. Block cipher definitions, design, and security are explained in separate sections. Attacks on block ciphers such as linear cryptanalysis, differential cryptanalysis, and integral cryptanalysis are intensively covered within the chapter [42,43]. The developments in the conventional block cipher attacks along with the newly surfaced ones are presented. The chapter concludes that block ciphers and their security are still hot research topics.

Chapter 12, 'Image provenance inference through content-based device fingerprint analysis', focuses on digital forensics as a relevant domain of information security. It offers a technical study on image provenance inference that aims to determine the source of a digital image. The chapter highlights the current challenges in image provenance [44,45], and it goes further by introducing different intrinsic device fingerprints and their applications in image provenance inference. The chapter ends by a comprehensive outlook to the future of image provenance inferences in the light of Internet development and Big-Data proliferation [46].

Chapter 13, 'EEG-based biometrics for person identification and continuous authentication', offers a study of the usage of electroencephalogram (EEG) signals as a biometric identifier for human identification and authentication [47]. The chapter offers detailed descriptions on human brain, types of EEG signals, EEG sensing techniques and EEG analysis [48,49]. A separate section is devoted for EEG signals as a biometric trait, including the selection criteria and EEG feature extraction [50]. Human continuous authentication, using EEG in multi-modal biometric systems, and the current challenges of EEG-related research are explained at the end of this chapter [51]. The chapter is well connected with Chapters 4, 6, and 8.

Chapter 14, 'Data security and privacy in the Internet-of-Things', bridges information security with the IoT paradigm [52]. Nowadays, IoT model has plenty of applications in many domains, including healthcare, smart cities, smart homes, and automation and controls [53]. The chapter presents the IoT infrastructure and the emerging security risks from deploying IoT. Security solutions and countermeasures for IoT systems are studied and discussed throughout the chapter. The chapter tackles a social security aspect by connecting human factors with other aspects in IoT security and privacy [54]. The chapter has a good balance between technical and conceptual aspects, and it is well connected to Big-Data security in Chapter 7.

Chapter 15, 'Information security algorithm on embedded hardware', presents a study on the deployment of information security algorithms on embedded hardware [55,56]. The chapter opens by a general introduction and moves forward to the classification of embedded systems [57]. The chapter explains the security requirements and deployment mechanisms for embedded hardware with a little focus on hardware security vulnerabilities [58]. This part of the chapter is well connected with Chapter 9 about side-channel attacks. The chapter closes by discussing the implementation strategies of a security algorithm on embedded hardware. This chapter is considered as a reference point for future applications of information security algorithms on different types of embedded hardware.

References

[1] King J, and Awad AI. 'A distributed security mechanism for resource-constrained IoT devices'. *Informatica (Slovenia)*. 2016;40(1):133–143.
[2] Grzenda M, Furtak J, Legierski J, and Awad AI. Network Architectures, Security, and Applications: An Introduction. Grzenda M, Awad AI, Furtak J, and Legierski J, editors. Advances in Network Systems : Architectures, Security, and Applications. Cham: Springer International Publishing; 2017. pp. 1–10. Available from: https://doi.org/10.1007/978-3-319-44354-6_1.
[3] Grzenda M, Awad AI, Furtak J, and Legierski J. *Advances in Network Systems: Architectures, Security, and Applications*. Advances in Intelligent Systems and Computing; Springer International Publishing Switzerland; 2017.

[4]   Charif B, and Awad AI. Business and Government Organizations' Adoption of Cloud Computing. Corchado E, Lozano JA, Quintián H, and Yin H, editors. Intelligent Data Engineering and Automated Learning – IDEAL 2014: 15th International Conference, Salamanca, Spain, September 10–12, 2014. Proceedings. Cham: Springer International Publishing; 2014. pp. 492–501. Available from: https://doi.org/10.1007/978-3-319-10840-7_59.

[5]   Charif B, and Awad AI. 'Towards smooth organisational adoption of cloud computing a customer-provider security adaptation'. *Computer Fraud & Security*. 2016;2016(2):7–15. Available from: http://dx.doi.org/10.1016/S1361-3723(16)30016-1.

[6]   Okoh E, Makame MH, and Awad AI. 'Toward online education for fingerprint recognition: A proof-of-concept web platform'. *Information Security Journal: A Global Perspective*. 2017;26(4):186–197. Available from: http://dx.doi.org/10.1080/19393555.2017.1329462.

[7]   Kissel R, Kissel R, Blank R, and Secretary A. 'Glossary of key information security terms'. NIST Interagency Reports NIST IR 7298 Revision 1, National Institute of Standards and Technology; 2011.

[8]   McGuire MR, and Holt TJ. *The Routledge Handbook of Technology, Crime and Justice*. Routledge International Handbooks. Routledge; UK, 2017.

[9]   Kim D, and Solomon MG. *Fundamentals of Information Systems Security*. Information Systems Security & Assurance Series. Jones & Bartlett Learning; 2010.

[10] Bwalya KJ, and Mutula S. 'A conceptual framework for e-government development in resource-constrained countries'. *Information Development*. 2016;32(4):1183–1198. Available from: http://dx.doi.org/10.1177/0266666915593786.

[11] Jain AK, Ross AA, and Nandakumar K. *Introduction to Biometrics*. 1st ed. Springer US; 2011.

[12] Unar JA, Seng WC, and Abbasi A. 'A review of biometric technology along with trends and prospects'. *Pattern Recognition*. 2014;47(8):2673–2688.

[13] Awad AI, and Hassanien AE. Impact of Some Biometric Modalities on Forensic Science. Muda AK, Choo YH, Abraham A, and N Srihari S, editors. Computational Intelligence in Digital Forensics: Forensic Investigation and Applications. Cham: Springer International Publishing; 2014. pp. 47–62. Available from: https://doi.org/10.1007/978-3-319-05885-6_3.

[14] Dunstone T, and Yager N. *Biometric System and Data Analysis: Design, Evaluation, and Data Mining*. 1st ed. Springer US; 2008.

[15] Gavrilova ML, and Monwar M. *Multimodal Biometrics and Intelligent Image Processing for Security Systems*. 1st ed. Hershey, PA, USA: IGI Global; 2013.

[16] Dong N, Jonker H, and Pang J. Formal Analysis of Privacy in an eHealth Protocol. Foresti S, Yung M, and Martinelli F, editors. Computer Security – ESORICS 2012: 17th European Symposium on Research in Computer Security, Pisa, Italy, September 10–12, 2012. Proceedings. Berlin, Heidelberg: Springer Berlin Heidelberg; 2012. pp. 325–342. Available from: https://doi.org/ 10.1007/978-3-642-33167-1_19.

[17]   Mansfield-Devine S. 'Your life in your hands: The security issues with healthcare apps'. *Network Security*. 2016;2016(4):14–18.

[18]   York TW, and MacAlister D. *Hospital and Healthcare Security*. 6th ed. Butterworth-Heinemann; 2015.

[19]   Okoh E, and Awad AI. Biometrics Applications in e-Health Security: A Preliminary Survey. Yin X, Ho K, Zeng D, Aickelin U, Zhou R, and Wang H, editors. Health Information Science: 4th International Conference, HIS 2015, Melbourne, Australia, May 28–30, 2015, Proceedings. Cham: Springer International Publishing; 2015. pp. 92–103. Available from: https://doi.org/10.1007/978-3-319-19156-0_10.

[20]   Hinde S. 'Privacy and security the drivers for growth of E-commerce'. *Computers & Security*. 1998;17(6):475–478. Available from: http://dx.doi.org/10.1016/S0167-4048(98)80069-2.

[21]   Nabi F. 'Secure business application logic for e-commerce systems'. *Computers & Security*. 2005;24(3):208–217. Available from: http://dx.doi.org/10.1016/j.cose.2004.08.008.

[22]   Zhang D, and Yu L. *Payment Technologies for E-commerce*. New York, NY, USA: Springer-Verlag New York, Inc.; 2003. pp. 71–94.

[23]   Awad AI, and Baba K. 'Evaluation of a Fingerprint Identification Algorithm with SIFT Features'. *Proceedings of the 3rd 2012 IIAI International Conference on Advanced Applied Informatics*. Fukuoka, Japan: IEEE; 2012. pp. 129–132.

[24]   Egawa S, Awad AI, and Baba K. Evaluation of Acceleration Algorithm for Biometric Identification. Benlamri R, editor. Networked Digital Technologies. Vol. 294 of Communications in Computer and Information Science. Berlin, Heidelberg: Springer; 2012. pp. 231–242. Available from: http://dx.doi.org/10.1007/978-3-642-30567-2_19.

[25]   Zheng Q, Li S, Han Y, Dong J, Yan L, and Qin J. Security Technologies in E-commerce. Zheng Q, editor. Introduction to E-commerce. Berlin, Heidelberg: Springer, Berlin, Heidelberg; 2009. pp. 135–168. Available from: https://doi.org/10.1007/978-3-540-49645-8_4.

[26]   Kennedy SE. 'The pathway to security mitigating user negligence'. *Information and Computer Security*. 2016;24(3):255–264. Available from: https://doi.org/10.1108/ICS-10-2014-0065.

[27]   Hashem IAT, Yaqoob I, Anuar NB, Mokhtar S, Gani A, and Khan SU. 'The rise of "big data" on cloud computing: Review and open research issues'. *Information Systems*. 2015;47:98–115. Available from: http://dx.doi.org/10.1016/j.is.2014.07.006.

[28]   Bertino E. 'Big Data – Security and Privacy'. *2015 IEEE International Congress on Big Data*; 2015. pp. 757–761.

[29]   Weber AS. 'Suggested legal framework for student data privacy in the age of big data and smart devices'. *Frontiers in Artificial Intelligence and Applications*. 2014;262:669–678.

[30]   Zeng Z, Pantic M, Roisman GI, and Huang TS. 'A survey of affect recognition methods: Audio, visual, and spontaneous expressions'. *IEEE Transactions on Pattern Analysis and Machine Intelligence*. 2009;31(1):39–58.

[31]   Wolf L, Hassner T, and Maoz I. 'Face recognition in unconstrained videos with matched background similarity'. *Proceedings of IEEE International Conference on Computer Vision and Pattern Recognition.* (CVPR'11); 2011. pp. 529–534.

[32]   Cao Q, Ying Y, and Li P. 'Similarity Metric Learning for Face Recognition'. *2013 IEEE International Conference on Computer Vision*; 2013. pp. 2408–2415.

[33]   Sun Y, Wang X, and Tang X. 'Deep Learning Face Representation from Predicting 10,000 Classes'. *Proceedings of the 2014 IEEE Conference on Computer Vision and Pattern Recognition.* (CVPR'14). Washington, DC, USA: IEEE Computer Society; 2014. pp. 1891–1898. Available from: http://dx.doi.org/10.1109/CVPR.2014.244.

[34]   Tehranipoor M, and Wang C. *Introduction to Hardware Security and Trust.* Springer-Verlag New York; 2011.

[35]   Lumbiarres-Lopez R, Lopez-Garcia M, and Canto-Navarro E. 'Hardware architecture implemented on FPGA for protecting cryptographic keys against side-channel attacks'. *IEEE Transactions on Dependable and Secure Computing.* 2017;In Press(99):1–1. DOI: https://doi.org/10.1109/TDSC.2016.2610966

[36]   Tehranipoor M, and Koushanfar F. 'A survey of hardware Trojan taxonomy and detection'. *IEEE Design Test of Computers.* 2010 January;27(1):10–25.

[37]   Singer PW, and Friedman A. *Cybersecurity and Cyberwar: What Everyone Needs to Know®.* Oxford University Press; UK, 2013.

[38]   Lee N. *Counterterrorism and Cybersecurity: Total Information Awareness.* Springer International Publishing Switzerland; 2015.

[39]   Islam R, Tian R, Batten LM, and Versteeg S. 'Classification of malware based on integrated static and dynamic features'. *Journal of Network and Computer Applications.* 2013;36(2):646–656. Available from: http://dx.doi.org/10.1016/j.jnca.2012.10.004.

[40]   Menezes AJ, Vanstone SA, and Oorschot PCV. *Handbook of Applied Cryptography.* 1st ed. Boca Raton, FL: CRC Press, Inc.; 1996.

[41]   Tilborg HCA, and Jajodia S. *Encyclopedia of Cryptography and Security.* 2nd ed. Springer US; 2011.

[42]   Kim J, Hong S, and Lim J. 'Impossible differential cryptanalysis using matrix method'. *Discrete Mathematics.* 2010;310(5):988–1002. Available from: http://dx.doi.org/10.1016/j.disc.2009.10.019.

[43]   Peeters E. *Side-Channel Cryptanalysis: A Brief Survey.* New York, NY: Springer New York; 2013. pp. 11–19. Available from: https://doi.org/10.1007/978-1-4614-6783-0_2.

[44]   Zhu X, Ho ATS, and Marziliano P. 'A new semi-fragile image watermarking with robust tampering restoration using irregular sampling'. *Signal Processing: Image Communication.* 2007;22(5):515–528. Available from: http://dx.doi.org/10.1016/j.image.2007.03.004.

[45]   Kee E, Johnson MK, and Farid H. 'Digital image authentication from JPEG headers'. *IEEE Transactions on Information Forensics and Security.* 2011 September;6(3):1066–1075.

[46] Lin X, and Li CT. 'Large-scale image clustering based on camera finger-prints'. *IEEE Transactions on Information Forensics and Security*. 2017 April;12(4):793–808.

[47] Armstrong BC, Ruiz-Blondet MV, Khalifian N, Kurtz KJ, Jin Z, and Las-zlo S. 'Brainprint: Assessing the uniqueness, collectability, and permanence of a novel method for ERP biometrics'. *Neurocomputing*. 2015;166:59–67. Available from: http://dx.doi.org/10.1016/j.neucom.2015.04.025.

[48] Logothetis NK, Pauls J, Augath M, Trinath T, and Oeltermann A. 'Neu-rophysiological investigation of the basis of the fMRI signal'. *Nature*. 2001;412(6843):150.

[49] Tadel F, Baillet S, Mosher JC, Pantazis D, and Leahy RM. 'Brainstorm: A user-friendly application for MEG/EEG analysis'. *Intell Neuroscience*. 2011;2011:8:1–8:13. Available from: http://dx.doi.org/10.1155/2011/879716.

[50] He C, and Wang J. 'An independent component analysis (ICA) based approach for EEG person authentication'. *2009 3rd International Conference on Bioinformatics and Biomedical Engineering*; 2009. pp. 1–4.

[51] Wang M, Abbass HA, and Hu J. 'Continuous authentication using EEG and face images for trusted autonomous systems'. *2016 14th Annual Conference on Privacy, Security and Trust (PST)*; 2016. pp. 368–375.

[52] Arias O, Wurm J, Hoang K, and Jin Y. 'Privacy and security in internet of things and wearable devices'. *IEEE Transactions on Multi-Scale Computing Systems*. 2015 April;1(2):99–109.

[53] Wilson DH, Atkeson C. Gellersen HW, Want R, and Schmidt A, editors. Simultaneous Tracking and Activity Recognition (STAR) Using Many Anony-mous, Binary Sensors. Berlin, Heidelberg: Springer Berlin Heidelberg; 2005. pp. 62–79. Available from: https://doi.org/10.1007/11428572_5.

[54] Li N, Zhang N, Das SK, and Thuraisingham B. 'Privacy preservation in wire-less sensor networks: A state-of-the-art survey'. *Ad Hoc Networks*. 2009;7(8): 1501–1514.

[55] Rakers P, Connell L, Collins T, and Russell D. 'Secure contactless smart-card ASIC with DPA protection'. *IEEE Journal of Solid-State Circuits*. 2001 March;36(3):559–565.

[56] Fathy A, Tarrad IF, Hamed HFA, and Awad AI. Advanced Encryption Standard Algorithm: Issues and Implementation Aspects. Hassanien AE, Salem ABM, Ramadan R, and Kim Th, editors. Advanced Machine Learning Technologies and Applications: First International Conference, AMLTA 2012, Cairo, Egypt, December 8–10, 2012. Proceedings. Berlin, Heidelberg: Springer Berlin Heidelberg; 2012. pp. 516–523. Available from: https://doi.org/10.1007/978-3-642-35326-0_51.

[57] Zhang J, and Qu G. 'A survey on security and trust of FPGA-based sys-tems'. *2014 International Conference on Field-Programmable Technology (FPT)*; 2014. pp. 147–152.

[58] Elfatah AFA, Tarrad IF, Awad AI, and Hamed HFA. 'Optimized hardware implementation of the advanced encryption standard algorithm'. *2013 8th International Conference on Computer Engineering Systems (ICCES)*; 2013. pp. 197–201.

Chapter 2
Information security foundation, theories and future vision

Steven Furnell[1]

Information security is an essential aspect of modern life for organisations and individuals using information technology (IT) systems. These systems, and more particularly the information that they store and share, require protection against a range of accidental and deliberate threats, which in turn demand a variety of security controls. However, while technology is implicitly involved, an important point to appreciate about information security is the broad range of considerations that it encompasses, both within and beyond the IT domain.

As its name suggests, the aim of this chapter is to establish some of the baseline principles and to show the breadth of the topic. Other chapters will then build upon this by exploring at least some of the issues in further depth. As will become apparent, there is not a single and simple way to look at security that easily captures all the various dimensions of interest. As such, much of this chapter is devoted to considering the issue from different angles, with the intention that by doing so a sufficiently comprehensive picture will ultimately have been presented to set the scene for the various discussions in later chapters.

2.1 Defining the problem

To begin our discussion, it makes sense to start by looking at what we mean by information security. At the core it is fundamentally about protecting information, which by implication also means protecting the devices and services that store and use it. It is notable that this book has eschewed the current trend of morphing the term into *cyber security* (or *cybersecurity* – without a space – if we adopt the US naming convention), but if we take a look at some of the definitions from sources such as standards bodies it becomes clear that both terms are now commonplace. Moreover, there is commonality of the definitions of other terms, such as Information Assurance.

---

[1]Centre for Security, Communications and Network Research, University of Plymouth, UK

Cybersecurity is the collection of tools, policies, security concepts, security safeguards, guidelines, risk management approaches, actions, training, best practices, assurance and technologies that can be used to protect the cyber environment and organization and user's assets. Organization and user's assets include connected computing devices, personnel, infrastructure, applications, services, telecommunications systems and the totality of transmitted and/or stored information in the cyber environment. Cybersecurity strives to ensure the attainment and maintenance of the security properties of the organization and user's assets against relevant security risks in the cyber environment. The general security objectives comprise the following:

- Availability
- Integrity, which may include authenticity and non-repudiation
- Confidentiality'. [1]

International Telecommunication Union
ITU-T X.1205, Overview of Cybersecurity, 2008

Cybersecurity: The process of protecting information by preventing, detecting, and responding to attacks. [2]

National Institute of Standards and Technology (USA)
Framework for Improving Critical Infrastructure Cybersecurity, 2014

Information assurance: Measures that protect and defend information and information systems by ensuring their availability, integrity, authentication, confidentiality, and non-repudiation. These measures include provision for restoration of information systems by incorporating protection, detection, and reaction capabilities. [3]

Committee on National Security Systems (USA)
National Information Assurance Glossary, 2010

Information security: Preservation of confidentiality, integrity and availability of information. In addition, other properties, such as authenticity, accountability, non-repudiation, and reliability can also be involved. [4]

International Organization for Standardization
ISO/IEC 27000 – Overview and Vocabulary, 2016

Security of network and information systems means the ability of network and information systems to resist, at a given level of confidence, any action that compromises the availability, authenticity, integrity or confidentiality of stored or transmitted or processed data or the related services offered by, or accessible via, those network and information systems. [5]

European Union
Directive on Security of Network and Information Systems, 2016

In considering these definitions, it is relevant to observe the varying aspects that they encompass. Some talk about what security involves (e.g. the types of controls), some about why it is needed (e.g. preventing attacks) and others about the principles it seeks to maintain. As such, all are actually correct, and this already starts to evidence the earlier claim that the true breadth of security is not easy to capture in a single statement.

Having observed that similar descriptions are being used to define different names (cyber security, information security, information assurance), it is worth briefly pausing to consider any significance here. Looking at this set, it is clearly difficult to pick a real distinction between what is meant by information security and what is regarded as cyber security. Indeed, looking at the National Institute of Standards and Technology (NIST) definition, we can see that cybersecurity is specifically defined in terms of 'protecting information', and so infosec would clearly work as a synonym here. So, is cybersecurity really something different? While there are some definitions that insist upon specific points of distinction, it is clear that many tend to view the terms synonymously.

If nothing else, the varying examples provide a clear indication that there is no single, universally agreed definition. Moreover, there can even be some variation amongst the same sources. For example, picking on the NIST definition again, it actually differs from a version presented a year earlier in NIST's Glossary of Key Information Security Terms, which defined it as 'the ability to protect or defend the use of cyberspace from cyber attacks' [6]. This in turn had actually been reproduced from the Committee on National Security Systems' National Information Assurance Glossary, which (as can be seen from the list given earlier) was consequently defining 'cybersecurity' as being something different from 'Information Assurance'. While all of this is intentionally labouring the point, it does serve to illustrate the difficulty that those actually wanting to protect their information can face when trying to understand the nature of the issue. Indeed, for those wanting an even more comprehensive discussion of the issue, a more detailed examination is presented in a related report from the European Network and Information Security Agency [7].

Regardless of whether the top-line label is cybersec, infosec, or IA, the definitions *do* serve to highlight that there are clearly some recurring themes in terms of the keywords Confidentiality, Integrity and Availability. These are fairly constant features within any security literature, and often referred to as the CIA Triad. Moreover, as the ISO definition identifies, there are a number of other keywords that often crop up, and so it is useful to get a sense of what these mean as well. However, perhaps unsurprisingly given the experience of defining information security itself, there is no single accepted definition. So, for good measure, Table 2.1 presents examples from both the ISO and NIST sources as an illustration (noting that in some cases the NIST document presents several definitions, each drawn from other sources, and that the ISO version, despite having mentioned 'accountability' in its list of additional keywords when defining security, does not actually define the term in its own glossary). Whichever definition you choose to subscribe to, these are terms that recur throughout the security field and will doubtless appear numerous times in the chapters that follow. Moreover, all of the security controls and countermeasures that we may introduce will ultimately be there in service of one of more of these goals.

Table 2.1   Definitions of key information security principles and properties

Term	ISO definition [4]	NIST definition(s) [6]
Confidentiality	• Property that information is not made available or disclosed to unauthorised individuals, entities or *processes*	• Preserving authorized restrictions on information access and disclosure, including means for protecting personal privacy and proprietary information. • The property that sensitive information is not disclosed to unauthorised individuals, entities or processes. • The property that information is not disclosed to system entities (users, processes, devices) unless they have been authorised to access the information.
Integrity	• Property of accuracy and completeness	• Guarding against improper information, modification or destruction, and includes ensuring information non-repudiation and authenticity. • The property that sensitive data has not been modified or deleted in an unauthorised and undetected manner. • The property whereby an entity has not been modified in an unauthorised manner.
Availability	• Property of being accessible and usable upon demand by an authorised entity	• Ensuring timely and reliable access to and use of information • The property of being accessible and usable upon demand by an authorised entity.
Authenticity	• Property that an entity is what it claims to be	• The property of being genuine and being able to be verified and trusted; confidence in the validity of a transmission, a message or message originator.
Accountability	–	• The security goal that generates the requirement for actions of an entity to be traced uniquely to that entity. This supports non-repudiation, deterrence, fault isolation, intrusion detection and prevention and after-action recovery and legal action. • Principle that an individual is entrusted to safeguard and control equipment, keying material and information and is answerable to proper authority for the loss or misuse of that equipment or information.

(Continues)

Table 2.1   Continued

Term	ISO definition [4]	NIST definition(s) [6]
Non-repudiation	• Ability to prove the occurrence of a claimed event or action and its originating entities	• Assurance that the sender of information is provided with proof of delivery and the recipient is provided with proof of the sender's identity, so neither can later deny having processed the information • Protection against an individual falsely denying having performed a particular action. Provides the capability to determine whether a given individual took a particular action such as creating information, sending a message, approving and information receiving a message. • Is the security service by which the entities involved in a communication cannot deny having participated. Specifically, the sending entity cannot deny having sent a message (non-repudiation with proof of origin), and the receiving entity cannot deny having received a message (non-repudiation with proof of delivery). • A service that is used to provide assurance of the integrity and origin of data in such a way that the integrity and origin can be verified and validated by a third party as having originated from a specific entity in possession of the private key (i.e. the signatory).
Reliability	• Property of consistent intended behaviour and results	–

There are also further properties that security ideally needs to possess when fulfilling the earlier principles. For example, the controls and processes that are introduced to support security ought to be

• *Robust*: Security safeguards should not be susceptible to failure or compromise, directly or as a result of other system components. If security can be disrupted by accidental events such as software crashes or power failures, undermined by deliberate interference from malicious processes, or bypassed via workarounds from users who would prefer to avoid, then it is clearly not providing the level of resilience and reliability intended of it.

- *Usable*: This means being understandable and tolerable to the user. Users need to be able to make sense of any security controls on offer to them, or any security-related decisions that they are required to make, and the use of security should not become intrusive or burdensome to the extent that it drives people away from being willing to use it [8].
- *Trusted*: People need to be able to believe in the protection, in the sense that it is working correctly and effectively to provide the level of safeguard that is claimed. Ensuring the aforementioned perception of robustness will be one contributor towards this, but other factors such as having a level of visibility to show that security is present and 'at work' can also assist here (although too much of this can end up impacting negatively upon usability, and care is needed to strike the right balance).

Some of these are clearly more subjective than others, and factors such as an individual's risk appetite, IT experience and general confidence, can end up having an influence (e.g. someone who is quite risk averse and lacking IT experience may find it more difficult to use and trust the technology than someone with prior experience and the confidence to experiment). This effectively adds another complication when providing security controls because what is considered effective and satisfactory for one user is not guaranteed to work for others. Security is definitely *not* a one-size-fits-all solution.

Taking things yet further, it is also worth recognising that the various principles and properties can apply at different phases of a security lifecycle. Looking around the literature there are different variations of these, but for the purposes of illustration we can use those proposed by NIST, which can be briefly summarised as follows [2]:

- *Identify* – developing the organisational understanding to manage cybersecurity risk to systems, assets, data and capabilities.
- *Prevent* – safeguards to ensure delivery of critical infrastructure services.
- *Detect* – activities to identify the occurrence of a cybersecurity event.
- *Respond* – activities to take action regarding a detected cybersecurity event.
- *Recover* – maintaining plans for resilience and restoring any capabilities or services impaired due to a cybersecurity event.

Having presented the list, it is useful to recognise a couple of further points. Firstly, all underlying security controls will again be looking to do things within at least one of these areas. Secondly, a lack of attention in the earlier phases can lead to there being more to attend to in the later ones (a point that is well-illustrated by the theme of software vulnerabilities, as discussed later in the chapter). So, a technology such as user authentication very much fits into the Prevent stage; if we get this right then there will not be impostor-related incidents to detect, respond to and recover from. Meanwhile, if we think of a control such as backup, it clearly has a role to play in the Recover stage (although you have to have considered it before reaching that point if any such backups are to be available!).

From these examples, it may be tempting to regard information security as a technology-based problem. However, in reality this is only one element of a bigger

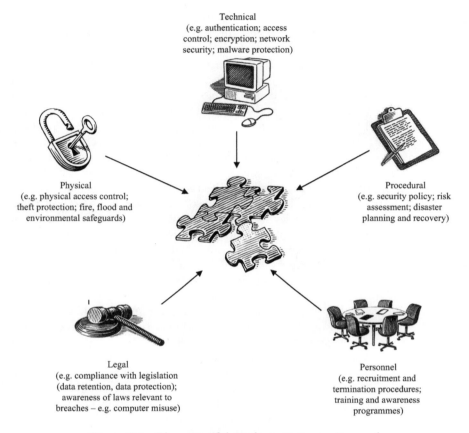

Figure 2.1   Elements of the information security puzzle

picture, and a holistic approach to security actually involves the introduction and utilisation of controls across several areas, as illustrated in Figure 2.1 [9].

The examples listed in the figure are far from exhaustive, but already provide a good indication that information security is actually a multifaceted problem and can consequently demand a range of inputs and expertise to enable appropriate solutions. With this in mind, later discussion takes a further look at the range of topic areas that information security can actually find itself drawing upon and overlapping with. Before that, however, it is relevant to take a closer look at some of the reasons why security is needed in the first place, and some of the forms it can take.

2.2   Security threats and protection

Security would not be needed at all were it not for the existence of threats. These may be accidental or deliberate in nature, although it is likely the latter that we tend to think about most readily, as these are the ones arising from attacks and misuse-related activities. Common keywords such as hacking and phishing and malware threats such as viruses, worms and Trojan horses all fit into this category.

As time has passed, the threat landscape has become considerably broader. If we look back to the 1980s, we already had IT systems but they were of a very different nature to those of today, and the threat categories were correspondingly fewer. For example, looking at the reporting categories in the UK Audit Commission's Computer Fraud Survey in 1981, we would see only two categories of related incident: fraud and theft. Repeated every 3–4 years until 2005, the survey saw the categories of incident progressively broadening until the final list also encompassed the following alongside the original two: accessing pornographic/inappropriate material; hacking; invasion of privacy; private work; sabotage; use of unlicensed software and virus/denial of service [10]. And the trend continues. Since 2005, the lexicon of threat types has broadened yet further, and if conducted today such a survey would doubtless refer to Advanced Persistent Threats, Botnets, Phishing and Ransomware, to name but a few [11].

More broadly speaking, *threats* are basically anything that can go wrong in order to violate the principles of security. *Vulnerabilities* are how exposed we are to them. So, to give a simple example, many systems will face a threat from malware. However, the vulnerability to this threat will depend upon whether the system has got controls in place to address the problem (e.g. up-to-date antivirus protection). In some cases, vulnerabilities are the result of whether or not we have such controls in place. In other cases, they are an inherent factor of software that we run, within which flaws can be discovered and exploited. This can include the operating system, server platforms or applications and tools. As can be seen in Figure 2.2 (drawing upon the raw number of vulnerabilities recorded per annum across all vendors/products in the annual vulnerability review reports published by Secunia), the problem is certainly not diminishing over time. Indeed, the scale of the issue is seen to have almost doubled over the more recent five years compared to the average of the five years preceding them. Having said this, in reading the chart, it should not necessarily be taken to mean that software development practices are becoming markedly worse. Part of the increase is also likely to be attributable to the fact that the market has become more attuned to seeking and reporting vulnerabilities (and similarly, attackers have become no less enthusiastic in terms of exploiting them). Nonetheless, it does not give a great deal of cause for optimism that the problem is going away anytime soon!

This leads us to the concept of *risk*, which we can think of as being a factor of our vulnerability to a given set of threats, the likelihood of those threats occurring and the resulting impact if this were to happen. It is worth noting that risk is only meaningful when considered in the context of particular asset(s) that need to be protected. So, for example, two different PCs both protected with the same antivirus are arguably the same in terms of their vulnerability to the threat of malware. However, if one PC is simply used as an end-user workstation, whereas the other hosts a customer database, the value of the latter is potentially higher and so the impact of a breach would similarly be greater. As such, one PC is considered at more risk than the other.

We introduce security controls (also commonly known as safeguards or countermeasures) to mitigate risk – ideally to remove it, but more typically to reduce it

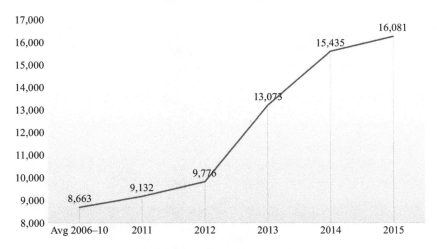

Figure 2.2   *The year-on-year increase in software vulnerabilities*
Source: Flexera/Secunia Vulnerability Reviews 2011–2016.

(or sometimes, in the case of approaches such as insurance, to transfer it to another party). However, if the controls are insufficient or ineffective, then we can find ourselves in the position of facing a security breach. Of course, security breaches only matter because something negative happens as a result, and these are typically termed as *impacts*. Using the categories from the CRAMM risk analysis methodology, the impacts upon data (arguably the key underlying asset in any system) can be of four types [12]:

- disclosure – data is disclosed to an unauthorised party;
- denial of access – data, or a system containing it, becomes unavailable;
- modification – data is changed as a result of the breach;
- destruction – data is lost as a result of the breach.

Staying with the CRAMM approach, each of these impacts may then introduce one or more resulting *consequences*, which can ultimately affect individuals (e.g. an organisation's clients or customers) or the organisation itself:

- disclosure of commercial information/breach of commercial confidentiality;
- infringement of personal privacy;
- embarrassment, loss of reputation or goodwill;
- disruption to activities;
- financial loss;
- failure to meet legal obligations;
- danger to personal safety.

So, to summarise all of these in a single sentence: threats and vulnerabilities lead to a level of risk, which can in turn lead to a security breach having potential impacts and consequences.

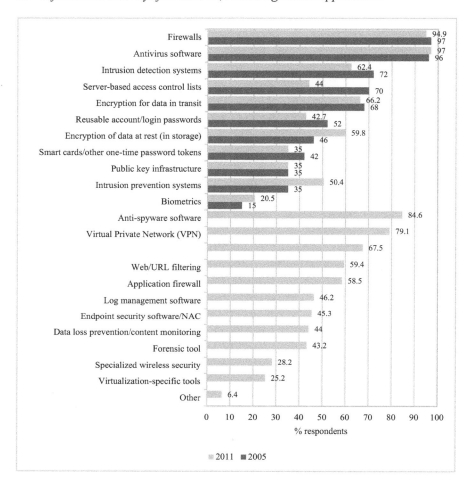

Figure 2.3   Evolving use of security technologies
        Source: CSI Surveys.

In response to the growing range of threats, and particularly those linked to deliberate attacks, the core set of security controls that needs to be considered has become ever-wider and spread over more devices. On the technology front, we have gone from basic password-style authentication, antivirus and firewalls to routine use of technologies such as biometrics, Security Information and Event Management, Data Loss Prevention and Insider Threat Detection. Meanwhile, if we look at technologies such as cryptography, which were once largely the preserve of government, military and financial applications, they are now a standard aspect of network communication and file storage, with the strength of protection also having increased as the underlying algorithms have advanced.

To illustrate the point regarding technology evolution, Figure 2.3 contrasts the claimed use of security technologies based upon CSI Computer Crime and Security

Surveys from 2005 [13] to 2011 [14], and gives an indication of how the landscape evolved over a relatively short period of time. Many of the technologies, such as antivirus and firewalls, were already well-established by 2005, but others clearly became more prominent as time went on. However, the key thing to note is not the varying use of a particular technology from one survey to the next, but rather that in the intervening 5–6 years the number of security options listed had actually doubled (and hence the bottom half of the chart lists a set of 2011 results for which there was no comparable sample in the earlier survey). The CSI survey series did not continue beyond this point, but had it done so then the list would only have extended further. Moreover, as time goes on, we see the technologies being needed across a growing range of devices, spanning traditional PCs and laptops to other mobile devices, as well as recognising elements within the network (e.g. router-based controls), an increased volume of endpoint devices, thanks to the Internet of Things, and specialised technologies such as Industrial Control Systems.

The consequent impact upon our use of IT systems is significant. If we look back to the mid-1990s, the repertoire of regularly used *end-user* security technologies may not have extended much beyond dealing with passwords, and running periodic backups and virus scans. In contrast, the baseline considerations for users today – whether for personal use or in the workplace – now routinely encompass the aspects described in Table 2.2 [15].

With all these points applying to an individual end-user, it is perhaps not surprising to find that the challenge facing organisations as a whole is even more diverse. As an example, we can consider the range of recommendations offered by the ISO Code of Practice for Information Security Controls, or ISO 27002 for short. This aims to provide a baseline standard for all organisations, regardless of their size and sector of business, with the intention that by following it they have a common basis for mutual trust. The 2013 edition of the Code of Practice (the most recent at the time of writing) is structured into 14 main control clauses, each addressing a different aspect of security, as follows [16]:

- Information security policies
- Organisation of information security
- Human resource security
- Asset management
- Access control
- Cryptography
- Physical and environmental security
- Operations security
- Communications security
- Systems acquisition, development and maintenance
- Supplier relationships
- Information security incident management
- Information security aspects of business continuity management
- Compliance

Table 2.2   Examples of baseline security literacy for end-users

Issue	Users should understand ...	Users should be able to ...
Authentication	The role of authentication in preventing unauthorised access	Choose and use suitable passwords, and then follow good practice in terms of managing them
Backup	The risks to systems and devices that may result in data loss, and the impact that such a loss may have for them	Utilise appropriate means to backup their data and devices, and appreciate the need for these to be stored away from the original copies
Malware protection	The potential impacts of malware and the possible routes for infection	Check that appropriate antivirus protection is installed and enabled
Mobile devices	The risks that devices can face from both technical threats and the physical environment	Employ available features for security and privacy, and take appropriate precautions to safeguard devices when on the move
Privacy and data leakage	The sensitivity of different types of data, and the ways in which they could be misused (e.g. to support identity theft)	Configure privacy and access settings in contexts where personal data may be most readily shared (e.g. in social networks, between apps or within cloud services), and make informed decisions about what to divulge
Safe Internet access and web browsing	The existence of threats such as phishing, malicious sites and unsafe downloads	How to spot the signs of scams and social engineering, alongside recognising the indicators that denote security and trustworthiness
Secure networking	The risks posed by using unprotected or unknown networks	Ensure that their own networks are protected and make informed decisions about when it is safe to connect to others
Software updates	The reason why software updates are released and the importance of patching vulnerabilities	Configure the system to handle updates in the most appropriate manner

Within the control clauses are a total of 35 main security categories, each of which then contains a control objective, stating what is to be achieved, followed by one or more controls that can be applied to achieve it. The 2013 standard has a grand total of 114 underlying controls, each including a general control statement, some more detailed implementation guidance and potentially other information (such as legal considerations and references to other standards). The length of the resulting control descriptions ranges from a few lines to over a page, but as with any standard, they are ultimately addressing *what* needs to be done rather than any real details on *how* to do it. As such, any organisation wishing to *follow* the code of practice will need to have (or buy in) appropriate expertise to support it, in terms of understanding how the broader statements and recommendations can be implemented in practice. This means not only having the underlying security knowledge, but also the ability to map it onto the specific systems, environment and operations of the target organisation.

This can represent a challenge in its own right, and picked up in the discussion of security skills later in this chapter.

The ISO Code of Practice is far from the only view of the issue, and indeed further dimensions are addressed by other standards in the wider ISO 27000 series (e.g. ISO 27001 provides the requirements for an information security management system, 27003 covers implementation guidance, 27004 considers metrics and measuring effectiveness and 27005 covers risk management), as well as by those from other standards bodies such as NIST. However, it is recognised that such broad standards can be daunting for many organisations (particularly small and medium enterprises), and so attempts have also been made to break the problem down into core elements that are potentially more actionable. Relevant examples in this respect, drawn from the UK context, are the *10 Steps to Cyber Security*[1] and the *Cyber Essentials* scheme[2], as discussed in the paragraphs that follow.

Originally published in 2012, and then re-launched in 2015, the *10 Steps to Cyber Security* are proposed by the Government Communications Headquarters (GCHQ), the UK's National Technical Authority for Information Assurance. They identify a series of key areas in which organisations may be vulnerable and provide advice on how to address them. The motivation for GCHQ to offer the guidance, as outlined in the original release by its then Director, Ian Lobban, was that 'about 80 per cent of known attacks would be defeated by embedding basic information security practices for your people, processes and technology' [17]. The aim of the 10 steps is therefore to reduce this opportunity. At the core is the need to have an Information Risk Management Regime, and this is supported by nine further steps as follows:

- secure configuration;
- network security;
- managing user privileges;
- user education and awareness;
- incident management;
- malware prevention;
- monitoring;
- removable media controls;
- home and mobile working.

It is fair to say that describing these various areas as *steps* is probably at risk of underselling the effort that may be involved in achieving them. All can certainly involve a number of sub-activities in order to address the headline issue, and so the path towards them may not be as straightforward as the name suggests. Nonetheless, they are certainly valid areas for attention and again highlight the need for controls to be introduced beyond just the technical level.

By contrast, the accompanying *Cyber Essentials* scheme intentionally adopts a technology-only focus. Specifically, it identifies five key areas of controls that

---

[1] See https://www.cesg.gov.uk/10-steps-cyber-security
[2] See https://www.cyberstreetwise.com/cyberessentials/

organisations must have in place if they are to have confidence that they are giving adequate attention towards the risks arising from Internet-based threats:

- boundary firewalls and internet gateways;
- secure configuration;
- access control;
- malware protection;
- patch management.

The scheme asserts that by addressing these five areas organisations can achieve 'basic cyber hygiene', and as a result be more confident about being protected against the most common cyber threats (particularly in an online context). A key element of Cyber Essentials is that organisations can get certified against it and can then use the resulting badge as a basis to signify their compliance. There are actually two levels that can be earned:

- Cyber Essentials – organisations self-assess against the scheme, and their assessment is then independently verified via a review by an external certifying body.
- Cyber Essentials Plus – an external certifying body independently tests the organisation's systems to confirm compliance.

The underlying idea here is for the Cyber Essentials badges to become a form of trustmark, in the hope that organisations will actually look for others to hold the badge if they are to become business partners. Indeed, the UK government has already adopted this approach, mandating that Cyber Essentials is now a requirement in certain areas of contracting and procurement. Nonetheless, while it serves to provide the basic hygiene as described, Cyber Essentials is very much a baseline step towards addressing information security. If you pare it down that much and that's all you do, then it's almost certainly not enough. As such, following the more comprehensive code of practice, and conducting a formal risk assessment to more specifically identify the security needs of the organisation in question, provides a far more robust approach.

2.3 Appreciating the breadth of information security

While it is assumed that many readers will be coming to this book from an IT perspective, it is important to realise that information security can actually be a truly multidisciplinary topic. This is illustrated by Figure 2.4, which identifies examples of discipline areas that contribute to the ability to understand and address it in a comprehensive manner. This does not claim to be an exhaustive list of topics, and moreover the diagram does not attempt to indicate the extent of the relationships that may exist (which in any case could vary depending upon the organisation concerned), but it already starts to show the wider breadth of the issue to be faced.

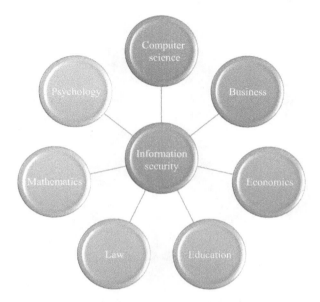

Figure 2.4 Disciplines contributing to information security

Leaving computer science aside for a moment, let's consider the relevance of the other areas, providing an example or two of how each of the non-computing disciplines can be considered security-relevant:

- *Business* – appreciating the organisational context in which the protection is required and the importance of security in terms of areas such as maintaining brand reputation, supporting business continuity and minimising business risk.
- *Economics* – understanding the value of security controls relative to costs of exposure and linking to factors such as return on (security) investment.
- *Education* – supporting areas such as user awareness and training, each being steps towards the boarder goal of achieving a security culture amongst the staff community.
- *Law* – recognising the laws that require us to preserve security, and those relevant in a response to incidents, as well as linking to criminology in relation to understanding the nature and motivation of some of the attackers that may be faced.
- *Mathematics* – providing the underpinnings for a variety of security techniques, including cryptography and access control.
- *Psychology* – helping us to understand how users perceive issues such as security and trust, as well as predicting how users may behave in risk scenarios and the factors that may influence their responses.

Taking things further, we could add yet more disciplines, including facets of civil engineering, in relation to physical and environmental protection, and electronics,

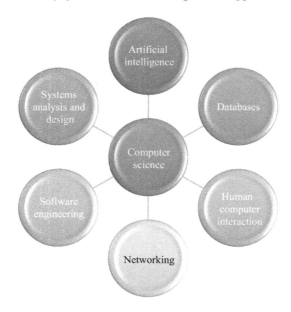

Figure 2.5   Security-related aspects of computer science

which has a clear relationship to underlying devices that hold and process much of the data. As a result, then, it becomes easy to appreciate that security is indeed wide-reaching, and from the diversity of topic linkages, it becomes clearly apparent that these are all not technical disciplines.

Having said all this, it remains fair to regard computer science as being central to the issue given that we are dealing with systems underpinned by IT. As such, let us decompose computer science (again non-exhaustively) and identify areas that have clear touchpoints with security. Some examples are identified in Figure 2.5, and these can relate to areas in which the techniques can be used to support security, as well as the topics having security issues that need to be addressed.

The following text again give a brief narrative to explain the security relevance of each of the areas.

- *Artificial intelligence (AI)* – AI techniques have significant potential to aid security technologies and decision processes (e.g. identifying and responding to suspected intrusions by spotting patterns of anomalous behaviour). In addition, the techniques themselves need to be secure against compromise, given the increasing trust and reliance that is placed on them in other contexts.
- *Databases* – Given that database technologies are often used to store the most valuable asset (the data), the security considerations here include preventing unauthorised disclosure and modification of the stored data, as well as preventing subtler breaches such as being able to determine things by inference across successive queries.

- *Human–computer interaction* – This links to a fundamental requirement for systems to be understandable and usable for the target audience. Systems that are designed and implemented without taking their users into account can often end up causing mistakes, which in turn could compromise security. It is also important for security-specific tools and features to be understandable in order to increase the chance of people using them and applying them correctly.
- *Networking* – Recognising that much of our data is sent over the network, and the network connections also establish paths between the systems we are seeking to protect, it is important to consider the security at the networking level in terms of protecting data in transit and controlling the permitted connectivity between the end-systems and devices.
- *Software engineering* – Recognising that many vulnerabilities can also occur as a result of the way code was written rather than a fundamental design flaw, this refers to knowledge and use of security-aware coding practices, particularly around areas such as memory management.
- *Systems analysis and design* – Security needs to be considered within the specification and design of new systems, such that it is recognised and incorporated from the outset rather than needing to be retrofitted at a later stage.

As a result of all this, information security is an area in which a variety of theories can have a role to play. Some of these are directly in the domain (e.g. the mathematical basis underpinning public key cryptography), some from more broadly from computer science (e.g. AI) and others can be drawn in from wider areas such as human and social sciences (e.g. the Theory of Planned Behaviour). It is not the intention to go into detail on these here (although later chapters will certainly pick up on some in more depth), but even at this level it further illustrates the rich tapestry that is created around the security area.

Given the breadth and complexity of security, it is clearly an area in which many organisations find themselves in need of specialist support. At the same time, offering such support demands appropriate knowledge and expertise, and it is therefore worthwhile to consider what someone needs to know about security in order to be recognised as a competent practitioner. In contrast to the software engineering domain, where the IEEE has established an agreed Body of Knowledge [18], there is currently no similarly agreed specification for the security discipline. Having said that, there is a long-established and widely recognised Common Body of Knowledge (CBK) from the International Information Systems Security Certification Consortium, Inc. [or (ISC)^2 for short], which is used to underpin similarly well-recognised professional certifications such as Certified Information Systems Security Professional (CISSP). To quote (ISC)^2, the CBK is intended to provide 'a vendor neutral and internationally understood common framework upon which the practice of information security can be discussed, taught and otherwise advanced across geographic and geopolitical boundaries. The broad spectrum of topics … ensure its relevancy across all disciplines in the field of information security and the high level of detail provided in each domain ensures that credential holders possess the depth of skills and knowledge expected of a seasoned security professional' [19].

The CBK is structured around eight security domains, as given next. Each of these then has several Key Areas of Knowledge associated with it (many of which also decompose into further sub-areas), but simply flagging the domains themselves is sufficient for the purposes of this discussion:

1. Security and risk management (e.g. security, risk, compliance, law, regulations, business continuity)
2. Asset security (protecting security of assets)
3. Security engineering (engineering and management of security)
4. Communication and network security (designing and protecting network security)
5. Identity and access management (controlling access and managing identity)
6. Security assessment and testing (designing, performing and analysing security testing)
7. Security operations (e.g. foundational concepts, investigations, incident management, disaster recovery)
8. Software development security (understanding, applying and enforcing software security)

It can already be seen that this is presenting a greater level of decomposition than we saw in Figure 2.1. However, parallels can be drawn with the ISO Code of Practice, where it may be noted that, while the topics are structured rather differently, the breadth of coverage is similar. The key thing is that it shows the broad range of topics that a security practitioner may be expected to know about and points to a need for competent and qualified professionals to handle the tasks. This, of course, is the reason why $(ISC)^2$ has the accompanying professional certifications, such as CISSP, and why other bodies such as ISACA also offer related certifications of their own as well. A further view of the issue can be seen by looking at Skills Framework produced by the Institute of Information Security Professionals (IISP). This was originally established in 2007 and then revised in 2016, and Figure 2.6 depicts the structure of the latest version. This is organised as 10 *Security Disciplines*, each of which then has a number of underlying *Skills Groups*[3]. Looking at this breakdown, it is very notable that the skills of interest are not restricted to the security-specific topics, and the disciplines denoted towards the right of the diagram are linked to business skills and professionalism. This recognises that rounded security practitioners will often require more than just knowledge and expertise in the security-related topics, and that successfully taking this into the organisation requires a number of other skills to support and enable the process.

The IISP Framework also recognises that individuals are likely to have different levels of familiarity and experience across the different disciplines, and so someone's ability in relation to each of the skills groups can be classified to one of six levels:

• Level 1: (Follow) Basic knowledge of principles/follow good user practice
• Level 2: (Assist) Basic application

---

[3]A full copy of the Framework can be obtained upon request via www.iisp.org.

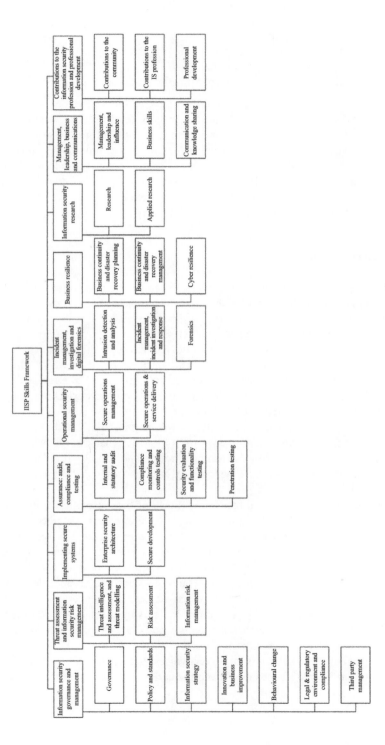

Figure 2.6 Top-level structure of the IISP Skills Framework

- Level 3: (Apply) Practitioner
- Level 4: (Enable) Senior practitioner
- Level 5: (Advise) Principal practitioner
- Level 6: (Initiate, enable, ensure) Expert/lead practitioner

Each level has differing expectations in terms of the knowledge and practical experience that someone would expected to have, and the full version of the Framework presents indicative descriptions against each level for each skill group.

The advantage of the Skills Framework is that it provides individuals and organisations with an opportunity to understand the skills that they need and to what level they possess them. The IISP itself uses it as a basis for assessing professional membership applications, and it has also been used (in adapted form) as the basis for the certification schemes for academic degree programmes by GCHQ[4].

2.4   Future vision

The scope of security changes as the technology changes. As computing has evolved from mainframes, through PCs and mobile devices, to the Cloud and the Internet of Things, all have required security in some way. In some cases, it is thanks to known threats that continue to exist in the new context. For example, the threat of impostor access typically applies in all cases to some degree, and so motivates having some level of user authentication and access control. In other cases, however, the new technologies add new threat dimensions. For example, the threat of large-scale data leakage or theft is very much a consideration with the Cloud and exists in a way that did not apply for the earlier forms of technology.

It is, of course, rather difficult to predict the future, particularly in the technology space. However, it is possible – and indeed useful – to step back to the past and see what the future looked like from that vantage point. The value particularly comes from seeing lessons that could have been learnt, and ensuring that these points are taken on board for the future.

One of the real challenges we face is that many of those leading the charge for technological advancement often appear to have little appreciation or concern for the security perspective. As a result, we are forming an unfortunately well-trodden path of innovating and deploying new technologies, while the risks are given little or no consideration. A good illustration of this is provided by the rise of mobile devices such as smartphones and tablets, which have become an accepted part of everyday technology usage without the associated security concerns having been fully recognised by the organisations or individuals using them. Specific examples that can be examined here are user authentication and malware protection, and there are lessons to be learnt in both cases.

Looking at authentication, it is fair to recognise that there had been some form of authentication on mobile phones even from the early days. However, the traditional

---

[4]See www.cesg.gov.uk/articles/gchq-certification-master-s-degrees-cyber-security

form that this took was the Personal Identification Number (PIN), with four digits being the typical default. Back in the mid-1990s of course, this was reasonable enough, and arguably commensurate with what was being protected (e.g. preventing unauthorised users from making calls on the device or accessing stored content in the form of contacts and text messages). However, as time went by, the devices of course became far more capable, with inbuilt applications and then downloadable apps encouraging a far greater array of data to be stored, and with faster data access enabling their use as full Internet devices. At this stage, there was clearly far more to protect and prevent impostors from accessing, but the point-of-entry authentication provision on most devices still remained resolutely PIN-based (and it was certainly still the default, even if alternative methods such as full-text passwords were available). As such, the level of protection that users' data and access to services was receiving on their mobile device was progressively falling out of alignment with the security that the same data/services would have received on a desktop PC (particularly within a workplace context, with appropriate password policies being enforced). Moreover, the data was now *less* protected on a device that was actually *more* physically vulnerable (i.e. the risk of loss or theft for smartphones and tablets is by its very nature greater than for a desktop PC because they are mobile devices), and there was a heightened chance of the device holding content that was not only relevant to the user but also of value to their employer (ushering in a significant debate around the issue of Bring Your Own Device security, which was not really aired until the issue was already a reality facing many organisations).

In a way, the fact that the PIN remained dominant was not surprising because the only alternative for much of this period had been the password. While this is arguably fine in the context of a desktop or laptop PC (subject to the caveats of actually following good password selection and usage practices!), the approach does not really translate so well for use on phones and tablets. On the smartphone in particular, the size of the device often militates against being able to type the password easily, especially if it involves multiple character types, and thereby necessitates switching between different keyboard views to get at the necessary characters. In addition, the style of use of both smartphones and tablets often means that we want quick access for a brief activity, rather than sitting for a more prolonged period of use that is the norm on a PC. As such, while entering a short PIN might be considered tolerable, doing keyboard acrobatics to enter a longer and more complex password could be judged too much of an overhead. What was needed was a means of authentication that was actually provided with the nature of the device in mind, and while this did ultimately happen (with touchscreen gesture-based techniques such as Android's Pattern Unlock or Windows' Picture Password, and the use of biometrics such as fingerprint and face recognition, all of which serve to make authentication more user-friendly) it was a long time coming in comparison to the advancement of the other capabilities of the devices concerned. Even then, these alternatives were being provided as options rather than the default provision, and in this sense mobile devices still lag considerably behind what the user would be expected to use even with the laxest of password-protection policies. It was only in 2015, for example, that Apple changed the default passcode length on iOS to being six digits instead of four [20]. And so, while clearly a step in the right direction, it was still hardly comparable to the level of password protection that the same data and services would be expected to receive if they were on a workplace PC.

So, the lesson from the authentication example is that the provision of security needs to keep pace with the rest of the technology. If we now move on to consider the problem of mobile malware, we see a rather different situation as the technology evolved.

In the early days of mobile phones, malware really was not an issue at all. The devices offered no option to download and run code, and so there was basically no way for malware to infect and spread. Again, however, as the technology of the devices advanced, this opened up possibilities that were also relevant in the malware context. From the technological perspective, malware needed a means to run on the devices, and a means to reach them. As the devices matured to offer full Internet access and enabled downloadable apps to be installed, both of these criteria were met. Meanwhile, from a practical perspective, malware also needed a target that was popular enough to make it worth the effort of writing it, which basically meant having enough users on a particular mobile platform to give the malware something to go after. This again took time, but it ultimately occurred. In the meantime, however, the warnings were there, but relatively little was done to heed them. For example, looking back to 2005, there were already *predictions* that mobile phones would become a future battleground for malware [21], but there was nothing much to report in terms of an *actual* problem. We had Personal Digital Assistants (PDAs), many of which had the ability to install new software onto them, but the idea of the smartphone was not well-established. Meanwhile, although the concept of the tablet computer had been realised in early forms, we were a good five years away from the point at which they would become popularised and mainstream with the launch of Apple's iPad. There were *some* examples of malware on PDAs, as well as some instances on earlier phones as their communication capabilities began to expand to include Bluetooth and Wi-Fi. However, these were essentially proof-of-concept, and the user base for such devices was not significant enough to distract the mainstream of malware activity away from the core business of infecting Windows-based PCs.

It was around 2011 that the real arrival of mobile malware was first seen, as illustrated by the chart in Figure 2.7, based upon data collated from reports released by Kaspersky Lab over this period [22–24]. As can be seen, back in early 2011 the problem existed but was rather small, with only eight distinct malware strains being identified on mobile platforms during the whole of January (by contrast, the volume of PC malware seen in the same period would have extended to many thousands of samples per day). However, as time went on, it is clear that the problem was significantly on the rise, with the monthly average for 2011 as a whole being a 100-fold increase on the average for January, and the average for 2015 getting close to being a 100-fold increase on that from 2011!

More worryingly, even once the problem of mobile malware was clearly real, many people remained exposed to it. The culture of mobile device usage had become established without having to be concerned about malware, and many remained unaware that the ground was shifting under them. For example, a survey of over

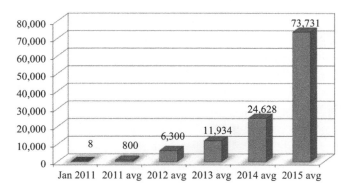

Figure 2.7   The rise of mobile malware
  Source: Kaspersky Lab data.

1,220 end-users conducted by Plymouth University in 2013/14 revealed that while 91 per cent of them claimed to have antivirus protection on their desktop or laptop PC, only 10 per cent claimed to do so on their smartphones. Narrowing this down to specifically the 688 respondents using the Android platform (which accounted for almost all of the mobile malware identified in the sample period), it was found that only 14 per cent had protection. So, while the extent of mobile malware is still miniscule compared to the millions of strains that are recognised on PCs (where, for example, Kaspersky Lab's report for Q2 2016 indicated over 16.1 million unique malware objects [25]), this does not count for much if you are not protected against any of it.

The ultimate lesson from the malware example is that if threats are foreseeable then they *will* eventually come to pass, and it is far better to be prepared in advance than fighting a rear-guard action later on. However, this is again a lesson that seems not to be taken forward as fully as it should be.

The mobile device revolution was quickly followed by the rise of the Internet of Things, and security was again flagged as an issue that would merit attention. Nonetheless, it did not take long for devices to emerge that lacked sufficient security provision, or indeed contained weaknesses that increased the vulnerability of the wider environment in which they were used. As an example of the former, we can consider the case of Internet-enabled surveillance cameras, which enable remote physical security monitoring via the network. This is a perfectly fine idea until the point where they are deployed with default passwords, meaning that anyone who knows (or does some quick investigation to discover) these defaults is able to tap into the video being captured [26]. Meanwhile, as an example of how a vulnerable IoT device can introduce wider problems, a series of nine vulnerabilities discovered in a particular smart lighting solution offered (amongst other things) the potential to facilitate unauthorised access to a user's home Wi-Fi network and other devices connected to it [27].

Based upon the past evidence and thinking back to the trend illustrated in Figure 2.2, it would seem unwise to predict a future in which security concerns have been fully addressed. What we *can* confidently predict is that

- IT will continue to advance in terms of both capability and availability;
- people will continue to reap – and enthusiastically seek – the benefits that this technology can offer;
- our expectation of technology (and our consequent reliance upon it) will continue to increase.

Set against this backdrop, security will clearly assume an increased level of importance. Indeed, if technology is involved in more and more areas in our business and personal lives, then more is implicitly being put at stake.

So, from one perspective, when we look to the future we can only see a bigger problem. It is rather notable that none of the cyber threats from the past has ever really gone away, and so the new issues are adding to a growing threat landscape. Putting it even more bluntly, the future can basically be summarised as 'threats everywhere'. There will be more to steal, attack and infect, and more entry points into our world. Using the problem of ransomware as an example, it first appeared on PCs, and within a relatively short time became a problem on mobile platforms as well. So, what might it look like in the future? How about ransomware on our TVs, in our cars and in our smart homes? Basically, when everything is connected, everything can work against you!

The history of technology adoption to date seems to tell us that the potential risks are rarely fully appreciated upfront, and first-generation technologies are generally not the secure ones. As such, security almost inevitably involves a degree of ensuring that protection is able to catch up with practice. Moreover, as we have seen with a succession of technologies (from mobiles, to the Cloud, to the use of big data) every business opportunity can also become a threat vector. Every technology we adopt can increase vulnerability and amplify risk. Of course, we can still adopt them, but we need to do so with both eyes open; seeing only the benefits is a direct path to falling foul of the threats. The fact that businesses today are still getting hit by attacks that exploit vulnerabilities from years ago does not paint a positive picture. It doesn't have to be this way, but there's still a lot of facing-up that remains to be done if the problem is to come under control. So, as we move forward, the clear advice for the future would be to stop ignoring the security lessons of the past.

Having said all this, the advancement of technology can also offer a benefit to security itself. As we move forward, for example, the incorporation of techniques such as AI is likely to enable security to have a greater degree of automation and intelligence. AI has advantages in key areas such as spotting things that we would not ordinarily notice, and automating activities that would otherwise rely upon manual intervention. For example, behavioural profiling and anomaly detection do not have much scope without AI. Statistical measures can work to some degree (e.g. if we know the average traffic, then we can flag departures falling outside certain bounds around it), but AI can pull out subtle patterns and can help to derive new rules that would have been unlikely to be identified if security administrators were asked to specify them directly. It is also useful for addressing the needle in the haystack challenge that would otherwise face humans when confronted with performing analysis and correlation across increasingly large and diverse data sets. Meanwhile, from the automation perspective, AI can be linked to areas such as incident monitoring, recognising that the speed of response is often critical in limiting impact. This is particularly important as we consider the rise of the Internet of Things and face the challenge of monitoring and responding to larger attacks affecting an increasingly diverse sets of targets. AI can help to reduce the dependency upon human involvement to spot problems and decide how to respond. There will, of course, still be some points at which human judgement is relevant, offering insights and information that the AI system will not know about. People bring elements such as intuition and creativity (e.g. the ability to spot things by thinking like at attacker) that an AI system would not be able to replicate. As a result, the system can handle the more mundane alerts (and can progressively learn the most effective responses), reducing the workload for security administrators and saving their attentions for the incidents that merit their intervention.

Automation is also linked to the potential for security technology to become more transparent from the user perspective, such that it is no longer something that people need to think about and act upon explicitly. We have already seen elements of this transition in the past, with areas such as malware scanning and software updates becoming largely background tasks unless they require user decisions or confirmations to be made. Similarly, in areas such as authentication, there is a move towards less intrusive techniques such as biometrics, with the consequence that security is seen as more tolerable and less demanding from the perspective of those required to use it.

One final advantage for security as we move forward is that it holds a higher profile than it did in the past. It is much more widely recognised as something that businesses (and individuals) need to be aware of and attending to. As such, there is the corresponding chance that it will also end up as a higher priority in their plans as well.

References

[1] ITU. *X.1205: Overview of cybersecurity*. International Telecommunication Union, Recommendation X.1205 (04/08), 18 April 2008.

[2] NIST. *Framework for Improving Critical Infrastructure Cybersecurity*, Version 1.0, National Institute of Standards and Technology, 12 February 2014.

[3] CNSS. *National Information Assurance (IA) Glossary*. Committee on National Security Systems, CNSS Instruction No. 4009, 26 April 2010.

[4] International Organisation for Standardisation. *Information Technology— Security Techniques—Information Security Management Systems—Overview and Vocabulary*. ISO/IEC 27000:2016. Fourth Edition, 15 February 2016.

[5] European Union. *Directive (EU) 2016/1148 of the European Parliament and of the Council of 6 July 2016 Concerning Measures for a High Common Level of Security of Network and Information Systems across the Union*. 6 July 2016. data.europa.eu/eli/dir/2016/1148/oj [Accessed 24 Aug 2016].

[6] NIST. *Glossary of Key Information Security Terms*. NISTIR 7298 Revision 2, Kissel R (ed.). National Institute of Standards and Technology, May 2013.

[7]   ENISA. *Definition of Cybersecurity – Gaps and Overlaps in Standardisation*. European Network and Information Security Agency. 18 December 2015.

[8]   Furnell, S.M. 'Security usability challenges for end-users', in Gupta M. and Sharman R. (eds.). *Social and Human Elements of Information Security: Emerging Trends and Countermeasures*. Information Science Reference, Hershey PA; 2008. pp. 196–219.

[9]   Furnell S.M. *Computer Insecurity: Risking the System*. London, UK, Springer; 2005. p. 7.

[10]   Audit Commission. *ICT fraud and abuse 2004 – An Update to Yourbusiness@risk. Public Sector Update*. June 2005. ISBN 186240 507 7.

[11]   Furnell S. 'The evolving landscape of technology-dependent crime', in McGuire M.R. and Holt T.J. (eds.). *The Routledge Handbook of Technology, Crime and Justice*. Abingdon, UK, Routledge International Handbooks; 2017.

[12]   Maguire S. 'Identifying risks during information system development: managing the process'. *Information Management & Computer Security*. 2002;**10**(3): 126–134.

[13]   Gordon L.A., Loeb M.P., Lucyshyn W. and Richardson R. *Tenth Annual CSI/FBI Computer Crime and Security Survey*, Computer Security Institute, 2005.

[14]   Richardson R. *2010/2011 CSI Computer Crime and Security Survey*, Computer Security Institute, 2011.

[15]   Furnell S. and Moore L. 'Security literacy: the missing link in today's online society?' *Computer Fraud & Security*, May 2014: 12–18.

[16]   International Organisation for Standardisation. *Information Technology – Security Techniques – Code of Practice for Information Security Controls*. ISO/IEC 27002:2013. 1 October 2013.

[17]   CESG. *10 Steps to Cyber Security – Executive Companion*. Crown Copyright, 2012.

[18]   Bourque P. and Fairley R.E. *SWEBOK V3.0 – Guide to the Software Engineering Body of Knowledge*. IEEE Computer Society. 0-7695-5166-1; 2014.

[19]   (ISC)^2. 'Exam Outline – Candidate Information Bulletin'. Revised 2.2.15 V11. 15 April 2015. www.isc2.org/uploadedfiles/(isc)2_public_content/exam_outlines/cissp-exam-outline-april-2015.pdf [Accessed 24 Aug 2016].

[20]   Thompson C. 'Apple made a simple change in iOS 9 that will make your iPhone a lot safer', Tech Insider, 16 September 2015. www.techinsider.io/ios-9-defaults-to-6-digit-passcode-2015-9 [Accessed 24 Aug 2016].

[21]   Furnell S. 'Handheld hazards: the rise of malware on mobile devices', *Computer Fraud & Security*, May 2005: 4–8.

[22]   Kaspersky Lab. '99% of all mobile threats target Android devices', Virus News, 7 January 2013. www.kaspersky.com/about/news/virus/2013/99_of_all_mobile_threats_target_Android_devices [Accessed 24 Aug 2016].

[23]   Kaspersky Lab. 'Mobile cyber-threats: a joint study by Kaspersky Lab and INTERPOL', October 2014. https://securelist.com/files/2014/10/report_mobile_cyberthreats_web.pdf [Accessed 24 Aug 2016].

[24]   Kaspersky Lab. 'The volume of new mobile malware tripled in 2015', Virus News, 23 February 2016. http://www.kaspersky.com/about/news/virus/2016/The_Volume_of_New_Mobile_Malware_Tripled_in_2015   [Accessed 24 Aug 2016].

[25]   Unuchek R., Garnaeva M., Ivanov A., Makrushin D. and Sinitsyn F. 'IT threat evolution in Q2 2016. Statistics', Securelist, 11 August 2016. https://securelist.com/analysis/quarterly-malware-reports/75640/it-threat-evolution-in-q2-2016-statistics/ [Accessed 24 Aug 2016].

[26]   Network World. 'Peeping into 73,000 unsecured security cameras thanks to default passwords', Network World, 6 November 2014. http://www.networkworld.com/article/2844283/microsoft-subnet/peeping-into-73-000-unsecured-security-cameras-thanks-to-default-passwords.html [Accessed 24 Aug 2016].

[27]   RAPID7. 'R7-2016-10: Multiple OSRAM SYLVANIA Osram Lightify vulnerabilities (CVE-2016-5051 through 5059)', RAPID7 Community, 20 July 2016. https://community.rapid7.com/community/infosec/blog/2016/07/26/r7-2016-10-multiple-osram-sylvania-osram-lightify-vulnerabilities-cve-2016-5051-through-5059 [Accessed 24 Aug 2016].

Chapter 3
Information systems security issues in the context of developing countries[1]
Devinder Thapa*, Samar Fumudoh**, and Usha Vishwanathan***

Abstract

This chapter explores the current state of information systems security (ISS) in developing countries and suggests a way forward. A systematic literature review is conducted applying the approach suggested in reference [1]. In total, 41 articles were evaluated, 17 of which were analysed as part of the review. The review shows that the proliferation of technology in developing countries is increasing; however, ISS risk is also increasing in tandem. The reasons are lack of robust infrastructure, security education and skilled manpower. The review also revealed that while most of the technologies created are for the organizations in the developed world, developing countries are blindly implementing the same technology without considering their own limitations resulting from lack of resources combined with unique cultural and social set-ups.

Keywords: Information systems security, Education, Developing countries

3.1 Introduction

While searching for the research on information systems (IS) in general, the nature of research happening in developing countries is well understood but only by a limited group of people who are aware of the social, cultural and infrastructure limitations of the developing world [2]. Furthermore, a study noted that information technology (IT) in developing countries is generally under-represented in the open literature and while a few publications concede that there can be major issues with transitional countries in developing their IS, the subject is not treated in any depth or breadth [3]. Also, in a

[1]A full version of this chapter has been published as a Master's thesis at Luleå University of Technology
*Department of Information Systems, University of Agder, Norway
**Swedish Police Authority, Sweden
***Aerospace Engineering Department, Indian Institute of Technology Bombay, India

study conducted by Whitman, the top two threats faced by IS were deliberate acts of espionage and trespass [4]. This is perhaps another reason why developing countries, although faced with other pressing issues, should make securing their information assets a high priority. For developing countries to gain the same degree of trust they must be able to show that they too have sturdy security measures in place protecting their assets and are ready, knowledgeable and capable. Furthermore, if developing countries are to be able to grow their economy, improve their health services, education and other services to become an industrialized and developed nation, they will need to address the information systems security (ISS) vulnerabilities that they face.

The current state and growth of ISS is of significant importance. In order to assist or advise developing nations on implementing robust ISS measures, one must understand where the developing countries are and where they should be going in terms of technological advancements. Countries which fail to embrace the use of IT will suffer significant disadvantages in the form of information poverty that could further widen the gap in economic status and competitiveness [5]. It is also important that developing countries are given focus and assisted in their efforts of developing their ISS in order to catch up with industrial nations and improve their prospects. However before leaping into the details we briefly describe what ISS means in this chapter.

3.1.1   What is ISS?

ISS is the protection of information and other critical elements either hardware or software from unauthorized use, access, disclosure, disruption, modification or destruction so as to ensure the confidentiality, integrity and availability of the information being stored [6]. ISS is the collection of activities that protect the IS and the data that is stored within it [7]. ISS could also be defined as a process of protecting the intellectual property of any organization.

The practice of ISS is critical and has been around for some time. In the early 1960s, ISS was mainly about the physical security of information but as the Internet was born and the ability to connect networks to networks emerged, securing information has become more complex. With the advances in technology, the dependence on electronic transactions and communications has increased [7]. With that said, the necessity of securing information physically has shifted to securing information technically. Nowadays, an IS consists of the hardware, operating systems, networks and application software that work together to collect process and store data for individuals' and organizations' benefits [7]. These IS play a vital role in supporting business operations, managerial decision-making and strategic competitive advantages, and it is the framework around which today's knowledge-based organizations are formed [8].

While organizations are increasingly relying on IS to enhance business operations and facilitate management decision-making [9], the ability to implement efficient ISS requires increased financial resources and also people who have the skills and the abilities to implement various security measures to protect these electronic assets. Together with the fact that the Internet today is used not only by organizations to increase their competitiveness, but also by criminals, ISS is crucial to protect and ensure the safety and integrity of the assets at hand [10].

3.1.2 ISS in the context of developing countries

The growth of IS has come together with the advancements in IT and these two are in a way reliant on one another. Today we are practically dependent on IT networks, and the development of these networks has led us to an information revolution. The methods of creating and sharing knowledge have become dependent on concrete and stable IT networks. Developing countries should not be left out of this information revolution and measures need to be put into place to address the digital divide between different nations. IS have transcended organizational and national boundaries and now support both global economic and political activities [2]; it is no surprise that countries, both developed and developing, must be vigilant and take necessary steps to protect their information assets.

Developing countries compared to developed countries have their own bespoke limitations. Developing countries lack resources, technical and scientific capabilities to develop and implement modern IS [11]. Also, there appears to be a lack of local context in adapting the global IT-based practices while implementing them in developing countries [12,13]. It is important that these problems do not prevent developing countries from acquiring the capabilities for using new Information and communication technology (ICT) applications, so that they can participate in the global information society [14].

3.2 Problem area

In a developing country, health and education systems are poor and technological innovation is scarce. Developing countries have far more pressing issues which make the implementation of adequate IS measures less important. Simply providing ICT to developing countries will not solve their problems, while providing new technologies to people who do not have the knowledge or skill to manipulate, it is meaningless. As rightly pointed out in reference [15], in developing countries, IT is developing faster than the knowledge, skill and awareness of the people [15]. That is to say, implementation of sufficient ISS goes hand in hand with raising the awareness and educating the people who will be using it. It is therefore paramount that the implementation of ISS in developing countries is instigated in hindsight of other pressing issues the countries might be facing.

In an article published in the *New Scientist*, it is clear to see that the lack of IS within developing countries is a concern. Additionally, it was noted that a current worry among computer security experts is the legal vacuum within developing countries. This vacuum is a vulnerability which might make developing countries susceptible to cybercrime [16]. The lack of legal backdrop relating to ISS or even Internet usage can be a burden, not just for the developing countries, but for many other developed nations. If a hacker is indeed based in a developing country where there are no laws in relation to Internet usage, it would be troublesome for developed countries that might consequently become targets. In another article published by the BBC in 2009, it is clear to see how people in Africa are now using their mobile phones to do all their money transactions [17]. It is therefore obvious that the effortless and simple things that the Internet can be used for are being grasped by developing countries. As such, the governments need to act and begin implementing robust IS measures before vulnerabilities are attacked.

In order for developing countries to progress, it is important that the issue of IS should be addressed seriously and sufficiently. According to the Insight Report on Global Risks by World Economic Forum, cyber-attacks are the fourth highest global risk in terms of likelihood. Given this figure together with the borderless nature of today's information, in order for solutions to work, all nations must act together. With nearly 80 per cent of the world's population living in developing countries [3], good security measures would lead to trustworthiness and thereby more business opportunities and further economic growth for the developing nation.

The problem area driving the research for this chapter is the current state of knowledge with regards to ISS within developing countries. It is clear that plenty of research has been done in this field but each piece of work seems to look at a different aspect of IS within developing countries. It is difficult for researchers, businesses, governments or nations to clearly understand the current situation as there seems to have been little effort to combine all the relevant studies into one single holistic viewpoint and it is this problem which this chapter will address. The specific research question that this chapter addresses is: *what are the prevailing ISS issues in the context of developing countries?*

3.3 Methodology

The methodological approach applied for answering the research question is literature review. The literature review was based on a qualitative approach and was loosely tied with the eight-step plan to conduct a literature review suggested by reference [1]. Considering the complexity of the topic, the research was guided by the following five-step process:

Step 1: Define the purpose of literature review
The purpose of this literature review was to highlight work that has been carried out by other researchers in this field. The review was focused on identifying the ISS issues in the context of developing countries. Particularly, the areas where extensive research is carried out and the fields which are yet to be explored.

Step 2: Collect the relevant literature
In this step, we collected information from various sources like IS journals, confer-ence proceedings and relevant news articles. Most of the information was obtained from the EBSCOHOST, Scopus, IEEE explore and Google Scholar.

Step 3: Do quality check and group according to the theme
A checklist was created to help us decide upon the quality of the collected resources. After the quality check, the information resources were grouped according to themes that are amassed in the process of the review.

Step 4: Evaluate the collected data
Once the relevant information is grouped, the resources were critically evaluated and compared. The fields where extensive researches have been conducted were identified along with the fields where research still needs to be done.

Step 5: Report submission with relevant conclusions and suggestions
The findings of the research were presented in the Master's thesis [18]. The report presented the length and breadth of the current research in the field of ISS in the context of developing countries as well as scope for further research is also suggested.

3.3.1   Analysing the data

Once the initial phases of the literature review were completed, the next step was to analyse the 17 articles that were selected in the Quality Appraisal. Given the quantity of data that was gathered, the techniques of open and axial coding from grounded theory approach were used as a backdrop to scrutinize the data. Developed by [19], grounded theory is a set of iterative techniques designed to identify categories and concepts within text that are then linked into theoretical models [20]. This approach was seen as most suitable for evaluating the data as it was systematic yet flexible in nature. It allowed the data to be evaluated in an open manner and also for themes to be created as the data was examined and the review progressed. To assist in the evaluation, qualitative research software NVivo was used. This allowed for the data to be managed and provided a workspace and tools to easily work through the information. The NVivo helped in keeping track of the analysis and also to ascertain that we were using the same coding patterns. To maintain consistency throughout the review, we divided the 17 articles between us and commenced the work by scanning the documents independently. While screening and coding, the following themes emerged:

- Policy – this included anything in the dataset relating to policy and polices.
- Legislation – this included anything in the dataset relating to laws or legal frameworks.
- Education – this included anything in the dataset relating to the education, skills and awareness of the people.
- Culture – this included anything in the dataset relating to the cultural or social factors that might be influencing the implementation of efficient ISS.
- Dependencies – this included anything in the dataset that was considered relevant in terms of positively or negatively influencing information's systems security but did not fit into any of the four main categories.

It is worth noting that the process of selecting and coding relevant text throughout each document was done repeatedly and exhaustively until it was evident that there was no more data available that could be included in the respective codes. The data that was coded was then individually extracted into separate word documents allowing for the text to then be structured accordingly. On a positive note, the NVivo always linked extracted data back to its original source which made for easier and more concise referencing.

3.4   Findings

This section discusses the findings that arise out of the literature review. We have excluded the technical issues intentionally because most of the technical issues that we identified were similar to developed countries'. Hence, we presented non-technical issues those were peculiar to developing countries' context.

3.4.1   *Legislation*

The formation of a concrete legal framework relating to ISS in developing countries is still somewhat lacking and more needs to be done to address this issue. In fact, many developing countries have yet to consider adopting adequate legislation related to information security management, laws that criminalize cyber-attacks and enable police to adequately investigate and prosecute such activities [21].

The lack of laws and legal frameworks means that not only are developing countries limited in taking action against intruders who are targeting their information assets but also against intruders who might use their country's information network as a base to perform illegal activities globally [3]. While IS laws exist in some developing countries, these need to be enhanced to effectively address the legal challenges of the present borderless cyber environment [22].

While little research has been done on the overall situation surrounding ISS legislation within developing countries, one can draw some form of understanding from the fragments of studies that have been done. For instance, in reference [23] noted users were unaware of ISS legislations, similarly a case study in Tanzania found that the country was lacking the necessary legal framework to assist in ICT security issues and controls [24]. Similarly, another work found that in many developing countries e-business and e-government laws were not yet available [5].

Although some of these findings are not directly in relation to ISS, they are somewhat reliant on one another. ISS is made up of both information and the systems required to protect it. As most information is held electronically and on IT systems, the security of the information has to encompass the legislation regarding the attainment of the data as well as the storage and onward distribution of the data. Throughout this process of ISS, people need to be aware of what is allowed and what is not [24]. As highlighted by reference [25] the main problems brought about by cyberspace are the lack of universal understanding of the rules, regulations and laws in relation to it. Ironically, even in the United States some police departments lack the necessary skills to tackle cybercrimes [26]. The situation is no better in developing countries. In a crime investigation in India, a police officer seized the hacker's computer monitor as the evidence. While in another instance the police seized the CD-ROM drive of the hacker [27]. All these instances point to the low awareness of law-enforcing officials.

Furthermore, even though many developing countries have the necessary laws and regulations in place, there are not enough lawyers, judges and other officials who understand cybercrimes. An article noted that out of a total of 4,400 police officers in Mumbai, there are only 5 who work in the field of cybercrime [28]. This article also points out some of the loopholes in 'India's IT Act 2000', like cyber theft, cyber stalking, cyber harassment and cyber defamation are presently not covered under the act. In addition, while cyber-attacks originate in overseas locations (normally in developing countries), the local police stations where the victims are located do not have the power to make an arrest [26].

It is clear that legal reforms particularly within developing countries must also allow room for national culture. As will be discussed in Section 3.4, national culture is an important backdrop for the implementation of ISS in developing countries. The national culture is unique to each country and so creating a legal framework that is adaptable to the nation is fundamental. In fact, even though the country has a judiciary system, culture may sometimes take precedent over the law [23].

3.4.2 Policy

While ensuring a legal framework to help prevent people from abusing the information system in place, policy is perhaps just as important. Policy provides a solid foundation for any ISS. According to the British Standards Institute, the IS policy of any organization is made up of the processes and procedures that the employees of the organization should follow in order to protect the confidentiality, integrity and availability of the information assets [29]. In simpler terms, a security policy incorporates a set of clear guidelines to which people should adhere to. In the field of ISS, and perhaps for any other field, simply having policies is not adequate. Proper steps need to be taken by the organizations to ensure that the policies are being implemented. It is only when people in organizations are aware of the ISS policies and fully comply with them that an affluent ISS culture can be created [30]. While it may seem like a straightforward task, researchers argue that many organizations find making employees comply with the security policies to be a major challenge [31]. Furthermore, in reference [32] it was found that organizations have to constantly monitor and impose the employee behaviour for policy compliance.

One of the examples which bring out the importance of security policies is the Security Breach at TJX, in 2005. In this security breach, around 45.6 million credit and debit card numbers were stolen from the company's system over a period of 18 months. Around 40 million records were compromised at Card Systems Solutions. The company also announced that the payment systems were assessed illegally and the attackers made off with card data belonging to a number of customers. When analysed, the security breach brought to light many security lapses. Amongst them was the lack of a coordinated security policy, and that the policies in place were not being followed [33]. This was a case that happened in the United States, a developed country where IS are well developed, with strong legal foundation, infrastructure and resources. Developing countries with their limitations are at a higher risk.

Although the importance of IS policies is evident, developing countries are lacking in both the creation and the implementation of adequate policies. For example, research found that the business sector in Thailand overlooked ISS, and not surprisingly only a very few businesses in Thailand had any supporting security policies in place [34]. Similarly, research into the educational sector in Tanzania and the United Arab Emirates confirmed that there were no IS policies in place in the respective educational institutions where the studies were conducted [23,24]. Also, in two separate studies – one from Nigeria and another from Kuwait – relating to IS outsourcing (where the task of ensuring the systems security is contracted to a third party), it was found that even though management were well aware of the risks involved, there was no structured outsourcing strategies or security policies in place [8,35].

One possible reason why ISS policies are lacking is perhaps the allocation of responsibility. For instance, a study in Tanzania showed that IS policies were seen as the responsibility of the IT department or merely as a technical issue [24], while another research highlighted that ISS responsibilities stopped at technical controls and so no security policies were in force [36]. Without the proper backing of ISS policies, security breaches which result in monetary losses can easily happen [37]. Developing countries, whose frail economies are very much dependent on the well-being of its various organizations, cannot withstand such losses [38]. Encouragingly, it appears that some developing countries are slowly moving in the right direction. In Malaysia, the National Cyber Security Policy provides the perspective of how cyber security should be implemented in an integrated manner [22]. Nowadays, the economic competitiveness of countries depends on two important assets: information and knowledge.

Most organizations are catching up with the developments such as internet banking, e-government and e-commerce. In this process, organizations as well as governments are putting forth a lot of sensitive data online. These progressions form part of the critical information infrastructure of the country and protecting them is critical. In reference [37] the author argues that given the importance of these advances combined with the lack of security awareness, parliaments, which are the highest bodies elected by citizens, should oversee the county's cyber health and assist in creating policies relating to ISS. In other words, while organizations should each have their own policies, the threat posed by cyberspace is something that should be overseen by an overarching national cyber policy which would help ensure the protection of the country's overall assets [37].

3.4.3   Education

Even if developing countries had a sound legal framework and robust policies, little can be achieved if the people are not educated about the risks associated with ISS and taught the skills required to attain optimum ISS. Developing countries, unlike the developed countries, face a unique problem in that they have not had a gradual exposure to cyberspace. In developing countries, a whole new generation is growing up venturing directly into cyber space via mobile devices without being made aware of the potential risks of using the Internet [37]. For example, in 2004, a British-based technology research firm Infosecurity did a survey with nearly 200 average workers who were using the subway to commute to work. It showed that over 70 per cent were ready to divulge their business password to a complete stranger in exchange for a candy bar. Another Infosecurity survey in 2003 found that 90 per cent of workers will give out their password for a free pen [39].

Several researchers have acknowledged that the human factor plays a significant role in ISS [30,40,41]. It is without doubt that the awareness of the people is critical to the success of ISS. In fact, research has found that one of the top threats for ISS is the errors committed by employees [42]. Although awareness among employees is low, little effort is being made to improve the situation [42]. This tendency to ignore instead of tackle was evident in several other studies [23,36,43]. Similarly, research on IS outsourcing in private and public organizations in Kuwait claimed that one of the important drivers for outsourcing, even though the management was well aware of all the risks involved, was the lack of security awareness [35].

It is obvious that ICT plays an increasingly important role in all walks of life, be it in education, business or government matters (e-governance). Developing countries are also embracing ICT at a fast pace, so it is only natural that developing countries must engage in educating the people and raise their awareness about the threats related to ISS. Developing countries generally lag behind in the modern education system. Insufficient training can lead to misuse of the electronic processes hindering the potential benefits that might be attained if used safely. Research highlights the need for people to be educated in terms of not only technical abilities, but also the non-technical issues such as safeguarding an organization's or a country's sensitive information [3].

Researchers agree that the development of human skills and capabilities through education and training is very important [3,5,23]. British Standards Institute recommends the promoting of security awareness through education and training which can help users of IS systems be aware of potential threats [29]. These awareness programmes must make users aware of not only the security risks and remedies, but also the organizations' ISS policy [23]. Of course, education and training programmes will increase the security awareness of users, but organizations should aim for a security culture where users are aware of all the security issues and are capable and skilled enough to make appropriate decisions [36,44].

3.4.4   Culture

Combined with the struggles brought about by limited legislation, insufficient policies and lack of skills in the field of ISS, developing countries are also faced with the citizen's resistance to change. While one could argue that organizational culture is autonomous to national culture, reference [45] argued that organizational cultures are nested within a national culture. That is to say that national culture influences people's practices and thereby their organizational behaviour. Reference [30] conducted an exploratory study in IS culture in Saudi Arabia and found that national culture played a vital role in encouraging people to adopt new ways of working as well as accepting and adjusting to new technologies. Transferring technology created abroad and putting it into practice at home creates numerous cultural and social issues [5]. According to reference [3] one reason why organizations regularly encountered this internal resistance, particularly when implementing new technological systems, is the view by employees that this change is a potential threat to their jobs. This was also noted in the work of [5], which found that resistance was driven by the fear of possible job losses due to traditional jobs being taken over by technology, the fear that technological advancements would lead to loss of income from bribes and also the apprehension posed by the possible new work practices that they would need to adhere to.

For example, in their study on IS awareness in higher education reference [10] sought to investigate the different IS threats faced by a typical higher education institution within the context of a developing country. The focus of the study conducted was Zayed University. The university is based in the United Arab Emirates, and although founded on an educational model from the west, it is embedded within a conservative environment which is rooted in the deep cultural and religious beliefs of its surrounding environment. The findings of the study indicated that in general reported IS threats were like those conveyed in similar investigations in developed countries [46]. The difference however was the perceived causes and sources of these threats together with the ways in which these threats were dealt with. In particular, it was found that the majority of threats were assumed to be external and not in any way connected to university employees or its resources.

While IS awareness is crucial to the overall security of an organization, it must be addressed in hindsight of the national culture. Similarly, while policies and legal frameworks are the foundation for effective IS system, little can be achieved without the full-fledged support and eagerness of the people. The difficulty in addressing the cultural obstacles hindering the implementation of a valuable information system is that each country has a unique culture. Every country has its own culture that subsequently influences the behaviour of the people. Research finding cannot be generalized to other developing countries since national culture affects IS culture in a distinctive way [30].

3.4.5 Dependencies

Apart from the above-mentioned factors there are other factors which influence the security of IS. Reference [25] pointed out that mostly software and hardware systems are manufactured in developed countries and developing countries do not have any control over the security of these components. Another argument presented by [47] is that ICT components developed in developed countries are adapted to meet the local conditions of developing countries. Most ICT products are the low-cost versions and lack the advanced features as it makes them expensive. These all are critical drawbacks when we consider the ISS in developing countries.

3.5 Discussion

Although there appears to be a sense of desire and will to achieve a satisfactory level of ISS, it is evident that ISS in developing countries is lagging behind. For the implementation of efficient and properly functioning ISS systems, particularly in developing countries, there is a basic need for a clear and sound foundation that is built upon lucid policy and transparent legislation. However, there is also a need to educate the people, not only in using new advanced technologies, but also in the risks that these new technologies create. Furthermore, there appears to be a barrier that must be overcome and that is the cultural and social hindrance created as a result of implementing more technical solutions to rather traditional nations.

In carrying out the review, five reoccurring themes or factors were identified – legislation, policy, education, culture and dependencies. While each of these factors was looked at individually, one finds that there is a lack of overall common goals, uncertainty and perhaps some chaos amongst everything else. For instance, research suggested that although awareness of the people is a problem, little was being done to address this issue. At the same time, some countries are choosing to outsource the management of their ISS to more capable companies instead of addressing the lack of awareness within their own organization. Understandably, the path to achieving adequate ISS is not easy flowing, and in a way, on completing of this review, there is a sense that there are no ground rules to follow and decisions are being made on the go. There does not seem to be a clear direction or a defined goal in terms of what the country(s) would like to achieve.

Of course, some countries have attempted to make progress, the United Arab Emirates with its introduction of new laws and Malaysia with its defined cyber policy. While these might seem like small steps to the developed world, they are applaudable advancements for the developing countries. Nevertheless, this is still a fraction of what needs to be done. While organizations and businesses seem to take the brunt of the disarray caused by the lack of laws, policies and awareness, it is evident that a bottleneck exists somewhere. The governments of developing countries must do more to make the changes happen. As mentioned earlier, without the proper backing of ISS, breaches which could result in financial losses can easily happen and this could be a huge burden for the frail economies of developing countries. While analysing the findings of the review, it is worth reiterating that ISS is made up of both information and the systems required to protect it. Basically, ISS is same technologically in both developed and developing nations, but it is the non-technical environmental factors which affect the implementation.

The overarching research questions that were used as a backdrop during the course of the review were

1. *What are the setbacks or vulnerabilities affecting developing countries in terms of ISS?*

This study found a number of different factors that are hindering the progression of developing countries in terms of ISS. To begin with, developing countries are lacking a concrete legal framework in relation to ISS. The laws are not fully established and in some instances, where the laws do exist, users are unaware of them. Secondly, developing countries do not have enough (if any) adequate ISS policies in place. Even when policies have been drafted and put into place, they tend to be overlooked (perhaps because they are not seen as important). Thirdly, ISS awareness amongst the people and general employees is low. Even so, little is being done to improve the situation or address the issue. The tendency to ignore the problem (that of lack of awareness amongst the people) instead of tackling it was evident in many studies.

Finally, one of the toughest setbacks faced by the developing countries was viewed to be the resistance of the people, sustained by strong and unique national cultures. While several reasons were identified as the possible basis of the resistance (for instance, the threat to jobs), addressing ISS issues of each particular nation's from a cultural perspective is complex. Nevertheless, while each of these factors could be identified separately, they are indeed interrelated to one another, and whilst it would be easier to address each of them individually, they must each be considered together but separately for each developing country.

2. *What considerations need to be made in terms of the future aspirations of developing countries?*

In terms of legislation, it is clear that developing countries are in need of some legal reforms in relation to ISS; however, these must be implemented while also educating the citizens on their importance and in hindsight of the national culture. In addition, employees and also the general public should be educated not only in terms of technical skills and abilities, but also on issues such as safeguarding an organization's or a country's sensitive information. Furthermore, more consideration and effort needs to be given to the creation and implementation of acceptable policies – both as a nation and also as an organization. Policymakers should show sensitivity towards local realities and should consider different alternatives before implementing any new technologies. ISS is a global responsibility and is not merely a technical issue. It encompasses all five factors that were identified in this review, namely legislation, policy, education, culture and dependencies. Finally, it is paramount that the threat posed by cyberspace is overseen by an overarching national cyber policy under the national parliament, which would help ensure the protection of the country's overall assets. This chapter in general contributes to the open literature. It also assists ICT policy developers in developing information security systems which are more sensitive to the unique cultural background, which is also typical of the developing nations.

3.6　Conclusion

The driving force behind this research was the uncertainty in regards to the current state of ISS within developing countries. The overall aim of the review was to evaluate the current available literature with the view of identifying different areas of research while providing a holistic viewpoint of the current situation and providing some concrete recommendations in terms of further research. Based on the review, it is suggested that ISS in developing countries should be examined more closely in terms of their political, social and cultural systems rather than just on technical systems.

References

[1]　Okoli, C., and Schabram, K. A guide to conducting a systematic liter-ature review of information systems research. Sprouts: Working Papers

on Information Systems, 2010; 10 (26), http://sprouts.aisnet.org/10-26, on January 2014.

[2] Avgerou, C. Information systems in developing countries: a critical research review. Journal of information Technology, 2008; 23(3), 133–146.

[3] Alfawaz, S., May, L. J., and Mohanak, K. E-government security in developing countries: a managerial conceptual framework. International Research Society for Public Management Conference, Brisbane, 2008.

[4] Whitman, M. E. Enemy at the gate: threats to information security. Communications of the ACM, 2003; 46(8), 91–95.

[5] Ndou, V. E-government for developing countries: opportunities and challenges. The Electronic Journal of Information Systems in Developing Countries, 2004; 18(1), 1–24.

[6] ISACA. Glossary of terms, 2008. Retrieved from http://www.isaca.org/Knowledge-Center/Documents/Glossary/glossary.pdf, on 10 July 2014.

[7] Kim, D., and Solomon, M. G. Fundamentals of Information System Security. 1st edition. USA: Jones and Barlett Publishers Inc., 2010.

[8] Adeleye, B. C., Annansingh, F., and Nunes, M. B. Risk management practices in IS outsourcing: an investigation into commercial banks in Nigeria. International Journal of Information Management, 2004; 24(2), 167–180.

[9] Kankanhalli, A., Teo, H. H., Tan, B. C., and Wei, K. K. An integrative study of information systems security effectiveness. International Journal of Information Management, 2003; 23(2), 139–154.

[10] Rezgui, Y., and Marks, A. Information security awareness in higher education: an exploratory study. Computers & Security, 2008; 27(7), 241–253.

[11] Avgerou, C. Recognising alternative rationalities in the deployment of information systems. The Electronic Journal on Information Systems in Developing Countries, 2000; 3(7), 1–15.

[12] Bada, A. O. Local adaptations to global trends: a study of an IT-based organizational change program in a Nigerian bank. The Information Society, 2002; 18, 77–86.

[13] Sahay, S., and Avgerou, C. Introducing the special issue on information and communication technologies in developing countries. The Information Society, 2002; 18, 73–76.

[14] Mansell, R. Information and communication technologies for development: assessing the potential and the risks. Telecommunications Policy, 1999, 23(1), 35–50.

[15] Ahmad, A. A. Evaluating the security controls of CAIS in developing countries: an empirical investigation. Information Management & Computer Security, 2007; 15(2), 128–148.

[16] Reilly, M. Beware, botnets have your PC in their sights. New Scientist, 2007; 196(2634), 22–23.

[17] Greenwood, L. Africa's mobile banking revolution. BBC News, 2009. Retrieved from http://news.bbc.co.uk/2/hi/business/8194241.stm, on 20 March 2014.

[18]   Fumudoh, S., and Viswanathan, U. En litteraturstudie av informations sys-
       tem säkerhet i utvecklingsländer (Dissertation), 2014. Retrieved from http://
       urn.kb.se/resolve?urn=urn:nbn:se:ltu:diva-58863, http://www.diva-portal.org/
       smash/get/diva2:1032251/FULLTEXT02.pdf.
[19]   Glaser, B., and Strauss, A. The Discovery of Grounded Theory: Strategies for
       Qualitative Research. New Brunswick, NJ: Aldine Transaction, 1967.
[20]   Corbin, J., and Strauss, A. Basics of Qualitative Research: Techniques and
       Procedures for Developing Grounded Theory. Thousand Oaks, CA: Sage, 2008.
[21]   UN. Information Economy Report, 2005. Retrieved from http://www.
       unctad.org/ecommerce/, on 20 March 2014.
[22]   Hashim, M. S. Malaysia's national cyber security policy: the country's cyber
       defence initiatives. In Cybersecurity Summit (WCS), 2011 Second Worldwide
       (pp. 1–7). IEEE.
[23]   Rezgui, Y., and Marks, A. Information security awareness in higher education:
       an exploratory study. Computers & Security, 2008; 27(7), 241–253.
[24]   Bakari, J. K., Tarimo, C. N., Yngstrom, L., and Magnusson, C. State of ICT
       security management in the institutions of higher learning in developing
       countries: Tanzania case study. Fifth IEEE International Conference on
       Advanced Learning Technologies (ICALT), 2005; 1007–1011.
[25]   Zareen, M. S., Akhlaq, M., Tariq, M., and Khalid, U. Cyber security chal-
       lenges and way forward for developing countries. 2nd National Conference
       on Information Assurance (NCIA), 2013; 7–14.
[26]   Computer Crime Research Center. Police grapple with cybercrime. 2014.
       Retrieved from http://www.crime-research.org/news/29.04.2014/3966/, on 10
       June 2014.
[27]   Aggarwal, V. Cyber crime's rampant. 2009. Express Computer. Retrieved
       from http://computer.financialexpress.com/20090803/market01.shtml, on 30
       May 2014.
[28]   Duggal, P. What's wrong with our cyber laws? Express Computer,
       2004. Retrieved from http://computer.financialexpress.com/20040705/
       newsanalysis01.shtml, on 30 May 2014.
[29]   British Standards Institute. Information Security Management- BS
       7799-1:1999. London: BSI.
[30]   Alnatheer M. A. Understanding and measuring information security culture
       in developing countries: case of Saudi Arabia. Research thesis submitted at
       Queensland University of Technology, Brisbane, Australia, 2013.
[31]   Beautement, A., Sasse, M. A., and Wonham, W. The compliance budget:
       managing security behavior in organizations. Proceedings of the 2008
       Workshop on New Security Paradigms (NSPW), 2008; 47–58.
[32]   Adams, A., and Sasse, A. Users are not the enemy: why users compromise
       security mechanisms and how to take remedial measures. Communications
       of the ACM, 1999; 42(12), 40–46.
[33]   Ayyagari, R., and Tyks, J. Disaster at a university: a case study in information
       security. Journal of Information Technology Education: Innovations in
       Practice, 2012; 11, 85–96.

[34] Vorakulpipat, C., Siwamogsatham, S., and Pibulyarojana, K. Exploring information security practices in Thailand using ISM-Benchmark. Technology Management for Global Economic Growth (PICMET), 2010; 1–4.

[35] Khalfan, A. M. Information security considerations in IS/IT outsourcing projects: a descriptive case study of two sectors. International Journal of Information Management, 2004; 24, 29–42.

[36] Tarimo, C. M. ICT security readiness checklist for developing countries: a social-technical approach. Research thesis submitted at Philosophy, Department of Computer and System Sciences, Stockholm University, 2006.

[37] Von Solms, B. Parliamentary oversight of cyber security and critical information infrastructures in developing countries. Science and Information Conference, London, 2013; 335–339.

[38] Raynard, P., and Forstater, M. Corporate social responsibility: implications for small and medium enterprises in developing countries. Technical report submitted at United Nations Industrial Development Organization, 2002.

[39] Wade, J. The weak link in IT security: what good is cutting-edge network security if your own employees sabotage the system by mistake? Risk Management, 2004; 51(6), 32–36.

[40] Parker, D. B. Fighting Computer Crime: A New Framework for Protecting Information. USA: John Wiley & Sons, 1998.

[41] Siponen, M., and Vance, A. Neutralization: new insights into the problem of employee information systems security policy violations. MIS Quarterly, 2010; 34(3), 487–502.

[42] Von Solms, S., and Von Solms, R. The 10 deadly sins of Information Security Management. Computer and Security, 2004; 23, 371–376.

[43] Katz, F. H. The effect of a university information security survey on instructing methods in information security. Second Annual Conference on Information Security Curriculum Development, 2005; 43–48.

[44] Van Niekerk, J., and von Solms, R. Corporate information security education: is outcomes based education the solution? International Information Security Workshops, 2005; 3–18

[45] Hofstede, G. Culture's Consequences: International Differences in Work Related Values. Beverly Hills: Sage Publications, 1984.

[46] Updegrove, D., and Wishon, G. Computers and network security in higher education. EDUCAUSE, 2003.

[47] Kshetri, N. Diffusion and effects of cyber-crime in developing economies. Third World Quarterly, 2010; 31(7), 1057–1079.

Chapter 4

Biometric systems, modalities and attacks

Nathan Clarke[1]

4.1 Introduction

The ability for computer systems to recognize individuals is referred to as biometrics. The need for them to do so has largely been to enable authentication – with weaknesses in other approaches such as secret-knowledge and tokens being well documented in the literature. However, many other reasons exist, they help border control agencies in providing an automated mechanism for passport verification, government agencies to reduce fraud through double claiming of social welfare and enable law enforcement to track terrorists through widespread distributed CCTV.

Whilst biometric systems offer the potential to solve a number of authentication and identification problems, biometrics themselves are complex systems with a variety of factors that affect their ability to operate successfully. Indeed, the use of a specific biometric technique will often largely be dependent upon the application or environment within which it will be used. For example, whilst fingerprint recognition is an ideal choice for use within the context of a mobile phone, it would not be a suitable choice when looking to remotely/covertly identify an individual – as might be required for law enforcement monitoring terrorists. There are also a wide variety of other factors that need consideration such as the availability of the biometric characteristic in the desired population, the uniqueness of the sample, how long the sample remains similar/consistent (referred to as permanence), the usability and acceptance of the approach by the user population, the ease of collecting the sample and the ability to circumvent the approach through forgery. No biometric technique (currently) has a perfect set of characteristics or attributes and therefore, careful selection, design and implementation are required in order to ensure success.

This chapter will present a detailed overview of biometric systems and how they work. The system attributes, performance metrics, modalities are all discussed, alongside an analysis of attacks that exist against biometric systems. Given the limitations that exist in all biometric systems, a trend in biometric research is towards the use of multibiometric systems, which seek to overcome the issues through the application of multiple modalities, algorithms, instances or samples. These systems and the approaches that exist are presented. The chapter ends with a discussion of

[1]University of Plymouth, Centre for Security, Communications & Network Research, UK

the efforts being made with the standardization of the domain – which has been the essential factor in bringing biometrics from a niche into the mainstream.

4.2   Biometric components and attributes

Biometrics are fundamentally concerned with the ability to recognize an individual. Such a recognition can then be used to permit access, whether that be to computer systems or at passport control. However, this explanation oversimplifies the definition and subsequently the underlying system that is required to support the biometric. Biometric systems are split based upon their primary objective: to verify a claimed identity or to identify an individual. The former typically relates to scenarios where the individual states who they are through a username when accessing an IT system or through the presentation of a passport. In such applications, the system need only to compare the biometric sample against the individual who they claim to be – a 1:1 comparison. In the latter case however, the comparison is not 1:1 but rather 1:N (where N is the sample population). The system needs to compare the sample against the whole population to identify whether the person is present. This approach would also likely be required at passport control to ensure the individual is not listed on a watch list (of known criminals/terrorists).

The International Standards Organization (ISO) Joint Technical Committee (JTC) 1 Special Committee 37 defines biometrics as 'automated recognition of individuals based upon on their biological and behavioural characteristics' [1]. It is therefore not appropriate to refer to a biometric where the completed automated system is not present. For example, DNA is not a biometric (as literature often suggests) but rather merely a biometric characteristic which in this case might have the potential to become a biometric in the future once automated. The definition refers to the complete system rather than simply the unique characteristics utilized. The definition also refers to biological and behavioural characteristics which seek to highlight the two subcategories of biometric modalities. The former, also frequently referred to as physiological biometrics, utilizes unique physical features of a person (such as the fingerprint, iris, face or hand) as a means of identifying an individual. Behavioural characteristics utilize features that are dependent upon our environment and learnt behaviour. For example, a person's voice, the way in which they type or provide a signature. The two categories offer a different set of opportunities and risks.

Literature classifies identification into two further modes, open-set and closed-set identification. Open-set identification refers to identifying *if* someone is in the database and if so finding the record. In closed-set identification, it is assumed the person is in the database, and the system needs to find the correct record. Whilst they appear similar in operation, the slight difference in assumptions of whether the individual is in the database or not results in a significant difference in system complexity, with the open-set identification being a far more challenging system to develop. The system need not only provide a person (or more typically a list of persons) who result in the closest match but must also make a determination of whether it is a sufficient match.

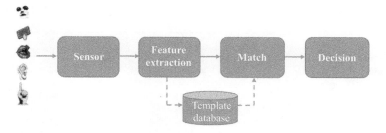

Figure 4.1   A generic model of a biometric system

A biometric system comprises four core components; sample capture, feature extraction, matching and decision. As illustrated in Figure 4.1, these components operate serially with the capture device or sensor providing the basis for collecting the raw sample. In many cases this is not the biometric characteristics themselves but merely a sample that can derive the unique attributes. For example, in facial recognition, the raw sample is a photograph of the face – which itself is suitable to use directly. Rather a set of features, such as facial measurements are derived from it. The second phase, feature extraction is present to achieve this. Once the unique or discriminative features have been identified and extracted these can then be processed by the matching algorithm which provides a measure of similarity between the new sample and a previous stored sample. The final component, decision, takes the matching score and makes a decision as to accept or reject the sample. In most biometric systems, this is merely based upon applying a threshold to the matching score – above the threshold, the sample is accepted, below rejected.

Similarly, with all authentication technologies, the base secret has to be setup prior to use (e.g. the initial setting of the password). In biometrics, this process is referred to as enrolment. The process of enrolment is identical to the first two stages of the biometric system, but rather than matching, the sample is stored as a template for use in the verification and identification processes (also illustrated in Figure 4.1). Given the sample provided in enrolment is utilized to compare all other samples, it is imperative that several additional criteria are met:

- The sample is indeed from the legitimate individual and not fraudulent. This often requires further confirmation of the individual (e.g. physical verification via a passport or driver's licence).
- The quality of the sample is excellent. A poor quality sample will impact each and every subsequent comparison leading to rejection of the approach by the authorized user. To aid this process, additional samples are typically obtained with a view to merging or selecting the best quality samples.

The realization of the biometric system can take a variety of forms depending upon the requirements. For instance, it is possible to have a biometric system where all components are highly integrated into a single device: capture, extraction, storage and classification are all performed locally. This has the advantage that the device is

Table 4.1   Attributes of a biometric approach

Attribute	Description
Uniqueness	The ability to successfully discriminate people. More unique features will enable more successful discrimination of a user from a larger population than techniques with less distinctiveness.
Universal	The ability for a technique to be applied to a whole population of users. Do all users have the characteristics required? For instance, users without fingerprints.
Permanence	The ability for the characteristics not to change with time. An approach where the characteristics change with time will require more frequent updating of the biometric template and result in increased cost to maintain.
Collectable	The ease with which a sensor is able to collect the sample. Does the technique require physical contact with the sensor or can the sample be taken with little or no explicit interaction from a person? What happens when a user has broken their arm and is subsequently unable to present their finger or hand to the system?
Acceptable	The degree to which the technique is found to be acceptable by a person. Is the technique too invasive? Techniques not acceptable will experience poor adoption and high levels of circumvention and abuse.
Circumventable/unforgeability	The ability not to duplicate or copy a sample. Approaches that utilize additional characteristics, such as liveness testing, can improve the protection against forging the sample.

less prone to various attacks as the sensitive biometric data never leaves the device. This is particularly useful in standalone applications such as a high school library for checking books out or a personal mobile phone. However, if there is a need for many biometric sensing devices, for example, at border/passport control, a network-based solution is necessary where the captured sample is sent to central server for verification/identification. If this was not the case, the system administrator would be responsible for ensuring each of the biometric devices are loaded with the necessary biometric templates and this would need updating continuously to reflect changes in employees. It would also prevent any central monitoring of the system. However, network-based solutions also open the door to various network-based attacks. It is important therefore to ensure an appropriate architecture is designed to meet the specific requirements of the deployment.

The selection of which biometric technique or modality to utilize is not necessarily straightforward. There are a number of attributes or characteristics of a biometric modality to consider in conjunction with its specific application. As illustrated in Table 4.1, each of the attributes has a degree of variance. Even with what may be considered the most important attribute, uniqueness, biometric modalities vary considerably in the level of uniqueness that might be present. Physiological approaches tend to have a larger degree of uniqueness in comparison to their behavioural counterparts, which result in them being able to successfully identify individuals in systems that have large population samples. For this reason, most applications that involve identification tend to focus upon the use of physiological modalities. Each biometric modality has a different constitution of the attributes. Retina and iris recognition are unique approaches with very time-invariant or permanent features. However, they are also the most challenging to collect and frequently have issues with acceptability. With regards to how universal a biometric is, this will also tend to vary as there is always a population of people that are unable to successfully provide a sample. For instance, techniques that rely upon a limb being present, such as fingerprint, hand geometry and vascular pattern recognition, would not be possible for individuals missing those particular limbs. Facial recognition is possibly the most universal of the techniques; however, it can suffer from low levels of permanence, with people's faces changing in relatively short periods of time due to weight gain or loss or perhaps hair growth. Furthermore, in societies where people cover their faces, facial recognition would only be acceptable if absolutely essential rather than the norm. The degree to which each technique is susceptible to circumvention through spoofing (the creation of a fraudulent sample) does vary between techniques. However, those approaches that obtain samples from within the body rather on the surface are far more challenging to spoof. For instance, vascular pattern recognition and retina scanning are both very difficult to spoof. Fingerprint and facial recognition are less so, as the process of coping the trait is simpler.

The level of entropy (a measure of the uniqueness) that exists within biometrics is neither fixed at the biometric level, nor fixed at the individual modality. It is wholly dependent upon the feature vector produced (which is intrinsically coupled to the method of classification). Even within a biometric technique, the entropy achieved can vary considerably. Moreover, with many proprietary approaches it is difficult to determine the actual level of entropy. This situation is further complicated by the fact that within biometric systems an exact match between samples is not required – merely a sufficient level of similarity, with sufficient being determined by the threshold level, which is defined on a system-by-system basis. It is therefore not easy to determine the precise entropy levels for biometric systems for a direct comparison. It is however generally understood that the more unique biometrics have extremely high levels of entropy. For instance, iris recognition can have up to 400 data points, with each data point consisting of a large range of values (for illustrative purposes, say, 100), this provides an entropy of 865 bits. Entropy is important because it provides a basis for appreciating the probability that an attacker can successfully predict the feature vector. Whilst an attack is not necessarily achievable merely by knowing the feature vector, the feature vector is in essence equivalent to a password, and thus an essential piece of information in order to successfully attack the system.

4.3   Biometric performance characteristics

Biometrics operate on the basis of comparing a biometric sample against a predetermined template, which is securely acquired from the user when they are initially enrolled on the system. This results in a matching process which provides a measure of similarity between the two samples. As such, misclassifications of both the authorized user and the impostors are possible. In verification systems, these errors rates are referred to as the

- *False acceptance rate* (FAR), or rate at which an impostor is accepted by the system, and the
- *False rejection rate* (FRR), or rate at which the authorized user is rejected from the system.

The error rates share a mutually exclusive relationship where neither of the error rates are typically both at 0% and one will increase as the other decreases. Figure 4.1 illustrates an example of this relationship. This relationship translates into a trade-off for the system designer between high security and low user-convenience (tight threshold setting) or low security and high user-convenience (slack threshold setting). Typically, a threshold setting that meets the joint requirements of security and user convenience is usually set. A third error rate, the *equal error rate* (EER), equates to the point at which the FAR and FRR meet and is typically used as a means of comparing the performance of different biometric techniques. These performance rates when presented are the averaged results across a test population, therefore presenting the performance a typical user might expect to achieve. It is therefore important when looking to understand how well a modality performs; an appreciation of the circumstances under which the performance metrics were determined is key to ensuring the stated values are credible.

The FAR and FRR metrics refer to the overall system performance of the biometric as determined at the decision stage. These rates are also accompanied by the

- *True acceptance rate* (TAR), the rate at which the system correctly verifies the claimed individual, and the
- *True rejection rate* (TRR), the rate at which the system correctly rejects a false claim.

It is more common for biometric vendors to publish their rates in terms of the FAR and FRR. There are, however, a number of other metrics commonly used when testing and evaluating biometric systems. These are calculated at extraction and matching stages of the biometric process. At the extraction phase the following metrics are established:

- *Failure to acquire* (FTA), the rate at which either the capture or extraction stages are unable to create a valid template, and the
- *Failure to enrol* (FTE), the rate at which the user is unable to successfully enrol onto the system.

Reasons for failure are numerous but can include problems with the physical sample such as dirty or scarred fingerprints; problems with the sensor such as swiping the finger too quickly; and environment factors, such as poor illumination for facial recognition. Both error rates are typically associated with problems capturing the sample due to poor human–computer interaction (or lack of education of how to use the system) and the sensitivity of the capture device. The FTA is a contributing factor of the FTE as it measures the proportion of the population that does not have a particular trait or is unable to provide one of sufficient quality. FTA errors can also appear for individuals that have successfully enrolled. As such the FRR and FAR metrics include the FTA errors. The FAR metric also includes the FTE. The FTE is not included within the FRR because if the user is never enrolled they are unable to be falsely rejected.

The remaining error rates are associated with the matching or classification stage. These mirror the FRR and FAR and are referred to as the

- *False match rate* (FMR), the rate at which impostors are falsely verified against the claimed identity; and the
- *False non-match rate* (FNMR), the rate at which authorized users are incorrectly rejected.

The key difference between the FMR/FNMR and the FAR/FRR metrics is the latter includes other errors that appear in the system – for instance, the FAR includes the FMR, FTA and FTE errors; and therefore presents the overall system performance. The metrics are related as follows:

FNMR = 1 – TAR
FMR = 1 – TRR
FRR = FNMR + FTA + *decision error*
FAR = FMR + FTA + FTE + *decision error*

It should be noted, however, that both the FRR and FAR metrics can also include an error generated by the decision phase should it introduce additional information such as sample quality scores into the decision-making process. Whilst the FAR, FRR and FMR and FNMR have specific definitions, it is common in literature for these terms to be used interchangeably. Care should therefore be taken in interpreting the results correctly.

There are also metrics utilized when the system operates in identification. These include

- True positive identification rate (TPIR), the rate at which the users' correct identifier is amongst those returned by the system. In identification systems, a ranked list of users mostly closely associated with the profile can be returned instead of only one user. It is assumed the user is enrolled in the system. As such, it is common to see several sets of the TPIR presented in rank 1, rank 3 and rank 5 (i.e. the identification is deemed successful if it appears in the first, first three or first five results, respectively).
- False positive identification rate, the rate at which users not enrolled onto the system are falsely identified. This error rate is only present in open-set identification, as in closed-set identification all users are enrolled onto the system.
- False negative identification rate (FNIR), the rate at which users' correct identifier is not amongst those returned by the system. It is assumed that the user is enrolled and is directly related to the TPIR (FNIR = 1 – TPIR).

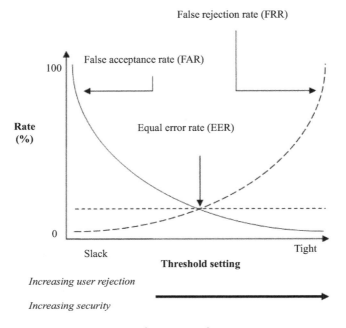

Figure 4.2   Verification performance curves

The actual performance of different biometric modalities varies considerably with the uniqueness and sophistication of the pattern classification engine. In addition, published performances from companies often portray a better performance than can typically be achieved. This is due to the tightly controlled conditions in which they perform their test, often taking into consideration any particular strengths their approach might have. Care must be taken when interpreting results to ensure they meet the required levels of performance for the system. On behalf of the US government, the National Institute for Standards and Technology (NIST) has played an active role in providing independent evolutions of many biometric systems [2].

In addition to the performance metrics, a number of performance graphs are also utilized to graphically assist the designer in understanding the relationship between the metrics and provide a mechanism for selecting the optimum threshold. Figure 4.2 illustrates the relationship between the FAR and FRR against varying thresholds. This provides a mechanism for establishing the threshold given acceptable levels of FAR and FRR error. The receiver operating characteristic (ROC) curve is also a standard graph that relates the FMR with the TAR (or FNMR). Examples of the ROC are illustrated in Figures 4.3 and 4.4. These charts map the error rates as a function of the threshold and enable a simpler mechanism for comparing biometric techniques or algorithms.

Determining an appropriate threshold between performance metrics is no simple task. Unfortunately, the graphs depicting system performance and trade-off merely present the averaged performance across a test population and hide the underlying

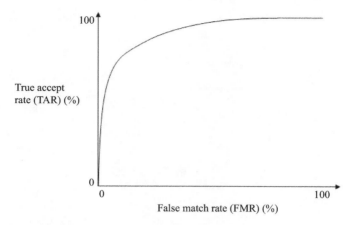

Figure 4.3   ROC curve (TAR against FMR)

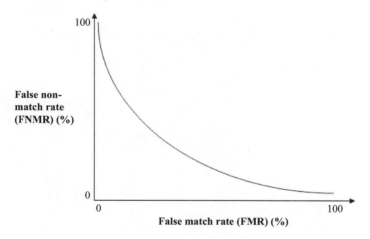

Figure 4.4   ROC curve (FNMR against FMR)

characteristics of individual levels of performance. The reality of the system is that the FAR and FRR convey very uncharacteristic relationships which can vary significantly between users. To illustrate the problem, Figures 4.5 and 4.6 fictitiously represent two users whose individual performance characteristics differ significantly. Had a system designer selected a threshold (say at the mid-point on the *x*-axis) because they had deemed this appropriate given the overall average performance the need to balance security with convenience, then neither of these users would experience the same level of performance. For the user displaying the characteristics in Figure 4.5, the choice of threshold level would result in a high level of user inconvenience and a higher level of security than was deemed appropriate. For the user in Figure 4.6, the level of security provided will be far lower than the system designer had set.

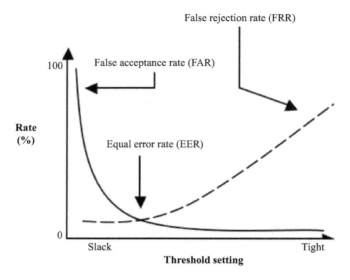

Figure 4.5   User A performance characteristics

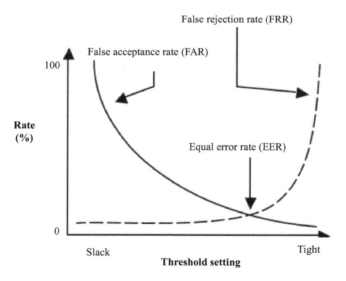

Figure 4.6   User B performance characteristics

In practice, the setting of a threshold can be achieved by setting either a global or a local level. If the former, it must be understood that significant variations might exist in the population, yet the latter can only really be determined by the user themselves – which will often result in the user fine-tuning the threshold to provide low levels of security in favour of usability. Given this problem, time and effort have been put into finding methods of normalizing the output of the pattern classification process – so that an output value of, say, 0.6 means the same across a population of users. Other efforts have gone into finding methods of automating the threshold decision based on a number of authorized and impostor samples – determining the performance of the biometric technique for each and every user prior to operation.

4.4   Physiological biometric approaches

The majority of core biometric techniques commercially available are physiologically based and tend to have a more mature and proven technology. In addition, physiological biometrics typically have more discriminative and characteristic invariant features, and as such are often utilized in both verification and identification systems. This section will briefly provide a background to the following physiological approaches:

- Ear geometry
- Facial recognition
- Facial thermogram
- Fingerprint recognition
- Hand geometry
- Iris recognition
- Retinal recognition
- Vascular pattern recognition

Please take care when considering the performance of the biometric approaches. Many of the statistics presented are based upon studies undertaken by researchers and industry bodies that vary in the nature and quality of methodology deployed. The results are therefore not directly comparable but do provide a basis for appreciating the level of recognition performance that can be achieved.

4.4.1   Ear geometry

The human ear is a structure that contains a rich canvas of information that changes little over time. As illustrated in Figure 4.7, the ear is made up of several components, including the helix, antihelix, concha and intertragic-notch, which result in a fairly unique pattern. Studies have reported recognition rates of between 93% and 99.6% under (specific) experimental conditions [3–5]. More recent research has sought to utilize 3D images of the ear, and Yan demonstrated an approach that provided a rank-one recognition rate of 97.6% [4].

It is also an approach that performs well against the criteria of being universal in nature – few people are born without an ear. Little evidence exists to its acceptability amongst users particularly as no large-scale commercial biometric systems exist. The approach has almost exclusively been used in the domain of law enforcement and forensics – where acceptability is not a requirement. Whilst collecting the sample might have its difficulties, studies have argued that ear geometry does not suffer so badly from environmental factors in comparison to other modalities such as facial

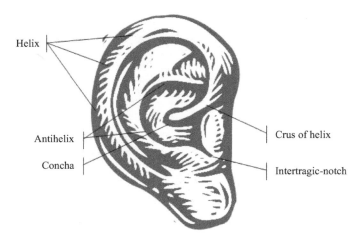

Figure 4.7   Anatomy of the ear

recognition. It is also large enough to be captured from a distance which is a problem
with other modalities such as iris and retina recognition [6].

4.4.2   Facial recognition

Utilizing the distinctive features of a face, facial recognition has found increasing
popularity in both computer/access security and crowd surveillance applications, due
in part to the increasing performance of the more recent algorithms and its covert
nature (i.e. authentication of the user can happen without their explicit interaction
with a device or sensor). Whilst the approach performs well against the criteria of
universality and acceptability (in most scenarios), it is an approach that suffers from
issues surrounding permanence and collectability. Obviously over longer periods of
time (decades) the nature of the face and subsequently the facial features can change
dramatically. However, shorter-term changes such as weight loss or gain can also
affect the performance of the system. Facial characteristics of the very young are
also likely to have not matured and be subject to change over shorter periods of time.
Collectability issues can result from objects obscuring the capture (e.g. beards, glasses
and hats) and the environment (e.g. illumination, position of face and distance from
camera). The actual features utilized tend to change between proprietary algorithms
but include measurements that tend not to change over time, such as the distance
between the eyes and nose, areas around cheekbones and the sides of the mouth.

   The performance of facial recognition algorithms can vary considerably depending upon the context (e.g. high-resolution images versus low-resolution, position
and environment) and the extraction and classification algorithms employed. NIST's
large-scale experimental results from the Face Recognition Vendor Test put the approx-
imate FAR at 0.001% with a FRR of 0.01% [7]. Whilst front-facing 2D images were
traditionally used in the capturing process, more recent research has focused upon
3D imagery. A key advantage of the 3D image is that it is capable of authenticating

users with an angle of up to 90°, rather than up to 20° with traditional 2D images. 3D capture also provides additional liveness detection to prevent forgery.

4.4.3   Facial thermogram

Facial thermogram is an approach that has evolved from the facial recognition domain and the problem where poor illumination results in increased errors. The need for sufficient light restricts the applicability of facial recognition in a number of application scenarios where such control over light is not possible. Facial thermogram utilizes an infrared camera to capture the heat pattern of a face caused by the blood flow under the skin. The uniqueness is present through the vein and tissue structure of a user's face. The use of an infrared camera removes the necessity for any illumination (although in practice many studies have also used intensified near-infrared sources which require some ambient light). Studies have shown that external factors such as surrounding temperature play an important role in the performance of the recognition [8]. Studies have also demonstrated that the performance achieved is between 84% and 93% [8]. However, the majority of research has combined thermogram with visible sensors to augment standard recognition performance, suggesting limited scope for the approach in a unimodal fashion.

4.4.4   Fingerprint recognition

Fingerprint recognition is the most widely utilized technique, with obvious applications in law enforcement as well as computer systems. They can utilize a number of approaches to classification including minutiae-based (irregularities within fingerprint ridges), ridge-based and correlation-based [9]. The 2006 Fingerprint Verification Competition best result obtained an average EER of 2.155% for one of the algorithms [10]. The image capture process does require specialized hardware, based upon one of four core techniques: capacitive, optical, thermal and ultrasound, with each device producing an image of the fingerprint. Figure 4.8 illustrates the more common optical

Figure 4.8   Fingerprint sensor devices

and capacitive scanners, the latter comprising a smaller form factor than the former but frequently resulting in a poorer image.

Fingerprint recognition is a mature and proven technology with very solid and time-invariant discriminative features suitable for identification systems. Although the uniqueness of fingerprints is not in question, with identical twins even having different prints, fingerprint systems do suffer from usability problems such as fingerprint placement, dirt and small cuts on the finger. To date fingerprint recognition has been deployed in a wide variety of scenarios from physical access security to computer security on laptops, mobile phones and Personal Digital Assistants (PDAs). Acceptability overall is quite good as people have a better understanding of the technique – largely derived from its use within law enforcement. Fingerprints are one of three accepted modalities for use within electronic passports (formally known as Machine Readable Travel Documents) (as defined by the International Civil Aviation Organisation (ICAO)) – with facial and iris recognition being the other two [11].

4.4.5   Hand geometry

Hand geometry involves the use of a specialist scanner, which takes a number of measurements such as length, width, thickness and surface area of the fingers and hand [12]. Different proprietary systems take differing numbers of measurements but all the systems are loosely based on the same set of characteristics. Unfortunately, these characteristics do not tend to be unique enough for large-scale identification systems, but are often used for time and attendance systems [13]. The sensor and hardware required to capture the image tends to be relatively large and arguably not suitable for many applications such as computer-based login [14].

4.4.6   Iris recognition

The iris is the coloured tissue surrounding the pupil of the eye and is composed of intricate patterns with many furrows and ridges, as illustrated in Figure 4.9. The iris is an ideal biometric in terms of both its uniqueness and stability (variation with time), with extremely fast and accurate results [15].

Traditionally, iris systems required a very short focal length for capturing the image (e.g. physical access systems), increasing the intrusiveness of the approach. However, a range of commercial desktop-based systems for logical access are acquiring images at distances up to 40 cm [16]. In the research domain, studies purport to be able to acquire iris images up to 10 m away with no degradation of performance [17]. Cameras are still however sensitive to eye alignment causing inconvenience to users. In terms of performance, Daugman reports a best EER of 0.0011 from the NIST Iris Competition Evaluation [6]. Iris recognition is therefore suited to identification scenarios and this is where the majority of implementations to date have been deployed. For example, the UK utilized iris recognition for expediting passport checks at airports [18].

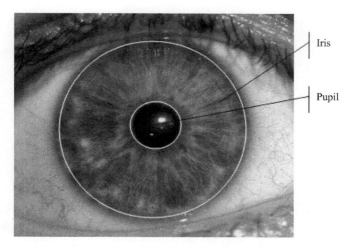

Figure 4.9   Anatomy of an iris. Modified from original: Wikimedia Commons, 2016

4.4.7   Retinal recognition

Retina scanning utilizes the distinctive characteristics of the retina and can be deployed in both identification and verification modes. An infrared camera is used to take a picture of the retina highlighting the unique pattern of veins at the back of the eye. Similar to iris recognition, this technique suffers from the problems of user inconvenience, intrusiveness and limited application as the person is required to carefully present their eyes to the camera at a very close proximity. In addition, hardware has been traditionally prohibitively expensive. As such, the technique tends to be most often deployed within physical access solutions with very high security requirements [16]. The approach does have excellent performance characteristics with the extraction phase producing upward of 240 data points (30–40 points for fingerprint minutiae) [19].

4.4.8   Vascular pattern recognition

This technique utilizes the subcutaneous vascular network on the back of the hand to verify an individual's identity. The patterns are highly distinctive and different in identical twins. The subcutaneous nature of the technique, like retinal recognition, is difficult to falsify or spoof. Vascular pattern recognition does not suffer from the same usability issues however. As such, this technique has experienced significant focus with commercial products available.

The requirement to capture the hand results in a fairly large sensor, which in turn makes it an inappropriate technology for computer access (in the most part). Applications of the technology include physical access and specific scenarios such as ATM authentication, where the technology has the opportunity to be developed within the system itself. The performance of the approach, as reported by studies, suggests an EER in the region of 0.145% (with some reporting even better performances [20]. Finger-based Vascular Pattern Recognition (VPR)s has become particularly popular – with a form factor similar to fingerprint recognition capture sensors but with the additional forgery protection afforded to VPR-based approaches.

4.5   Behavioural biometric approaches

Behavioural biometrics classify a person on some unique behaviour. However, as behaviours tend to change over time due to, for instance, environmental, societal and health variations, the discriminating characteristics used in recognition also change. This is not necessarily a major issue if the behavioural biometric has built-in counter-measures that constantly monitor the reference template and new samples to ensure its continued validity over time, without compromising the security of the technique. In general, behavioural biometrics tend to be more transparent and user convenient than their physiological counterparts, however, at the expense of a lower authentication performance.

This section will briefly explain the following behavioural approaches to biometrics:

- Behavioural profiling
- Gait recognition
- Keystroke analysis
- Signature recognition
- Speaker recognition

4.5.1   Behavioural profiling

Behavioural profiling (also referred to as service utilization) describes the process of authenticating a person based upon their specific interactions with applications and or services. For instance, within a PC, service utilization would determine the authenticity of the person dependent upon which applications they used, when and for how long, in addition to also utilizing other factors. The permanence of the features is poor with the variance experienced within a user's reference template being a significant inhibiting factor. It is suggested however that sufficient discriminative traits exist within our day-to-day interactions to authenticate a person (Figure 4.10).

Although not unique and distinct enough to be used within an identification system, this technique is non-intrusive and can be used to continuously monitor the identity of users whilst they work on their computer system. However, this very advantage also has a disadvantage with regard to users' privacy as their actions will be continually monitored, and such information has the potential to be misused (e.g. the capturing of passwords). Acceptability is therefore going to be determined by how these two factors play out in practice. Although no authentication mechanisms exist utilizing this technique, a number of companies are utilizing profiling as a means of fraud protection on credit card and mobile telephony systems [21,22]. Within these

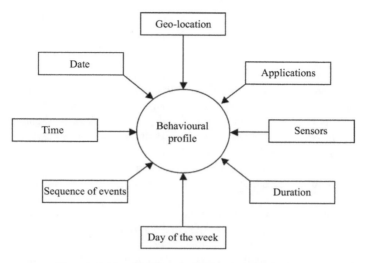

Figure 4.10   Attributes of behavioural profiling

systems, which are very specific to a subset of tasks, studies have reported detection rates exceeding 90% with false alarm rates as low as 3% [23].

4.5.2   Gait recognition

Utilizing the way in which an individual walks to determine their identity, gait recognition has an obvious advantage from the collection perspective in that it can be achieved from quite a distance, more so than any other biometric approach (most of which require physical contact with the sensor). This leads to it being used almost exclusively for identification purposes (as no opportunity to provide a claimed identity is available) and several unique applications where discrete monitoring of the individuals is required, such as airports. However, like all behavioural biometrics, external factors play a significant role in the variance of samples. Footwear, walking surface and clothing all play a role, as well as indoor versus outdoors and the mindset of the person. Gait recognition also suffers from issues with regards to its universality and permanence. It would not work on those who are wheelchair bound and disabled. Ignoring the already fairly large day-to-day variance that exists in our gait due to carrying bags and environmental facts, long-term recognition will also be an issue as age and illness play a role.

The process of classification is generally categorized into two approaches: shape and dynamics. A gait sample includes the walking of an individual over two strides. The shape-based approach looks at the overall image shape of the individual over this cycle, whereas the dynamics approach looks at the rate of transition within the cycle. Performance rates vary considerably depending upon the study but identification rates can range from 78% to 3% depending upon the dataset [24].

With the popularity of mobile devices, mobile-based gait recognition has received significant attention in research laboratories – where the built-in accelerometer and gyroscopes are utilized to provide a basis for performing verification. Experiments are however largely constrained to very simply setups that do not reflect normal use in practice [25].

4.5.3   Keystroke analysis

The way in which a person types on a keyboard has been shown to demonstrate some unique properties [26]. The process of authenticating a person from their typing characteristic is known as Keystroke Analysis (or Dynamics). Authentication itself can be performed in both *static* (text dependent) and *dynamic* (text independent) modes, the former being the more reliable approach. The particular characteristics used to differentiate between people can vary, but often include the time between successive keystrokes, also known as the inter-keystroke latency and the hold time of a key press.

The unique factors of keystroke analysis are not discriminative enough for use within an identification system, but can be used within a verification system. Several commercial systems have been developed over the years with varying degrees of success. BehavioSec is a leading supplier of continuous authentication of which is based in part upon keystroke dynamics [27]. A major downside to keystroke analysis is the time and effort required to generate the reference template. As a person's typing characteristics are more variable than say a fingerprint, the number of samples required to create the template is greater, requiring the user to repetitively enter, for example, a username and password until a satisfactory quality level is obtained. The performance of keystroke analysis varies considerably amongst studies, but a notable study by Joyce and Gupta [28] managed to achieve an FRR of 16.36% with an FAR of 0.25% using a short-string.

4.5.4   Signature recognition

As the name implies, signature recognition systems attempt to authenticate a person based upon their signature. Although signatures have been used for decades as a means of verifying the identity of a person on paper, their use as a biometric is more recent. The use of touchscreen interfaces such as those on PDAs, mobile phones and tablets has made the acquisition of samples simpler (and cheaper). Authentication of the signature can be performed statically or/and dynamically. Static authentication involves utilizing the actual features of a signature, whereas dynamic authentication also uses information regarding how the signature was produced, such as the speed and pressure. The latter approaches are far more robust against forgery – an attack that has always plagued signature-based verification. Commercial applications exist, including for use within computer access and point-of-sale verification and are frequently utilized in the US. Performance rates for signature recognition are better than most behavioural approaches with an EER of 2.84% being reported [29].

4.5.5   Speaker recognition (or voice verification)

A natural biometric, and arguably the strongest behavioural option, voice verification utilizes many physical aspects of the mouth, nose and throat, but is considered a behavioural biometric as the pronunciation and manner of speech is inherently behavioural. Although similar, it is important not to confuse voice verification with voice recognition as both systems perform a distinctly different task. Voice recognition is the process of recognizing *what* a person says, whereas voice verification is recognizing *who* is saying it. Voice verification, similarly to keystroke analysis, can be performed in static (text dependent) and dynamic modes (text independent), again with the former being a simpler task than the latter. Pseudo-dynamic approaches do exist, which request the user to say a random two numbers, which have not been explicitly trained for during enrolment. Numerous companies exist providing various applications and systems that utilize voice verification. In terms of performance, speaker recognition is typically amongst the best performing behavioural approach with an EER of approximately 2% [30]. However, the authors from this study also demonstrate the variability of the performance characteristics depending upon the nature of the sample.

The list of biometrics provided should not be considered exhaustive as new techniques and measurable characteristics are constantly being identified. The common underlying trend that appears within behavioural approaches is that their performance is highly variable depending upon the scenario and external factors. The levels of uniqueness and permanence in comparison to their physical counterparts are poorer.

4.6 Attacks against biometrics

As with all authentication approaches, efforts have been made to hack, break and circumvent biometric systems. As these systems tend to be more complex than their secret-knowledge and token counterparts, in that they contain more components and rely upon probabilistic outcomes, they do offer a wider scope for possible misuse.

The simplest way to categorize the possible attack vectors against a biometric is to consider all the components that make up the system. In reality, each component, the sample, the sensor, the biometric algorithm, the system or any of the communication links in between can possibly be compromised (as illustrated in Figure 4.11).

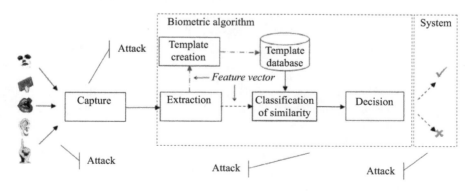

Figure 4.11   Attacks on a biometric system

The ability and difficulty for an attacker to compromise an element will greatly depend upon the implementation of the individual biometric. Biometric systems can come in a variety of forms from completely standalone devices that perform the capture, extraction, classification and decision process internally or locally (e.g. a USB memory device with a fingerprint sensor) to systems that perform various aspects of the process in physically disparate systems. For instance, an enterprise deployment of fingerprints to replace standard logins could have distributed functionality throughout the network. The sensor on the mouse or keyboard captures the biometric sample. The sample is then communicated to an authentication server via the desktop system. The authentication server will perform extraction and classification – possibly on multiple servers to allow for load balancing which is required when large volumes of authentications are necessary (e.g. when everyone arrives at 9 am to start work). The decision from the authentication server is then communicated to the enterprise server that controls access to all systems. That decision is then filtered down to the desktop system, which will subsequently login or deny access. The latter system has far more scope for misuse simply due to the larger number of systems that are involved and the various communication links between the systems that provide an opportunity for interception.

Standalone systems are typically far more resistant to attack as the complete process has been deployed into a single processing unit. An opportunity to sniff or capture information from bus lines (metal tracks and wires connecting components) or read the memory off of chips is more limited. Whilst they have good tamper-resistance, poor design still offers opportunities for misuse, with a number of USB memory keys with fingerprint sensors having been hacked. Notably, Apple in 2013 took the decision with its fingerprint solution (Touch ID) to implement a device-centric model with a dedicated chip to process and store the fingerprint information. It provided an approach that prioritized usability over cost and subsequently became an exemplar in usable security.

Considering each of the components in turn, the acquisition of a biometric sample via forceful means is an inevitable consequence, largely due to its simplicity versus the remaining more technical attacks. Fortunately, to date, few such attacks have occurred; however, one notable incident in Malaysia did result in a person losing his thumb [31]. The communication links are also an obvious target for attack. However, approaches to attacking and defending against these forms of attack fall under standard domain of network security (i.e. end-to-end cryptographic support) and therefore will not be considered.

Instead focus will be given to attacks on the sensor and the biometric algorithm. By far the most common attacks are those against the sensor itself. Spoofing is a technique where the attacker is able to provide a fake biometric sample to the sensor and convince it that it is indeed a legitimate sample. Attacking the system at the presentation stage removes many of the technical barriers that exist when compromising other aspects of the system. The nature of some biometric approaches is that either fragments or even complete copies are left behind. For instance, fingerprints are left behind on many objects people touch. An attacker can use the same techniques deployed by law enforcement agencies for lifting the prints. Once lifted, a duplicate

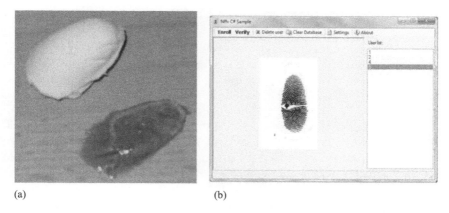

(a)   (b)

Figure 4.12   Examples of fake fingerprint: (a) silicon and jelly fingers; (b) image captured using silicon finger

can be from freely available modelling materials [32]. Figure 4.12 illustrates two examples of fake fingers created using silicon and jelly. The second image illustrates a successful capture and authentication using a fake silicon finger. Facial images are created every time a photograph is taken of you. A simple print-off can often be used to spoof a sensor. There have also been documented cases of attackers simply breathing on a fingerprint sensor and obtaining access – this works due to the latent oils from the finger remaining on the sensor from the previous person [33].

Behavioural biometrics techniques are subject to forgery, particularly if an action is observed previously. Signature recognition, keystroke analysis, voice verification and gait recognition all have the opportunity of being misused in this way. Although, as with traditional forgery, it often requires a specialist skill in its own right in order to mimic the behaviour of the authorized individual. For example, the way a TV impersonator is able to mimic the voice and mannerisms of celebrities.

As a consequence, biometric vendors are adding a level of sophistication to the approaches that assist in minimizing the threat posed by spoofing. For many approaches, a liveness component is included in the system to ensure the sample being provided is acquired from a live host. Approaches taken for fingerprint systems include temperature, pulse, blood pressure, perspiration and electrical resistance. Facial recognition systems have utilized approaches such as rapid eye movement and 3D imagery to determine liveness. Whilst practically different biometric techniques have differing levels of liveness implemented, some have fallen short in providing effective protection, with ingenious attackers circumventing even these measures. However, this continued battle between designers and hackers will persist and liveness detection will improve in time and become an inherent component of all biometric products.

Attacks against the biometric algorithm can be amongst the most technically challenging to achieve. A thorough analysis and understanding of the data extraction and classification elements can highlight possible weaknesses in the algorithm that can be exploited. For example, whilst a biometric approach might utilize a number of features to correctly classify an individual, some features' contribution to the unique discriminatory information that is provided could be more than others. Understanding which play a more important role provides a focus for the attacker. This information could then be either used to produce a sample that would conform to those features or more likely be injected into the system as a mechanism for bypassing the sensor.

Another approach to this type of attack is to analyse the performance characteristics of an approach at the individual user level. Whilst performance metrics are given in various forms such as EER, FAR or FRR, in reality for statistical reliability, these figures are actually average performances across a population of people. An examination of individual performance characteristics (the match score) will often highlight impostors with very high FAR against a particular authorized user. A demonstration of this is illustrated in Figure 4.13 where impostors 1 and 3 have characteristics that are closer to the authorized user than impostor 2. The collection and analysis of these will highlight potential weaknesses in the system.

These more technically challenging attacks do assume the attacker has free access to the technology – either the product or an Software Development Kit of the algorithm, so that repeated samples can be sent through the process and analysed. The final, rather non-technical approach is to simply attempt a brute-force attack against the feature vector. After all, the feature vector is simply a form of secret-knowledge. The key difference with biometric samples is that the attacker does not need to reproduce the feature vector exactly; just with sufficient similarity for the system to deem

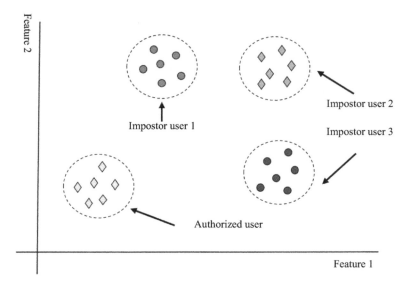

Figure 4.13   Demonstration of feature space

it an authorized sample. How similar depends upon the configuration of the threshold value and the level of security the administration wants to achieve.

4.7 Multibiometrics

The individual weaknesses of biometric approaches have resulted in more towards combining certain aspects in order to benefit constructively from the strengths whilst minimizing any negative consequences. Multibiometrics can be divided into six categories and each has its own set of advantages that help achieve a particular set of objectives:

- Multimodal
- Multi-sample
- Multi-algorithmic
- Multi-instance
- Multi-sensor
- Hybrid

Multimodal approaches seek to combine biometric techniques in order to overcome particular issues in any particular modality. Typically, this is related to improving upon the recognition performance, but can also be used to reduce the problem of universality. All biometric techniques suffer from a (typically small) proportion of the population unable to present the particular biometric trait. Facial recognition is perhaps one of the few exceptions. The use of multimodal approaches provides the ability of the system to rely upon more than one biometric technique. For instance, the ICAO suggests the use of fingerprint and facial recognition technologies. Should users be unable to present reliable and consistent fingerprint samples, a secondary measure is present. The performance of the overall approach, for users that can provide both traits, can also be improved. The need to provide more than one sample will also help in preventing spoofing attacking because an attacker needs to not only circumvent one technique but two or more. Whilst combining them does not increase the difficulty of circumventing the individual techniques, it does increase the workload and effort required from the attacker. After cost, which will be discussed later, the principal disadvantage with multimodal approaches is acceptability. The inclusion of multiple sensors from different modalities within the normal intrusive application scenario places an additional burden upon the individual.

Multi-sample approaches seek to improve overall recognition performance through the combination of matching scores from multiple samples. This has a positive effect in situations where a degree of variability exists within the sample collection (due to noise or other environmental factors). The use of multiple samples assists in reducing the impact of poor individual samples.

The third approach of multi-algorithmic refers to utilizing more than one algorithm during the matching phase. This can permit the system to capitalize upon the strengths of particular classification approaches and subsequently provide a more robust decision. For instance, some facial recognition algorithms have a better performance with images with more serve facial orientations or changes in illumination. For the same reasons as multi-sample, multi-algorithmic approaches also provide a more robust result. But rather than focusing upon the potential weaknesses between samples, multi-algorithmic approaches look to improve upon the weaknesses present in a classification algorithm. The use of multi-algorithmic approaches can also be referred to as a multi-classifier system and such systems have been widely recognized as providing significantly better performance over their uni-algorithmic counterparts. The basis for this improvement is largely based upon utilizing classification algorithms that base or weight their matching score on different attributes of the sample or feature vector. As highlighted in the previous chapter, each biometric technique has a variety of approaches to achieve classification. Each approach capitalizes upon particular attributes of the sample. If algorithms which focus upon different aspects are combined, they can complement each other. For instance, speaker recognition systems have relied upon either spectral or higher-level classification approaches. Both approaches look at different attributes of the biometric sample. A spectral approach focuses upon the vocal characteristics of the sample, whilst the higher-level language approach tends to focus upon how and what is being said. A combination of both approaches would constructively support each other.

Given the increasing trend towards multi-algorithmic approaches, many biometric vendors are likely to contain multi-algorithmic approaches in order to improve performance.

Multi-instance approaches are similar to multi-sample but refer to the use of multiple subtypes of the same biometric, for instance, the left and right iris or the index finger of the left and right hands. This approach is useful particularly in situations where the user population is particularly large. Rather than relying upon a single biometric instance to provide sufficient distinctiveness to discriminate the whole population, the use of multi-instances simplifies the problem.

Multi-sensor approaches utilize more than one sensor to capture a single biometric trait. This approach is useful when the different sensors are able to bring complementary information to the classification problem. For instance, in fingerprint recognition, the use of optical and capacitive sensors has been used with a significant improvement in overall performance [34].

Finally, hybrid systems utilize a combination of the aforementioned approaches, for example, the combination of a multimodal approach and multi-algorithmic. Each individual technique utilizes multiple classification algorithms to optimize the individual response, but those responses are also combined with other biometric techniques. Hybrid systems, if designed correctly, represent the most robust and strongest (in terms of recognition performance) biometric systems. They do however also represent the most complex, requiring increased storage, processing and architectural complexity.

The capture of samples can be performed in a synchronous and asynchronous approach. The former refers to capturing the biometric samples simultaneously or in parallel. The latter approach refers to the user interacting with each biometric capture device sequentially. There are also multiple approaches to actually using these

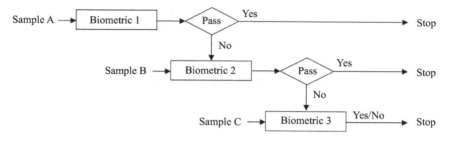

Figure 4.14   Cascade mode of processing of biometric samples

samples. It is possible to combine the output of the matching subsystems from multiple algorithms or the result from multiple approaches after the decision subsystem. It is also possible to take the output of one decision from a single biometric sample to inform whether a subsequent sample needs to be analysed. For instance, should the matching result of the first biometric result in a very high confidence in the authenticity of the user, there could be no need for further verification. Should the confidence be lower, further verification would be useful. As illustrated in Figure 4.14, if given sample A, the authenticity of the user cannot be verified, the system can move to sample B, sample C and so on. At any point during the process should the verification result be successful, the process can stop, removing the need to further process samples. If the order of samples presented to the system is prioritized based upon overall performance/confidence of the modality (i.e. facial recognition outperforms behavioural profiling in terms of performance), the level of processing could be reduced.

4.7.1   Fusion

In each of the multibiometric approaches a requirement exists to combine some data, for instance, the matching scores from multiple algorithms or the decisions from multiple biometric approaches. The term fusion is given to this combination or fusing of data in order to enhance the overall performance of biometrics. The nature of the data fusion can occur effectively at any point within the biometric system:

- Sensor image
- Feature extraction
- Matching subsystem
- Decision subsystem

The type of fusion that is required will depend upon a variety of factors. However, certain types of multibiometrics can only implement fusion later on in the biometric process. For example, a multi-algorithmic approach requires data fusion at either the matching or the decision subsystems. It would not be viable to fuse the data any earlier as it would not be possible to process the data through the different algorithms. Multi-sample approaches could utilize fusion at the sensor or feature extraction processes to produce a more robust image or feature vector for use by the matching subsystem.

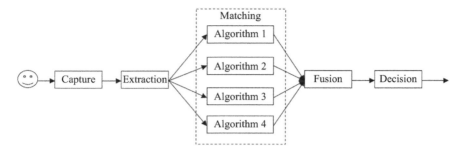

Figure 4.15   Matching score-level fusion

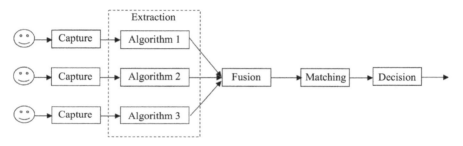

Figure 4.16   Feature-level fusion

Figure 4.15 illustrates one approach to achieving matching score-level fusion – where the outputs from multiple classifiers are combined to provide a single result that is presented to the decision subsystem.

Sensor-level fusion is useful in certain applications for establishing or developing a more effective sample, such as the creation of a 3D facial image from two 2D images. For approaches with multiple samples of the same biometric trait, fusion at the feature extraction process can enable a more robust feature vector to be developed based upon a weighted average of the feature vectors generated individually (or by any other combinational algorithm they wish). Rather than putting each sample through the complete biometric process and obtaining a decision, feature-level fusion allows the creation of a single-feature vector from a series of samples, as illustrated in Figure 4.16. The biometric process then only needs to be performed once – reducing computational overheads (assuming the fusion process is less computationally intensive than several runs of the matching subsystem process – which invariably it is).

Feature-level fusion can also be applied to different modalities – effectively concatenating or appending them together. Some biometric vendors may create matching subsystems based upon a variety of features derived from different modalities – rather than using separate matching subsystems. In such an approach, the feature vectors of the two independent approaches need to be combined in order to be inputted into the matching subsystem. Such systems typically also include measures for reducing the feature vector to the most efficient feature size for the combined modalities in order to achieve its task. The larger the feature vector, the more complex the resulting matching subsystem needs to be – a problem known as the curse of dimensionality [35]. Therefore, it is necessary to ensure the feature vector is as efficient as possible.

Matching or score-level fusion takes the output of the resulting matching subsystems and combines the results prior to presenting to the decision subsystem. Of all the fusion approaches, matching-level fusion is the most widely implemented. The approach enables multimodal authentication with each modality being classified by a dedicated matching subsystem designed specifically for that approach. The most challenging problem with score-level fusion is how to interpret the outputs. If all the outputs from the various classifiers are identical, the combination of those results is relatively simple. However, invariably the use of different classifiers results in a different output being produced. For instance:

- The output from one classifier might be a measure of the similarity between two samples. For instance, a statistical-based classifier that provides a probabilistic value of how similar the two samples are. The larger the value, the more similar the two samples. Another classifier, based upon minimal distance, would output a distance measure. The smaller the distance, the more similar the samples.
- The output from another classifier might be a measure of their dissimilarity. Conversely to levels of similarity, these classifiers are designed to output the opposite of similarity measures.
- The range of values available to a classifier might vary considerably. For instance, the output of two popular neural network classifiers, the feed-forward multi-layered perceptron and radial basis function networks have an output that varies from 0 to 1 and 0 to ∞.

There are various techniques to solving this problem [36]. A common approach is to develop some mechanism for normalizing the outputs so that they can be combined in a consistent manner. One such technique is the min–max approach, where each output is scaled based upon the minimum and maximum value within its own output range. The resulting values are therefore proportional to the range of values that its own particular classifier is able to output.

Decision-level fusion occurs at the end of the biometric process when each individual biometric system has provided an independent decision. Within a verification problem, this result is effectively a Boolean value. For that reason, decision-level fusion lacks the richness of information that match-level fusion has with raw scores. However, with some implementations, decision-level fusion is the only option. For example, in a multimodal system, a system designer might choose to select a series of vendor-specific algorithms, the output from which is a decision rather than a match-score.

A common technique used for fusion at the decision level is majority voting – each classifier has an equal weighting and the majority that agree with the decision win. A slight modification of that approach is the weighted majority voting – this approach takes into consideration the relative recognition performance of the underlying approaches. For example, a facial recognition approach performs better than a

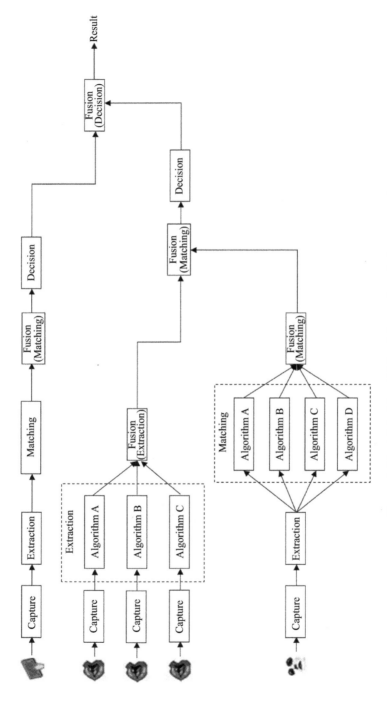

Figure 4.17 A hybrid model involving various fusion approaches

behavioural profiling approach and should therefore not have an equal weighting in the decision process.

A multibiometric approach could therefore benefit from a variety of these approaches being utilized. The multi-sample approach could utilize fusion at the feature, match or decision level or a different model for each biometric modality. Multi-algorithmic approaches would usefully utilize match-level fusion in order to benefit from the additional information stored in the result over their decision-level fusion counterparts. Figure 4.17 illustrates one of many possible models a multibiometric could implement. What the combination of approaches utilized are in terms of modes of multibiometrics or methods of fusion is actually dependent upon what recognition performance that is to be achieved. This type of approach is widely referenced in the literature in reference to transparent and continuous authentication approaches [37].

4.7.2 Performance of multimodal systems

Research into multimodal systems has increased considerably over the last decade due to the enhancements in performance that can be experienced. Literature is available that directly compares the performance of multimodal systems over their unimodal counterparts. To highlight these aspects, this section will describe the findings from three multimodal studies involving

1. finger and face modalities;
2. finger, face and hand modalities; and
3. face and ear modalities.

The first study is interesting because it involves a large population of users numbering almost 1,000 [38]. Few biometric studies tend to include such high levels of participation – particularly for multimodal applications. Utilizing a dataset with such a large number of participants provides for a more statistically reliable set of measurements and results. The application sourced datasets from two independent sources. The facial data was based upon the FERET database (a publicly accessible dataset used for testing facial recognition algorithms and the fingerprint data from a proprietary source). Whilst the two sets of data do not come from the same individual, their independent nature means that can be combined (i.e. an individual's face has no impact upon the resulting fingerprint image). A standard methodology was utilized in the study in terms of calculating the performance characteristics – one user acted as the authorized user and the remaining as impostors. All users were given the opportunity of playing the authorized user. The match-level fusion approach was applied using a simple sum function (applied after normalization). As illustrated in Table 4.2, the performance of the multimodal approach is better than either of the unimodal approaches.

The second study by [39] studied the performance of a multimodal system incorporating the finger, face and hand modalities. It utilized the Michigan State University multimodal database. A set of 100 virtual participants with finger, face and hand

Table 4.2   *Multimodal performance: finger and face*

Classifier	FRR		EER (%)
	FAR = 1%	FAR = 0.1%	
Fingerprint	25	32	2.16
Face	59	100	3.76
Multimodal	9	21	0.94

Table 4.3   *Multimodal performance: finger, face and hand modalities*

Classifier	FRR at a FAR = 0.1%
Finger	16.4
Face	32.3
Hand	53.2
Multimodal (Minmax norm)	2.2
Multimodal (Tanh norm)	1.5

Table 4.4   *Multimodal performance: face and ear modalities*

Classifier	TPIR (%)
Face	70.5
Ear	71.6
Multimodal	90.9

geometry samples. The study sought not only to evaluate the performance of the multimodal approach against their unimodal counterparts but also to compare different normalization strategies. The key results from the research are presented in Table 4.3. The fusion technique applied to the results was the sum of scores method. It can be seen from the table that the normalization approach does indeed have a significant role to play in the performance of the multimodal approach. Interestingly, all seven normalization approaches tested in the study returned better levels of performance than the unimodal systems. (The 'Tanh' function normalizes the output on a non-linear scale from −1 to +1.)

The third study utilized face and ear modalities [40]. This study is interesting for two reasons. It is one of a few studies that include the ear modality within the system. It also applies fusion at the sensor rather than the match level. The face and ear raw samples are concatenated together and processed by the feature extraction algorithm. An experiment based upon 197 participants found the multimodal approach significantly outperformed the unimodal systems. The methodology is based upon an identification rather than verification system, so the results are represented in terms of the TPIR based upon being returned in the rank 1 position (Table 4.4).

Whilst studies are somewhat limited in multimodal biometrics when compared to the unimodal biometrics, there is clear evidence that the performance of multimodal systems significantly outperforms the standard approaches.

4.8 Biometric standards

Historically, the implementation of biometric systems involved the creation of bespoke designs that were carefully crafted into enterprise management systems. The close coupling and incompatibility of biometric subsystems results in vendor lock-in and a lack of competition. The introduction of standards has revolutionized the domain of biometrics by decoupling the biometric system to provide flexibility to the provisioning of solutions. Through this evolution and maturing of the biometric market, more effective best-of-breed solutions can be adopted and approaches such as multibiometrics can truly be deployed in a cost-effective manner.

It is clear that standardization is a technology enabler and provides a mechanism for organizations to ensure they utilize the best configuration of components and future proof of the technology. The development of standards can be driven from a variety of directions including formal and informal Standards Development Organisations (SDOs) both within a national and international context, industry and consumers. From an international perspective, the ISO and International Electrotechnical Commission (IEC) play a significant role in biometric standards via a joint partnership as they do with many areas of joint interest. On a national front, there are SDOs such as American National Standards Institute, British Standards Institute and the NIST to name but a few. Informal SDOs such as the Biometric Consortium, BioAPI Consortium and the World Wide Web Consortium exist to serve their membership and typically provide very industry-specific guidelines. In a variety of consumer or industry-sector domains, organizations exist that develop standards to meet specific purposes. For instance, the ICAO mandates a standard regarding the use and storage of biometrics within international travel documents [11].

The primary coordination of biometric standards is performed by ISO/IEC under JTC 1 Subcommittee (SC) 37. As illustrated in Table 4.5, SC37 comprised six working groups covering key aspects: from harmonizing biometric vocabulary, developing data interchange formats to cross-jurisdictional and societal aspects. It is worth highlighting that the efforts of SC37 encompass the complete range of biometric applications: verification, identification, watch list and forensics.

Within each working group, standards are developed and published through international collaboration. ISO/IEC has developed an onion model to represent the relationships between standard efforts. As illustrated in Figure 4.18, the model has a series of seven layers, each one encapsulating the previous [41].

The innermost layer contains the Data Interchange Formats. These standards pertain to the interoperability of data between systems using the same modality. This will enable a common approach to the structure of biometric data and represents the lowest level of interoperability. The Data Structure layer refers to standards that define the wrappers for data exchange between systems or components. In order to appreciate

Table 4.5 ISO/IEC JTC1 SC37 working groups

Group	Focus area
ISO/IEC JTC1 SC37 WG 1	Harmonized biometric vocabulary
ISO/IEC JTC1 SC37 WG 2	Biometric technical interfaces
ISO/IEC JTC1 SC37 WG 3	Biometric data interchange formats
ISO/IEC JTC1 SC37 WG 4	Technical implementation of biometric systems
ISO/IEC JTC1 SC37 WG 5	Biometric testing and reporting
ISO/IEC JTC1 SC37 WG 6	Cross-jurisdictional and societal aspects of biometrics

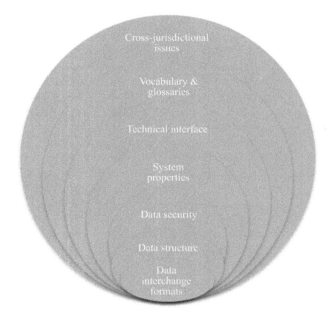

Figure 4.18 ISO/IEC onion model of data interchange formats

the difference between the two layers, an analogy to the IP protocol can be used. The IP protocol relates to the Data Structure standards and formally structuring the payload of the IP packet would involve the Data Interchange Format standards. The Data Security Standards layer provides protection for the previous two layers in terms of the vulnerability of the biometric data. ISO/IEC JTC1 SC 27 (IT Security Techniques) are responsible for defining these standards and they pertain to security countermeasures such as the appropriate use of cryptography to secure the communication channel. System properties standards assist in providing interoperability through the use of biometric profiles and evaluating the effectiveness of the approach within that context. The use of application-specific profiles permits more appropriate evaluations to be performed that enable uniform conformance testing. Without such profiles, comparing the performance of a biometric system, for example, in airport identification versus a system deployed for point-of-sale merchants, would be unreliable. The Technical Interface Standards provide the mechanisms for the various biometric components to interoperate. The standards provide a framework for hardware and software components to communicate, providing an ability to decouple the biometric systems subcomponents from a single vendor. The penultimate layer refers to the standardization of vocabulary and terms of reference to ensure all stakeholders have a uniform understanding of the terms. This avoids confusion and misunderstandings to develop over any aspect of the system and its performance. For instance, the FAR and FRR are frequently misquoted as the match/classification performance in studies rather than the decision performance. The final layer in the model refers to all the higher-level non-technical aspects such as the impact of laws and treaties, privacy concerns relating to the handling and storage of biometric data, ethical issues and health and safety.

4.9 Conclusions

Biometrics are arguably now a mainstream authentication approach with an ever-increasing appeal across a range of applications. Whilst there are certainly increased costs and complexity in comparison to other traditional user authentication approaches, the usability, convenience and level of security being provided in practice are driving factors that make biometrics a more effective solution. The introduction of TouchID by [42] in particular has illustrated how usable yet secure user authentication is through careful thought and design – closely integrating security with convenience. This approach is more widely applied in the research field as transparent and continuous user authentication and is arguably the way forward for user authentication technologies, seeking to remove the burden, inconvenience and insecurity of previous approaches.

It is worth highlighting of course that biometrics are not merely user authentication approaches and are also used in a range of identification applications such as terrorist watch lists at airports and monitoring of social security benefit claimants. Biometrics also have an increasing appeal in forensics – particularly fingerprint and facial recognition.

Whilst biometrics have matured and are in use on a daily basis, it is worth highlighting that continued research is essential to improve upon the biometric techniques across a range of attributes – performance, forgeability, acceptance and collection – to ensure they remain relevant and fit for purpose across the variety of applications to which they can be applied.

References

[1]   ISO. ISO/IEC 2382-37:2012. Information Technology – Vocabulary – Part 37: Biometrics. Available at: http://standards.iso.org/ittf/PubliclyAvailable Standards/index.html [Accessed 14 September 2016].

[2]   NIST. Biometric Evaluation Homepage. National Institute for Standards and Technology. Available at: https://www.nist.gov/itl/iad/ig/resources/biometrics-evaluations [Accessed 14 September 2016].

[3]   Moreno, B., and Sanchez, A. "On the use of outer ear images for personal identification in security applications". In proceedings of IEEE 33rd Annual International Conference on Security Technologies, pp. 469–476; 1999.

[4]   Yan, P. Ear Biometrics in Human Identification. PhD Thesis, University of Notre Dame. Available at: http://www3.nd.edu/~kwb/Ping_Yan_PhD.pdf [Accessed 14 September 2016].

[5]   Hurley, D., Nixon, M., and Carter, J. "Force field feature extraction for ear biometrics". Computer Vision and Image Understanding, vol. 98, pp. 491–512; 2005.

[6]   Jain, A., Patrick, F., and Arun, R. Handbook of Biometrics. New York, Springer. ISBN: 978-0-387-71040-2; 2008.

[7]   Phillips, J., Scruggs, T., O'Toole, A., *et al.* "FRVT 2006 and ICE 2006 Large-Scale Results". IEEE Transactions on Pattern Analysis and Machine Intelligence, vol. 32, no. 5; 2010.

[8]   Socolinsky, D., and Selinger, A. "Face detection with visible and thermal infrared imagery". Computer Vision and Image Understanding; 2003.

[9]   Maltoni, D., Maio, D., Jain, A., and Prabhakar, S. Handbook of Fingerprint Recognition. New York, Springer. ISBN: 978-0387954318; 2005.

[10]   FVC2006. "Open Category: Average Results over All Databases". Biometric System Laboratory. Available at: http://bias.csr.unibo.it/fvc2006/results/Open_resultsAvg.asp [Accessed 114 September 2016].

[11]   ICAO. Doc 9303 – Machine Readable Travel Documents, Part 9: Deployment of Biometric Identification and Electronic Storage of Data in eMRTDs. ICAO. Available at: http://www.icao.int/publications/Documents/9303_p9_cons_en.pdf [Accessed 14 September 2016].

[12]   Smith, R. Authentication: From Passwords to Public Keys. Michigan, Addison Wesley. ISBN: 0201615991; 2002.

[13]   Ashbourn, J. Biometrics: Advanced Identity Verification: The Complete Guide. Michigan, Springer. ISBN: 978-1852332433; 2000.

[14]   Honeywell. "HandKey". Honeywell Access Control Systems. Available at: https://www.honeywellaccess.com/products/access-control-systems/readers/biometric/52198.html [Accessed 14 September 2016].

[15]   Daugman, J. Biometric Personal Identification System Based on Iris Recognition. US Patent 5,291,560; 1994.

[16]   Nanavati, S., Thieme, M., and Nanavati, R. Biometrics: Identity Verification in a Networked World. New York, John Wiley & Sons. ISBN: 0471099457; 2002.

[17]   Fancourt, C., Bogoni, L., Hanna, K., *et al.* Iris Recognition at a Distance. In International Conference on Audio- and Video-Based Biometric Person Authentication (pp. 1–13). Springer: Berlin Heidelberg; 2005.

[18]   Associated Newspapers. "£9 Million Iris Recognition Scheme Introduced to Slash Queues at Airports Is Scrapped". Mail Online. Available at:

http://www.dailymail.co.uk/travel/article-2102489/Iris-recognition-scheme-airports-scrapped-years.html [Accessed 14 September 2016].

[19] Woodford, C. Iris Scans. Available at: http://www.explainthatstuff.com/how-iris-scans-work.html [Accessed 14 September 2016].

[20] Miura, N., Nagasaka, A., and Miyatake, T. "Feature Extraction of Finger-Vein Patterns Based Repeated Line Tracking and its Applications to Personal Identification". Machine Vision and Applications, vol. 15, pp. 194–203; 2004.

[21] Gosset, P (editor). ASPeCT: Fraud Detection Concepts: Final Report. Doc Ref. AC095/VOD/W22/DS/P/18/1; 1998.

[22] Stolfo, S.J., Wei F., Wenke L., Prodromidis, A., and Chan, P.K. "Cost-based modeling for fraud and intrusion detection: results from the JAM project". DARPA Information Survivability Conference and Exposition, 2000. DISCEX '00. Proceedings. Vol. 2, pp. 130–144; 2000.

[23] Stormann, C. Fraud Management Tool: Evaluation Report. Advanced Security for Personal Communications (ASePECT), Deliverable. 13, Doc Ref. AC095/SAG/W22/DS/P/13/2; 1997.

[24] Sarkar, S., Phillips, P., Liu, Z., Robledo-Vega, I., Grother P, and Bowyer, K. "The Human ID Gait Challenge Problem: Data Sets, Performance and Analysis". IEEE Transactions on Pattern Analysis and Machine Intelligence, II:162–177; 2005.

[25] Derawi, M.O., Nickel, C., Bours, P., and Busch, C. Unobtrusive User-Authentication on Mobile Phones Using Biometric Gait Recognition. In Intelligent Information Hiding and Multimedia Signal Processing (IIH-MSP), 2010 Sixth International Conference on (pp. 306–311). IEEE; 2010.

[26] Spillane, R. "Keyboard Apparatus for Personal Identification". IBM Technical Disclosure Bulletin, 17, 3346; 1975.

[27] BehavioSec. Continuous Authentication with Behavioural Biometrics. Available at: https://www.behaviosec.com [Accessed 14 September 2016].

[28] Joyce R., and Gupta, G. Identity Authentication Based on Keystroke Latencies. Communications of the ACM, vol. 39; pp. 168–176; 1990.

[29] Yeung, D., Chang, H., Xiong, Y., et al. "SVC2004: First International Signature Verification Competition". In Proceedings of ICBA, pp. 16–22. Springer LNCS-3072; 2004.

[30] Przybocki, M., Martin, A., and Le, A. "NIST Speaker Recognition Evaluations Utilising the Mixer Corpora – 2004, 2005, 2006". IEEE Transactions on Audio, Speech, and Language Processing, vol. 15, no. 7, pp. 1951–1959; 2007.

[31] Kent, J. "Malaysia Car Thieves Steal Finger". BBC News. Available at: http://news.bbc.co.uk/1/hi/world/asia-pacific/4396831.stm [Accessed 14 September 2016].

[32] Matsumoto, T., Matsumoto, H., Yamada, K., and Hoshino, S. "Impact of Artificial 'Gummy' Fingers on Fingerprint Systems". Proceedings of SPiE, vol. 4677; 2002.

[33] Dimitriadis, C., and Polemi, D. Biometric Authentication. Proceedings of the First International Conference on Biometric Authentication (ICBA). Springer LNCS-3072; 2004.

[34] Marcialis, G., and Roli, F. "Fingerprint Verification by Fusion of Optical and Capacitive Sensors". Pattern Recognition Letters, vol. 25 (11); 2004.

[35] Bishop, M. Pattern Classification and Machine Learning. New York, Springer; 2006.

[36] Ross, A., Nandakumar, K., and Jain, A. Handbook of Multibiometrics. New York, Springer; 2006.

[37] Clarke, N. Transparent User Authentication: Biometrics, RFID and Behavioural Profiling. London, Springer Science & Business Media; 2011.

[38] Snelick, R., Uludag, U., Mink, A., Indovina, M, and Jain, A. "Large Scale Evolution of Multimodal Biometric Authentication Using State-of-Art Systems". IEEE Transactions on Pattern Analysis and Machine Intelligence, vol. 27(3); 2005.

[39] Jain, A., Nandakumar, K., and Ross, A. "Score Normalisation in Multimodal Biometric Systems". Pattern Recognition, vol. 38 (12); 2005.

[40] Chang, K., Bowyer, K., Sarkar, S., and Victor, B. "Comparison and Combination of Ear and Face Images in Appearance-Based Biometrics". IEEE Transactions on Pattern Analysis and Machine Intelligence, vol. 25 (9); 2003.

[41] ISO. ISO/IEC 19784-1:2006 Information Technology – Biometric Application Programming Interface – Part 1: BioAPI Specification. International Standards Organisation. Available at: http://www.iso.org/iso/iso_catalogue/catalogue_tc/catalogue_detail.htm?csnumber=33922 [Accessed 14 September 2016].

[42] Apple Inc. Use Touch ID on iPhone and iPad. Apple Inc. Available at: https://support.apple.com/en-gb/HT201371 [Accessed 14 September 2016].

Chapter 5
Foundation of healthcare cybersecurity
Jemal H. Abawajy[1]

Abstract

Healthcare automation has brought significant benefits to health care in terms of operational cost reduction, quality of care, patient convenience and initiation of personalized care. It has also brought new and increasing security and privacy challenges. The recent spate of successful cyberattacks against healthcare systems demonstrate that the security and privacy threats in health care are more varied and capable of undermining patient care and diminish revenues of healthcare sector. Considering the role that the healthcare sector plays within our society, the importance of protecting this critical infrastructure cannot be overstated. In this chapter the foundation of healthcare cybersecurity is presented. Major components of the healthcare systems and the associated requirements in terms of security and privacy are discussed. The threat landscape, vulnerabilities exploited to perpetrate cyberattacks against healthcare organizations and the various cyberattack types are identified and presented. Countermeasures and tools to defend and mitigate cyberattacks are also discussed.

Keywords: Electronic healthcare record (EHR), Cybersecurity, Phishing, Ransomware, Threats, Vulnerabilities, Attacks, Risk Analysis, Business Continuity Planning

5.1 Introduction

Healthcare sectors are embracing information and communication technologies at a rapid pace. There have been significant efforts in integrating technological innovations such as electronic health record (EHRs), mobile health (mHealth), cloud computing and Internet of Things (IoT) into healthcare practices to diagnose, treat and rehabilitate patients [1]. These technological innovations have been rapidly transforming healthcare industry into a more patient-focused and economically sustainable service. By enabling healthcare providers timely access to accurate patient data when needed from anywhere, these technologies have enabled primary care providers to make

[1]Faculty of Science, Engineering and Built Environment, Deakin University, Australia

fast and accurate decisions as well as provide good medical outcomes to patients [2]. Furthermore, by making patient medical histories easily and quickly accessible, digitization has enabled healthcare professionals to quickly diagnose potential health issues. Moreover, these technologies offer healthcare providers the right level of actionable information at the point of care, thus greatly improving patient experiences.

Technological innovation in healthcare sectors has also established a platform for easily and quickly sharing health data across a variety of stakeholders (e.g. patients, doctors, insurance companies, government agencies, research institutes and other healthcare providers) [2]. Furthermore, they empowered patients to have real-time access to their clinical information online. This has enabled patients to engage in their care while increasing their understanding of their health and improving their ability to look after themselves. The adoption of technological innovations has benefited healthcare providers and patients tremendously through improving healthcare delivery and management, convenience, as well as making them economically sustainable [3].

Although there is ample evidence that digitization of healthcare workflow can enhance the quality of care and decrease the cost of care, technological innovation of healthcare systems brings with it potential privacy and security risks [4]. This is because health data contains extremely sensitive patient information and thus their collection, usage and storage raise serious patient privacy and data security issues. Healthcare data is exceedingly attractive to cybercriminals who have been working overtime to get their hands on it [2]. Recent high-profile cybersecurity incidents across the world in healthcare industry show that the sector is exceedingly coming under constant cyberattacks. These trends are expected to escalate in frequency and magnitude for the foreseeable future. The escalation of cyberattacks in health care could lead to serious safety concerns of the patients, eroding patient confidence and business reputation, productivity and financial losses. For example, the annual cost to healthcare sector due to data breaches is estimated to be about $6.2 billion and is expected to increase with adoption of new technologies by the healthcare industry [5].

With the recent health data breach incidents, cybersecurity has become a strategic issue for healthcare organizations. Therefore, the concerns of cybersecurity and privacy are taking a centre stage in modern digital healthcare system [4,6]. As health care is a critical infrastructure, guaranteeing adequate protection of the patient privacy and data security is a critical factor in realizing the benefits of the technological innovations in healthcare environment. Thus, the benefits that the technological innovations offer to healthcare organizations should be matched by the same measure of devotion and commitment to ensure the patient privacy and security of the digitized healthcare systems.

The principal aim of this chapter is to give an overview of the current cybersecurity trends in the healthcare domain. Specifically, the aim is to provide insight into the current cybersecurity landscape with emphases on cybersecurity threats and vulnerabilities to patient privacy and data security in healthcare settings. The important contribution is to provide an in-depth understanding of the potential security and privacy risks facing healthcare providers and vulnerabilities, as well as contemporary threats and the most effective countermeasures to ensure safe and secure operation of the healthcare systems. We will discuss how the speed and complexity of healthcare digitization complicate addressing patient privacy and data security challenges. The different types of assets likely to be targeted will be reviewed as well as the profile of the potential threat agents and their objectives. Advances in technologies and management issues to ensure the patient privacy and data security are highlighted. Also, regulations and acts that decree the standards for dealing with health information will be discussed.

5.2 Health system architecture

Healthcare organizations such as hospitals, health insurance agencies and healthcare manufacturing companies are experiencing rapid digitization. A wide range of hardware (personal computers, mobile devices, medical hardware, data storage facilities, inventory systems and power supply), software (custom software applications for a wide variety of healthcare industry customers) and Web-based applications are used in the healthcare settings. Figure 5.1 shows the high-level schematic representation of healthcare environment. In this section, we discuss healthcare datasets and the infrastructures used to collect, store, process and exchange the health information.

5.2.1 Healthcare infrastructure

Based on the functions performed by the various components of the systems, we classify the overall system into patient care systems, administrative systems and research systems. The patient care systems ensures continuity of care, including, among others, active/passive medical devices, medicine delivery systems and surgery equipment. The disruption of these services may have a devastating impact on patients' health. The administrative systems are dedicated to the smooth hospital workflow. Systems

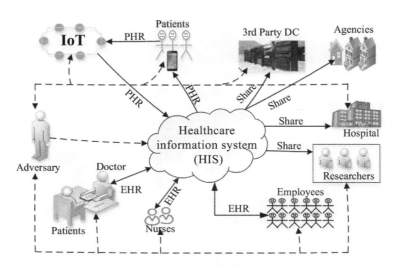

Figure 5.1   High-level healthcare system

handling work orders, medicine inventories, prescriptions, bills or appointments are part of these services. Their unavailability is however less critical as long as their downtime remains of short duration. Healthcare organizations also maintain intellectual properties such as experimental procedures for surgery, test and studies' results, test subject information or drug formulas.

Health data is the lifeblood of any healthcare provider. Therefore, health data collection is the single most important function of healthcare systems. There are a variety of ways in which the health data is collected from the patients. The conventional face-to-face approach during the normal course of business is still the prevailing approach. In this approach a healthcare professional (e.g. physicians and nurses) prompts patients for information and documents it. Also, a wide variety of technologies both within the hospital settings and outside hospitals such as patient homes are used to collect data. For example, wearables (e.g. smart watches and fitness trackers) are commonly used to gather patient-generated physiological health data such as temperature and heart rhythm. Financial and other data are also collected either in a traditional manner or online. Cloud computing is increasingly used as the main platform for personal health record (PHR) [7]. Cloud computing offers on-demand access to computational and storage resources from almost anywhere and when needed.

5.2.2   Healthcare dataset

Healthcare sectors collect, store, manage and analyse large amounts of patient data. In addition to treating patients, healthcare data is used for a wide variety of purposes such as public health and medical research. For healthcare sector, this data is the most important asset used for a wide variety of purposes mainly to provide the best possible care for patients. This health record typically contains extremely sensitive information including personally identifiable information (PII) and the protected health information (PHI). The PII constitutes information that identifies or can be used to identify the patient. This information includes social security number, information regarding healthcare provider, credit card data, patient name, address and date of birth as well as email addresses and employment information. The PHI includes information such as medical history records (e.g. current and past diagnoses, pathology results, vital sign data, medical test results, X-rays, treatments and medications), provision of health care and payment for health care that can be directly linked to a specific individual. Both PII and PHI often remain valid for years, if not decades.

With digitization process, the EHRs have been replacing the conventional paper-based health record. EHRs have numerous advantages including the reduction of medical errors, reliable prescription and quick access to records, fast data transfer and data sharing in unprecedented scale. They enable clinicians and nurses to be able to view patient records simultaneously from different locations, which is not possible with paper-based records. They also decrease the number of lost records and permit a complete set of backup records in a cost-effective manner.

EHRs make up-to-date and complete health information accessible to healthcare providers instantly. This enables healthcare providers to render good health care and timely treatment services to patients, thus enhancing quality of life and patient satisfaction. By replacing physicians' handwritten notes, EHRs decrease common problems with incorrect medication, dosages and procedure due to illegible handwritten notes. Healthcare providers can use the data for a wide variety of purposes such as making clinical decision support to decrease the readmission rates and hospital-contracted conditions, to prevent, detect and eliminate wastage, and to efficiently coordinate and manage patient care.

By design, healthcare providers share patient records (clinical, administrative or financial) with a variety of organizations such as public health and government agencies, insurance, clearinghouses, pharmaceuticals, research institutions and third-party vendors. Each organization may use the patient data for different purposes such as for research, disease surveillance, population health management and for healthcare policy development. Advances in information technology have also sparked patient and physician interest in sharing health data in social environments. Patients may share their health data with their healthcare providers, insurance companies, family members, etc. In this regard, patients use a variety of mobile devices such as smartphones running medical consumer apps to access, store and transmit their PHR as well as treatment in social environments. Similarly, some physicians started sharing their ideas about specific sicknesses related to their professional area on social environments. As health data sharing is one of the most desirable capabilities of healthcare systems [4], EHRs enable healthcare information to be shared within and between hospitals to provide better care and good outcomes for patients. It also enables healthcare information sharing with researchers to develop better treatments.

EHRs contain a wealth of highly regulated, mission-critical information. They are the lifeblood of every healthcare sector. They have also become cybercriminals' primary target for stealing at any cost. This is because, according to Ponemon Institute [8], EHRs are on average valued at $50 on the black market as they can be used to commit identity theft and other insurance frauds. Therefore, EHRs must be securely managed and used to reap the benefits (e.g. cost-effectiveness, high efficiency and performance demands) of the EHR.

5.2.3 Data access infrastructure

Healthcare systems are used for treating patients with a variety of health conditions and different stages of illness. Modern healthcare sectors deploy a wide variety of advanced medical devices both in hospital settings and outside hospitals to provide quality care to patients with acute and chronic conditions as well as for disease prevention and lifestyle changes in a cost-effective manner. Healthcare employees (e.g. doctors and nurses) in the medical practice use a myriad of devices for accessing and updating health records, prescribing medication, ordering tests or viewing results, medical decision-making and many important tasks. Healthcare providers also permit patients to access their PHR such that they participate in their own health care via electronic means.

The common devices used in accessing healthcare records include the standard workstation in offices and a wide variety of small handheld devices such as smartphones, tablets such as iPads and other mobile devices. Workstations are good for static situations such as at the nursing workspace. However, the workflow within the hospital environment is dynamic as the clinicians, nurses and patients continually move around the hospital. With its capability to enable mobility of the clinicians and access to the patient information wherever he/she is providing care or reviewing information to provide care, mobile devices have become part and parcel of healthcare digital system infrastructure. In addition to making patient care more efficient, it has enhanced healthcare professionals' workflow. As the number of healthcare providers using mobile devices for patient care keeps increasing, huge investment in the development of mobile EHR is currently underway.

5.2.4   Privacy and security requirements

Patients entrust their private information to healthcare providers with discrete expectation for privacy and security. Moreover, with the introduction of electronic healthcare records, security and privacy have been receiving more attention with the healthcare providers, researchers and government agencies. Thus, it is imperative to understand the potential security and privacy challenges the healthcare digitization poses so that appropriate and adequate controls can be deployed to successfully ensure security and privacy requirements of EHRs [9].

5.2.4.1   Health privacy

Privacy is the right of the individual patient to control the collection, use and sharing of his/her personal information. Health data collected as a result of clinical interaction is regarded as private information and must be safeguarded [10]. The fear for privacy breach keeps out many patients from seeking treatment. In the USA, for example, it is estimated that about 2 million patients with mental illnesses avoid getting treatment for their illness because of privacy concerns [11].

Patient privacy is a legally protected right with stringent consequences in almost all countries. For example, patient privacy protection is legally mandated in the form of legislations such as the Health Insurance Portability and Accountability Act (HIPAA) in the USA [12]. Therefore, healthcare institutions must comply with the existing privacy regulations and laws when they release sensitive medical data to others. For example, preserving the privacy of PII is extremely essential when using health data for clinical or health services-related research. Failure to prevent disclosure of PII to unauthorized entities may have serious financial and reputational consequences. The fine in the amount of $275,000 paid by Prime Health care Services Inc. for privacy breach is a good example that illustrates the financial impact that healthcare providers can face for noncompliance. Therefore, healthcare providers are obliged to express good judgement and discretion when sharing patient health records.

Multidisciplinary teams of healthcare professionals often treat patients, which necessitates electronic healthcare records sharing. Also, sharing health data among different healthcare providers, research institutions, government and public health agencies and insurance companies is an important trait of healthcare systems [4]. With the speed in which the healthcare has been undergoing changes towards interconnected care, the size of health data shared between healthcare providers and other institutions will only increase. While sharing of clinical data is greatly beneficial to provide quality

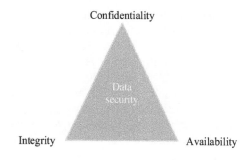

Figure 5.2   Properties of data security

care to patients, sharing of patient data must be done carefully to preserve patients' privacy. However, sharing health information with other institutions without the prior consent or authorization of the patient may constitute a breach of the patient's privacy rights. Therefore, patient data should only be released to entities outside the healthcare professionals that treated the patients, with the consent of the patients or as allowed by the law.

5.2.4.2   Health data security

Cybersecurity is the protection of valuable assets (e.g. proprietary information, personal information and financial information) from an adversary whose goal includes obtaining private information, undermining the system or preventing its legitimate use. Information security is as important for a small healthcare provider as it is for a large one.

As shown in Figure 5.2, the value of a digital information and the protection it is accorded is captured by confidentiality, integrity and availability (CIA) properties. As a result, the principle of CIA has become a fundamental expectation from patients, providers and other stakeholders such as regulatory agencies. Therefore, ensuring CIA are the core objectives of an information security program.

Confidentiality principle

The confidentiality principle states that patient health records must not be disclosed to unauthorized entity while it is in use, in transit or at rest. For instance, a clerk should not access prescription information, whereas a trauma doctor can access the emergency system when treating a patient in emergency room. In hospital setting, role-based access privileges with accountability are normally used to grant access to health data. The authorized users are accountable for proper use of the health information and must only use it for discharging their responsibilities. Further, authorized individuals should only access the information for the purpose of discharging their responsibilities. For example, a nurse should not access the health records of a patient that is not under her observation at the hospital.

Improper disclosure of the patient's data can be caused by insufficient security controls, outdated devices or poor organization of the hospital. Confidentiality breaches can also be due to carelessness, indiscretion or sometimes even malicious acts. Unfortunately, confidentiality breach can destroy the intrinsic duty in the doctor–patient relationship. Patients will only disclose information fully to their doctors if they are assured that their confidentiality is protected. Therefore, ensuring patient data confidentiality plays a significant role in the level and confidence of the clinician–patient relationship. Similarly, confidentiality is very important to safeguard the well-being of patients. For example, the public disclosure of mental health condition of a patient can seriously affect the well-being of the patient by causing embarrassment and humiliation at best. It can also affect patient's career, reputation and could lead to lost opportunities and financial commitments.

Integrity principle
The principle of data integrity deals with the quality, trustworthiness and reliability of the patient records created and maintained by the healthcare providers. The principle seeks to guarantee that the patient information is authentic (i.e. true and credible), accurate (i.e. meaningful, valid, correct and free of errors), complete (i.e. sufficient in breadth, depth and scope for its desired use) and timely (i.e. data is up to date and current). Major activities in health care (i.e. patient care, research and health management) require that the patient records are trustworthy and reliable. Therefore, data authenticity is critical for the trustworthiness of a healthcare system [13]. EHR can be assumed to be authentic if it is provable that it has not been tampered with following its creation. Accuracy indicates that the data is correct and free of errors. Making sure that the dosage in a patient record is accurate is an example of data accuracy. Health data collected as a result of clinical interaction must be captured completely as fast as possible during or immediately following the event or activity and must be accessible for the envisioned use within a reasonable time frame.

As data integrity breaches affect all decisions made along the patient care continuum, it is extremely imperative that the integrity of the patient records is ensured at all times. Breach of health record integrity can be life threatening, can dent the confidence of the patients and can compromise patient care. For example, patients assume that healthcare professionals make decisions based on high-quality and reliable information. However, inaccurate patient data can negatively influence the decision of treating clinicians (e.g. the clinicians may make treatment errors) as well as affect patient care coordination by different specialists' collaboration to treat patients. Similarly, altering patient health records and compromising medicine inventory systems are likely to have dramatic consequences on the health of the patients involved. For example, an incomplete health record can jeopardise patient's health as it can lead to misdiagnosis, deferred patient treatment and prescription of improper medicines. Integrity breaches can also have an impact on the quality of reporting and research results, and can lead to fraud and abuse. Therefore, ensuring integrity of patient records requires that patient data is protected from omission, tampering and unauthorized alteration.

Availability principle
The availability principle states that patient information should be available when and where it is rightly needed by authorized users to support patient care and health system management decisions. Unlike other industries such as financial institutions, a

healthcare facility generally needs to remain open round the clock. The availability of the system and the data to the authorized individuals when needed to care for patients is a crucial data security component. However, the system and the data can be rendered unavailable for a variety of reasons including cyberattacks. For example, the Medstar hospital chain CryptoLocker attack that paralyzed the systems for more than a week is the most recent example that demonstrates the consequences of unavailability of the critical system and data. The attack completely grounded the Medstar hospital systems to a halt, forcing the Medstar hospital staff to revert to paper-based processes and in most cases had to send patients to other hospitals. Therefore, the availability dimension of data security is concerned with the accessibility of the appropriate healthcare resources and patient records to support information needs and to influence service or decision-making.

Generally speaking, healthcare systems can be classified into two broad classes: critical systems and functions (e.g. active/passive medical devices, medicine delivery systems and surgery equipment) and less critical systems and functions (e.g. workflow management, medicine inventories, prescriptions, bills and appointments). It is quite possible to tolerate short-time unavailability of less critical systems and functions as most of these activities can be handled manually. However, the availability of critical functions and critical systems is crucial to effective healthcare delivery. There must be confidence that critical business functions on critical business systems will both be available and behave as expected. For example, compromising power supply in operating rooms is likely to have dramatic consequences on the health of the patients involved. Similarly, access to critical data and systems can be seriously impacted when the system is bombarded with malicious requests that seriously overload it. Any event that compromises the availability of the critical systems and functions, be it accident or a deliberate act, can have a devastating impact on patients' health.

5.3 Health data breach incidents

A cyberattack is defined as a deliberate and unlawful act purported by cybercriminals using a variety of 'exploit' to cause harms to the assets of an organization. An 'exploit' is a technique or mechanism to compromise a system. The ease with which the cyber-criminals can hack healthcare institutions as compared to banks and other financing firms, coupled with the fact that cybercriminals can make a lot more money from EHRs, has made healthcare institutions a prime target for cyberattacks. A variety of cyberattack methods such as insider attacks and denial of service (DoS) that enable cyberattackers to tamper with the patient data and information disclosure exist [14]. The growing use of healthcare digitization has created a whole new opportunity to compromise the health information and the recent health data breach incidents place healthcare sectors on the top of the cyberattacks' spectrum. The big motivation for cybercriminals targeting healthcare industry is the high prices that EHRs command. EHRs are far more valuable than other data such as financial data. EHRs can fetch $50, whereas a stolen social security number or credit card number fetches just $1 [15]. This is what is fuelling the increasing rate of cyberattacks against healthcare institutions.

Table 5.1   Data breach examples

Institution	Service	Records	Vulnerability
Anthem	Health insurer	80×10^7	
Community Health Systems	Network of acute care hospitals	4.5×10^7	Heartbleed
Banner Health	Hospital networks	3.7×10^7	
Tricare	Military health system	4.9×10^7	Policy lapse
Premera Blue Cross	Health insurer	11×10^7	
Australian Red Cross	Blood bank	1.28×10^7	Third party

5.3.1   Cyberattacks against health care

Generally, based on the type of exploit used, cyberattacks can be classified into technical and non-technical attacks. Technical attacks are perpetrated by circumventing or nullifying hardware and software protection mechanisms. Examples of such attacks include password attacks, malware attacks, ransomware attacks, crypto-ransomware attacks and DoS attacks. In contrast, non-technical attacks are usually performed by means of deception. Examples of such attacks include phishing and spam [16,17]. Cyberattacks can be generally divided into random attacks and targeted attacks [18]. In the random attacks, adversaries select the targets with high profit and the least effort. In contrast, the adversaries in targeted attacks focus on specific assets and are determined to reach them at any cost.

Table 5.1 shows some notable examples of data breaches in which cybercriminals were able to infiltrate the healthcare organization's servers and computer systems. Anthem suffered an attack in which 80 million patient records (names, social security numbers, addresses, income data and healthcare identification numbers) were stolen by the hackers [19]. In addition, and perhaps equally as concerning, was the fact that Anthem believed, but could not confirm, that medical records or credit cards of customers were compromised. Another health insurer, Premera Blue Cross was breached in 2015 in which over 11 million patient records were stolen. In 2011, Tricare reported data breach affecting 4.9 million patients. In 2014, Community Health Systems was breached and 4.5 million patient records were stolen. In 2016, Banner Health reported 3.7 million payment card transactions and patient data (e.g. patient names, dates of birth, addresses, names of doctors, service received dates, insurance claims data and social security numbers) were stolen. In 2016, a third party maintaining blood donors' information for the Australian Red Cross was hacked, exposing the personal details of 1.28 million blood donors online. The personal records included the names, email addresses, phone numbers and blood types; the records occasionally included sensitive medical information – such as whether a person had recently engaged in high-risk sexual activity. These cyberattack samples are just a small part of the actual number of cybersecurity attacks on healthcare sector which are much greater than the available statistics suggest.

The recent spate of cyberattacks on the healthcare industry shows that the healthcare sector is facing serious threats from cybercriminals. Such incidents stand as a looming security problem for all within reach of healthcare data. The healthcare sector is an appealing target for cybercriminals. The continued growth of cybercrimes specifically targeting the healthcare sector can be linked to the combination of several attributes. First, healthcare information is high-value data (each record fetches $50 on average), making them cybercriminals' primary target. The extremely high revenue potential serves as the motivational factor for cybercriminals who are determined to get to it at any cost. Because of this increased potential financial gains, cyber-criminals targeting healthcare sector are now more numerous and better-skilled. With outdated and weak security defences as compared to other industries [20], cybercrim-inals consider healthcare sectors as easy targets to infiltrate. Adversaries are initiating regular and targeted cyberattacks against healthcare sectors with unbelievable success rate. Another factor favouring the cybercriminals is that healthcare institutions have mission-critical systems that must be online at all time. Therefore, new cybersecurity threats in healthcare environment are both more probable and hard to detect.

5.3.2 Impact of cyberattacks

The pricy nature of health records has rendered them the most sought after by the cybercriminals. As a result, health records have become the most hacked in the world [15] and mainly used for identity theft purposes. As cyberattacks are capable of undermining patient care and diminishing revenues of the healthcare sector, they can cause significant tangible and intangible impacts on the healthcare providers, staff and patients.

5.3.2.1 Financial loss

Health data is critical to the mission of the health organization and its breach can lead to serious financial consequences both to the service provider and patients. In fact, both the healthcare providers and the victims will suffer significant financial losses. Availability compromise can degrade the capability of the healthcare providers to deliver services to patients and at worst it can cause failure of the system. It can also lead to a loss of operating capability, which can lead to regulatory compliance breach and have adverse effects on stakeholders and loss of control over activities. According to Ponemon Institute [8], distributed denial of service (DDoS) attacks are costing healthcare organizations on average $1.32 million per year. Healthcare providers may experience serious rectification costs, legal liabilities, lost entitlements, patient churn and other unforeseen costs. Identity theft can be financially devastating to the victim as well. It can also lead to loss of patient employment, miss out on career opportunities, as well as devastating financial lose for re-claiming their stolen identity. The stolen PII can be used to dishonestly obtain health services, purchase prescription drugs, obtain credit in the name of the victim, etc. Thus, the victimized person may be billed for medical services he/she did not obtain or merchandise he/she did not purchase. Moreover, an imposter can create a criminal record for the legitimate person.

5.3.2.2 Reputational damage

A cyberattack can affect the reputation of the healthcare provider, healthcare professional, patients, as well as the government of the day. The loss of reputation can result in ruined reputations and shattered patient–doctor relationships. For example, it can cause embarrassment to patients due to revelation of confidential private health conditions. Due to lack of confidence, patients may not be at ease to voluntarily and openly release pertinent information to their caregiver, which can compromise their treatment. In the case of blood bank services like those offered by the Red Cross, a lack of trust can be deadly, with fewer people ready to hand over their personal details along with their blood. Regaining reputation is a costly process and includes publicity campaigns to rebuild reputation or gain confidence.

5.3.2.3 Danger to patients

Tampering with the EHR can lead to injury or death. For example, a patient's EHR may be altered improperly to indicate that a patient has hypertension and takes medication for it. If this change to EHR is undetected, a physician treating the patient is working with incorrect or conflicting information about the patient's medical history as well as prescribed medications. Similarly, identity theft can be emotionally draining as it can have long-term negative impact on the victim's credit rating and future insurance costs. Identity theft refers to the unlawful use of another person's information to impersonate the legitimate persons. The time to repair the damage caused by the identity theft generally depends on when the identity theft is discovered and the extent of damage incurred. Therefore, some victims quickly solve the problems caused by identity theft with minimal cost while for others it can take a long time and become very expensive to recover from the damage. While repairing the damage, victims may experience side effects such as being refused medical care and declined loans. Thus, it is important to re-emphasize the ever-evolving threats to patient data and the misfortune that can occur when this information lands in the wrong hands.

5.4 Healthcare vulnerability landscape

Healthcare systems suffer from a variety of flaws [15,21]. Thus, adversaries often exploit unnoticed security vulnerabilities of the healthcare systems to perpetrate an attack on them. Therefore, in order to counter cybercriminal attacks, the first critical step is to have a good vulnerability assessment process in place. In this section, we highlight some of the main sources of healthcare system vulnerabilities.

5.4.1 Medical device vulnerability

The necessities to decrease the cost of providing health care have introduced a wide variety of software-controlled medical devices in the healthcare systems. These medical devices are increasingly capable of interconnecting with other devices through the Internet or over local area networks. Moreover, a variety of devices such as laptops, mobile devices and thumb drives are often used for simplifying internal distribution of EHRs. As the medical devices evolve, so do the threats to the security and reliability of these devices. Specifically, the increasing number of medical devices and systems within the healthcare settings opens more points of entry for cybercriminals to exploit. Also, the loss and theft of devices is a common occurrence and has become a significant problem in the healthcare sector.

A wide variety of medical devices such as insulin pumps, defibrillators, pacemakers, and other medical electronics are commonly used in healthcare. Although these medical device functions can be life critical, security is mainly relegated to an afterthought. Therefore, medical devices without the necessary security features are quite common in healthcare environment. With the cyberattacks becoming prevalent within the healthcare sector, medical device hacking has become a mainstream concern. This is because medical devices (e.g. anaesthesia devices, medication infusion systems and pacemakers) with known inherent vulnerabilities are quite commonly deployed in healthcare environment [22]. Moreover, many healthcare providers use aged systems with obsolete hardware and software, with inherent vulnerabilities, that could inadvertently put patients in danger. Furthermore, as the IoT penetrates the health care deeply, the security concerns of health care systems will exacerbate since the devices in IoT are vulnerable to malicious exploitations [23,24]. Another serious concern is that malware are widespread on medical devices [25].

5.4.2 Outsourcing vulnerabilities

File-sharing applications and cloud computing are increasingly used for maintaining and processing patient health data, financial and billing information [7]. They also enabled patients to access their information online through their doctor or hospital using Web-based systems. Technically, the adoption of cloud computing has enabled healthcare service providers to shift the security problems and costs of having infrastructures to cloud service providers. The file-sharing applications and cloud computing have the potential to create new problems as well.

As healthcare providers increasingly rely on hosted services, they are placing themselves at even greater risk from cybercriminals. For example, the data breach incident at Medical Informatics Engineering (MIE) in July 2015 that exposed the patients' personal records was an example in which MIE outsourced its healthcare data and the data breach occurred through the third party that was infiltrated. As this example illustrates, the healthcare providers automatically inherit the vulnerabilities inherent in the cloud computing and file-sharing applications. While the healthcare providers stand to save some costs associated with the purchase and maintenance of infrastructures, they are still responsible for ensuring the security of the patient data.

5.4.3 Software and hardware vulnerabilities

Exploits of existing software and hardware vulnerabilities such as structured query language injection vulnerabilities [26,27] are the most common security incidents in healthcare environment. Medical devices for patient care such as wireless heart pumps, mammogram imaging and insulin pumps are often based on outdated computers. They also use operating systems which are vulnerable to cyberattacks. There has been an increased report in medical device software and hardware vulnerabilities such as the malware infection of high-risk pregnancy monitor [28]. Similarly, TrapX [29] reported that cybercriminals were able to permeate and control older devices such as 'X-ray machines, medical lasers and even life support systems'. Deploying medical devices manufactured without adequate security standards in healthcare environment continues to pose a serious risk to the healthcare sector or individuals using these devices. Cybercriminals can hack these unprotected devices easily and cause the device to malfunction with serious consequences to the patients. They can also make use of the hacked device as a back door to hack into other healthcare resources.

5.4.4   End user vulnerability

There is an alarming laxity in many healthcare organizations' approach to data security. Health data is frequently exposed through employee negligence and/or general lack of awareness about privacy and security. For instance, ransomware attack that hijacked the Hollywood Presbyterian Medical Center is believed to have been triggered by an employee who clicked on an attachment containing malware in an email. The main factor attributing to such lack of awareness and assiduousness by healthcare staff is often due to the lack of an appropriate organizational security culture (i.e. values, norms, etc.) that respects privacy of the patients and data security. Many studies have shown that the healthcare sector lacks a culture of security. As the level of success ultimately depends on the prevailing organizational culture, it is imperative that the healthcare sector understands that the untrained staff can act as a serious vulnerability to the organization. The healthcare providers should engage all their staff (both managers and employees) in continuous learning, evaluation and enhancement to establish a workplace that values and respects patients' rights to privacy and data security. Another concern is that, in the healthcare settings, clinicians and nurses do not have designated computers and workstations as they often move around and use nearby workstations to access patient data. Therefore, the healthcare employees have access to large amounts of personal information using an ever-increasing myriad of devices. As cybersecurity is a business risk as much as it is a technology risk, the healthcare providers have the due diligence and due care to ensuring an increased cybersecurity awareness at all levels within the healthcare centres.

5.4.5   Business vulnerability

Another cause of vulnerabilities arises from systemic business failures. One of the reasons why the healthcare industry is vulnerable to cyberattacks is the limited budget allocated by healthcare institutions to cybersecurity investment. Specifically, information security and privacy preservation are not considered a priority, thus there is lack of investment in cybersecurity [8]. Although the threat against healthcare system is growing substantially, investment in cybersecurity has not always followed proportionally. In addition to the value of the healthcare data, the lack of qualified cybersecurity professionals in the healthcare sector quite often is one of the main reasons that cybercriminals target healthcare organizations. Cybersecurity does not commend a high priority in healthcare industry and thus they do not budget for hiring qualified IT security personnel as well as purchasing quality security tools that could help them set up solid information security programs. As a result, solid incident response plan and vulnerability management processes are absent in most healthcare organizations.

5.5 Healthcare threat landscape

Cybercriminals (inside and outside of healthcare walls) deploy various threat vectors and ingenious strategies to infiltrate the inherent vulnerabilities in the healthcare systems. The digitally enabled healthcare environments face diverse, dangerous and constantly evolving cyber threat landscape. Understanding both existing and emerging cybersecurity threats is vital to defend security and privacy of the healthcare data as well as comply with pertinent healthcare regulations.

5.5.1 Cyber threat

Cyber threat is a potential risk to an asset that can originate from nature, people, processes and technology. Cyber threat agent is an adversary (internal or external person or entity such as malware and a disgruntled employee) that poses a threat to the organization's assets either maliciously or unknowingly. Malicious threat agents use a variety of threat vectors and ingenious tactics to hack the healthcare providers. Unfortunately, the high potential financial gains of health data have attracted numerous and better-skilled cyber threat agents. Therefore, understanding the profile, motivation and sophistication of the actual adversaries is therefore paramount to adopt the appropriate security policy.

New cyber threat vectors continue to emerge in the healthcare systems due to the introduction of many new applications such as physician mobility, mobile devices, wearable sensors, health information sharing and cloud computing. Also, the increasing level of interconnectedness between physical and virtual systems, people and processes, as well as the ease in which health records is distributed both internally through devices such as laptops, mobile devices, thumb drives and externally through cloud computing are contributing to the increasing magnitude of threats facing healthcare sectors. Further, these cyber threats have become more diverse and distributed in nature while growing in sophistication with lower barriers to entry increasing both in the frequency and impact of cyberattacks. Unfortunately, healthcare organizations have difficulties in 'understanding, tracking, reporting and managing' these threats in an efficient manner [20].

5.5.2 Social engineering threat

Social engineering threat is the most frequent and lethal threat to healthcare systems. Social engineering exploits human psychology using a variety of smart ways that include phone calls, emails and platforms such as social media [16] to trick people into divulging sensitive information such as login information offering them access to the system. Phishing scams [26] might be the simplest and most common types of social engineering attacks used today. The phishers send purposefully crafted spam emails to the medical staff to steal personal data such as password. Normally, the spam email is embedded with malevolent link that points to fraudulent websites where the medical staff would be prompted to enter their confidential information such as a username and password. The spam email may also come with document attachment bearing malware to staff with attractive email subject such as a medical invoice. The aim of the phishers is to be able to convince just one staff member to act on the spam email. Normally, a busy healthcare administrator or doctor may unwittingly fall prey to the phishers by acting on the spam email and share their login information. This gives cybercriminals access to the healthcare networked system from where they can infiltrate other systems and steal data, and potentially install ransomware on the system.

5.5.3   Employee threat

Employees can be both the strongest firewall and the weakest link in the information security chain. The threats from the employees assume different forms, such as staff who access patient data without any genuine need for it, malicious staff who steal data or render the organization's system inoperable, staff who unintentionally breach security policy and staff who get exploited by an external cyber attacker. There are many different possible risks associated with employee threats. However, mishandling of health records by healthcare employee can disclose it to unauthorized individuals. The impact of the disclosure on both the healthcare provider and the affected patients will include financial, social and psychological consequences.

Inadequate security awareness and training is a major source of the employee threat to information systems. Generally speaking, healthcare employees tend to exhibit lack of basic good security practices and the standard mistakes to avoid. In addition, they exhibit a weak security risk awareness and comprehension of the prevailing threat landscape [20]. Therefore, healthcare staff tend to be the weakest link in the security chain as they have shown to be highly susceptible to social engineering attacks such as phishing, spear phishing and other social engineering attacks. For example, Baystate Health reported that several employees responded to a phishing email compromising patient information.

5.5.4   Malicious software threats

Malicious software (malware) is a significant type of cybersecurity threat facing the healthcare vertical. Recent study shows that the healthcare sector is as much as four times likely to be attacked by malware than any other industry [30]. These malware can perform DoS and DDoS cyberattacks, which are serious threats to healthcare providers. Essentially, these attacks overwhelm the network to the point of making the system useless, causing harmful delays in access to critical information and information systems. For example, in January 2016, the Melbourne Health networks was attacked by the Qbot malware, causing chaos in the pathology unit and compelling the staff to resort to manual workarounds to process blood tissue and urine samples.

Ransomware is the latest data security threat with the healthcare industry being the prime target. Ransomware (e.g. locky, cryptolocker, cryptowall, Cerber or teslacrypt ransomware) is a malware variant used for extortion attack. Specifically, ransomware take data on your system as hostage by encrypting the file and charging a ransom to unlock it. Ransomware has targeted and victimized a number of healthcare institutions in recent years. In fact, many of the recent high-profile healthcare institution data breaches (e.g. British Association for Counselling and Psychotherapy) have been attributed to ransomware attack. The new, easy-to-use ransomware tools and services, the ease of implementation (e.g. all you need is a spam email acted on by an employee) and the high success rate of extortion have made ransomware very popular and responsible for the increasing ransomware attacks on the healthcare industry. The fact that health care is a critical infrastructure and any downtime can lead to serious consequences has not lost on cybercriminals as well. Also, because of the nature of healthcare institution, cybercriminals believe that they can demand a much higher pay from healthcare organizations, which explains the exponentially rising ransom attacks. They also believe that healthcare institutions are highly likely to pay out. For example, a Hollywood Presbyterian Medical Centre suffered a ransomware attack in early 2016 that forced the staff to revert to pen and paper to continue operations. It ultimately paid $17,000 in bitcoin in order to regain access to their medical files [31]. As a result, the healthcare industry is hit significantly harder by ransomware than in any other industry and the list of healthcare providers falling prey to ransomware attacks is growing.

5.5.5 Mobile health technologies threats

A wide variety of wireless network enabled mobile devices, such as smartphones and tablets capable of sensing, computing and networking, have proliferated the healthcare environment. These devices are used for handling emergency situation management as well as collecting and monitoring a number of physiological data such as temperature and heart rhythm. They are also used for accessing healthcare data and EHRs. While greatly aiding medical personnel in performing their duties, the mobile devices introduce a whole new and greater cybersecurity threat to the healthcare industry. This is because security implementations on mobile devices are often not adequate mainly because of resource constraints.

Although mobile devices could improve productivity, their ability to install third-party apps from a variety of sources poses the biggest security and privacy risk to healthcare systems. This is because third-party apps can carry malware, which gives hackers easy access to private information. With increasing proliferation of mobile devices in healthcare setting and the rampant state of malware in current mobile devices [32], the probability of healthcare system infection through mobile device malware is highly likely. Since many of these malware use complex techniques purposely designed to circumvent security architectures currently in use [32], it is necessary that the healthcare providers are made aware of the concealed risks that lurk in third-party apps on mobile devices.

Mobile devices contain sensitive information, which is a major magnet for cybercriminals. The potential for being lost or stolen is quite high. In addition, they are prone to all wireless network-related threats such as eavesdropping, data interception, rogue access points and snooping. For example, medical prescriptions contain personal health information, and if an adversary captures the medical prescription data on the wireless network and misuses it, breach of patient privacy could result. Other medical devices such as wireless heart pumps, mammogram imaging and insulin pumps also face a wide variety of threats. The main cause of the threats emanates from the fact that functionality has always been a focus in the development of EHR, especially when it comes to medical devices because the functions can be life critical.

5.5.6 Managing vendor security threats

In healthcare industry, it is a common practice to outsource data to managed services providers. Outside vendors can leave the healthcare organization open to privacy and data breaches and theft of patient information. For example, Mass General Hospital (MGH) contracted with Patterson Dental Supply, Inc. (PDSI), specifically for the purpose of safely and securely managing their patients' data. Instead, MGH found that even the outsourcing of patients' data is not immune from cyberattacks and data breaches; specifically, PDSI databases were hacked and 4,300 patient dental records, medical id numbers, social security numbers and other identifying information were stolen and/or compromised. The Australian Red Cross case is another example that illustrates threats due to managed services providers' threats.

5.5.7 Social media and BYOD threats

Online social media and bring your own device (BYOD) have altered the conventional workplace and work habits worldwide. Employees use a wide variety of online social media platforms [33] to connect and interact with people, share information with colleagues, research new developments and read news articles. Similarly, employees are increasingly using employee-owned devices to access enterprise data and systems. Although there are many practical benefits of both online social media and BYOD in enhancing patient care, for example, through enriching healthcare professional networking, the prevalence of both BYOD and social media usage by employees at workplace can pose serious threats to privacy [34] and data security as well as ethical and legal issues. For example, social media platforms such as Twitter and Facebook have become the prime avenues for cybercriminals to spread spam and malware as well as locating personal employee information and use it to target specific individuals in an organization. Similarly, confidential information leakage is a real possibility in which employees can post seemingly uncritical information or using incorrect account to inadvertently post sensitive information on the social media.

5.6 Cybersecurity controls

Cybersecurity controls are cyber defence tools and recommended set of standard actions deployed by organizations to preserve patient privacy and protect data security (i.e. CIA) from today's most pervasive cyber threats. Healthcare organizations deploy various security controls to maximize the protection of privacy and security (i.e. CIA) without impacting functionality and usability.

5.6.1 Regulatory authorities

Health data is usually collected by healthcare professionals such as clinicians, nurses or other clinical professionals. Thus it represents a trusted and professional relationship between patients and their team (e.g. doctors and nurses) responsible for treating them [35]. This relationship is very sensitive that deserves proper control in place to safeguard it. As result, health data security and privacy are legislated as privileged information that must be safeguarded from unauthorized disclosure. Moreover, healthcare professional associations have developed codes of ethics that spell out healthcare professionals' obligation to ensure that the confidentiality of their patients' data is protected from unlawful use and disclosure [36].

There are many regulations (i.e. legislation, codes of practice and guidelines) and conventions that mandate healthcare providers and associated organizations in their jurisdictions to adopt rigorous standards for preventing misuse of personal information. The European Commission's Data Protection Directive and the European Commission's General Data Protection Regulation, the HIPAA and the Health Information Technology for Economic and Clinical Health Act are examples of regulatory bodies empowered to regulate the use of personal health data that include the collection, storage, disclosure and exchanging. The main purpose of these regulatory bodies is to strike a balance between the lawful use/disclosure of health data and the public interest in privacy protection.

Although the regulations of health information are country specific in some cases, they all support broad data security and privacy measures. Normally these regulations place restrictions or specific conditions on the collection and management (i.e. storage, access, use and disclosure) of PHRs. For example, HIPPA requires that policies and documentation regarding patient privacy are put into place, that there is ongoing monitoring of appropriate access to patient's PHI and to investigate potential HIPAA violations. Furthermore, HIPAA requires that healthcare organizations, regardless of their size, designate a privacy officer whose primary duty is to protect the confidentially and privacy of patients' PHI. The privacy officer or anyone acting in that capacity is ultimately responsible for protecting patient privacy. It is important to note that compliance does not assure security performance [37].

5.6.2 Healthcare data protection

With the threat landscape changing constantly, preserving privacy and securing patient data is not an easy proposition. However, there exist a range of 'best practices' that healthcare sectors can adopt to defend themselves against cyberattacks [39]. A variety of privacy preserving mechanisms for EHRs have been developed [9]. For example, data anonymization techniques are deployed to hide patient identity and obscure contents of health data from unauthorized third parties.

Confidentiality is supported by technical tools such as encryption and access control (i.e. authentication and authorization) as well as cybersecurity policy and legal protections. The access control mechanisms control access to medical information systems, whereas the access accountability ensures who accessed what, when and where. Physical access control mechanisms ensure that high-security locations such as server rooms are restricted to authorized individuals only. Authentication involves users to identify themselves to the system through specific identity such as usernames and passwords, biometrics (e.g. palm, finger, retina or face recognition) or the combination of the previous two methods before accessing the resources on the system. In contrast, authorization ensures that only users with appropriate access permission and entity can use a resource or access a file. For healthcare environment, critical systems and data must remain available round-the-clock in the face of natural disasters, system failures and cyberattacks such as DoS attacks. The availability of the system and the data to the authorized individuals when needed to care for patients is a crucial data security component. Redundancy (primary backup) techniques are commonly used to ensure that if the primary server becomes inoperable the system will switch to a backup server to quickly resume the operation.

Healthcare staff are essential in mitigating the privacy and security issues. Trust in healthcare environment is extremely important. Patients share their health data with healthcare providers under the assumption that the healthcare providers use their health data to treat them. They also expect that the healthcare providers will have mechanisms in place to safeguard their data from inappropriate use. Therefore, healthcare workforce (i.e. permanent, temporary and even volunteer employees) must be aware of the cybersecurity measures required to safeguard privacy and security of data they use for patient care and management. Specifically, all healthcare staff who have access (i.e. use, view or share) to health data receive ongoing regular awareness and training concerning data security and patient privacy [6]. A wide variety of approaches can be used to raise awareness of the employees [40] by providing training opportunities about important security and privacy measures. Indeed, cybersecurity cannot be addressed without training employees to use devices properly, raising their awareness on cyber threats and ensuring their compliance with security policies.

5.6.3 Planning for cybersecurity

Cybersecurity programs driven by strategic planning that emphasizes strategic solutions are required. Cybersecurity programs include technical cybersecurity solutions and management processes for handling cybersecurity risks and ensures regulatory compliance. Healthcare organizations are confronted with dynamically varying cybersecurity risks and legal compliance challenges [41].

5.6.3.1 Cybersecurity strategic planning

There exist rich technical, administrative and operational controls for attending to the cybersecurity threats and vulnerabilities facing the healthcare sectors. Healthcare organizations need to follow strategic approach to implement them in a balanced and cost-effective manner. Therefore, given the sensitive nature of health information and the social and legal repercussions for its disclosure to unauthorized parties, healthcare organizations need to implement sustainable cybersecurity strategies to defend patient information and ensure regulatory compliance on a long-term basis. There is ample evidence that healthcare providers that attain this objective will possess an effective cybersecurity strategy [37,42]. Therefore, with so many cases of healthcare breaches recently, healthcare providers are becoming more and more aware of the strategic importance of developing a thorough cybersecurity strategy. For instance, healthcare providers need to observe the pertinent regulations and conventions governing the collection, storage, disclosure and exchanging of health data. In order to keep abreast of their obligations with legal and regulatory requirements, it is crucial that healthcare providers perform thorough planning.

5.6.3.2   Contingency planning

With the healthcare industry considered by cybercriminals as the most economically profitable target, cybersecurity and privacy assurance in healthcare sector is very complicated. Although the privacy and security of personal health data are of utmost importance, the alarming frequency with which healthcare data breaches are occurring raises serious questions about the preparedness of the healthcare sector in tackling this problem. As healthcare sectors more and more rely on information technology to provide care to patients, contingency planning to ensure business continuity has become increasingly important. These facilities face unplanned disruptions varying from simple incident to disaster and business failures. Note that data security includes assurance of confidentiality, integrity and availability, thus contingency planning is a vital component in cybersecurity defence strategies. Therefore, healthcare providers should have a plan for contingency to ensure continuity and speedy recovery of critical services or functions to mitigate any unplanned disruptions. Contingency planning is a crucial process that must be embedded in the cybersecurity program of the healthcare organization. Moreover, having in place capability to ensure business continuity and timely recovery from disasters and incidents for healthcare organizations has become mandatory in many countries. Therefore, healthcare providers should create and keep them up to date an incident response plan, disaster recovery plan and business continuity plan in order to quickly respond to security incidents and quickly recover from unplanned disruptions that threaten core assets of the healthcare organization.

5.6.3.3   Planning for risk analysis and management

Healthcare systems are indispensable critical infrastructures and thus risk-based active defence strategies to protect them against increasing cyberattacks are imperative. Planning and performing risk analysis and management is necessary to ensure that the healthcare providers' assets are protected in a cost-effective manner. Moreover, risk analysis and management is key for healthcare organizations to develop effective information security programs. As threats and vulnerabilities are evolving constantly, regular risk analysis and management is indispensable to protect healthcare infrastructures and information from cyberattacks. It is important to note that risk analysis and management are mandated by HIPAA regulations.

5.6.4 Cybersecurity policies

Looking from the potential consequences perspective, the protection of healthcare data and systems is often critical as it can endanger the well-being of the patients. Strong and robust privacy and cybersecurity policies are crucial to ensure that patient data are secure from unlawful usage and disclosure [43]. Therefore, healthcare organizations need to develop and implement robust information security policies in order to prevent potential exposures or leaks of healthcare information. Generally speaking, these policies create the objectives of the cybersecurity program. They establish clear rules regarding the proper use of cybersecurity controls, acceptable uses of resources and data, acceptable sharing and releasing of health data, monitoring adherence for avoiding and detecting breaches, and disciplinary procedures for delinquents. However, having a cybersecurity policy in place does not necessarily guarantee security and privacy. A number of factors determine the success of cybersecurity policies. The most important factor for the cybersecurity policy to succeed is the senior managers' interest. Given poor obedience to cybersecurity policies by employees in many organizations, strong commitment of the top managements is necessary. Senior management engagement and guiding of the development and implementation in their organization will act as a catalyst for the employees to consider the policy seriously and comply. Also, easily accessible and understandable policies can encourage employees to abide by them. Moreover, policies that can balance usability of the health data for care against the protection of the patient privacy and data security are attractive. Overly restrictive policies are inviting the staff to find novel ways to circumvent the policy to accomplish their work. Finally, it is necessary to ensure that cybersecurity policies are regularly updated, monitored and enforced.

5.7 Analysis of cyberattack impacts

Cyberattacks will have serious financial consequences on the healthcare providers in addition to a possible damaged reputation as well as decrease in employee morale. In this section an analysis of some prominent financial impacts to the healthcare providers and patients is presented.

5.7.1 Revenue loss

A recent study from Accenture [5] predicts, based on historical security breach data, that more than 25 million patients will have their medical identity stolen from their healthcare providers over 5 years.

Figure 5.3 shows the projected number of patients impacted by healthcare provider data breaches from 2015 to 2019. Accenture estimates that a healthcare provider stands to lose an average of $113 million of lifetime patient revenue for every data breach it suffered. Furthermore, patients affected by medical identity theft will most likely leave a healthcare provider, which stands to lose about $305 billion in cumulative lifetime patient revenue [5].

5.7.2 Financial impact on patients

Medical identity theft is not only complex to resolve but also very costly for the patients to restore their identity. Victims generally report spending an average of $13,500 to reclaim their identities, restore their credit, reimburse providers for fraudulent claims and correct inaccuracies in their health records.

Figure 5.4 shows that the medical identity theft victims suffer significant financial consequences for reclaiming their stolen identities. Even if only 20% of the patients

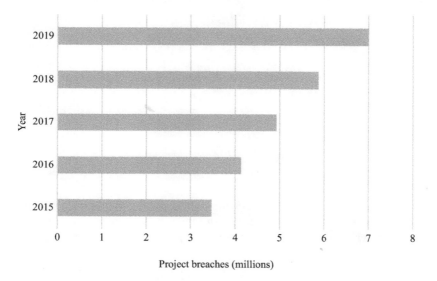

Figure 5.3 Medical identity theft projection

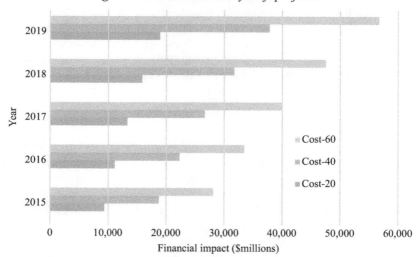

Figure 5.4 Projected financial impact on patients

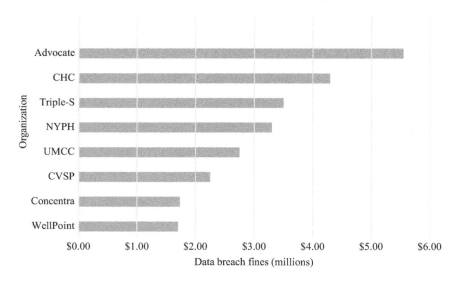

Figure 5.5   HIPAA settlement fines

(Cost-20) spend out of pocket to reclaim their identities, this is a significant sum. Therefore, as resolution of medical identity theft is time consuming and costly to patients, it is critical for healthcare providers to prevent medical identity theft.

5.7.3   Regulatory costs

Figure 5.5 shows a sample of fines imposed on covered entities for violating HIPAA regulations such as data breach that exposed the PHI due to lack of policies or safeguards. The result shows that the penalties and fines for noncompliance are substantial. It also shows that HHS is getting aggressive in handing out fines to violators. As organizations failing to comply with HIPAA are exposed to multimillion dollar fines, it is imperative that healthcare providers develop effective information security programs taking into account the appropriate regulations to ensure compliance.

5.7.4   Cost of downtime

Healthcare facilities can experience an unplanned downtime for a variety of reasons. The recent spate of ransomware attacks that brought many healthcare organizations offline for several days is an example of threats that healthcare organizations constantly face. Figure 5.6 shows the cost that a healthcare provider can potentially suffer from unplanned downtime based on the determination by Ponemon Institute that an unplanned downtime at healthcare organization costs an average of $7,900 a minute per incident [44].

The high cost of downtime underscores the importance of effective and up-to-date contingency planning to recover and restore system in the shortest possible

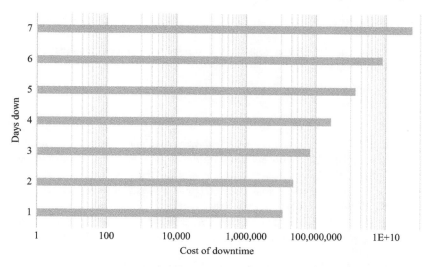

Figure 5.6   Cost of unplanned system downtime

timeframe. As no system is fail proof, measures can be taken to reduce the likelihood of experiencing an unplanned downtime by developing preventative measures that allows them to ensure business continues and recovers as quickly as possible.

5.8   Conclusion

There are business and regulatory reasons to protect and prevent unauthorized access to patient records that the healthcare providers generate, receive, maintain or transmit. This chapter highlighted the potential challenges to privacy and security posed by digitization of health data. Although healthcare digitization will enable patient data to be used to positively enhance the quality of care and reduce operational expenses, digitalization has introduced new trends such as healthcare professional mobility, cloud computing and possibility of instantly sharing PHRs from anywhere at any time. In return, these have posed serious risks to the data security and patient privacy. The recent spate of security breaches suggests that cyber threats against healthcare industry are growing and that much of the healthcare organizations are unprepared to deal with them. Unless healthcare sector takes a proactive approach to protect its critical assets from cyberattacks, the sector stands to lose patients and billions in revenue. Therefore, healthcare providers must deal with the security and privacy risks associated with healthcare information as well as remain compliant to various regulatory requirements. In order to realize these, healthcare providers should have appropriately funded cybersecurity programs. Cybersecurity policies and cybersecurity controls based on risk analysis and management need to be implemented.

Acknowledgment

This chapter will not have been possible without the assistance of Maliha Omar.

References

[1]   Abawajy J.H., and Hassan M.M. *'Federated Internet of Things and cloud computing pervasive patient health monitoring system'.* IEEE Communications Magazine. 2017; 55(1):48–53.

[2]   Steve M.-D. *'Your life in your hands: the security issues with healthcare apps'.* Network Security. 2016; (4):14–18.

[3]   John H., John B., Tamara S., John K, and Shanna H. *A Consumer-Driven Culture of Health: The Path to Sustainability and Growth.* Deloitte University Press, 2015.

[4]   Buket Y., Alptekin K., and Öznur Ö. *'Research issues for privacy and security of electronic health services'.* Future Generation Computer Systems. 2017; (68):1–13.

[5]   Accenture. *The $300 billion attack: the revenue risk and human impact of healthcare provider cyber security inaction* [online]. 2015. Available at www.accenture.com. [Accessed 17 June 2016].

[6]   Farzandipour M., Sadoughi F., Ahmadi M., and Karimi I. *'Security requirements and solutions in electronic health records: Lessons learned from a comparative study'.* Journal of Medical Systems, 2010; 34(4):629–642.

[7]   Xuhui L., Qin L., Tao P., and Jie W. *'Dynamic access policy in cloud-based personal health record (PHR) systems'.* Information Sciences. 2017; 379: 62–81.

[8]   Ponemon Institute, *The state of cybersecurity in healthcare organizations in 2016.* Ponemon Institute Research Report, 2016.

[9]   Harsha P., and Vladimir O. *'Privacy preserving mechanisms for enforcing security and privacy requirements in E-health solutions'.* International Journal of Information Management. 2016; 36:1161–1173.

[10]   Rinehart-Thompson A., and Harman B. Privacy and confidentiality. In: Harman LB, editor. *Ethical Challenges in the Management of Health Information.* 2nd edition. Sudbury, MA: Jones and Bartlett; 2006. p. 53.

[11]   Peel D.C. *Electronic health records vs. patient privacy: Who will win?* [online]. 2012. Available at http://www2.idexpertscorp.com/blog/single/electronic-health-records-vs.-patient-privacy-who-will-win [Accessed 20 February 2017].

[12]   Solove D. *'HIPAA turns 10. Analyzing the past, present and future impact'.* Journal of AHIMA. 2013; 84(4):22–28.

[13]   Dimitrios L., and Dimitris G. *'Long-term verifiability of healthcare records authenticity'.* International Journal of Medical Informatics, 2007; 76(5–6): 442–448.

[14] Ashley C., and Jemal A. *'Detecting and mitigating HX-DoS attacks against cloud web services'*. Proceedings of 15th International Conference on Network-Based Information Systems; Melbourne, Australia, September 2012 (California, IEEE, 2012), pp. 429–434.

[15] Caroline H., and Jim F. *Your Medical Record Is Worth More to Hackers than Your Credit Card.* Reuters. 2014.

[16] Hamid I., and Abawajy J. *'An approach for profiling phishing activities'*. Computers and Security. 2014; 45:27–41.

[17] Islam R., and Abawajy J. *'A multi-tier phishing detection and filtering approach'*. Journal of Network and Computer Applications. 2013; 36(1): 324–335.

[18] Independent Security Evaluators. *Securing hospitals: A research study and blueprint* [online].2016. Available at www.securityevaluators.com. [Accessed 22 May 2016].

[19] Hackett R. *Anthem, a major health insurer, suffered a massive hack* [online]. 2015. Available at http://fortune.com/2015/02/05/anthem-suffers-hack/ [Accessed 22 May 2016].

[20] Greg B., and Michael E. *Health care and cyber security: increasing threats require increased capabilities.* KPMG report, 2015.

[21] Tony Y., and Don M. *Healthcare Security Risks and Vulnerabilities. Hospital and Healthcare Security.* 6th edition. 2015, pp. 49–77.

[22] Abawajy J., and Kelarev K. *'Iterative classifier fusion system for the detection of android malware'*. IEEE Transactions on Big Data, 2017; pp. 1–1, 2 March 2017, doi: 10.1109/TBDATA.2017.2676100.

[23] Biplob R., Morshed C., and Jemal A. *'Secure object tracking protocol for the Internet of Things'*. IEEE Internet of Things Journal. 2016; 3(4):544–553.

[24] Sanaz M., Tuan G. Ethiopia N., Amir R., *et al.* *'End-to-end security scheme for mobility enabled healthcare Internet of Things'*. Future Generation Computer Systems. 2016; (64):108–124.

[25] Albot D. *Computer viruses are 'rampant' on medical devices in hospitals* [online]. MIT Technology Review, 2012. Available at https://www.technologyreview.com/s/429616/computer-viruses-are-rampant-on-medical-devices-in-hospitals/ [Accessed 25 July 2016].

[26] Abawajy J.H. *'Human-computer interaction in ubiquitous computing environments'*. International Journal of Pervasive Computing and Communications. 2009; 5(1):61–77.

[27] Jemal A. *'SQLIA detection and prevention approach for RFID systems'*. Journal of Systems and Software. 2013; 86(3):751–758.

[28] Fu K., and Blum J. *'Controlling for cybersecurity risks of medical device software'*. Communication of ACM 2013; (56):35–37.

[29] TrapX Security, *TrapX reveals 2016 healthcare breaches increased 63 percent year-over-year: medical device hijacks and ransomware on the rise* [online]. 2016. Available at https://trapx.com/trapx-reveals-2016-healthcare-breaches-increased-63-percent-year-over-year-medical-device-hijacks-and-ransomware-on-the-rise/ [Accessed 25 July 2016].

[30] Healthcare Information and Management Systems Society (USA). Healthcare Environmental Security Scan Report. vol. 1. Chicago: HIMSS; 2016.

[31] Trevor M. *Hollywood hospital pays $17,000 to ransomware hackers* [online]. 2016. Available at http://www.digitaltrends.com/computing/hollywood-hospital-ransomware-attack/ [Accessed 17 June 2016].

[32] Guillermo S.-T., Juan T., Pedro P.-L., and Arturo E. *'Detection and analysis of malware for smart devices'*. IEEE Communications Surveys and Tutorials, 2014; 16(2):961–987.

[33] Luo, E. Liu, Q., Abawajy, J., and Wang, G. *'Privacy-preserving multi-hop profile-matching protocol for proximity mobile social networks'*. Future Generation Computer Systems 2017; (68):222–233.

[34] Jemal H. Abawajy, Mohd Izuan Hafez Ninggal, and Tutut Herawan. *'Privacy Preserving Social Network Data Publication'*. IEEE Communications Surveys and Tutorials. 2016; 18(3):1974–1997.

[35] Brodnik M., Rinehart-Thompson L., and Reynolds R. *Fundamentals of Law for Health Informatics and Information Management Professionals*. 2nd edition. Chicago: AHIMA Press; 2012. p. 3.

[36] McWay, D. *Legal and Ethical Aspects of Health Information, Third Edition*. New York: Cengage Learning; 2010.

[37] Juhee K., and Johnson M. *'Security practices and regulatory compliance in the healthcare industry'*. Journal of the American Medical Informatics Association. 2013; 20(1):44–51.

[38] Naipeng D., Hugo J., and Jun P. *'Formal analysis of privacy in an eHealth protocol'*. Proceedings of the 17th European Symposium on Research in Computer Security. Pisa, Italy, September 10–12, 2012 (Springer-Verlag, Berlin Heidelberg, 2012), pp. 325–342.

[39] David H., and Peter Y. *'Cyberterrorism: Is the U.S. Healthcare System Safe?'* Telemedicine and e-Health. 2013; 19(1):61–66.

[40] Abawajy J. *'User preference of cyber security awareness delivery methods'*. Behaviour and Information Technology. 2014; 33(3):237–248.

[41] Beard L., Schein R., Morra D., Wilson K., and Keelan J. *'The challenges in making electronic health records accessible to patients'*. Journal of the American Medical Informatics Association. 2012; 19(1):116–120.

[42] Murphy N., Gainer V., Mendis M., Churchill S., and Kohane I. *'Strategies for maintaining patient privacy in i2b2'*. Journal of the American Medical Informatics Association. 2011; 18(Suppl 1):103–108.

[43] Al-Nayadi F., and Abawajy J.H. (eds.). *'An authorization policy management framework for dynamic medical data sharing'*. Proceedings of the International Conference on Intelligent Pervasive Computing; Jeju Island, Korea, Oct. 2007 (California, IEEE, 2007), pp. 313–318.

[44] The Ponemon Institute, *The cost of data center outages* [online]. 2017. Available at http://www.ponemon.org/blog/2013-cost-of-data-center-outages. [Accessed 17 June 2016].

Chapter 6

Security challenges and solutions for e-business

Anne James[1], Waleed Bulajoul[2,3], Yahaya Shehu[2,4], Yinsheng Li[5], and Godwin Obande[2]

Abstract

The advantages of economic growth and increasing ease of operation afforded by e-business and e-commerce developments are unfortunately matched by growth in cyberattacks. This chapter outlines the common attacks faced by e-business and describes the defenses that can be used against them. It also reviews the development of newer security defense methods. These are (1) biometrics for authentication, (2) parallel processing to increase power and speed of defenses, (3) data mining and machine learning to identify attacks, (4) peer-to-peer security using blockchains, (5) enterprise security modeling and security as a service, and (6) user education and engagement. The review finds overall that one of the most prevalent dangers is social engineering in the form of phishing attacks. Recommended counteractions include education and training, and the development of new machine learning and data sharing approaches so that attacks can be quickly discovered and mitigated.

Keywords: E-business security; e-commerce security; security solutions

6.1 Introduction

Electronic business (e-business) is the use of the internet, intranet, extranet, or other networks to support business processes. It includes various activities such as buying and selling electronically, electronic procurement, electronic distribution, online customer service, electronic marketing, secure transactions, automation of processes, and electronic collaboration. E-commerce, on the other hand, generally refers to the buying and selling, marketing and servicing, and delivery and payment of products,

[1]School of Science and Technology, Nottingham Trent University, UK
[2]Faculty of Engineering, Environment and Computing, Coventry University, UK
[3]Faculty of Engineering, Omar Almukhtar University, Libya
[4]Shehu Shagari College of Education, Nigeria
[5]Software School of Fudan University, Fudan University, China

services and information over the internet, although other electronic mediums can be used. It is part of e-business.

The advantages of economic growth and increasing ease of operation afforded by e-business and e-commerce developments are unfortunately matched by growth in cyberattacks [1,2]. The aim of these attacks is usually financial gain. Sadly the Anti-Phishing Working Group (APWG) recorded more phishing in 2016 than in any year since it began monitoring in 2004 [1] with a 65% increase on 2015 figures. According to the latest APWG Activity Report, over 80% of phishing attacks target retail services, financial institutions, Internet Service Provider, or payment services. These attacks are normally not mitigated quickly, with average uptime of 29 h and 51 min in 2014 [3]. Thus the fake interfaces have plenty of time to trap victims before they are removed.

The Symantec 2016 Internet Threat Report [2] highlighted that over the previous year there was a 125% increase in zero-day attacks where vulnerabilities are exploited before the software owners are aware of them. It also reported that 78% of websites have unpatched vulnerabilities and that there is a rise of ransomware attacks where attackers encrypt or lock owner's data and do not release it until a ransom is paid. A recent example of a ransom attack is the WannaCry malware, which affected many organizations around the world in 2017. The report also noted a rise in attacks against small business (those with 250 or fewer employees), although there was a decrease in the number of small businesses attacked, evidencing more targeted attack campaigns. Indeed increased by 55% are spear phishing attacks. In these attacks individuals or organizations are targeted after the attacker has obtained information about them and then uses that information to gain trust. The report also stated that the Internet of Things presents greater risks as the technology develops and becomes more widespread.

There have been significant technological advancements in developing tools to prevent attacks on electronic communication over the internet. Examples include tools that alert users of potentially fraudulent emails and websites but, as also extensively reported in literature, these tools are not entirely reliable in protecting users against attacks [4,5]. Security experts and attackers compete against each other. Experts, with the help of developers, continue to develop software to prevent attacks while attackers are constantly learning new techniques and changing tactics to make attacks more successful. Furthermore, the "human" is often the weakest link in information security chain rendering technical innovations powerless when successfully attacked through social engineering [6].

In the following sections, a review is provided of security in e-business, concentrating on the e-commerce area as this area is the most targeted and vulnerable. In Section 6.2, current security threats are reviewed. Section 6.3 looks at current solutions, while Section 6.4 discusses new developing approaches. Section 6.5 offers a conclusion to the chapter.

6.2   Current security threats in e-commerce

Many of the current security threats are especially damaging in the e-commerce side of e-business. This is the area where exchanges of money for goods or services occur and thus are of particular interest to users with bad intent for financial gain. There are a number of common vulnerabilities. As early as 2001, a survey by Udo [7] showed that the major hurdles to using e-commerce were privacy and security concerns. In 2014, Hartono *et al.* [8] found that buyer concern about website security is still a critical issue when it comes to maximizing the potential for electronic commerce transactions. Furthermore in 2016, Jotwani and Dutta highlighted e-commerce security threats, emphasizing the importance of information security in the financial transactions of e-commerce [9]. Security threats in e-commerce can be divided into three main types: denial of service (DoS), spying attacks, and unauthorized access. Within these types, there are many methods of attack and there are overlaps between the areas, with some methods being common to more than one type of threat. The following sections discuss these three main threats.

6.2.1   Denial of service

A DoS attack aims to make the target service overwhelmed with messages such that it is no longer able to execute satisfactorily, thus denying users access to the service. It is achieved by bombarding the service with requests usually generated automatically. IP spoofing may be used to start a DoS attack. IP spoofing involves changing the source address of a data packet so that it looks like it has come from a recognized and trusted source. Since the server logs will already contain the spoof address, it is difficult to find the source of the attack. The DoS attack these days is usually a distributed attack called a distributed denial of service (DDoS) attack where requests are sent from many sites, often as a result of participating attack sites being compromised after being infected with malicious software (see description of Trojan attacks in Section 6.2.2). The participating sites act maliciously without the owner's knowledge.

Another type of DoS attack is to infect the target with a virus such that it is no longer able to function. A computer virus is a malware program that replicates itself and spreads through a network and might be set up to deliberately corrupt or delete data. The virus is usually spread via attachments in emails or via downloads. When the user opens the file, the virus will be activated. It may then continue to spread its code into other programs and files stored on the victim computer. A computer worm operates similarly to a virus but does not carry a payload to cause damage to the victim system. A worm can however still cause problems by taking up valuable bandwidth and thus denying service.

6.2.2   Unauthorized access

Unauthorized access means accessing a system without permission. There are various ways in which this might be achieved. One method is through back doors. A back door is an access channel to a site that bypasses normal authentication methods. They are used by developers to enable quick and easy access during development and should be removed before the software is released. Any which remain are a threat to security as attackers often attempt to access the site through the server side. Back doors are sometimes in place for legitimate reasons such as troubleshooting or restoring user passwords but they are not recommended since they become an area of vulnerability regarding security. Open ports are another vulnerability. A port scanner might be used to find open serviced ports through which a DDoS attack can be launched. Port scanning is also a method used legitimately by administrators to check security of their systems. At a higher level, a ping sweep can be used to find which IP addresses map to live hosts. A live host sends an echo-reply and can then be probed further by an attacker.

The attacker may obtain credentials by social engineering, which refers to persuading or tricking humans into passing on their credentials. This can be achieved by person-to person contact, often over the phone with the attacker posing as a legitimate agent for an entity with which the victim has a relationship, or by machine-to-person contact through phishing. Phishing attacks are used to illegitimately gain credentials by presenting what seems to be a trusted and recognizable system interface to the user but it is actually false and linked to the attacker's domain. The legitimate user thinks they are accessing the real system but unfortunately they are not. Instead the user's credentials get passed to the attacker's site while the user receives a benign message generated by the attacker so that suspicions are not aroused. By this time the attacker has the user credentials and can access the system.

Often social engineering is used to launch a Trojan horse or Trojan attack where the victim is duped into opening an email attachment or downloading some software. The Trojan attack takes the form of a malicious computer program, which creates a back door to the affected computer. It does this by connecting to a controller that can then have unauthorized access to the victim machine enabling the attacker to access everything in the affected computer, modify or delete data and upload further software. Personal information such as banking information, passwords, or personal identity (IP address) can be stolen. The controller might gradually gain control of a number of machines, collectively termed a Botnet, which it can use to create a DDoS attack (see Section 6.2.1).

Another category of attack worth mentioning is that of stealth attacks [10,11]. A stealth attack is one that remains undetected by the client computer. Stealth attackers targeting a victim may move patiently through computer networks, taking days, weeks, or months to accomplish their objectives, in order to avoid detection. As networks scale up in size and speed, monitoring for such attack attempts is increasingly a challenge [12]. Other methods of unauthorized access include brute-force attacks where the attacker gains access by trial and error, continually attempting to guess the password. A predeveloped list of possible passwords or automated software may be used to generate a large number of consecutive guesses.

6.2.3 Spying attacks

Spying attacks include sniffing. Sniffers are applications or devices that can read, monitor, and capture network data exchanges and read network packets. Without strong encryption, data can be read by sniffers as they traverse the network. Having access to the data gives attackers the ability to gain sensitive information, which can be used for criminal offences. The man-in-the-middle (MITM) attack is where an attacker intercepts a conversation between two parties and relays messages

Table 6.1   Attacks and methods

Category	Attack	Contributing method
(Distributed) Denial of service	Stops legitimate users being able to access the service or impairs performance of a service	Message bombardment Botnet IP spoofing Virus Worm
Spyware	Discovers sensitive information	Sniffer Man-in-the-middle Key logger
Unauthorized access	Commits crimes like manipulating records for financial gain, carrying out unauthorized operations, placing viruses or malware	Social engineering (including phishing) Password cracking Back door Stealth attack

between the parties impersonating each of them. The attacker thus gains access to information that the two parties were exchanging and may also change messages or send false messages. The MITM attack could be used to send a Trojan horse (see Section 6.2.2).

Another type of spying attack is key logging. A key logger is a hardware device or small program that monitors each keystroke a user types on a specific computer's keyboard. As a hardware device, a key logger is a small battery-sized plug that serves as a connector between the user's keyboard and computer. As the user types, the device collects each keystroke and saves it as text in its own miniature hard drive. At a later point in time, the person who installed the key logger must return and physically remove the device in order to access the harvested information. A key logger program, on the other hand, does not require physical access to the user's computer. It can be downloaded on purpose by someone who wants to monitor activity on a particular computer or it can be downloaded unwittingly as spyware and executed as part of a rootkit (software designed to enable access to areas of system software that would not otherwise be allowed) or through a remote administration Trojan (see Section 6.2.2). A key logger program typically consists of two files that get installed in the same directory: a dynamic link library (DLL) file (which does all the recording) and an executable file that installs the DLL file and triggers it to work. The key logger program records each keystroke the user types and uploads the information over the internet to the installer.

6.2.4   Summary of attacks and methods

Table 6.1 shows categories of attack and methods that are commonly used and that were discussed in the previous sections.

6.3 Current security solutions

Generally, security can be defined as an organized framework consisting of concepts, beliefs, principles, policies, procedures, techniques, and measures that are required in order to protect the individual system assets as well as the system as a whole against any deliberate or accidental threat [13]. The AIC triangle (availability, integrity, and confidentiality) is a model designed to guide the development of policies for information security in organizations (see Figure 6.1). Availability means ensuring that data needed is available at all times to those that need it. Integrity means ensuring that the data is correct and protected from unauthorized modification or unintended corruption. Confidentiality means that data stored on the computer must only be accessible to those with a right or need to see it. The AIC model is widely accepted in organizations and considered to be a cornerstone of security maintenance. Various methods can be used to support the AIC objectives. These include authentication, encryption, access control, firewalls, intrusion detection and prevention systems, message digest or checksum, honeypot, digital signature, and digital certificate. Table 6.2 shows the approaches used and how they relate to the AIC model.

Authentication is the process of proving the identity of the user or process to the receiving system. It is commonly implemented through names and passwords. Cards, tokens, or biometrics may also be used but the standard legacy password offers a good balance of security versus convenience. Bonneau *et al.* [14] evaluated two decades of proposals to replace text passwords for general-purpose user authentication on the web using 25 usability, deployability, and security benefits that an ideal scheme might provide. The scope of proposals surveyed included password management software, federated login protocols, graphical password schemes, cognitive authentication schemes, one-time passwords, hardware tokens, and phone-aided schemes and biometrics. The authors found that no known scheme came close to providing all desired benefits and none even retained the full set of benefits that legacy passwords already provide. They found a wide range of schemes from those offering minor security benefits beyond legacy passwords, to those offering significant security benefits in return for being more costly to deploy or more difficult to use.

Encryption is the conversion of plain text to code or cypher-text in order to make it non-intelligible to anyone who views it without the necessary access rights. The

Figure 6.1 AIC model

cypher-text can only be decoded through the use of a key that only authorized users or processes should possess. Various methods of encryption can be used and research efforts continue to seek stronger solutions to combat the efforts of attackers [15]. Access control is the use of rules that state which users are allowed access to which objects. A principle is that users should only be able to access systems needed to carry out their assigned functions. Access control lists (ACLs) are widely used in organizations and are usually role based.

Firewalls are hardware or software devices that protect a local network by monitoring and controlling the incoming and outgoing traffic based on predetermined security rules. They sit between a local network and the internet. Intrusion detection and prevention systems (IDPS) work similarly but the latter have more functionality. They sit either on the local network (NIDPS) or on the host (HIDPS) and report, detect, or protect systems. Intrusion detection and prevention systems (IDS, IPS, or IDPS) monitor, detect, analyze, and prevent intrusions. A system that protects important operating system files is an example of an HIDPS, while a system that analyzes incoming network traffic is an example of an NIDPS. IDPS can also be classified by detection approach. The detection method might be signature-based detection (recognizing bad patterns, such as malware) or anomaly-based detection (detecting deviations from a model of "good" traffic). Selecting the right response to an attack

Table 6.2   Approaches to security defense and the AIC model

Method	Purpose	AIC model relationship
Authentication	Makes sure only legitimate users can access the system	Confidentiality Integrity
Encryption	Makes sure data cannot be read by unauthorized people	Confidentiality
Access control	Makes sure users only access parts of the system they need	Confidentiality Integrity
Message digest or checksum	Enables data to be checked for tampering	Integrity
Firewall	Prevents attackers from getting into the system	Confidentiality Integrity Availability
Intrusion detection and prevention systems	Detects, analyzes, and prevents intrusions from outside and within a system	Confidentiality Integrity Availability
Antivirus and antispyware	Detects, blocks, and removes virus and spyware	Confidentiality Integrity Availability
Honeypot	Attracts attacks away from proper site and learns about them	Confidentiality Integrity Availability
PKI – digital signature and certificate	Ensures non-repudiation and that data can be sent securely over the internet using encryption	Confidentiality Integrity

is an important part of intrusion detection. Responses include generating a report or alarm, isolation, relocation, no punishment, service denial, account locking, ICMP messaging, remote logging, IP address blocking, host shut down, disconnecting from the network, disabling attack port, or creating backup [16].

Message digests are secure one-way hash functions that take arbitrary-sized data and output a fixed-length hash value. Examples are the SHA algorithms [17]. They protect the integrity and of data since they can be used to check whether or not data has been modified. Any modification would produce a different hash value. Checksum is a similar method for protecting integrity. In this case a sum is made of the values of bytes in a piece of data to create a sum that can be checked. Any modification of the data would produce a different sum value. Honeypots are decoy systems intended to deflect attackers. They mimic the real systems and appear to have data attractive to attackers but they are isolated from the real site. They can be used to learn more about attacks and to keep the attackers away from the real system. Once an attacker is identified, they can be blocked from the real site.

Digital signature is part of Public Key Infrastructure (PKI). It manifests as a code that is attached to an electronically transmitted document to verify its contents and the sender's identity. In PKI, a user has a public key and a private key that are generated mathematically and verified by a certifying authority. The digital signature is used to sign documents. A user encrypts the signed document with the private key and sends it together with the public key to the receiver. The receiver decodes the message with the sender's public key and is thus able to verify the sender. It would not be possible to decrypt the document with the public key if it had not been encrypted with the private key. Digital signature therefore provides non-repudiation, which means that the sender cannot deny having sent the document.

Digital certificates are also part of PKI. Digital certificates are electronic documents used to prove the ownership of a public key. Information about its owner's identity, as well as the digital signature of an entity that has verified the certificate's contents, is included in the certificate. A potential sender can examine the certificate and check whether the signature is valid by using the verifying entity's public key. If the signature is valid, the sender will be reassured that they can use the certificate holder's public key to securely send a message to the certificate holder. On receipt of the message the certificate holder uses their private key to decrypt the message.

Based on PKI and having evolved from Netscape's Secure Sockets Layer (SSL) protocol, Transport Layer Security (TLS) is the most commonly used security technology for establishing an encrypted link between a web server and a browser. The terms SSL or SSL/TLS are used to refer to the same protocol. TLS provides privacy and data integrity between two communicating applications. It differs from the earlier SSL by providing more secure methods as part of its protocol. Key differences between SSL and TLS that make TLS a more secure and efficient protocol are message authentication, key generation, and the supported cipher suites, with TLS supporting newer and more secure algorithms. A common higher-level protocol used in e-commerce is HTTPS. It uses TLS to secure the communication as opposed to HTTP, which does not. An important standard for a PKI to manage digital certificates and public-key encryption is X.509 [18]. The standard is a key part of the TLS protocol and includes formats for public key certificates, certificate revocation lists, attribute certificates, and a certification path validation algorithm.

6.4 New developments in security for e-business

In this section, we discuss newer solutions to security defenses. Included are biometrics for authentication; parallelism to increase power and speed of defenses; data mining and machine learning to identify attacks; peer-to-peer security using blockchains; enterprise security modeling and security as a service; and user education and engagement.

6.4.1 Biometrics for authentication

Biometrics [19] are becoming popular in user identification systems [20]. Biometrics are technologies for measuring and analyzing a person's physiological or behavioral characteristics. These characteristics are unique to individuals, hence can be used to verify or identify a person. Arguably, biometrics provide a very convenient method of identification because a person always carries their biometrics with them and does not therefore need a card token or to remember a long password. However, there are some issues with biometrics that hinder take-up [21–23] including accuracy and privacy concerns.

Biometric technologies for authentication are increasingly being adopted in e-business, particularly in developing nations. Nigeria is a country with an estimated population of over 167 million people [24]. A number of biometric initiatives have been introduced in recent years [25]. Banks were recently given directives to collate fingerprints of all their existing customers after which a unique Bank Verification Number was issued to all customers. The reason for this was to enable checks and reduce fraud. Mobile phone operators in the country make it a policy that all their customers must register their SIM card (a registration that involves fingerprints) before they can have access to the network as directed by the Nigerian Communication Commission. The aim is to reduce fraud and criminal activity. In some states, ministries, or agencies, fingerprints are used to uniquely identify genuine employees. The idea behind this is to check the rampant cases of ghost workers. These are workers who are on the payroll but who will never be seen because they do not exist. However, there have been issues with accuracy and confidence in some of these use cases. Coventry University, UK, is developing a system to increase confidence and performance in biometric authentication methods in partnership with a state government in Nigeria [26]. Nigeria is not the only country adopting widespread national use of biometrics. The Brazilian bank Bradesco uses a palm vein biometric system called Palm of Your Hand to provide secure log-in on its ATM machines. Clients can choose to use this biometric instead of their PINs. The national government of India is aiming to reduce benefit fraud with the roll out of a biometric identification database that will contain biometric details of all of its citizens. Nigeria, Brazil, and India are nations that, in spite of rapid development, have many citizens still living in poverty. Some citizens do not have a birth certificate and in these cases biometrics can provide a good solution for proving identity. In the developed world we see fingerprints used at Disney parks in the USA and thumb prints are commonly used across schools in the UK for lunch and refreshment purchase. Biometrics are also increasingly used in passports and national identity cards in many countries around the world. It is a technology that will be increasingly adopted. A standard biometric authentication procedure typically runs as follows. First a user registers their biometrics via a sensor, a template is generated, and stored in a database. Subsequently to access the system, a user provides their biometrics again via a sensor, a new template is generated, and compared to the previously stored template. If there is a match, access is allowed. If not, access is denied.

The fundamental objective of a biometric system is to recognize individuals accurately. This in turn implies that a biometric system must have low recognition error rates. False Acceptance Rate (FAR) and False Reject Rate (FRR) are used to quantify errors in verification systems. Many research efforts are devoted to creating systems that decrease false outcomes for varying modes of biometrics. A Detection Error Tradeoff (DET) curve is a plot that has FRR on the y-axis and the FAR on the x-axis. FAR and FRR are useful because the Equal Error Rate (EER) is deduced based on these two parameters. EER is a unique operating point where FAR=FRR. This summarizes the entire DET curve and can be interpreted to achieve the accuracy of detection by subtracting the EER value from 100. EER is commonly used as a measure to compare performance of different biometric systems.

There are many modes of biometrics that can be used for identification in authentication systems [27]. They include physical biometrics such as fingerprints [28], face recognition [29], hand geometry [30], iris recognition [31], and palm vein identification [32]. Keystroke is an example of a behavioral biometric. Jain, Ross, and Prabhakar [33] identified seven factors for assessing the suitability of any trait for use in biometric authentication. These are universality, uniqueness, permanence, measurability, performance, acceptability, and circumvention. Table 6.3 shows comparative performance in terms of EER of some popular biometric modalities.

Since biometrics are unique to the person, they are more reliable in identifying individuals than passwords. However, some biometrics change over time. Finger surfaces may wear or get damaged and irises may age and change [60]. Furthermore, performance in terms of false results can be an issue. In case of the latter, multimodal biometrics, where more than one method is used, could offer a more robust and better performing identification method [33]. There are privacy and accuracy concerns about collecting biometrics but, in spite of this, they are gradually gaining acceptance and increasingly being taken up by applications. Table 6.4 presents a comparison of some biometric modalities in terms of the seven comparison criteria introduced by [33] and based on the authors' viewpoint following research review.

Following analysis of the various biometrics, the authors consider that palm vein technology offers great potential for use in biometric authentication in e-business. The liveness factor, namely the palm vein technology is based on thermal scanning and as such only works with a live palm, is very important as this avoids circumvention. It also seems to have higher acceptability than iris scanning, another technology with

Table 6.3   Performance evaluation of different biometric techniques

Biometrics	EER	Subjects	Comments	Research source
Voice	≈10%	234	Recorded speech, gender characteristic aware algorithm. Better results obtained when gender specific features were used. ALBAYZIN and MOBIO speech corpora.	[34]
Keystroke	≈8%	300	Keystroke Biometrics Ongoing Competition (KBOC). Average of 15 best systems.	[35]
Face	≈5%	Over 2M	Average from a number of research works. Images and videos. Deep learning methods. Average score for images ≈2%. Average score for videos ≈8% Best result for images ≈1% (1.05) Best result for videos ≈3% [36].	[36–42]
Fingerprint	≈3%	Various	FVC2002 database. Average from a number of research works. Best result 0.44% [43].	[43–46]
Hand geometry	≈1.5%	≈1,250 images	Based on two recent works. Best result achieved with genetic algorithm ≈0.9% [47].	[47, 48]
Iris	≈1.5%	Various	Reported EER from experiments on CASIA v3 Interval data set. Higher EER reported on CASIA v3 Lamp data set. Much lower EER reported on earlier data sets e.g., ≈0.001% EER on NIST Iris image base [49].	[49–54]
Palm vein	≈0.5%	Various	Average from a number of research works.	[55–59]

high performance. At Coventry University, UK, there is an ongoing research project that is investigating the development of a BioPKI system, which uses palm vein technology [61].

6.4.2   Parallelism to increase power and speed of defenses

Many studies on improving security have led to research into how parallel and multicore technologies could benefit the efficiency and effectiveness of such systems.

Vasiliadis *et al.* [62] proposed a new model for a multiparallel IDS architecture for high-performance processing and stateful analysis of network traffic. Their solution offers parallelism at a subcomponent level, with processors within a host machine carrying out specialized tasks to improve scalability and running time. They showed that

Table 6.4 Comparison of different biometric technologies based on the authors' viewpoint

Biometric	Universality	Uniqueness	Collectability	Permanence	Performance	Acceptability	Circumvention
Fingerprint	H	H	M	M	M	H	M
Face	H	M	H	M	L	H	H
Iris	H	H	H	H	H	M	L
Hand geometry	H	M	H	L	H	H	M
Keystroke	L	L	M	L	L	L	M
Voice	M	H	M	L	L	H	H
Palm vein	H	H	M	H	H	H	L

H = High, M = Medium, L = Low.

processing speeds can reach up to 5.2 Gbps with zero packet loss in a multiprocessor system. Jiang *et al.* [63] proposed a parallel design for a NIDS on a TILERAGX36 many-core processor. They explored data and pipeline parallelism and optimized the architecture by exploiting existing features of the processor to break the bottlenecks in the parallel design. The system was designed according to two strategies: first a hybrid parallel architecture was used, combining data and pipeline parallelism; and second a hybrid load-balancing scheme was used. They took advantage of the parallelism offered by combining data, pipeline parallelism, and multiple cores, using both rule-set and flow space partitioning. They showed that processing speeds can handle and reach up to 7.2 Gbps with 100-byte packets and 13.5 Gbps for 512-byte. Jamshed *et al.* [64] presented the Kargus system that exploits high-processing parallelism by balancing the pattern matching workloads with multicore CPUs and heterogeneous GPUs. Kargus adapts its resource usage depending on the input rate, to save power. The research shows that Kargus handles up to 33 Gbps of normal traffic and achieves 9–10 Gbps even when all packets contain attack signatures.

Bul'ajoul *et al.* [65,66] proposed an NIDPS solution for high-speed malicious traffic using quality of service (QoS) configuration and parallel technology. They designed a novel security architecture to increase the analytical, detection, and prevention performance of the NIDPS when facing high-speed traffic. Their study investigated the impact of parallelism in high-speed environments and how to achieve improvement through parallelization using industry-standard software systems and standard desktop processors. The study showed that security performance can be weak in the face of high-speed and high-load malicious traffic in terms of packet drops, outstanding packets, and failing to detect/prevent unwanted traffic. Their solution used a novel QoS configuration in a multilayer switch to organize and improve network traffic performance in order to reduce the number of packets dropped. The NIDPS used was Snort. Parallel techniques were used to increase processing speed performance. Results are shown in Figures 6.2 (processing time) and 6.3 (processing speed).

The solution is based on configuring the network switch to shape traffic into queues, each queue having its own NIDPS, the complete set operating in parallel (see Figure 6.4). A differentiated services technology was used to modify, organize, and control traffic based on the differentiated services code point (DSCP) value, which can offer more precise handling of traffic and classify each packet upon entry into the network interface, allowing for adjustments to be made for different traffic speed and loads. Incoming traffic was classified through a class map that enabled packets to be processed as a group of bytes defined by policy and ACLs that were matched with DSCP values to allow each traffic group to be processed by separate queue.

The novel architecture was tested under different traffic speeds, types, and tasks. The experimental results show that the novel architecture along with the introduction of parallel technologies can increase the efficiency and effectiveness of security platforms and so improve overall security. By using 2× quad core machines connected to 2× 1 GB interfaces, the new architecture processed up to 8 Gbps traffic speed with 1 kB packets. This solution is a more accessible way of receiving good results as it can be activated at a higher level, namely at the level of configuring the multicore

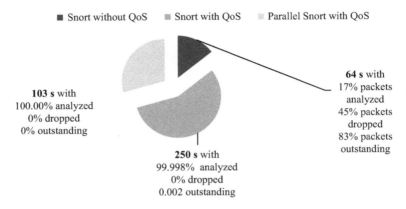

Processing time (for 40,000 kB at 1 kB/1 ms)

■ Snort without QoS   ■ Snort with QoS   ▨ Parallel Snort with QoS

103 s with
100.00% analyzed
0% dropped
0% outstanding

250 s with
99.998% analyzed
0% dropped
0.002 outstanding

64 s with
17% packets
analyzed
45% packets
dropped
83% packets
outstanding

*Figure 6.2   Parallel Snort NIDPS processing time for 40,000 1 kB packets sent at
1 ms intervals*

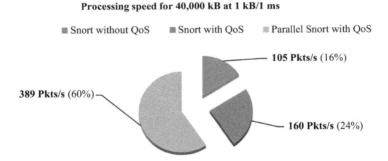

Processing speed for 40,000 kB at 1 kB/1 ms

▨ Snort without QoS   ■ Snort with QoS   ▨ Parallel Snort with QoS

389 Pkts/s (60%)

105 Pkts/s (16%)

160 Pkts/s (24%)

*Figure 6.3   Parallel Snort NIDPS processing speed for 40,000 1 kB packets sent at
1 ms intervals*

switch and replicating NIDPS on multicore machines. Further improvements could
be made if higher performance equipment were used. The solution can be extended
to the idea of an elastic NIDPS, which can grow as the traffic grows. This is achieved
by varying number of queues and NIDPS machines according to traffic. As traffic
gets higher more NIDPS are engaged. The emergence of cloud computing provides
the infrastructure for this type of solution. While traffic becomes heavier the number
of NIDPS increases, while in the background, services search for anomalies to find
the source of a possible malicious DDoS attack. Once sources are discovered, they
can be blocked, traffic will decrease to normal levels, and the number of operational
NIDPS can be decreased.

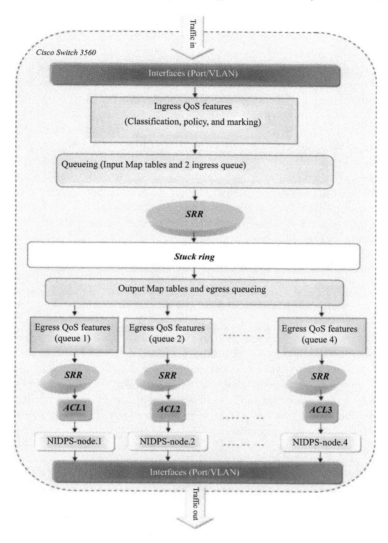

Figure 6.4   Novel architecture for NIDPS

6.4.3   Data mining and machine learning to identify attacks

Data mining and machine learning offer good potential for increasing the power of intrusion detection and attack signature learning [67]. Stealth attacks, normally difficult to counteract, may be detected through the use of data mining techniques. Tran *et al*. [68] argue that due to the complex and dynamic nature of computer networks and hacking techniques, detecting malicious activities remains a challenging task for security experts. They proposed a novel machine learning algorithm that integrates an adaptive boosting technique and a semiparametric neural network to obtain good tradeoff between accuracy and generality. Feng *et al.* [69] proposed combining state vector machine and ant colony networks to mine network data for intrusion detection.

Finding anomalies in access or data logs through data mining can indicate an attack. However, since launching stealthy attacks is a sophisticated technique that may take place over months, it is theoretically necessary to keep a long history of activities in order to identify these attacks. Kalutarage *et al.* [12,70] have proposed a technique based on anomaly detection and sampling in order to overcome this issue. Using peer and discord analysis, a monitoring algorithm based on Bayes probability is used to monitor network nodes at regular intervals and generate profiles with probabilities of whether a node is an attacker or not. A node showing an out-of-line profile can be further investigated. The approach maintains long-term estimates computed on sampled data rather than retaining event data for post-facto analysis, thus it significantly reduces the amount of data to handle and maintain, thereby increasing the chances of detecting the stealth attack.

6.4.4   Peer-to-peer security using blockchains

A new method that is gaining interest as a security defense is peer-to-peer security through blockchains [71].

> With blockchain, we can imagine a world in which contracts are embedded in digital code and stored in transparent, shared databases, where they are protected from deletion, tampering, and revision. In this world every agreement, every process, every task, and every payment would have a digital record and signature that could be identified, validated, stored, and shared. Intermediaries like lawyers, brokers, and bankers might no longer be necessary. Individuals, organizations, machines, and algorithms would freely transact and interact with one another with little friction. This is the immense potential of blockchain.
>
> Lansiti and Lakhani [72]

The blockchain approach has been used in transaction processing for bitcoin, a decentralized crypto-currency, to provide financial data security on a distributed peer-to-peer platform [73]. No third parties are needed. This avoids issues of vulnerability of having all data in one place and also allows transactions to be cleared quickly. Public key cryptography is used for security together with a distributed secure ledger. Each coin is associated with its current owner's public key. When bitcoins are sent by an owner, a transaction is created, attaching the new owner's public key to the sent coins. The transaction is signed with the previous owner's (the sender's) private key. When this transaction is broadcast to the bitcoin network, the new owner of these coins is publicized. The signature on the message verifies that the message is authentic. The complete history of transactions is kept by everyone, so anyone can verify current ownership of coins. The approach works by having a public ledger in the form of a blockchain replicated and viewable by all. Each block contains a timestamp and a link to a previous blockchain. Every 10 min new transactions have to be secured as a block and added to the public blockchain. They are then considered cleared. Peers called data miners compete to create a message hash of the new transaction block such that it cannot subsequently be altered. SHA256 is used as the underlying cryptographic hash function. To make the problem harder there are constraints on the form of the hash code. Thus the problem becomes finding a suitable key that will generate a compliant hash code. The data miner who completes first is rewarded with bitcoins. A majority of miners have to agree that the hash is correct before it is accepted. Once accepted, the new block is added to the chain and cannot ever be altered. This stops fraudulent activity. The approach is considered very secure. However, there have been breaches [74]. Ethereum [75], a platform for smart contracts, is taking a similar approach and the traditional banking sector is now interested in the technology [76,77]. An issue however is that the blockchain as implemented with bitcoin is based on anonymity of users. This would not be acceptable for the traditional banking sector. Therefore, a modified version of the approach where the identities of users are knowable would be necessary. There have been questions about scalability too [78,79].

6.4.5   Enterprise security modeling and security as a service

Given the wide range of attacks and the various mechanisms available to counteract them, we see how important it is for enterprises to devote attention to their security profile. An organizational security model that maps business processes, application systems, systems software, servers, and network topology against possible attacks and their defenses provides a good foundation for security management. This is particularly pertinent now that enterprises are moving their infrastructure to the cloud that increases, while at the same time obscuring, the network complexity. Establishing the correct security services involves detailed analysis of need, and sound knowledge of all relevant system components and processes. Making these entities explicit creates a better overall understanding.

Aulkemeier *et al.* [80] have produced a service-oriented e-commerce reference architecture based on the three layers of technology, application, and business. Relevant system components are specified at each level. Their architecture does not contain a security model but it is well placed to form the basis on which a security model could be built. Luhach *et al.* [81] proposed a logical security framework for the small- and medium-sized e-commerce systems. The proposed logical security framework is based on a service-oriented architecture model of e-commerce transactions. The framework includes authentication certificates, code filters, web services SOAP access, HTTPS, IDS, IPS, access control rules, database protection and encryption, as well as having business data on a separate server to the e-commerce site. The use of a service-oriented and architecture-centric approach for security engineering can lead to the development of more secure service-oriented applications. The approach develops clearer understanding and exploits security solution reuse where applicable. Dikanski and Abeck [82] developed a service-oriented security architecture view model, with a security engineering view for development artifacts, a security service view for security services, and a security integration view for the integration and centralization of an organization's security infrastructure.

From viewpoint of service engineering, the composition of services into applications in the Internet of Services raises further questions on security and trust. Can discovered services be trusted and are they secure? Security preservation within a composition of services is important. Dwivedi and Rath [83] considered six security patterns (identification and access management, check point, data confidentiality, policy, proxy-based firewall, and secure service proxy) and proposed to incorporate security features in a service-oriented architecture with the help of software security patterns. This scheme is described by developing an architectural model integrated with security goals and security patterns. The structural and behavioral aspects of web services composition incorporated with security features were presented using a Unified Modeling Language class diagram and sequence diagram, respectively. Formal validation technologies can have a decisive impact for the trust and security of services composition. Armando *et al*. [84] developed a validation platform, which is an integrated toolset for the formal specification and automated validation of trust and security of service-oriented architectures. The goal was to ensure global security of dynamically composed services and their integration into complex architectures by developing an integrated platform of automated reasoning techniques and tools.

The development of architectural models for enterprise security, particularly those based on service-oriented architecture, increases understanding and can yield a solid framework to support future requirements such as handling increasing number of attacks, knowledge transfer, technology upgrade, system migration, or moves to outsourcing.

Analyzing security requirements systematically leads to the prospect of adopting security as a service (SECaaS) [85,86]. SECaaS is a business model in which a large service provider integrates their security services into a corporate infrastructure, thereby providing security as a service for the corporation on the basis that this is a more cost-effective solution. In this scenario, security is provided as a cloud service. Typical security service provision includes authentication, antivirus, antimalware/spyware, intrusion detection, and security event management. In 2011 the Cloud Security Alliance [87] identified the following areas as feasible SECaaS offerings: identity and access management; data loss prevention; web security; email security; security assessments; intrusion management; security information and event management; encryption; business continuity and disaster recovery; and network security.

The cloud SECaaS market is growing rapidly [88]. Advantages of outsourcing security to the cloud include cost, consistency, uniformity, more reliable virus definition updates, greater security expertise, and fewer security administrative tasks. An issue is that each security request would require an exchange with the security provider exposing the request to a possible network attack but secure communication should mitigate this. Furthermore, with current trends such as mobile and location independent working, the on-premises in-house maintenance of uniform security becomes very difficult. SECaaS may offer an attractive means to manage enterprise security. Additionally cloud services can be developed to share information about attacks and defenses and well as to provide extra resource to fighting attacks when needed (see Section 6.4.2).

6.4.6 User education and engagement

The role of training and education in the fight against security breaches has long been recognized. In 2003, The National Institute of Standards and Technology (NIST) proposed a learning continuum model for information security, starting from awareness, through training to education [89]. Their model focused on enhancing security knowledge for end-users. As cyberattacks increase, the role of education and training is becoming increasingly important. The British Retail Consortium [90] produces guidance for retailers on how to protect their online systems. Some non-profit organizations such as the APWG and the US Computer Emergency Readiness Team offer educational interventions to enhance public understanding of the threats posed by attackers and how to protect systems from attacks. Significant efforts have been made to provide user education to enable public understanding of security. Such efforts must be sustained.

Previous research has shown that well designed end-user security education can be effective in mitigating against IT infrastructure issues [91–93]. This could be in the form of web-based training materials, contextual training, and embedded training to enhance users' ability to avoid attacks. It is argued by Kirlappos and Sasse [94] that the aim of security education should be on the drivers of end-user behavior rather than on warning users of dangers. This means that a well-designed security education should develop threat perception so that users become genuinely aware of the danger. Amankwa *et al.* [95] discussed the development of end-user education, training, and awareness programs by categorizing known models for enhancing security education, training, and awareness based on the stakeholder domains, which included end-users, institutions, and industry. They acknowledged the fact that approaches for enhancing end-users' security knowledge exist but that there has been insufficient research on models for enhancing security knowledge of end-users based on need.

Aware that attacks cannot be prevented by technology alone, researchers have devoted attention to the development of innovative educational media based on the principle that user engagement and education provide a powerful means of preventing electronic attacks, both at the employee and at the customer levels [96,97]. Arachchilage *et al.* [98] investigated how one can develop a mobile game that, through increasing motivation, enhances users' avoidance behavior in order to protect themselves against phishing attacks. The study was based on the notion that computer games offer a natural learning environment that motivates the user to continue whilst also providing education to users. The results from their study showed a significant improvement of participants' phishing avoidance behavior and suggested that participants' threat perception, safeguard effectiveness, self-efficacy, perceived severity, and perceived susceptibility positively impact threat avoidance behavior, whereas safeguard cost had a negative impact on it.

It is important that employees and users are educated, encouraging them to be vigilant at all times. They should be taught what qualifies as sensitive data and how to identify threats and avoid them. Acceptable use and security policies must be promoted and enforced at organizational level. It is also crucial that end-users understand their roles and responsibilities in maintaining the organization's compliance with relevant regulations operating in its domain. In short, educating the workforce is critical and is a key requirement of information security standards such as ISO27001. There are a number of ways that security awareness training can be delivered to end-users. The most popular tends to be the e-learning variety, where online courses covering the essentials of security awareness are mandated for all employees. In this way, users are taught they are potential targets and they learn how to look out for social engineering and phishing, how to increase password security, how to handle sensitive data, as well as about any specific compliance-driven requirements.

6.5   Conclusion

This chapter has provided a review of current threats and solutions facing e-business and in particular e-commerce. Phishing remains a dominant attack and in particular spear fishing where individual employees or organizations are targeted. It is extremely important that employees and organizations are trained in how to recognize and counter such attacks. User engagement and education is therefore a vital component of the e-business security defense response. Increased collaboration and sharing of attack information is also important. Cloud computing can offer a useful means of facilitating this. Scalable use of resources to counter DDoS attacks offers a useful direction of travel, together with the development of machine learning algorithms for better and quicker recognition of new attacks and anomalies in usage patterns.

References

[1]   Anti-Phishing Working Group. Phishing Activity Trends Report. 4th Quarter 2016. [Online available at: http://docs.apwg.org/reports/apwg_trends_report_q4_2016.pdf, accessed 13-3-2017].

[2]   Symantec. 2016 Internet Threat Report. 2016. [Online available at: https://www.symantec.com/security-center/threat-report, accessed 13-3-17].

[3]   Anti-Phishing Working Group. Phishing Activity Trends Report. 2nd Quarter 2014. [Online available at: http://docs.apwg.org/reports/apwg_trends_report_q2_2014.pdf, accessed 26-2-2016].

[4]   Moghimi M, and Varjani AY. New rule-based phishing detection method. Expert Systems with Applications. 2016 Jul 1;53:231–42.

[5]   Li L, Berki E, Helenius M, and Ovaska S. Towards a contingency approach with whitelist-and blacklist-based anti-phishing applications: what do usability tests indicate? Behaviour and Information Technology. 2014 Nov 2;33(11): 1136–47.

[6]   Gupta S, Singhal A, and Kapoor A. A literature survey on social engineering attacks: Phishing attack. In: 2016 International Conference on Computing,

Communication and Automation (ICCCA). 2016 Apr 29 (pp. 537–540). IEEE.

[7]   Udo GJ. Privacy and security concerns as major barriers for e-commerce: a survey study. Information Management and Computer Security. 2001 Oct 1;9(4):165–74.

[8]   Hartono E, Holsapple CW, Kim KY, Na KS, and Simpson JT. Measuring perceived security in B2C electronic commerce website usage: a respecification and validation. Decision Support Systems. 2014 Jun 30;62:11–21.

[9]   Jotwani V, and Dutta A. An analysis of e-commerce security threats and its related effective measures. International Journal. 2016 Jun;4(6):116–121.

[10] Ficco M, and Rak M. Intrusion tolerance of stealth DoS attacks to web services. In: IFIP International Information Security Conference. 2012 Jun 4 (pp. 579–584). Springer, Berlin, Heidelberg.

[11] Kapoor A, and Mathur R. Predicting the future of stealth attacks. In: Virus Bulletin Conference. 2011 Oct (pp. 1–9).

[12] Kalutarage HK, Shaikh SA, Wickramasinghe IP, Zhou Q., and James AE. Detecting stealthy attacks: efficient monitoring of suspicious activities on computer networks. Computers and Electrical Engineering. 2015 Oct 31;47: 327–44.

[13] Kiountouzis E. Approaches to the security of information systems. Information Systems Security, New Technologies Publications, Athens, Greece. 2004.

[14] Bonneau J, Herley C, Van Oorschot PC, and Stajano F. The quest to replace passwords: A framework for comparative evaluation of web authentication schemes. In: 2012 IEEE Symposium on Security and Privacy (SP). 2012 May 20 (pp. 553–567). IEEE.

[15] Darwish A, El-Gendy MM, and Hassanien AE. A new hybrid cryptosystem for Internet of Things applications. In: Multimedia Forensics and Security. 2017 (pp. 365–380). Springer, Cham.

[16] Anwar S, Zain JM, Zolkipli MF, Inayat Z, Jabir AN, and Odili JB. Response option for attacks detected by intrusion detection system. In: 2015 4th International Conference on Software Engineering and Computer Systems (ICSECS). 2015 Aug 19 (pp. 195–200). IEEE.

[17] Dworkin MJ. SHA-3 standard: permutation-based hash and extendable-output functions. Federal Inf. Process. Stds. (NIST FIPS)-202. 2015 Aug 4.

[18] Adams C, Farrell S, Kause T, and Mononen T. Internet X. 509 public key infrastructure certificate management protocol (CMP). 2005.

[19] Jain AK, Ross AA, and Nandakumar K. Introduction. In: Introduction to Biometrics. 2011 (pp. 1–49). Springer, USA.

[20] Duarte T, Pimentão JP, Sousa P, and Onofre S. Biometric access control systems: A review on technologies to improve their efficiency. In: 2016 IEEE International Power Electronics and Motion Control Conference (PEMC). 2016 Sep 25 (pp. 795–800). IEEE.

[21] Sabharwal M. The assessment of concerns, opinions and perceptions of bank customers to find the significant metrics for deployment of biometrics in

e-banking. International Journal of Computer Applications. 2016 April; 140(5):28–41.

[22]   Carpenter D, McLeod A, Hicks C, and Maasberg M. Privacy and biometrics: an empirical examination of employee concerns. Information Systems Frontiers. 2016:1–20.

[23]   Li QY, and Zhang L. The public security and personal privacy survey: biometric technology in Hong Kong. IEEE Security and Privacy. 2016 Jul;14(4): 12–21.

[24]   National Population Commission, Nigeria. Nigeria over 167 million population: implication and challenges. 2016. [Online available at: http://www.population.gov.ng/index.php/84- news/latest/106-nigeria-over-167-million-population-implications-and-challenges, accessed 26-7-16].

[25]   Biometric Update. Nigeria. 2017. [Online available at: http://www. biometricupdate.com/tag/nigeria, accessed, 8/8/2017].

[26]   James A, and Shehu Y. Security and Integrity of Fingerprint Templates. Project. Researchgate. 2017. [Online available at: https://www.researchgate.net/ project/Security-and-Integrity-of-Fingerprint-Templates, accessed 8-8-17].

[27]   Le C, and Jain R. A survey of biometrics security systems. EEUU. Washington University in St. Louis. 2009.

[28]   Jain AK, Hong L, Pankanti S, and Bolle R. An identity-authentication system using fingerprints. Proceedings of the IEEE. 1997 Sep;85(9):1365–88.

[29]   Savvides M, Kumar BV, and Khosla PK. Cancelable biometric filters for face recognition. In: Proceedings of the 17th International Conference on Pattern Recognition, 2004. ICPR 2004. 2004 Aug 23 (Vol. 3, pp. 922–5). IEEE.

[30]   Mathivanan B, Palanisamy V, and Selvarajan S. Multi dimensional hand geometry based biometric verification and recognition system. International Journal of Emerging Technology and Advanced Engineering. 2012;2(7): 348–54.

[31]   Daugman J. How iris recognition works. IEEE Transactions on Circuits and Systems for Video Technology. 2004 Jan;14(1):21–30.

[32]   Dere SN, Gurjar AA, and Sipna CO. Human identification using palm-vein images: a new trend in biometrics. International Journal of Engineering Science. 2016 Mar;2298.

[33]   Jain AK, Ross A, and Prabhakar S. An introduction to biometric recognition. IEEE Transactions on Circuits and Systems for Video Technology. 2004 Jan;14(1): 4–20.

[34]   Mazaira-Fernandez LM, Álvarez-Marquina A, and Gómez-Vilda P. Improving speaker recognition by biometric voice deconstruction. Frontiers in Bioengineering and Biotechnology. 2015;3.

[35]   Monaco J. Robust keystroke biometric anomaly detection. U.S. Army Research Laboratory Aberdeen Proving Ground, MD 21005, USA. 2016. [Online available at: https://arxiv.org/abs/1606.09075, accessed 8-8-17].

[36]   Parkhi OM, Vedaldi A, and Zisserman A. Deep face recognition. In: BMVC 2015 Sep (Vol. 1, No. 3, p. 6).

[37] Simonyan K, Vedaldi A, and Zisserman A. Learning local feature descriptors using convex optimisation. IEEE Transactions on Pattern Analysis and Machine Intelligence. 2014 Aug;36(8):1573–85.

[38] Parkhi OM, Simonyan K, Vedaldi A, and Zisserman A. A compact and discriminative face track descriptor. In: Proceedings of the IEEE Conference on Computer Vision and Pattern Recognition. 2014 (pp. 1693–1700).

[39] Taigman Y, Yang M, Ranzato MA, and Wolf L. Deepface: closing the gap to human-level performance in face verification. In: Proceedings of the IEEE Conference on Computer Vision and Pattern Recognition. 2014 (pp. 1701–8).

[40] Taigman Y, Yang M, Ranzato MA, and Wolf L. Web-scale training for face identification. In: Proceedings of the IEEE Conference on Computer Vision and Pattern Recognition. 2015 (pp. 2746–54).

[41] Schroff F, Kalenichenko D, and Philbin J. Facenet: a unified embedding for face recognition and clustering. In: Proceedings of the IEEE Conference on Computer Vision and Pattern Recognition. 2015 (pp. 815–23).

[42] Sun Y, Liang D, Wang X, and Tang X. Deepid3: face recognition with very deep neural networks. arXiv preprint arXiv:1502.00873. 2015 Feb 3.

[43] Flores M, Torres G, Garcia G, and Licona M. Fingerprint verification methods using Delaunay triangulations. International Arab Journal of e-Technology. 2017 May 1;14(3):346–54.

[44] Yang W, Hu J, and Wang S. A Delaunay triangle-based fuzzy extractor for fingerprint authentication. In: 2012 IEEE 11th International Conference on Trust, Security and Privacy in Computing and Communications (TrustCom). 2012 Jun 25 (pp. 66–70). IEEE.

[45] Ross A, Jain A, and Reisman J. A hybrid fingerprint matcher. Pattern Recognition. 2003 Jul 31;36(7):1661–73.

[46] Deng H, and Huo Q. Minutiae matching based fingerprint verification using Delaunay triangulation and aligned-edge-guided triangle matching. In: Audio-and Video-Based Biometric Person Authentication. 2005 (pp. 357–72). Springer Berlin/Heidelberg.

[47] Silva AG, Barbosa IA, Nascimento MV, Rego TG, and Batista LV. Analysis of the performance improvement obtained by a genetic algorithm-based approach on a hand geometry dataset. In: Proceedings of the International Conference on Artificial Intelligence (ICAI). 2015 Jan 1 (pp. 125–30).

[48] Park G, and Kim S. Hand biometric recognition based on fused hand geometry and vascular patterns. Sensors. 2013 Feb 28;13(3):2895–910.

[49] Daugman J. Evolving methods in iris recognition and implications from 200 billion iris comparisons: presentation. The First International Conference on Biometrics: Theory, Applications and Systems (BTAS 07). 2017. [Online available at: http://www.cse.nd.edu/BTAS_07/John_Daugman_BTAS.pdf, accessed 8-8-2017].

[50] Daugman JG. High confidence visual recognition of persons by a test of statistical independence. IEEE Transactions on Pattern Analysis and Machine Intelligence. 1993 Nov;15(11):1148–61.

[51]   Roy K, Bhattacharya P, and Suen CY. Iris recognition using shape-guided approach and game theory. Pattern Analysis and Applications. 2011 Nov 1;14(4):329–48.

[52]   Bouraoui I, Chitroub S, and Bouridane A. Does independent component analysis perform well for iris recognition? Intelligent Data Analysis. 2012 Jan 1;16(3):409–26.

[53]   Tsai CC, Lin HY, Taur J, and Tao CW. Iris recognition using possibilistic fuzzy matching on local features. IEEE Transactions on Systems, Man, and Cybernetics, Part B (Cybernetics). 2012 Feb;42(1):150–62.

[54]   Chen Y, Liu Y, Zhu X, He F, Wang H, and Deng N. Efficient iris recognition based on optimal subfeature selection and weighted subregion fusion. The Scientific World Journal. 2014;2014, Article id 157173.

[55]   Zhang D, Guo Z, Lu G, Zhang L, Liu Y, and Zuo W. Online joint palm-print and palmvein verification. Expert Systems with Applications. 2011 Mar 31;38(3):2621–31.

[56]   Lee JC. A novel biometric system based on palm vein image. Pattern Recognition Letters. 2012 Sep 1;33(12):1520–8.

[57]   Sun J, and Abdulla W. Palm vein recognition using curvelet transform. In: Proceedings of the 27th Conference on Image and Vision Computing New Zealand. 2012 Nov 26 (pp. 435–439). ACM.

[58]   Al-Juboori AM, Bu W, Wu X, and Zhao Q. Palm vein verification using Gabor filter. International Journal of Computer Science Issues. 2013 Jan;10(1): 678–84.

[59]   Al-Juboori AM, Bu W, Wu X, and Zhao Q. Palm vein verification using multiple features and locality preserving projections. The Scientific World Journal. 2014 Feb 17;2014.

[60]   Mehrotra H, Vatsa M, Singh R, and Majhi B. Does iris change over time? PloS One. 2013 Nov 7;8(11):e78333.

[61]   James A, Obande G, and Bentahar K, Development-of-a-secure-BioPKI-using-Palm-Vein-Technology. Project. Researchgate. 2017. [Online available at: https://www.researchgate.net/project/Development-of-a-secure-BioPKI-using-Palm-Vein-Technology, accessed 9-8-17].

[62]   Vasiliadis G, Polychronakis M, and Ioannidis S. MIDeA: a multi-parallel intrusion detection architecture. In: Proceedings of the 18th ACM conference on computer and Communications Security. 2011 Oct 17 (pp. 297–308). ACM.

[63]   Jiang H, Zhang G, Xie G, Salamatian K, and Mathy L. Scalable high-performance parallel design for network intrusion detection systems on many-core processors. In: Proceedings of the Ninth ACM/IEEE Symposium on Architectures for Networking and Communications Systems. 2013 Oct 21 (pp. 137–46). IEEE Press.

[64]   Jamshed MA, Lee J, Moon S, *et al.* Kargus: a highly-scalable software-based intrusion detection system. In: Proceedings of the 2012 ACM Conference on Computer and Communications Security. 2012 Oct 16 (pp. 317–28). ACM.

[65]   Bul'ajoul W, James A, and Pannu M. Improving network intrusion detection system performance through quality of service configuration and parallel technology. Journal of Computer and System Sciences. 2015 Sep 30;81(6):981–99.

[66]   Bul'ajoul W, James A, Shaikh S, and Pannu M. Using CISCO network components to improve NIDPS performance. Third International Conference on Computer Science and Engineering. Computer Science and Information Technology (CS and IT) 2017:6(10):137–57. 2016. [Online available at: http://airccj.org/CSCP/vol6/csit65712.pdf, accessed 8-8-2017].

[67]   Buczak AL, and Guven E. A survey of data mining and machine learning methods for cyber security intrusion detection. IEEE Communications Surveys and Tutorials. 2016 Jan 1;18(2):1153–76.

[68]   Tran TP, Nguyen TT, Tsai P, and Kong X. BSPNN: boosted subspace probabilistic neural network for email security. Artificial Intelligence Review. 2011 Apr 1;35(4):369–82.

[69]   Feng W, Zhang Q, Hu G, and Huang JX. Mining network data for intrusion detection through combining SVMs with ant colony networks. Future Generation Computer Systems. 2014 Jul 31;37:127–40.

[70]   Kalutarage HK, Shaikh SA, Zhou Q, and James AE. Sensing for suspicion at scale: a Bayesian approach for cyber conflict attribution and reasoning. In: 2012 4th International Conference on Cyber conflict (CYCON), 2012 Jun 5 (pp. 1–19). IEEE.

[71]   Pilkington M. Blockchain technology: principles and applications. In: Olleros FX and Zhegu, M, editors. Research Handbook on Digital Transformations. Edward Elgar, 2016. [Online available at: https://papers.ssrn.com/sol3/Papers.cfm?abstract_id=2662660, accessed 8-8-17].

[72]   Lansiti M, and Lakhani KR. The truth about blockchain. Harvard Business Review. 2017 Jan 1;95(1):119–27.

[73]   Nakamoto, S. Bitcoin: a peer-to-peer electronic cash system. 2008. [Online available at: https://bitcoin.org/bitcoin.pdf, accessed 8-8-17].

[74]   Morabito V. The security of blockchain systems. In: Business Innovation Through Blockchain. 2017 (pp. 61–78). Springer, Cham.

[75]   Wood G. Ethereum: A secure decentralised generalised transaction ledger. Ethereum Project Yellow Paper. 2014 Apr;151.

[76]   Financial Times. Blockchain can create financial sector jobs as well as kill them. 2016. [Online available at: https://www.ft.com/content/3a9ef8d8-33d5-11e6-bda0-04585c31b153, accessed 8-8-17].

[77]   PwC. Blockchain technology: is the banking sector ready for FinTech? 2016. [Online available at: http://pwc.blogs.com/fintech/2016/11/blockchain-technology-is-the-banking-sector-ready-for-fintech.html, accessed 13-3-17].

[78]   Croman K, Decker C, Eyal I, *et al*. On scaling decentralized blockchains. In: International Conference on Financial Cryptography and Data Security 2016. Feb 26 (pp. 106–25). Springer, Berlin, Heidelberg.

[79]   Vukolić M. The quest for scalable blockchain fabric: proof-of-work vs. BFT replication. In: International Workshop on Open Problems in Network Security. 2015 Oct 29 (pp. 112–25). Springer, Cham.

[80]   Aulkemeier F, Schramm M, Iacob ME, and Van Hillegersberg J. A service-oriented e-commerce reference architecture. Journal of Theoretical and Applied Electronic Commerce Research. 2016 Jan;11(1):26–45.

[81]   Luhach AK, Dwivedi SK, and Jha CK. Implementing the logical security framework for e-commerce based on service-oriented architecture. In: Proceedings of International Conference on ICT for Sustainable Development. 2016 (pp. 1–13). Springer, Singapore.

[82]   Dikanski A, and Abeck S. A view-based approach for service-oriented security architecture specification. In: The Sixth International Conference on Internet and Web Applications and Services (ICIW2011), St. Maarten, The Netherland Antilles. 2011 Mar 20 (pp. 2017–2013). IIARIA.

[83]   Dwivedi AK and Rath SK. Incorporating security features in service-oriented architecture using security patterns. ACM SIGSOFT Software Engineering Notes. 2015 Feb 6;40(1):1–6.

[84]   Armando A, Arsac W, Avanesov T, *et al.* The AVANTSSAR platform for the automated validation of trust and security of service-oriented architectures. Tools and Algorithms for the Construction and Analysis of Systems. 2012: 267–82.

[85]   Sharma DH, Dhote CA, and Potey MM. Security-as-a-service from clouds: a comprehensive analysis. International Journal of Computer Applications. 2013 Jan 1;67(3).

[86]   Furfaro A, Garro A, and Tundis A. Towards security as a service (SECaaS): On the modeling of security services for cloud computing. In: 2014 International Carnahan Conference on Security Technology (ICCST). 2014 Oct 13 (pp. 1–6). IEEE.

[87]   Cloud Security Alliance. Security guidance for critical areas of focus in cloud computing v 3.0. Cloud Security Alliance. 2011:15.

[88]   Cloud Pro. The rise of cloud-based security is an indication of how trustworthy cloud computing has now become. 2014. [Online available at: http://www.cloudpro.co.uk/cloud-essentials/cloud-security/3671/security-as-a-service-really-has-become-a-no-brainer, accessed 12-3-17].

[89]   Wilson M, and Hash J. Building an information technology security awareness and training program. NIST Special publication. 2003 Oct;800(50): 1–39.

[90]   British Retail Consortium. Cyber security toolkit: a guide for retailers. 2017. [Online available at: http://brc.org.uk/media/120731/brc-cyber-security-toolkit_final.pdf, accessed 14-3-2017].

[91]   Jafari S. Enhancing security culture through user-engagement: an organisational perspective. International Journal of ICT Research in Africa and the Middle East (IJICTRAME). 2017 Jan 1;6(1):31–39.

[92]   Kennedy SE. The pathway to security – mitigating user negligence. Information and Computer Security. 2016 Jul 11;24(3):255–64.

[93]   Le Compte A, Elizondo D, and Watson T. A renewed approach to serious games for cyber security. In: 7th International Conference on Cyber Conflict: Architectures in Cyberspace (CyCon). 2015 May 26 (pp. 203–16). IEEE.

[94] Kirlappos I, and Sasse MA. Security education against phishing: a modest proposal for a major rethink. IEEE Security and Privacy. 2012 Mar;10(2): 24–32.

[95] Amankwa E, Loock M, and Kritzinger E. A conceptual analysis of information security education, information security training and information security awareness definitions. In: 9th International Conference for Internet Technology and Secured Transactions (ICITST). 2014 Dec 8 (pp. 248–52). IEEE.

[96] Arachchilage NA, Love S, and Beznosov K. Phishing threat avoidance behaviour: an empirical investigation. Computers in Human Behavior. 2016 Jul 31;60:185–97.

[97] Sanchez F, and Duan Z. A sender-centric approach to detecting phishing emails. In: International Conference on Cyber Security (CyberSecurity). 2012 Dec 14 (pp. 32–9). IEEE.

[98] Arachchilage NA, Tarhini A, and Love S. Designing a mobile game to thwarts malicious IT threats: a phishing threat avoidance perspective. arXiv preprint arXiv:1511.07093. 2015 Nov 23.

Chapter 7

Recent security issues in Big Data: from past to the future of information systems

Julio Moreno[1], Manuel A. Serrano[1], and Eduardo Fernández-Medina[1]

It is a reality, we live in the world of Big Data. The use of Big Data creates new issues in different ways as the volume, velocity, and variety of the data that processes. However, many other problems are related to how to secure the data privacy and the data itself. In this chapter, we will describe a full perspective of the problematic. Furthermore, we will explain the main international proposals that address the security and privacy in Big Data environments.

7.1 Introduction

Over the last few years, data has become one of the most important assets for organizations in almost every field. It is important not only for companies related to the field of computer science industry but also for organizations such as countries' governments, healthcare, education, or the engineering sector. For all of them, data is essential to conduct their daily activities, and not only that, data can also help the businesses' management to achieve their goals and make the best decisions on the basis of the information extracted from them [1].

Moreover, every day, we generate a bigger volume of data. In fact, it is estimated that 90 percent of all the data in recorded human history has been created in the last few years. In 2003, five exabytes of data were generated by humans, while this amount of information is, at present, created within 2 days [2]. This tendency toward increasing the volume and detail of the data that is collected by companies will not change in the near future; in fact, the importance given to social networks, multimedia, and the Internet of Things (IoT) has risen, producing an overwhelming flow of data [3]. As a consequence, we can claim that we are living in the era of Big Data.

In addition, this data is mostly unstructured, signifying that traditional systems are not capable of analyzing it. However, this difficulty does not discourage the companies, quite the contrary. Organizations are willing to extract more beneficial

[1] Grupo de Seguridad y Auditoría (GSyA Research Group), Universidad de Castilla-La Mancha, Spain

information from this high volume and variety of data [4]. In order to solve all these problems, a new analysis paradigm with which to analyze and better understand this data, therefore, emerged to obtain not only private but also public benefits. This new paradigm was Big Data [5].

Companies are gaining more and more acceptance of the Big Data technology. According to a study conducted by the *Forbes* American business magazine in the year 2014 [6], 87 percent of companies believe that Big Data analytics will change their industry landscape in the following year. Furthermore, the organizations that do not implement a data analysis strategy based on Big Data will be in danger of losing market and relevancy.

Each new disruptive technology brings new issues with it, and Big Data is not an exception. In the case of Big Data, these issues are related not only to the volume or the variety of data but also to data quality, data privacy, and data security. This chapter will focus on the subjects of Big Data privacy and security.

Big Data not only increases the scale of the challenges related to privacy and security as they are addressed in traditional analysis systems, but also creates new ones, related to the inherent characteristics of Big Data that need to be approached in a new way [7]. The more data that is stored and analyzed by organizations or governments, the more regulations are needed to address these concerns.

Thus, achieving security in Big Data has, therefore, become one of the most important barriers that could decelerate the spread of this technology: without an adequate level of security, Big Data will not achieve the required level of trust [8]. Big Data brings big responsibility [9].

In this chapter, we will first explain what is and how a Big Data environment works. After that, we will focus on describing the main issues and challenges related to the security in a Big Data environment and how to address these concerns. Finally, it is important to know the different approaches as regards security and privacy in this technology that have been done by the international organizations.

7.2 Big Data basis

The term Big Data refers to a framework that allows the analysis and management of a larger amount of data than the traditional data analysis technologies [10]. Big Data supposes a change from those traditional techniques in three different ways: the amount of data (volume), the rate of data generation and transmission (velocity), and the types of structured and unstructured data (variety) [11]. These properties are known as the three basic Vs of Big Data.

Some authors have added new characteristics to the initial group such as variability (the meaning of the data is constantly changing), veracity (the truthfulness of data), or value (extract the most advantage possible from the outcome of Big Data processing) of data [12]. Figure 7.1 shows an overview of the different Vs of Big Data.

One of the most important characteristics of a Big Data environment is the use of the new technologies to obtain valuable information from the data, in addition to its ability to mix data from different sources and formats (both structured, semistructured,

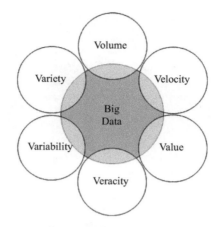

Figure 7.1   Vs of Big Data

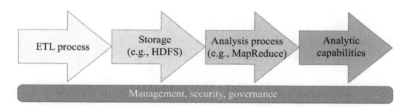

Figure 7.2   Typical architecture of a Big Data environment

and unstructured data). Therefore, Big Data means a change in how organizations using this technology store the data [13]. Moreover, the fact that a company is implementing Big Data allows them to improve their knowledge about their own business, which can mean achieving great profits in the near future [14].

Traditionally, data were stored in a structured format, like a relational database, in order to improve its processing and understanding. However, nowadays, a new tendency appears: storing huge amounts of data without a specific structure or with a semistructured format [15]. This unstructured format is even more important due to the current maturity of technologies as cloud computing or the ubiquitous connectivity that provides a platform where it is easy to collect, to store, and to process the data [16].

These sets of characteristics have allowed the fast expansion of the Big Data techniques. In addition to this, something that could make easier the expansion of this technology is the fact that not only big companies can afford to use a Big Data environment but also small companies can obtain benefits from the use of a Big Data environment [17]. Figure 7.2 shows a general scheme of how a Big Data system works.

To understand this high-level architecture of a Big Data environment, the elements of the figure will be explained. First of all, data enters in the environment through

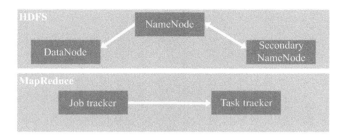

Figure 7.3   Typical Apache Hadoop architecture

an Extract Transform Load process; with this technique, the data is transferred into a Database Management System (DBMS) data warehouse of operational data store. Once the data is stored in the environment, it is possible to create specific analysis processes that allow to obtain information from that raw data. Finally, by using the wide variety of analytical capabilities, it is possible to obtain valuable information. Furthermore, this whole process should be well managed, properly governed, and performed in a secure way [18].

In this section, we will describe the main technologies for implementing a Big Data environment, including a more in-depth description of the Apache Hadoop technology. Moreover, it will be explained how the programming framework MapReduce, typical in Big Data environments, works. Finally, we will provide an explanation of the main proposals made by international organizations and the scientific community as regards security and privacy in Big Data.

7.2.1 Big Data technologies

There is a wide range of different possibilities for implementing a Big Data environment. Notwithstanding, there is one that stands out among the others: Apache Hadoop. Hadoop is a technology developed by Apache that allows the distributed processing of big sets of data along computer cluster using programming frameworks. It is designed to be scalable from one single server to thousands of them; each of them offers local computation and storage [19]. Currently, Apache Hadoop can be considered as a de facto standard because of its huge significance among the companies that implement a Big Data environment [20].

As an input, a Hadoop system receives the same data that feeds the Big Data environment. As we explained before, these data are usually originated in different sources and have different formats. Apache Hadoop has its own file system called Hadoop Distributed File System (HDFS) that stores the data in different server with different functions. For example, the NameNode is used for storing the metadata, or the DataNodes where the applications' data is stored [21]. Figure 7.3 illustrates a summary of the main elements of an Apache Hadoop architecture.

Nevertheless, as we explained before, Apache Hadoop is not the only option for implementing a Big Data environment, even though it is the most common one. These are the most known alternatives to Apache Hadoop:

- **Apache Spark** [22] is an open-source distributed computation environment. Apache Spark is known for being much faster than Hadoop in terms of processing tasks. To accomplish that, Apache Spark stores the data that is being analyzed in memory in order to minimize the number of readings and writings in the disk that burden the MapReduce performance. Apache Spark can be used as a part of the Apache Hadoop environment or be implemented as stand-alone. The biggest difference with Apache Hadoop is that Spark is more focused on processing stream datasets.
- **Google BigQuery** [23] is a RESTful web service, a way of providing interoperability between computer systems on the Internet that is designed to do queries against massive datasets. Those queries can be quite slow and very expensive without the proper software and infrastructure. To address this problem, BigQuery allows to enable very fast Structured Query Language (SQL)-kind queries, thanks to its table format and the infrastructure provided by Google.
- **PrestoDB** [24] is an open-source distributed SQL-king query engine that allows the execution of interactive analytic queries against data storage systems of every size. While Apache Hadoop needs to create a MapReduce algorithm to obtain value from the data, PrestoDB directly uses the NameNode and the HDFS, executing the queries in parallel. As Apache Spark, this process occurs entirely in memory, as a consequence, the latency of readings and writings to the disk is reduced.
- **Apache Flink** [25] is a scalable and open-source platform for processing huge amounts of stream datasets. Apache Flink was designed bearing in mind the idea of being an alternative of the MapReduce algorithms used by Apache Hadoop. In a first look, it can seem very similar to Apache Spark because of its purpose of processing stream datasets, but the programming model behind it is totally different. While Spark does a quick batch processing that simulates to be done in real time, Flink is truly capable of doing stream processing in real time. To do so, it is based on two main Application Programming Interfaces (APIs): DataSet and DataStream API.

7.2.2 MapReduce

MapReduce plays a pivotal role in Big Data. It is a programming framework typically used in Big Data environments for obtaining valuable information from the data. MapReduce is particularly focused on processing and generating large datasets. The MapReduce paradigm accomplishes this goal by describing two different functions [26]:

- The **map** function, which processes the key/value pair needed to create a set of intermediate key/value pairs.
- The **reduce** function, which processes the intermediate values generated and merges them to produce a solution.

A very typical example to explain how MapReduce works is doing the count of the different words that appear in a book. In order to accomplish that goal, the chapters

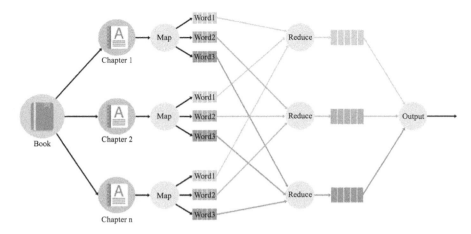

Figure 7.4   How MapReduce works

that form the book will be divided into the different mappers that form the system. Once all the chapters have been processed, the different words that form the output of the map function will be sorted and sent to the different reducers of the system. These reduce functions will be in charge of adding one each time that the same word appears. As a result of this process, the number of times that each word appears in the book is obtained. Figure 7.4 depicts a summary of how MapReduce works.

7.3   Main challenges in Big Data security

As we explained in the introductory section, Big Data brings new security and privacy problems. Those problems are not only related to the inherent characteristics of Big Data. In fact, the truth is that most of the security and privacy problems come from the origin of the Big Data technology itself. Actually, when Big Data was created, those topics were not kept in mind. For that reason, addressing the main security and privacy problems in Big Data is not an easy task. To accomplish that goal, we will divide the issues in six different categories which are shown in Figure 7.5.

7.3.1   Infrastructure security

When discussing infrastructure security issues in Big Data, it is necessary to describe the main problems as regards securing the architecture of a Big Data system. In particular, this topic is most of the time related to how to protect a Hadoop topic, since it is most frequently used for implementing a Big Data environment.

Therefore, the security problems that can be found in an Apache Hadoop topic are mainly related to the fact that Apache Hadoop was not developed having in mind the idea of being a secure system. Consequently, Hadoop lacks advanced authentication methods or a secure access control system [27]. Furthermore, the HDFS typical of

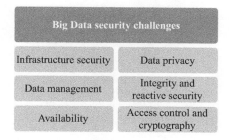

Figure 7.5   Main security challenges in Big Data security

this kind of systems can be a target for the attackers, so it is important to properly protect the data that is stored there [28].

Moreover, concerning the infrastructure security problems, it is important to highlight the security as regards communications between different parts of the Big Data ecosystem, since it is a topic often ignored.

Another different approach is describing a new Big Data architecture, or modifying the typical one, in order to improve the security of the environment. These changes are mainly done by creating certain protocols or by changing the infrastructure of function of the different nodes that form the Big Data environment [29].

In summary, with regard to the topic of infrastructure security, the main problems are related to how to secure a Hadoop system. This is not surprising since, as stated previously, Apache Hadoop can be considered as a de facto standard in industry. Those problems are usually solved by modifying the usual scheme of a Big Data system through the addition of new security layers.

7.3.2   Data privacy

Data privacy is probably the topic about which ordinary people are most concerned, but it should also be one of the greatest concerns for the organizations using Big Data techniques. A Big Data system usually contains an enormous amount of personal information that organizations use in order to obtain benefit from that data. However, we should ask ourselves where is the limit regarding the use of that information.

This is not a new topic, and it was also a problem present in the traditional analytics systems, but with Big Data, not only the issue gets bigger but also new privacy problems need to be addressed. It is important to highlight that although privacy is traditionally treated as a part of confidentiality, in the case of Big Data, privacy has a tremendous impact on the general public's perception of this technology.

Furthermore, the popularity of social networks is currently huge, and almost everyone with access to the Internet has at least one account with them. People share a lot of personal information in these networks without actually worrying about what the organization behind them will do with their data. This data, along with the strong analysis capability of Big Data, is a huge threat to our personal privacy. This fact has caused that many governments have started to worry about the legislation regarding the data protection and privacy.

Figure 7.6   How anonymization works

In addition to this, the predictive analysis of the data, which is possible to do with a Big Data environment, increases the privacy threats. For instance, a Big Data system was capable of predicting if a teen girl was pregnant even before her father did. To do so, the system analyzed all the searches that the girl did, and after a data mining analysis, it came to the conclusion that she was pregnant [30].

Managing this big amount of data is by itself an important problem to address but if the data protection and privacy are considered as well, the problem gets very difficult to handle. For that reason, there are many different techniques and methods developed in order to address the privacy problem:

- Creating **privacy-preserving queries**. This can be used in order to manipulate the data whilst simultaneously not violating the privacy of the data [31].
- **Anonymization of the data**. This is probably one of the most extended ways to protect the privacy of data. This consists of applying some kind of technique or mechanism to the data in order to remove the sensitive information from it or to hide it. There are mainly two different anonymization schemes: top-down specialization and bottom-up generalization [32]. In Figure 7.6, there is a typical schema of how anonymization works.
- Using **differential privacy**. The objective of differential privacy is to provide a method with which to maximize the value of analysis of a set of data while minimizing the chances of identifying users' identities. To accomplish this goal, there are techniques based on adding noise to the set of data [33].

In summary, the privacy of the data can be considered as one of the most important concerns as regards securing Big Data. This is related to the fact that Big Data can be used as a powerful tool for analyzing huge amounts of data and with the information extracted from it can even predict tendencies.

As a consequence, there are many different perspectives as concerns ensuring privacy, most of them are variations of traditional techniques that have been adjusted to the inherent characteristics of Big Data.

7.3.3   Integrity and reactive security

One of the bases on which Big Data is supported is the capacity to receive streams of data from many different origins and with distinct formats: either structural data or nonstructural data. This increases the importance of checking that the data's integrity is good so that it can be used properly. This topic also covers the use case of applying Big Data in order to monitor security so as to detect whether a system is being attacked.

Integrity has traditionally been defined as the maintenance of consistency, accuracy, and trustworthiness of data. It protects data from unauthorized alterations during its life cycle. Integrity is considered as one of the three basic dimensions of security (along with confidentiality and availability).

Due to its inherent characteristics, ensuring integrity is critical in a Big Data environment. In order to address this problem, there are different perspectives. For example, data can be checked by an external source in order to ensure its integrity [34]. Another situation where the data integrity can be compromised is after performing a MapReduce analytic algorithm [35].

As we explained before, as occurs with all systems, Big Data may be attacked by malicious users. In order to protect the environment from these malicious users, it is interesting to highlight a certain indicators that may be a sign that the Big Data environment in under attack. For instance, monitoring the provenance data related to a MapReduce process [36].

Furthermore, the Big Data environment can collapse for some reason and, in that scenario, it is important to count with particular policies and controls that ensure that the system will recover as soon as possible when a disaster occurs. This is very important due to the fact that many organizations currently store their data in Big Data systems, signifying that if a catastrophe occurs the entire company could be in danger.

In summary, in this section, we have discussed the main key points related to the integrity of data, the detection of malicious attacks against a Big Data environment, and how to properly recover the system in case a disaster occurs.

7.3.4 Availability

Availability, as integrity, is considered as one of the three basic dimensions of security. The problem of availability in a Big Data environment is not a trivial topic. This is because one of the main characteristics of Big Data environments, and by extension of a Hadoop implementation, is the availability attained by the use of hundreds of computers in which the datasets are not only stored but also replicated along the cluster.

Even so, there are different solutions in order to fully guarantee the full-time availability of a Big Data environment. For instance, one point of failure in an Apache Hadoop implementation is its NameNode. If the metadata that is contained in this node gets corrupted or lost, then the entire cluster will go down. In order to solve this problem, the most updated versions of Apache Hadoop includes a secondary NameNode that stores the latest checkpoint in a directory, which is structured the same way as the primary NameNode's directory [37]. In case, the primary NameNode is corrupted or down for some reason, the checkpointed image will be ready if necessary.

Another way to address the problem is by increasing the fault tolerance of the system. This solution is motivated for the long time that takes to restart an enormous system as the Big Data environment when a failure occurs [38].

To sum up, availability can be considered as an inherent characteristic of a Big Data environment. However, it is still difficult to claim that the perfect high availability pretended by Big Data is completely achieved. In order to improve this situation, there are a few techniques like replication or fault tolerance that can be used.

7.3.5   *Access control and cryptography*

Access control and cryptography are two of the basic traditional techniques used to achieve the security of a system. Due to the inherent characteristics of the Big Data environment, new techniques of access control and cryptography need to be developed or updated in order to address the new security problems derived from the use of Big Data.

The main objective of an access control technique is to restrict undesirable users' access to the system. In the case of Big Data, the access control problem is related to the fact that there are only basic forms of it. As we explained before, this is related with the fact that Big Data (and by extension Apache Hadoop) was not conceived with the idea of being a secure environment. In order to solve this problem, it is important to implement new security policies that deal with this new scenario. For example, it is possible to enforce the security on the MapReduce process itself by using security policies at the key-value level [39].

On the other hand, cryptography can be considered as the most frequently employed solution as regards securing data privacy in a Big Data system. Cryptography has been used to protect data for a considerable amount of time. This tendency continues in the case of Big Data, but it has a few inherent characteristics that make the direct application of traditional cryptography techniques impossible. In order to use cryptography in Big Data, it is necessary to adapt it with the creation of new schemas. For example, by creating a bitmap encryption that guarantees users' privacy [40].

However, cryptography is not only important as a method for ensuring the privacy of the data. This topic also covers how to process data that is already encrypted. In that case, it is important to follow some schemes that allow the system to directly work with that encrypted data without losing too much efficiency [41].

To summarize, access control and cryptography are both techniques that have traditionally been used to protect the security of the systems. Big Data is not an exception, but due to its inherent set of characteristics, it is necessary to create new techniques or to update the previous ones.

7.3.6   *Data management*

Data management covers many different topics related to the security in Big Data. It addresses not only how to secure the data that is stored in the Big Data system but also how to share that data along the different parts of the environment. Furthermore, we shall also discuss the different policies and legislation that is suggested in order to ensure the data protection.

As mentioned previously, Big Data usually implies a huge amount of data, and it was not initially conceived to be a secure system. It is, therefore, of prime importance not only to find a means to protect data when it is stored in a Big Data environment but also to know how to initially collect that data. Protecting this storage system can cover different perspectives, from achieving an acceptable level of privacy of the data stored in the environment [42] to secure the data, by dividing the data stored in the Big Data system into sequenced parts and storing them in different cloud storage service providers [43].

Additionally, in order to obtain the maximum possible value from data, it is necessary to share that data among the cluster in which Big Data is running or to share those results for collaboration. However, again, there is the problem of how to guarantee security and privacy when the sharing process is taking place. In order to solve these problems, there are a few sharing algorithms specifically conceived to adapt to the Big Data inherent set of characteristics [44].

Furthermore, it is essential to have in mind the idea that with every disruptive technology, new problems appeared, and Big Data is no exception. The problems related to Big Data are mostly related to the increase in the use of this technique to obtain value from a large amount of data by using its powerful analysis characteristics. This could imply a threat to people's privacy. In order to reduce that risk, many organizations, companies, and even governments propose the creation of new legislation and laws that will allow these new problems to be confronted in an effective manner [45].

On the other hand, it is imperative the creation of a government security framework in the Big Data environment that allows the top management of every company that makes use of the Big Data technology to properly manage this kind of system during its entire life cycle.

All things considered, in this section, we have discussed almost the entire life cycle used in a Big Data system, from its collection to its sharing, and also include how to properly govern the security of that data. As a response to this necessity, we have created a proposal for a security government framework for Big Data named security governance in Big Data environments (SGB) framework that will be explained in the next section.

7.3.7 SGB framework

Our governance framework proposal called SGB [46] aims to cover the security governance in the Big Data environment throughout their life cycle. It is based on three main pillars:

- The structure of process domains and processes as means of generating the skeleton proposed by Control Objectives for Information and related Technology (COBIT) [47] will be used, but with changes in the same.
- Capability Maturity Model Integration (CMMI) [48] has been used as a way to make more accessible the implementation of COBIT processes (or in our case, the SGB framework) following its recommendations and good practices. Furthermore, they will serve to determine at what level of maturity is each of the processes that form the frame.
- The knowledge related to the security in a Big Data context will serve as a base to take into account when creating our governance framework proposal.

Taking as a basis the structure of four process domains identified by COBIT, it was decided to modify it to meet the specific needs of a Big Data. In addition to the modifications to these process domains, a fifth domain for analyzing Big Data security has been added. Then, each of the domains which creates our governance framework proposal is defined:

- **Planning and Organization (PO)**: in this case, both the name and the purpose of the domain are maintained regarding COBIT, but there will be changes in terms of the processes that form it since it will be necessary to implement a specific security plan for Big Data.
- **Security Analysis in Big Data (SA)**: this domain is a novelty with respect to COBIT. Its inclusion in the framework is due to the fact that COBIT is a framework of a more general nature and high level, which is contrary to our goal. Thus, in this domain, a series of processes required to address security issues in Big Data environments has been created more specifically.
- **Design and Safe implementation of Big Data (DI)**: this domain corresponds to the domain of "acquisition and implementation" of COBIT, but some changes, regarding the processes that form it, as well as the inclusion of new processes, are introduced. Thus, to achieve that, our framework is less generic than COBIT. This domain is intended to cover the design and implementation phase of a Big Data environment in a company.
- **Safe Operation of Big Data (SO)**: the domain of SO of Big Data seeks to address how the security of a Big Data environment is managed, once this has already been implemented in the company. In this case, most processes found in this domain are adaptations of processes already present in COBIT.
- **Monitoring and Evaluation (ME)**: finally, this domain evaluates the performance of the system in terms of security indicators, and it also includes an external audit process. Concerning COBIT, this domain adds the process of conducting audits and adapts the rest of processes to align them with the strategic security plan established in the first domain.

Once created the different process domains that form our proposal, the processes proposed by COBIT have been analyzed. As a result of this analysis, different processes that make our proposal have been obtained. These processes can remain the same as in COBIT, be modified to suit the specific security needs of a Big Data environment, or have been created from scratch to include some important aspects of security governance on Big Data that are part of COBIT. Figure 7.7 depicts a comparison between the different domains of the SGB framework and domains of COBIT.

Those processes are defined in a very high level of abstraction. In order to improve the understanding of our framework, these processes can be divided into different subprocesses. Furthermore, to ease the implementation of the SGB framework, we will use CMMI. The relationship between COBIT and CMMI enables an easier implementation of COBIT processes thanks to good practices proposed by the various process areas of CMMI. Our framework can take advantage of this relationship since it follows a similar structure of the proposal by COBIT. CMMI allows us to add a new dimension to our governance framework; in addition to facilitating the implementation of processes, it provides us the opportunity to assess the maturity of the different processes that form our proposal.

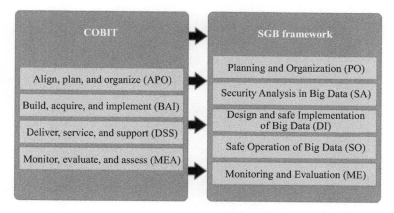

Figure 7.7   Comparison between the domains of COBIT and SGB framework

The process areas of CMMI can be, as well, divided into different tasks that are adapted from CMMI to meet our set of specific security characteristics. These tasks are composed by different subtasks and work products. The performance of these subtasks and the quality of the work products can be measured by means of KPIs (key performance indicators). The addition of the whole set of KPIs across the framework will allow us to measure not only the performance but also the maturity of the system. Figure 7.8 depicts a tree structure representation of our framework.

7.4   Scientific community reaction against Big Data security challenges

Big Data is not just a buzzword. The scientific community is probably the most important source for improving the security and privacy issues in Big Data environments. But not only is the scientific community concerned by those problematics, the most relevant organizations related to the information technologies (IT) have also done many reports about Big Data. These reports cover many aspects of this technology from how to properly implement it in a company to how the implementation can change the way the company works. As a consequence, how to achieve the adequate level of security in a Big Data environment has been thoroughly addressed. In this section, we will describe the main contributions in the field of the security in Big Data that have been done by the main organizations related to the IT sector and the scientific community perspective.

7.4.1   Cloud Security Alliance

Cloud Security Alliance (CSA) is a nonprofit organization that has the objective of promoting the use of best practices to provide security assurance within cloud computing and to provide education on the uses of new technologies to help secure all other

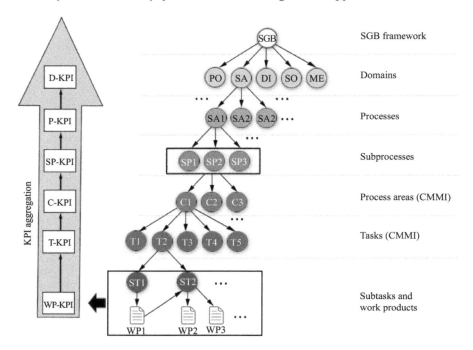

Figure 7.8   Tree structure of the SGB framework

forms of computing. It can be considered as a company more focused in achieving the best possible level of confidence in the technologies related to cloud computing. Regarding the Big Data topic and, more specifically, the security problems, CSA has created different reports that note the new security issues that need to be addressed in order to ensure Big Data.

Probably, the most important report is the one which is about the main Big Data security and privacy challenges [49]. CSA divides those challenges in four main categories that in turn can be divided in more specific problems, as Figure 7.9 shows.

This report is very important because it has been used as the base of several proposals to describe the security problems in Big Data and also how to properly address them, for instance, the National Institute of Standards and Technology (NIST) agency.

7.4.2   National Institute of Standards and Technology

NIST is a North American agency, whose main purpose is to promote the use of the industrial innovation and competitiveness by means of creating different metrics and standards related to the technology. To address the Big Data security problem, NIST adopts two different perspectives.

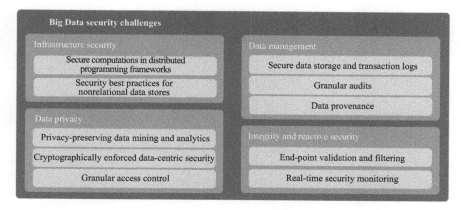

Figure 7.9   Main security challenges in Big Data according to CSA

On one hand, NIST highlights the security and privacy problems related to the inherent characteristics of a Big Data environment. In this case, NIST identifies the following "Vs" and problems:

- **Variety**: a new problem introduced by Big Data variety is the capability of inferring identity from anonymized datasets by making correlations between public databases.
- **Volume**: the huge amount of data that a Big Data is capable of processing can be also a threat. This volume of Big Data is usually stored in multitiered storage media. The movement of data between those tiers has led to a requirement of classification threat models and creates new techniques.
- **Veracity**: in this case, NIST describes the problematic by dividing this characteristic in three different subcharacteristics:
  - **Provenance** is crucial for protecting the quality, security, and privacy. Provenance addresses the problem of understanding the data's original source, for example, by using the metadata. But tracking and defining the metadata in Big Data is a very difficult problem that has not been properly resolved yet.
  - **Veracity** covers how the information was collected. For example, the time when the sensors were used or the configuration of the device. Curation is an integral notion that allows to improve the problems of provenance and veracity by using principles of governance.
  - **Validity** is defined as the accuracy and correctness of data. Usually, it is referred to data quality, but in the security scenario, variety refers to a number of assumptions about data from which analytics are being applied. When the data is not properly validated, wrong conclusions can be made by an analytical tool.

On the other hand, NIST also addresses the security and privacy challenges in Big Data by developing some use cases where the Big Data plays an important role and highlights the main security problems that can occur. These are the main scenarios identified:

- In the field of **marketing and retail,** there are different situations where the use of Big Data can have security and privacy challenges. These problems are related to the several uses that the companies that collect the individual data can do. These include the smartphone Global Positioning System (GPS) or the data related to the social media. One more specific scenario is the data collected from the usage of a website, where the problems related to the personal data get more complicated due to the different legislations over the different countries.
- In the field of **healthcare**, the problems of privacy get even more critical due to the fact that usually the data treated in these situations should have a special level of confidentiality. Therefore, to adequately ensure the privacy of these data, the systems must have specific encryption schemes for each type of sensitive record. On the other hand, NIST highlights the importance of implementing differential privacy techniques and the anonymization of patients' data.
- In the field of **cybersecurity**, the main problems are related to how to protect the network. This includes from the data collection to the monitoring. In this case, NIST highlights the fact that the security in this area is mature, but not the privacy. Hence, the companies should make an effort to protect the personal data.
- There are a few more use cases developed by NIST that will not be described here. For instance, the security problematic derived from the domestic surveillance performed by the institutional governments or the use of the data collected from different sensors.

7.4.3 Information Systems Audit and Control Association

Information Systems Audit and Control Association (ISACA) is an international organization that supports the development of methodologies and certifications with the objective of performing activities related to auditory and control of IT systems.

In the topic of security and privacy in Big Data, ISACA has done some reports about it. In order to accomplish that objective, ISACA addresses the problem as a consequence of the inherent characteristics of the Big Data environment, like the volume or the velocity. More specifically, ISACA is more focused on analyzing the different problems related to the treatment of data as regards privacy issues.

Furthermore, ISACA considers a topic that is not usually addressed in this kind of documents: the Big Data governance. ISACA claims that managing how the data is used is the best option for protecting it. For that reason, they propose the use of different agile methodologies and frameworks like COBIT to achieve an acceptable level of trust for the data. Without a proper data government, the same data that produces a great benefit for the company can generate detrimental outputs that can lead the company to bad strategic decisions.

7.4.4 Scientific community perspective

Notwithstanding, not only have big organizations done proposals related to the security and privacy in Big Data. The scientific community is probably the most important

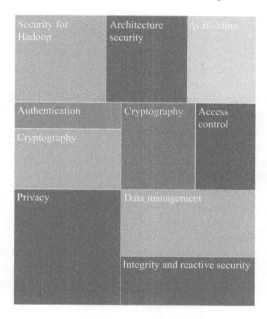

Figure 7.10 Main topics as regards security in Big Data

source with regard to this topic. In order to obtain a full perspective of the problem, we have conducted a systematic mapping study [50] about which are the main topics addressed by the authors. A summary of the results obtained can be seen in Figure 7.10.

The results obtained from that research show how many authors, therefore, focus their research on creating means to protect data, particularly with respect to privacy, but privacy is not the only security problem that can be found in a Big Data system; the traditional architecture itself and how to protect an Apache Hadoop system is also a huge concern for researchers. On the other hand, we have also detected a lack of solutions in the field of data management, especially with respect to government. We have considered that this fact is not acceptable, since having a government security framework will allow the rapid expansion of Big Data technology.

In addition to the solutions given by the scientific community, most of the organizations related to the IT, and more specifically with the Big Data, have their own products to achieve a proper level of security. For example, Apache has developed Eagle which provides security by analyzing the performance of Big Data platforms, like Hadoop or Spark [51], or the solution proposed by Hortonworks based on providing a centralized security across Hadoop which is actually a dashboard that allows the user control the Hadoop's performance [52]. The problem of these kinds of solutions is that they do not properly address the specific problems of Big Data. These are evolutions of previous techniques that work fine with the traditional systems but Big Data brings new problems that are usually not considered.

7.5   Case of use: how to use Big Data for security

There are two ways of addressing the security in Big Data: secure the Big Data system itself or using Big Data techniques to achieve security goals in other systems. In this chapter, we mainly focus on the first scenario about which are the main security problems in Big Data. In order to provide a wider vision of the second scenario, we will explain a specific prototype whose purpose is to use the analysis characteristics of Big Data to evaluate the security in a relational database [53].

To achieve that goal, we have developed a specific Big Data architecture and MapReduce algorithms that address the main security problems related to databases that are specified by the main international standards and methodologies like ISO/IEC 27000 or COBIT 5 for information security.

The developed architecture of our proposal is shown in Figure 7.11. The main component of this architecture is Apache Hadoop that will allow us to perform the different security evaluations implemented by means of MapReduce algorithms. Our prototype needs to import the data from the relational database to the HDFS; in order to achieve that aim, Apache Sqoop has been used. Apache Sqoop allows the transference of bulk data from databases to the HDFS. The system is implemented as a web application by means of the stack MEAN. This application permits to input the needed information for performing the evaluations. Finally, the results from the evaluations will be shown in a final report with graphics.

Once the architecture is defined, the different security evaluations that form our prototype were implemented. These evaluations are related to the recommendations and good practices specified by the main security standards and methodologies. Finally, the developed evaluations are

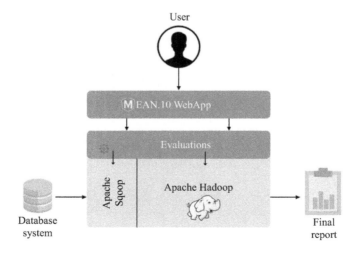

Figure 7.11   Prototype to evaluate the security in databases

- **Evaluation 1—Encryption**: to ensure that the records of a database are properly encrypted. ISO/IEC 27002 expresses the necessity of having an encryption politic.
- **Evaluation 2—Users' permission**: to guarantee which users have the proper permissions. COBIT 5 proposes the use of the principle of least privilege.
- **Evaluation 3—Users' privileges revoked**: to confirm that the privileges from former users have been revoked. ISO/IEC 27002 urges to protect data from former users.
- **Evaluation 4—Access time**: to check the allowed time to access the system. Insider attacks are one of the principal sources of threads.
- **Evaluation 5—Wrong accesses**: to monitor the wrong accesses made by each user. ISO/IEC 15408 describes controls about the importance of authentication and identification.

This is just an example to show the versatility of Big Data and how it is possible to use the inherent characteristics of it to improve the security of other systems. Of course, there are many of different possibilities that can address a wide range of security issues.

7.6 Conclusions

This chapter provides a high-level perspective of the different problems and challenges related to security and privacy in Big Data. It also explains some proposals that have been done in order to solve these problematics. These contributions are mostly from the scientific community but we have also considered the proposals made by the main organizations related to the field of the IT and the Big Data environment.

It can be concluded that the principal problems are related to the inherent characteristics of a Big Data system, and also to the fact that security issues were not contemplated when Big Data was initially conceived. For that reason, the proposals focus more on how to protect data, particularly with respect to privacy, but privacy is not the only security problem that can be found in a Big Data system; the traditional architecture itself and how to protect a Hadoop system is also a huge concern.

Furthermore, we have found that there is a lack of proposals in the field of data management, especially with respect to government. This is not acceptable, since having a government security framework will allow the rapid spread of Big Data technology considering that it will increase the level of trust in this technology.

In conclusion, the Big Data technology seems to be reaching a mature stage where the solutions proposed are more and more specific. However, that does not mean that it is a totally secure technology. Furthermore, Big Data can be useful as a base for the development of the future technologies that will change the world as we see it, like the IoT, or on-demand services, and that is the reason why Big Data is, after all, the future.

Acknowledgments

This work has been funded by the SEQUOIA project (Ministerio de Economía y Competitividad and the Fondo Europeo de Desarrollo Regional FEDER, TIN2015-63502-C3-1-R) and SERENIDAD project (Consejería de Educación, Ciencia y Cultura de la Junta de Comunidades de Castilla-La Mancha, y Fondo Europeo de Desarrollo Regional FEDER, PEII-2014-045-P).

References

[1]   Mayer-Schönberger V, and Cukier K. *Big Data: A Revolution That Will Transform How We Live, Work, and Think*. Houghton Mifflin Harcourt; 2013.

[2]   Sagiroglu S, and Sinanc D. 'Big data: A review'. *2013 International Conference on Collaboration Technologies and Systems (CTS)*. 2013 May; pp. 42–47.

[3]   Hashem IAT, Yaqoob I, Anuar NB, Mokhtar S, Gani A, and Ullah Khan S. 'The rise of "big data" on cloud computing: Review and open research issues'. *Information Systems*. 2015;47:98–115.

[4]   Sharma, S . 'Rise of Big Data and related issues'. *2015 Annual IEEE India Conference (INDICON)*. 2015 Dec; pp. 1–6.

[5]   Eynon R. 'The rise of Big Data: What does it mean for education, technology, and media research?' *Learning, Media and Technology*. 2013;38(3):237–240.

[6]   Columbus L. 84% of Enterprises See Big Data Analytics Changing Their Industries' Competitive Landscapes in the Next Year; 2014. Available from: http://www.forbes.com/sites/louiscolumbus/2014/10/19/84-of-enterprises-see-big-data-analytics -changing-their-industries-competitive-landscapes-in-the-next-year/.

[7]   Wang H, Jiang X, and Kambourakis G. 'Special issue on security, privacy and trust in network-based Big Data'. *Information Sciences: An International Journal*. 2015;318(C):48–50.

[8]   Thuraisingham B. 'Big data security and privacy'. *Proceedings of the 5th ACM Conference on Data and Application Security and Privacy*. ACM. 2015; pp. 279–280.

[9]   Rijmenam V. *Think Bigger: Developing a Successful Big Data Strategy for Your Business*. New York: Amacom; 2014.

[10]   Meng X, and Ci X. 'Big data management: Concepts, techniques and challenges'. *Jisuanji Yanjiu yu Fazhan/Computer Research and Development*. 2013;50(1):146–169.

[11]   Chen M, Mao S, and Liu Y. 'Big data: A survey'. *Mobile Networks and Applications*. 2014;19(2):171–209.

[12]   Ali-ud-din Khan M, Uddin MF, and Gupta N. 'Seven V's of Big Data understanding Big Data to extract value'. *American Society for Engineering Education (ASEE Zone 1), 2014 Zone 1 Conference of the*. IEEE. 2014; pp. 1–5.

[13]   Cumbley R, and Church P. 'Is "Big Data" creepy?' *Computer Law & Security Review*. 2013 Oct;29(5):601–609.

[14] Dijcks JP. 'Oracle: Big data for the enterprise'. *Oracle White Paper*. 2012. [Online]. Available from: http://www.oracle.com/us/products/database/big-data-for-enterprise-519135.pdf. [Accessed: 11 November 2017].

[15] Minelli M, Chambers M, and Dhiraj A. *Big Data, Big Analytics: Emerging Business Intelligence and Analytic Trends for Today's Businesses*. John Wiley & Sons; 2012.

[16] Demchenko Y, De Laat C, and Membrey P. 'Defining architecture components of the big data ecosystem'. *2014 International Conference on Collaboration Technologies and Systems (CTS)*. IEEE. 2014; pp. 104–112.

[17] Kumaresan A. 'Framework for building a big data platform for publishing industry'. *International Conference on Knowledge Management in Organizations*. Springer. 2015; pp. 377–388.

[18] Helen S, and Peter H. 'Oracle information architecture: An architect's guide to big data'. *USA: Oracle Corporation*. 2012.

[19] Apache Hadoop. Available from: http://hadoop.apache.org/.

[20] Cackett D. 'Information Management and Big Data: A Reference Architecture'. Oracle White Paper, Feb 2013. [Online]. Available from: http://www.oracle.com/technetwork/topics/entarch/articles/info-mgmt-big-data-ref-arch-1902853.pdf. [Accessed 11 November 2017].

[21] Shvachko K, Kuang H, Radia S, and Chansler R. 'The Hadoop distributed file system'. *2010 IEEE 26th Symposium on Mass Storage Systems and Technologies (MSST)*. IEEE; 2010; pp. 1–10.

[22] FAQ | Apache Spark. Available from: http://spark.apache.org/faq.html.

[23] What Is BigQuery? | BigQuery | Google Cloud Platform. Available from: https://cloud.google.com/bigquery/what-is-bigquery.

[24] Presto | Distributed SQL Query Engine for Big Data. Available from: https://prestodb.io/.

[25] Apache Flink: Scalable Batch and Stream Data Processing. Available from: https://flink.apache.org/.

[26] Dean J, and Ghemawat S. 'MapReduce: Simplified data processing on large clusters'. *Communications of the ACM*. 2004;51(1):107–113.

[27] Meye P, Raipin P, Tronel F, and Anceaume E. 'Mistore: A distributed storage system leveraging the DSL infrastructure of an ISP'. *2014 International Conference on High Performance Computing & Simulation (HPCS)*. 2014 Jul; pp. 260–267.

[28] Azeem MA, Sharfuddin M, and Ragunathan T. 'Support-based replication algorithm for cloud storage systems'. *Proceedings of the 7th ACM India Computing Conference*. Nagpur, India: ACM; 2014; pp. 1–9.

[29] He S, Wu Q, Qin B, Liu J, and Li Y. 'Efficient group key management for secure big data in predictable large-scale networks'. *Concurrency Computation*. 2016;28(4):1174–1192.

[30] Hill K. How Target Figured Out a Teen Girl Was Pregnant Before Her Father Did; 2012. Available from: http://www.forbes.com/sites/kashmirhill/2012/02/16/how-target-figured-out-a-teen-girl-was-pregnant-before-her-father-did/.

[31]   Kuzu M, Islam MS, and Kantarcioglu M. 'Distributed Search over Encrypted Big Data'. *Proceedings of the 5th ACM Conference on Data and Application Security and Privacy*. San Antonio, Texas, USA: ACM; 2015; pp. 271–278.

[32]   Irudayasamy A, and Arockiam L. 'Scalable multidimensional anonymization algorithm over big data using map reduce on public cloud'. *Journal of Theoretical and Applied Information Technology*. 2015;74(2):221–231.

[33]   Hongde R, Shuo W, and Hui L. 'Differential privacy data Aggregation Optimizing Method and application to data visualization'. *2014 IEEE Workshop on Electronics, Computer and Applications*. IEEE; 2014; pp. 54–58.

[34]   Liu C, Yang C, Zhang X, and Chen J. 'External integrity verification for outsourced big data in cloud and IoT'. *Future Generation Computer Systems*. 2015;49(C):58–67.

[35]   Wang Y, Wei J, Srivatsa M, Duan Y, and Du W. 'IntegrityMR: Integrity assurance framework for big data analytics and management applications'. *2013 IEEE International Conference on Big Data*. 2013 Oct; pp. 33–40.

[36]   Liao C, and Squicciarini A. 'Towards provenance-based anomaly detection in MapReduce'. *2015 15th IEEE/ACM International Symposium on Cluster, Cloud and Grid Computing (CCGrid)*. 2015 May; pp. 647–656.

[37]   Wang Z, and Wang D. 'NCluster: Using multiple active name nodes to achieve high availability for HDFS'. *2013 IEEE 10th International Conference on High Performance Computing and Communications & 2013 IEEE International Conference on Embedded and Ubiquitous Computing (HPCC_EUC)*. 2013 Nov; pp. 2291–2297.

[38]   Yang CT, Liu JC, Hsu CH, and Chou WL. 'On improvement of cloud virtual machine availability with virtualization fault tolerance mechanism'. *The Journal of Supercomputing*. 2014;69(3):1103–1122.

[39]   Ulusoy H, Colombo P, Ferrari E, Kantarcioglu M, and Pattuk E. 'GuardMR: Fine-grained security policy enforcement for MapReduce systems'. *Proceedings of the 10th ACM Symposium on Information, Computer and Communications Security*. Singapore, Republic of Singapore: ACM; 2015; pp. 285–296.

[40]   Yoon M, Cho A, Jang M, and Chang JW. 'A data encryption scheme and GPU-based query processing algorithm for spatial data outsourcing'. *2015 International Conference on Big Data and Smart Computing (BIGCOMP)*. 2015 Feb; pp. 202–209.

[41]   Stephen JJ, Savvides S, Seidel R, and Eugster P. 'Program analysis for secure big data processing'. *Proceedings of the 29th ACM/IEEE International Conference on Automated Software Engineering*. Vasteras, Sweden: ACM; 2014; pp. 277–288.

[42]   Xu L, Jiang C, Chen Y, Ren Y, and Liu KJR. 'Privacy or utility in data collection? A contract theoretic approach'. *IEEE Journal of Selected Topics in Signal Processing*. 2015 Oct; 9(7):1256–1269.

[43]   Cheng H, Rong C, Hwang K, Wang W, and Li Y. 'Secure big data storage and sharing scheme for cloud tenants'. *China Communications*. 2015 Jun;12(6):106–115.

[44]   Thilakanathan D, Calvo R, Chen S, and Nepal S. 'Secure and controlled sharing of data in distributed computing'. *2013 IEEE 16th International Conference on Computational Science and Engineering (CSE)*. IEEE; 2013; pp. 825–832.

[45]   Weber AS. 'Suggested legal framework for student data privacy in the age of big data and smart devices'. *Frontiers in Artificial Intelligence and Applications*. 2014; 262:669–678.

[46]   Moreno J, Serrano M, and Fernández-Medina E. 'Propuesta de Marco para el Gobierno de la Seguridad en Entornos Big Data'. *XXII Jornadas de Ingeniería del Software y Bases de Datos, JISBD*. 2017 Jul.

[47]   ISACA. COBIT 5: A Business Framework for the Governance and Management of Enterprise IT. ISACA, 2012.

[48]   Chrissis MB, Konrad M, and Shrum S. *CMMI for Development: Guidelines for Process Integration and Product Improvement*. Addison-Wesley Professional; 2011.

[49]   CSA. *Expanded Top Ten Big Data Security and Privacy*. CSA, Group BDWG; 2013. [Online]. Available from: https://downloads.cloudsecurity alliance.org/initiatives/bdwg/Expanded_Top_Ten_ Big_Data_Security_and_ Privacy_Challenges.pdf [Accessed 11 November 2017].

[50]   Kitchenham BA, Budgen D, and Pearl Brereton O. 'Using mapping studies as the basis for further research – A participant-observer case study'. *Information and Software Technology*. 2011 Jun;53(6):638–651.

[51]   Apache Eagle – Analyze Big Data Platforms for Security and Performance. Available from: http://eagle.incubator.apache.org/.

[52]   Comprehensive Security in Hadoop – Hortonworks. Available from: http://es.hortonworks.com/solutions/security/.

[53]   Moreno J, Serrano M, and Fernández-Medina E. 'Big Data para evaluar la seguridad en bases de datos'. *XIV Reunión Española sobre Criptología y Seguridad de la Información, RECSI*. 2016 Oct; pp. 163–167.

Chapter 8

Recent advances in unconstrained face recognition

Yunlian Sun[1] and Massimo Tistarelli[2]

Many face recognition systems have demonstrated promising results under well-controlled conditions with cooperative users. However, face recognition in real-world scenarios is still a challenging problem due to dramatic facial variations caused by different poses, lighting conditions, expressions, occlusion and so on. In this chapter, we summarize recent advances in unconstrained face recognition. We begin by introducing existing unconstrained face databases or benchmarks. We then provide an overview of recent techniques specifically developed for this task, including advanced face representations, metric learning approaches, background information investigation and pose-invariant approaches. Finally, we highlight some open issues to be addressed.

8.1 Introduction

The analysis of human faces has been a long-standing problem in biometrics and pattern recognition. It has received significant attention due to its wide applications in access control and video surveillance (e.g., for identity recognition) [1], human–computer interaction (e.g., for emotion analysis) [2] and human demographic analysis (e.g., for age estimation, gender classification and race categorization) [3]. Among these applications, face-based identity recognition (i.e., face recognition) has been one of the most extensively studied problems.

Early work in face recognition was mainly focused on recognizing faces collected in controlled lab environments. In order to study the effect of variability due to lighting conditions, head poses, expressions and occlusion, a number of face databases have been assembled (e.g., the Face Recognition Technology database (FERET) [4], the pose, illumination and expression database from Carnegie Mellon University (CMU PIE) [5] and the Face Recognition Grand Challenge database (FRGC) [6]). With these databases, many face recognition algorithms have been developed, and significant progress has been achieved for face recognition in constrained scenarios [1].

[1]School of Computer Science and Engineering, Nanjing University of Science and Technology, China
[2]Department of Sciences and Information Technology, University of Sassari, Italy

Though with significant progress, a number of face systems still fail to work in some practical applications. To improve the robustness of face recognition algorithms to diverse facial variations, the focus has been moved to unconstrained scenarios. The release of the Labeled Faces in the Wild (LFW) database made unconstrained face recognition a hot topic [7] in both the scientific and industrial communities. Following LFW, a number of challenging face databases or benchmarks have been collected and made publicly available in order to advance face recognition research in real-world scenarios. Over the years, great efforts have been devoted to tackling this problem. In this chapter, we summarize the results achieved in unconstrained face recognition, and we then list some challenges faced by today's research in face recognition.

8.2   Real-world databases

There are a large number of face databases publicly available to researchers for face recognition. These databases range in size, scope and purpose. Early face databases were generally acquired under controlled lab environments, where face samples were drawn from a narrow distribution with some parameters of variability controlled (e.g., pose, illumination, facial expression, occlusion). FERET [4], CMU PIE [5] and FRGC [6] are among these early databases. Over time, the advancement of bio-metric research allowed to achieve very impressive performance on these constrained datasets. For example, in 2012, the NIST Face Recognition Vendor Test reported a true acceptance rate of about 96% at a false acceptance rate of 0.1% on a database of face mug shots.

Even though with significant progress, a number of attributes, including the direct application of algorithms developed for these databases to face images captured in real application scenarios, cannot produce satisfactory results. Therefore, to improve the generalization of face recognition algorithms, the focus has been moved to unconstrained scenarios. The LFW database [7], made available in 2007, was the first attempt to provide a more realistic testing platform for face recognition research. Over time, several unconstrained face databases have been made publicly available.

8.2.1   LFW benchmark

In 2007, Huang *et al.* proposed the LFW benchmark with 13,233 face photos of 5,749 different individuals. It was collected by running the Viola–Jones face detector [8] on pictures taken from the Yahoo News website. Face images in this database exhibit natural variability in pose, illumination, focus, resolution, facial expression, age, gender, race, accessories, makeup, occlusion, background and image quality. Therefore, it represents an initial attempt to provide a set of labeled face pictures spanning the range of conditions typically encountered by people in their everyday lives. Face recognition in this benchmark is addressed as a pairwise matching problem, aiming to determine whether two face images represent the same individual or not. Two evaluation protocols are provided along with the dataset: image restricted and unrestricted. Under the image-restricted setting, it is not allowed to use the name of a person to infer the equivalence or nonequivalence of two face images that are

Matching pairs   Nonmatching pairs

Figure 8.1   Several challenging matching and nonmatching pairs from the LFW
database [7]

not explicitly given in the training set. On the contrary, in the unrestricted training paradigm, one may compose as many matching and nonmatching pairs as desired from a set of images labeled with identity. In Figure 8.1, several challenging matching and nonmatching face image pairs from this database are shown.

8.2.2 PubFig database

In 2009, Kumar *et al.* introduced the PubFig dataset with real-world face images of well-known individuals (celebrities and politicians) taken from the Internet [9]. This database includes 60,000 images of 200 subjects. The larger number of images per person (as compared to LFW) allows researchers to construct subsets of the data across different poses, lighting conditions and expressions, while still maintaining a sufficiently large number of images within each subset. Similarly based on face pair matching, the evaluation is performed on 20,000 pairs of images of 140 people following a 10-fold cross validation procedure.

8.2.3 YTF video database

The YouTube Faces (YTF) video database is a dataset collected from the YouTube web repository over the Internet, using the name list of LFW [10]. It was designed for video-based face recognition though. The database includes 3,425 videos of 1,595 subjects, with an average of 2.15 videos for each subject. The LFW pairwise matching protocol (matching/nonmatching) is adopted to test algorithms on the YTF dataset. The testing procedure involves a random selection of 5,000 video pairs for a 10-fold cross validation evaluation. Since videos in YouTube are compressed at a very high ratio, individual face images from this dataset are of very low quality. Figure 8.2 shows some example frames.

8.2.4 Point-and-shoot face recognition challenge

Given that most of today's face photos are generally taken by using point-and-shoot cameras and cell phones, Beveridge *et al.* produced the Point-and-Shoot Face Recognition Challenge to facilitate face recognition research in this context [11]. This dataset

Figure 8.2   Example frames from the YTF database [10]

includes 9,376 still images (both frontal and nonfrontal views) and 2,802 videos taken from 293 subjects. The dataset was captured both inside buildings and outdoors, by using different cameras and varying the distance from the captured subject. As a result, many face samples in this challenge are of low quality with poor lighting, motion blur and poor focus. The evaluation protocol is based on verification for three cases: comparing still images to still images, videos to videos and still images to videos.

8.2.5   MegaFace dataset

In 2015, Miller *et al.* collected from Flickr the MegaFace dataset [12] to evaluate the performance of current algorithms on large scale data. The dataset allows to perform face recognition tests with up to a million distractors, i.e., up to a million people that are not in the test set. Both identification and verification protocols are included. The distractor dataset with 1 million Flickr face images serves as the enrollment database, while the test set includes 4,000 face images of 80 individuals. And each test face image is randomly selected from the FaceScrub dataset [13].

8.2.6   IJB-A dataset

The rapid progress in unconstrained face recognition research has resulted in the saturation of recognition accuracy for benchmark datasets like LFW and YTF. One limitation in such unconstrained datasets is the lack of full pose variation, which is due to the use of a commodity face detector to select the face images to be included in the dataset. To well study face recognition with fully unconstrained faces, Klare *et al.* collected the IARPA Janus Benchmark A (IJB-A) dataset [14], which includes 5,712 images and 2,085 videos of 500 subjects. All the samples included in the dataset were collected "in the wild." A key difference between this dataset and the previous ones is that all human faces have been manually localized within each picture. This strategy results in an unprecedented amount of variation in pose, occlusion and illumination. The protocols support both open-set identification and verification. Some example faces from the IJB-A dataset are shown in Figure 8.3.

8.3   Face representations

Many early approaches for face recognition investigated global representations [15–18], which are built from a collected set of face images by employing subspace

Figure 8.3   Example faces from the IJB-A dataset [14]

learning techniques. These holistic methods represent each face image as a single high-dimensional vector by concatenating the gray values of all its pixels. Subspace learning algorithms are then employed to learn a low-dimensional representation, which can well capture the global information of the whole face. Though simple and efficient, they are not robust to local appearance variations caused by, e.g., different lighting conditions, pose, expression, occlusion and misalignment. Therefore, directly when applying these methods to face images captured in real-world scenarios, it may be extremely difficult to achieve satisfactory recognition performance. In order to overcome this problem, several representations have been specifically developed as face descriptors for unconstrained face recognition. These methods include: handcrafted local appearance features, descriptors learned by encoding local microstructures, aggregation of local appearance features and features learned by deep neural networks (DNNs).

8.3.1   Local appearance features

Local appearance models, as opposed to holistic representations, have several advantages. First of all, as these models take into account both the shape and texture of the human face, they are generally more stable to local appearance variations than holistic descriptors. Some of the local appearance models, successfully applied for unconstrained face recognition, include Gabor spatial frequency decomposition [19], local binary patterns (LBP) [20], scale-invariant feature transform (SIFT) [21], histogram of oriented gradient [22] and biologically inspired features [23]. These local representations and several adapted versions of the same have been widely used during the early stage of face recognition research and testing on the LFW dataset [23–29]. For example, in [24], Wolf *et al.* applied a family of patch-based LBPs to capture statistics of local patch similarities. These descriptors were extracted by using short bit strings to encode similarities between neighboring patches, thus capturing information which is complementary to pixel-based descriptors. Cox *et al.* [23] randomly generated a multitude of complex, nonlinear, multilayer neuromorphic feature representations from face images and then screened them to find those best suited for unconstrained face recognition. In [29], Seo and Milanfar developed a visual descriptor named locally adaptive regression kernel (LARK). This representation measures a self-similarity based on the geodesic distance between a center pixel and its surrounding pixels within a local neighborhood.

8.3.2   Descriptors learned by encoding local microstructures

Handcrafted models, such as those presented in Section 8.3.1, may not be well adapted to the underlying dataset and/or the application domain. In order to obtain descriptors more robust to complex variations in the face appearance, as commonly seen in real-world scenarios, researchers have exploited data-driven techniques. In [30], a learning-based encoding (LE) method was presented, which used unsupervised learning methods to encode the local microstructures of the face into a set of discrete codes. Hussain *et al.* [31] generalized local pattern features by using vector quantization and lookup table. In [32], higher order statistics of local nonbinarized pixel patterns were computed as a new image representation for face analysis. Cui *et al.* [37] divided each image/video into several spatial/spatial–temporal blocks and then represented each block by sum pooling the nonnegative sparse codes of position-free patches, sampled within the block. After applying Whitened Principal Component Analysis, a compact spatial face region descriptor for each face image/video is obtained. The discriminant face descriptor (DFD) proposed by Lei *et al.* [33] introduced discriminative learning into three steps of LBP-like feature extraction. The discriminant image filters, the optimal soft sampling matrix and the dominant patterns were all learned from training images.

8.3.3   Aggregation of local appearance features

Apart from learning representations directly from pixel intensities, there are also visual representations based on orderless aggregation of local appearance features. For example, in [34], a visual dictionary was obtained by pooling a large number of feature vectors, extracted by 2D discrete cosine transform decomposition, from training faces. Each test face was then described in terms of multiregion probabilistic histograms of visual words. The loss of spatial relation within each region, due to averaging, may result in an increased robustness to face misalignment. Simonyan *et al.* [35] employed the fisher vector (FV) encoding algorithm to aggregate a large set of feature vectors (dense SIFT) into a high-dimensional vector representation. By augmenting each local feature (e.g., LBP or SIFT) with its location, Li *et al.* [36] trained a Gaussian mixture model (GMM) to capture the spatial-appearance distribution of all face images in the training corpus. Each Gaussian component then contributes to match corresponding feature pairs between two face samples.

8.3.4   Features learned by deep neural networks

In recent years, social networks such as Facebook, Twitter and YouTube have contributed to accumulate an unprecedented volume of photos and videos in the Internet network. The large volume of face data, together with more and more powerful computational resources, required the application of more effective statistical models. However, traditional data-driven approaches have limited capacity to leverage such large amount of training data. To address this problem, researchers have turned to DNNs, which have been successfully applied in fields like computer vision, language modeling and speech analysis. For vision systems, deep models have significantly improved the system robustness to common variations caused by illumination changes, pose/view changes and occlusions.

In 2012, Huang *et al.* [38] applied convolutional deep belief networks to learn hierarchical representations from face images. To take advantage of the global structure of the human face, they developed local convolutional restricted Boltzmann machines, assuming stationarity of features across the whole face image. On the LFW benchmark, the designed deep networks, trained using unsupervised learning, achieved an accuracy comparable to a system based on the combination of handcrafted image descriptors. The surge of interest in using DNN for unconstrained face recognition started after DeepFace [39], where a nine-layer DNN was trained on an identity labeled dataset of 4 million face images belonging to more than 4,000 identities. Instead of using the standard convolutional layers, the DeepFace network used several locally connected layers without weight sharing. With the learned face representations, an accuracy of 97.35% was obtained on the LFW dataset, closely approaching human-level performance. DeepFace also achieved an impressive accuracy of 92.5% on the YTF dataset.

Following DeepFace, several deep models have been developed to learn robust face representations. Among these, variations of deep convolutional neural networks (CNNs) are the most widely used [40]. The convolution and pooling operations in CNNs are specially designed to extract visual features hierarchically, from local low-level to global high-level features. Different supervision signals have been used to guide the training process. For example, Sun *et al.* [41] learned the Deep hidden IDentity features (DeepID) by using the identification supervision signal, i.e., optimizing the softmax loss function, which allows the learned features to represent rich identity-related or interpersonal variations. In [42], to obtain more discriminative features, they further employed a verification signal for supervision (i.e., optimizing the contrastive loss). Consequently, the Deep IDentification-verification features (DeepID2) were learned in an attempt to both increase interpersonal variations and reduce intrapersonal variations.

In [43], Schroff *et al.* trained a FaceNet by using a triplet-based loss function. Each triplet consists of two matching face thumbnails and a nonmatching face thumbnail. The loss function is built to separate the positive pair from the negative one by a distance margin. In order to enhance the discriminative power of features learned by optimizing the softmax loss function, Wen *et al.* [44] applied the center loss to guide the deep learning process. This loss function allows to simultaneously learn a center for deep features of each class while penalizing the distances between deep features and their corresponding class centers. With the joint supervision of softmax loss and center loss, robust CNNs can be trained to obtain features with interclass separability and intraclass compactness.

8.4 Metric learning approaches

Once discriminative face representations are designed and built from the available face images, the next step to be performed is face matching. This is the task of computing the distance/similarity between two face descriptors. The performance of many face recognition algorithms critically depends upon the distance metric which has been used. In order to match faces captured from real-world scenarios, researchers have resorted to exploit metric learning approaches to learn a metric which is more suitable to the task at hand. Most of the developed works on metric learning rely on learning a Mahalanobis distance based on an objective function defined by means of a labeled training set or a set of positive (from the same class) and negative (from different classes) pairs. The difference among metric learning methods mainly lies in the objective functions, which are designed for specific tasks, e.g., clustering [45] and k-nearest neighbor (kNN) classification [46].

In 2009, Guillaumin *et al.* [25] investigated metric learning on matching challenging real-world face images, obtaining impressive performance. They proposed two methods for learning robust Mahalanobis metrics. The first is a logistic discriminant approach which learns the metric from a set of labeled image pairs. The second is a marginalized kNN approach, which computes the probability of two face images belonging to the same class. Nguyen *et al.* [26] presented a Cosine Similarity Metric Learning (CSML) approach. In [47], Cao *et al.* developed a regularization framework to learn similarity metrics over the intrapersonal subspace. The objective function was formulated by considering both the discriminative power and the robustness to large intrapersonal variations. The pairwise-constrained multiple metric learning in [37] was developed with the aim to effectively integrate multiple face region descriptors. In [48], Hu *et al.* developed a deep metric learning method to learn hierarchical nonlinear transformations through a DNN.

8.5   Background information investigation

For matching unconstrained face images, quite a few recent approaches have been focused on exploiting an additional set of face images. The images contained in this background dataset do not belong to the subject/subjects being compared or tested. This complementary face set has been referenced in the literature in several ways, including background database, cohort set, generic set, reference set, library, memory, etc.

From a set of background samples, Wolf *et al.* [24] defined several similarity functions to learn a discriminative model exclusive to the pair of images being compared. In [49], an additional identity dataset was employed for building a set of either attribute or simile classifiers. For comparing two faces under significantly different settings, Yin *et al.* [27] proposed to associate one input face with alike identities from an extra generic identity dataset. For the same purpose, Schroff *et al.* [50] proposed to describe an input face by an ordered list of identities from a library. In the ordered list, identities are ranked according to their similarity to the input face image. The similarity between two face images is then computed as the similarity of their corresponding ordered lists. To handle unconstrained face pair matching, Tistarelli *et al.* [51] developed a picture-specific cohort score normalization approach, by extracting discriminative cohort coefficients from a pool of sorted cohort samples using polynomial regression.

8.6   Pose-invariant face recognition

For face recognition in uncontrolled real-world scenarios, handling appearance variations caused by pose has always been a difficult problem. In order to address misalignment issues caused by pose changes, quite a few recent approaches focus on designing representations by pooling information over an image region. Visual representations based on orderless aggregation of local appearance features are among these techniques, e.g., the multiregion probabilistic histograms in [34] and the FV faces in [35]. Pooling operations, commonly used in CNNs, also belong to such approaches [41–44]. These approaches work well when faces are presented with small pose changes. However, more specialized techniques are needed when dealing with large pose variations.

In [52], for each gallery subject, a 3D model was estimated from a single frontal 2D image using the Generic Elastic Model approach. Given a test query, an initial estimate of the pose was obtained using a linear regression approach based on automatic facial landmark annotation. Each 3D gallery model was subsequently rendered at different poses within a limited search space about the estimated pose, and the resulting images were matched against the test query. In [54], Yi *et al.* built a 3D deformable model and defined many feature points on the 3D model. The pose and shape of a 2D input face image was obtained by fitting the 3D model to the image and then projecting the defined 3D feature points to the image plane. Finally, pose robust features are extracted at the projected feature points by using Gabor filters.

Many recent attempts focus on normalizing the pose of a profile face to a canonical frontal view. For example, in [53], Asthana *et al.* proposed to render a profile face to a frontal view by automatically fitting a 3D face model to the 2D input image. In this work, pose-dependent correspondences between 2D landmark points and 3D model vertices were investigated. Taigman *et al.* [39] presented a system to warp a detected 2D facial crop to a frontal one based on the explicit 3D modeling of faces. Similarly working on face frontalization, Hassner *et al.* [55] explored a simpler approach by using a single, unmodified 3D surface as an approximation to the shape of all input faces. In [56], a pose-adaptive 3D morphable model fitting algorithm was proposed to automatically generate a natural face image with frontal pose and neutral expression. The authors further developed an identity preserving 3D transformation method to normalize the pose and expression. Finally, an inpainting method, based on Possion editing, was used to fill the invisible region caused by self-occlusion. Instead of investigating 3D models, Zhu *et al.* [57] proposed a deep learning framework to recover the canonical view of face images.

8.7   Performance evaluation

In the above several sections, we talked about existing techniques developed for unconstrained face recognition. In Table 8.1, we summarize the performance these techniques can achieve on View 2 of the LFW benchmark under the restricted protocol. As is shown, deep learning-based models [39,41,43] lead to top performance. The success is largely due to the use of massive training data. In Table 8.2, we show the

Table 8.1   Verification accuracies (%) on View 2 of the LFW benchmark under the restricted protocol

	Algorithm	Accuracy
Wolf *et al.* [24]	One-shot similarity	83.98
Cao *et al.* [30]	Multiple LE descriptors	84.45
Nguyen *et al.* [26]	CSML	88.00
Seo *et al.* [29]	LARK	85.10
Cox *et al.* [23]	Biologically inspired model	88.10
Yin *et al.* [27]	Associate-predict model	90.57
Lei *et al.* [33]	DFD	84.02
Hussian *et al.* [31]	Local quantized patterns	86.20
Li *et al.* [36]	GMM encoding	84.08
Simonyan *et al.* [35]	FV encoding	87.47
Yi *et al.* [54]	3D model fitting	87.77
Hassner *et al.* [55]	3D face frontalization	85.63
Taigman *et al.* [39]	Deep neural network	97.15
Sun *et al.* [41]	CNN with softmax loss	97.45
Schroff *et al.* [43]	CNN with triplet loss	97.15

Table 8.2   The amount of training data used for building leading deep CNN models on the LFW benchmark together with verification accuracies (%)

System	# Training images	# Training identities	Accuracy
Human [39]	–	–	97.53
DeepFace [39]	4M	4K	97.15
DeepID [41]	203K	10K	97.45
DeepID2 [42]	203K	10K	99.15
DeepID3 [58]	290K	12K	99.53
FaceNet [43]	260M	8M	97.15
VGGFace [59]	2.6M	2.6K	98.95
Face++ [60]	5M	20K	99.50

amount of training data used for building leading deep CNN models on the LFW benchmark. By using a large amount of outside labeled data to train CNN models, many systems are able to achieve better than human performance. For example, in Table 8.1, the reported recognition accuracy of DeepID2, DeepID3, VGGFace and Face++ is always higher than the accuracy achieved by humans, when performing the same recognition task.

8.8   Open issues

As reviewed above, comprehensive efforts have been devoted to unconstrained face recognition. For some benchmarks, many systems have achieved performance better than humans. There are still some challenging issues remaining to be addressed.

8.8.1   Large-scale face recognition in real-world security scenarios

Recent face recognition algorithms applied to public benchmarks show that face recognition is performing stunningly well, surpassing human performance. However, face recognition at scale, especially in surveillance scenarios, is far from solved. The release of the MegaFace dataset and the Chinese ID benchmark [60] emphasized the importance and difficulty of this problem.

8.8.2   Pose-invariant face recognition

As reviewed in Section 8.6, several approaches have been proposed to tackle large pose variations. However, these techniques are limited, especially those based on 3D models. Since faces are 3D objects, researchers are encouraged to resort to 3D modeling techniques for pose-invariant face recognition.

8.8.3   Age-invariant face recognition

While considerable progress has been made on recognizing faces collected from the Internet, age-invariant face recognition has not received substantial attention compared to other facial variations due to pose, lighting and expression. Facial aging is a complex process that affects both the shape and texture of the human face. Thus, developing representations and matching schemes that are robust to changes due to facial aging is of vital importance to unconstrained face recognition.

8.8.4   Dependence on large amount of labeled training data

As shown in Table 8.1, most top-performing deep networks in the LFW benchmark need a large number of labeled training face images. Such large labeled training dataset may not always be available. Hence, techniques that work well with unlabeled data or small labeled dataset are needed.

Acknowledgments

This research work has been partially supported by a grant from the European Commission (H2020 MSCA RISE 690907 "IDENTITY") and partially supported by a grant from the National Natural Science Foundation of China (Grant No. 61603391).

References

[1]   Zhao W., Chellappa R., Phillips P.J., and Rosenfeld A. 'Face recognition: A literature survey'. *ACM Computing Survey*. 2003;35(4): 399–458.

[2]   Zeng Z., Pantic M., Roisman G.I., and Huang, T.S. 'A survey of affect recognition methods: Audio, visual, and spontaneous expressions'. *IEEE Transactions on Pattern Analysis and Machine Intelligence*. 2009;31(1): 39–58.

[3]   Sun Y., Zhang M., Sun Z., and Tan T. 'Demographic analysis from biometric data: Achievements, challenges, and new frontiers'. *IEEE Transactions on Pattern Analysis and Machine Intelligence*. 2017.

[4]   Phillips P.J., Moon H., Rizvi S.A., and Rauss P.J. 'The FERET evaluation methodology for face-recognition algorithms'. *IEEE Transactions on Pattern Analysis and Machine Intelligence*. 2000;22(10): 1090–1104.

[5]   Sim T., Baker S., and Bsat M. 'The CMU pose, illumination, and expression (PIE) database'. *Proceedings of IEEE International Conference on Automatic Face and Gesture Recognition*. 2000. pp. 53–58.

[6]   Phillips P.J., Flynn P.J., Scruggs T., *et al.* 'Overview of the face recognition grand challenge'. *Proceedings of IEEE International Conference on Computer Vision and Pattern Recognition*. 2005. pp. 947–954.

[7]   Huang G.B., Ramesh M., and Berg T., Learned-Miller E. *Labeled faces in the wild: A database for studying face recognition in unconstrained environments*. Technical Report 07-49, University of Massachusetts, Amherst, 2007.

[8]   Viola P., and Jones M.J. 'Robust real-time face detection'. *International Journal of Computer Vision*. 2004;57(2): 137–154.

[9]   Kumar N., Berg A.C., Belhumeur P.N., and Nayar S.K. 'Attribute and simile classifiers for face verification'. *Proceedings of IEEE International Conference on Computer Vision*. 2009. pp. 365–372.

[10]   Wolf L., Hassner T., and Maoz I. 'Face recognition in unconstrained videos with matched background similarity'. *Proceedings of IEEE International Conference on Computer Vision and Pattern Recognition*. 2011. pp. 529–534.

[11]   Beveridge J.R., Phillips P.J., Bolme D.S., *et al.* 'The challenge of face recognition from digital point-and-shoot cameras'. *Proceedings of IEEE International Conference on Biometrics: Theory, Applications and Systems*. 2013. pp. 1–8.

[12]   Miller D., Brossard E., Seitz S., and Kemelmacher-Shlizerman I. 'Megaface: A million faces for recognition at scale'. arXiv:1505.02108. 2015.

[13]   Ng H.W., and Winkler S. 'A data-driven approach to cleaning large face datasets'. *Proceedings of IEEE International Conference on Image Processing*. 2014. pp. 343–347.

[14]   Klare B.F., Klein B., Taborsky E., *et al.* 'Pushing the frontiers of unconstrained face detection and recognition: IARPA Janus Benchmark A'. *Proceedings of IEEE International Conference on Computer Vision and Pattern Recognition*. 2015. pp. 1931–1939.

[15]   Turk M.A., and Pentland A.P. 'Face recognition using eigenfaces'. *Proceedings of IEEE International Conference on Computer Vision and Pattern Recognition*. 1991. pp. 586–591.

[16]   Belhumeur P.N., Hespanha J.P., and Kriegman D.J. 'Eigenfaces vs. fisherfaces: Recognition using class specific linear projection'. *IEEE Transactions on Pattern Analysis and Machine Intelligence*. 1997;19(7): 711–720.

[17]   Yang J., Zhang D., Frangi A.F., and Yang J.Y. 'Two-dimensional PCA: A new approach to appearance-based face representation and recognition'. *IEEE Transactions on Pattern Analysis and Machine Intelligence*. 2004;26(1): 131–137.

[18] He X., Yan S., Hu Y., Niyogi P., and Zhang H.J. 'Face recognition using lapla-cianfaces'. *IEEE Transactions on Pattern Analysis and Machine Intelligence.* 2005;27(3): 328–340.

[19] Liu C., and Wechsler H. 'Gabor feature based classification using the enhanced fisher linear discriminant model for face recognition'. *IEEE Transactions on Image Processing.* 2002;11(4): 467–476.

[20] Ahonen T., Hadid A., and Pietikäinen M. 'Face description with local binary patterns: Application to face recognition'. *IEEE Transactions on Pattern Analysis and Machine Intelligence.* 2006;28(12): 2037–2041.

[21] Lowe D.G. 'Distinctive image features from scale-invariant keypoints'. *International Journal of Computer Vision.* 2004;60(2): 91–110.

[22] Dalal N., and Triggs B. 'Histograms of oriented gradients for human detection'. *Proceedings of IEEE International Conference on Computer Vision and Pattern Recognition.* 2005. pp. 886–893.

[23] Cox D., and Pinto N. 'Beyond simple features: A large-scale feature search approach to unconstrained face recognition'. *Proceedings of IEEE International Conference on Automatic Face & Gesture Recognition and Workshops.* 2011. pp. 8–15.

[24] Wolf L., Hassner T., and Taigman Y. 'Effective unconstrained face recognition by combining multiple descriptors and learned background statistics'. *IEEE Transactions on Pattern Analysis and Machine Intelligence.* 2011;33(10): 1978–1990.

[25] Guillaumin M., Verbeek J., and Schmid C. 'Is that you? Metric learning approaches for face identification'. *Proceedings of IEEE International Conference on Computer Vision.* 2009. pp. 498–505.

[26] Nguyen H.V., and Bai L. 'Cosine similarity metric learning for face verification'. *Proceedings of Asian Conference on Computer Vision.* 2010. pp. 709–720.

[27] Yin Q., Tang X., and Sun J. 'An associate-predict model for face recognition'. *Proceedings of IEEE International Conference on Computer vision and Pattern Recognition.* 2011. pp. 497–504.

[28] Taigman Y., Wolf L., and Hassner T. 'Multiple one-shots for utilizing class label information'. *Proceedings of British Machine Vision Conference.* 2009. pp. 1–12.

[29] Seo H.J., and Milanfar P. 'Face verification using the lark representation'. *IEEE Transactions on Information Forensics and Security.* 2011;6(4): 1275–1286.

[30] Cao Z., Yin Q., Tang X., and Sun J. 'Face recognition with learning-based descriptor'. *Proceedings of IEEE International Conference on Computer Vision and Pattern Recognition.* 2010. pp. 2707–2714.

[31] Hussain S.U., Napolén T., and Jurie F. 'Face recognition using local quantized patterns'. *Proceedings of British Machine Vision Conference.* 2012.

[32] Sharma G., ul Hussain S., and Jurie F. 'Local higher-order statistics (LHS) for texture categorization and facial analysis'. *Proceedings of European Conference on Computer Vision.* 2012. pp. 1–12.

[33]   Lei Z., Pietikäinen M., and Li S.Z. 'Learning discriminant face descriptor'. *IEEE Transactions on Pattern Analysis and Machine Intelligence*. 2014;36(2): 289–302.

[34]   Sanderson C., and Lovell B. 'Multi-region probabilistic histograms for robust and scalable identity inference'. *Proceedings of International Conference on Biometrics*. 2009. pp. 199–208.

[35]   Simonyan K., Parkhi O.M., Vedaldi A., and Zisserman A. 'Fisher vector faces in the wild'. *Proceedings of British Machine Vision Conference*. 2013.

[36]   Li H., Hua G., Lin Z., Brandt J., and Yang J. 'Probabilistic elastic matching for pose invariant face recognition'. *Proceedings of IEEE International Conference on Computer Vision and Pattern Recognition*. 2013. pp. 3499–3506.

[37]   Cui Z., Li W., Xu D., Shan S., and Chen X. 'Fusing robust face region descriptors via multiple metric learning for face recognition in the wild'. *Proceedings of IEEE International Conference on Computer Vision and Pattern Recognition*. 2013. pp. 3554–3561.

[38]   Huang G.B., Lee H., and Learned-Miller E. 'Learning hierarchical representations for face verification with convolutional deep belief networks'. *Proceedings of IEEE International Conference on Computer Vision and Pattern Recognition*. 2012. pp. 2518–2525.

[39]   Taigman Y., Yang M., Ranzato M.A., and Wolf L. 'Deepface: Closing the gap to human-level performance in face verification'. *Proceedings of IEEE International Conference on Computer Vision and Pattern Recognition*. 2014. pp. 1701–1708.

[40]   LeCun Y., Bottou L., Bengio Y., and Haffner P. 'Gradient-based learning applied to document recognition'. *IEEE*. 1998;86(11): 2278–2324.

[41]   Sun Y., Wang X., and Tang X. 'Deep learning face representation from predicting 10,000 classes'. *Proceedings of IEEE International Conference on Computer Vision and Pattern Recognition*. 2014. pp. 1891–1898.

[42]   Sun Y., Chen Y., Wang X., and Tang X. 'Deep learning face representation by joint identification-verification'. *Proceedings of Advances in Neural Information Processing Systems*. 2014. pp. 1988–1996.

[43]   Schroff F., Kalenichenko D., and Philbin J. 'Facenet: A unified embedding for face recognition and clustering'. *Proceedings of IEEE International Conference on Computer Vision and Pattern Recognition*. 2015. pp. 815–823.

[44]   Wen Y., Zhang K., Li Z., and Qiao Y. 'A discriminative feature learning approach for deep face recognition'. *Proceedings of European Conference on Computer Vision*. 2016. pp. 499–515.

[45]   Xing E.P., Jordan M.I., Russell S.J., and Ng A.Y. 'Distance metric learning with application to clustering with side-information'. *Proceedings of Advances in Neural Information Processing Systems*. 2003. pp. 521–528.

[46]   Weinberger K.Q., Blitzer J., and Saul L.K. 'Distance metric learning for large margin nearest neighbor classification'. *Proceedings of Advances in Neural Information Processing Systems*. 2006. pp. 1473–1480.

[47] Cao Q., Ying Y., and Li P. 'Similarity metric learning for face recognition'. *Proceedings of IEEE International Conference on Computer Vision.* 2013. pp. 2408–2415.

[48] Hu J., Lu J., and Tan Y.P. 'Discriminative deep metric learning for face verification in the wild'. *Proceedings of IEEE International Conference on Computer Vision and Pattern Recognition.* 2014. pp. 1875–1882.

[49] Kumar N., Berg A., Belhumeur P.N., and Nayar S.K. 'Describable visual attributes for face verification and image search'. *IEEE Transactions on Pattern Analysis and Machine Intelligence.* 2011;33(10): 1962–1977.

[50] Schroff F., Treibitz T., Kriegman D., and Belongie S. 'Pose, illumination and expression invariant pairwise face-similarity measure via Doppelgänger list comparison'. *Proceedings of IEEE International Conference on Computer Vision.* 2011. pp. 2494–2501.

[51] Tistarelli M., Sun Y., and Poh N. 'On the use of discriminative cohort score normalization for unconstrained face recognition'. *IEEE Transactions on Information Forensics and Security.* 2014;9(12): 2063–2075.

[52] Prabhu U., Heo J., and Savvides M. 'Unconstrained pose-invariant face recognition using 3D generic elastic models'. *IEEE Transactions on Pattern Analysis and Machine Intelligence.* 2011;33(10): 1952–1961.

[53] Asthana A., Marks T.K., Jones M.J., Tieu K.H., and Rohith M.V. 'Fully automatic pose-invariant face recognition via 3D pose normalization'. *Proceedings of IEEE International Conference on Computer Vision.* 2011. pp. 937–944.

[54] Yi D., Lei Z., and Li S.Z. 'Towards pose robust face recognition'. *Proceedings of IEEE International Conference on Computer Vision and Pattern Recognition.* 2013. pp. 3539–3545.

[55] Hassner T., Harel S., Paz E., and Enbar R. 'Effective face frontalization in unconstrained images'. *Proceedings of IEEE International Conference on Computer Vision and Pattern Recognition.* 2015. pp. 4295–4304.

[56] Zhu X., Lei Z., Yan J., Yi D., and Li S.Z. 'High-fidelity pose and expression normalization for face recognition in the wild'. *Proceedings of IEEE International Conference on Computer Vision and Pattern Recognition.* 2015. pp. 787–796.

[57] Zhu Z., Luo P., Wang X., and Tang X. 'Recover canonical-view faces in the wild with deep neural networks'. arXiv:1404.3543. 2014.

[58] Sun Y, Liang D, Wang X, and Tang X. 'Deepid3: Face recognition with very deep neural networks'. arXiv:1502.00873. 2015.

[59] Parkhi O.M., Vedaldi A., and Zisserman A. 'Deep face recognition'. *Proceedings of British Machine Vision Conference.* 2015.

[60] Zhou E., Cao Z., and Yin Q. 'Naive-deep face recognition: Touching the limit of LFW benchmark or not?' arXiv:1501.04690. 2015.

Part II

Technologies and applications

Chapter 9

Hardware security: side-channel attacks and hardware Trojans

Eslam Yahya[1,2] and Yehea Ismail[3]

9.1 Introduction

Modern information systems increasingly provide remote access to the users' data. Cloud computing, Internet of Things (IoT), smart cities, autonomous cars, vehicle-to-vehicle communication (V2V), smart homes, and many other applications rely on communicating devices through the internet and/or customized communication backbones. The network structure in many cases, such as IoT and V2V, are decentralized networks in which nodes can jump in and out in an ad hoc style. These systems must be secured against unauthorized data access to protect the users' privacy. In addition, very strong identity management is needed to prevent hackers to log into the network and issue harmful activities or false alarms [1–4].

In software-based security frameworks, it is relatively easy for experienced attackers to contaminate the software stack, and hence, compromise the system security. As shown in Figure 9.1(a), encryption keys and secret information are accessible within the software stack in the software-based security. If the software stack is contaminated, these secret keys can be transmitted to the attackers, and therefore, the system security can be compromised. In contrast, hardware-based security systems (Figure 9.1(b)) contain a specialized hardware to perform encryption and user-identity management algorithms. All secret information and encryption keys are kept inside this hardware, therefore, they are not accessible to the software stack and no secret information leakage can happen due to software contaminations. Most of the modern systems move toward hardware-based security frameworks such as hardware security modules [5], cryptoprocessors [6], and trusted computing modules.

Moving all security functions to hardware makes the system safer; however, it is still possible for a highly skilled attacker to extract confidential information. Side-channel attacks are security breaches based on information extracted from the physical implementation of the hardware [5,8,9]. Side-channel attacks do not try

[1]The Ohio State University, Electrical and Computer Engineering Department, USA
[2]Benha Faculty of Engineering, Electrical Engineering Department, Benha University, Egypt
[3]Center of Nanoelectronics and Devices (CND), American University in Cairo, Zewail City

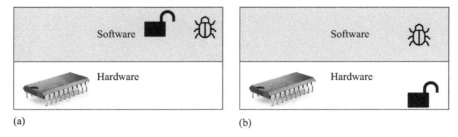

(a)   (b)

Figure 9.1   *(a) Software-based security (secret information is exposed to malicious software); (b) hardware-based security (secret information kept inside the hardware and protected from malicious software)*

Figure 9.2   *Common types of side-channel attacks (from right to left): fault attack, timing attack, power attack, EMI attack, and acoustic attack*

to break the theoretical strength of the cryptographic algorithm; they use leaked information through physical inspection of the hardware. Commonly used methods for side-channel attack, shown in Figure 9.2, are power analysis, fault attack, timing attack, electromagnetic attack, and acoustic attacks [7,10,26,39,45,50].

The objective of the attacker in this method is to identify the computation performed by the hardware through one of these phenomena. For example, by monitoring the power consumption of the hardware, the attacker can correlate different power traces with different instructions (multiplication, addition, etc.). More details about different side-channel attacks are discussed later in this chapter. Different countermeasures shall be applied to eliminate or reduce the emitted information (such as Electromagnetic Interference (EMI) or acoustics) or decorrelate the emitted information and the different processing performed by the hardware [10,16,33,35,49,56]. As shown in Figure 9.3, security systems must use side-channel attack-hardened hardware components to protect their confidential data.

Modern systems contain many hardware components. The trust in components supply chain is one of the major parameters judging the strength of the security system. Similar to software, hardware components can be contaminated by malicious

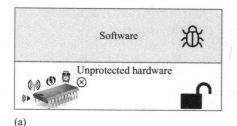 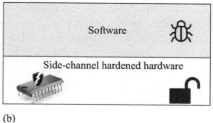

(a)   (b)

Figure 9.3   *(a) Using unprotected hardware can leak confidential information
through side-channel attacks; (b) side-channel hardened hardware is
safer for modern security systems*

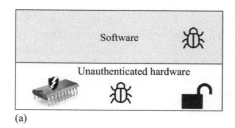 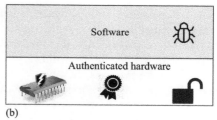

(a)   (b)

Figure 9.4   *(a) Unauthenticated hardware may contain hardware Trojans that leak
confidential information; (b) by authenticating the hardware, your
system shall be trusted to perform operations on plain text and
secret keys*

hardware Trojans (HT) [3,69,70]. HT are malicious modification of the IC design
to hide a hardware block that is able to leak confidential information, alter the chip
functionality, or entirely disable the chip. Modern systems are using huge number of
hardware IPs, which are delivered by different design houses and then implemented
by many fabrication companies. The supply chain is so long and not easy to be traced,
which make it complex to trust all the hardware components. Unlike the software,
HT must be shipped with your hardware; it is very hard to contaminate your hardware
after being deployed. An efficient procedure is to inspect your hardware before the
deployment. There are many techniques to detect HT such as physical inspection,
functional testing, and unclonable functions [71,72]. In hardware security, physical
unclonable functions (PUFs) use the random parameters introduced during fabrication
to implement a challenge-response authentication pairs, which are unique for every
chip. The uniqueness of these pairs comes from the fact that, even with the same
fabrication process, you can't produce exactly the same physical parameters for two
identical chips. PUFs can be used to authenticate the security chips to be sure they are
original chips (fabricated by a trusted vendor) and not cloned copy that might contain
some HT. As explained in Figure 9.4, verifying the originality of the used hardware is
a very important step to be sure that the hardware is not contaminated by any Trojans.

Information security in different systems is originally based on how the hardware is secured and trusted. By secured, we mean that the hardware is immune against hardware attacks such as side-channel attacks. By trusted, we mean that the hardware does not contain any malicious modules or HT, which are able to leak sensitive information to an unauthorized entity. The hardware security importance is extended to protect the IP rights and to detect any IP infringement.

9.2   Side-channel attacks and their countermeasures

Cryptographic algorithms and signing schemes are designed to make the attacker task very time/resources consuming to compromise the algorithm and retrieve the secret data. Cryptanalysis is the science of studying the crypto algorithm to breach the system through some mathematical vulnerabilities. Cryptanalysis attacks are generic and can be applied to any implementation since it is related to the algorithm itself. In contrast, side-channel attacks are based on physical observations of the algorithm implementation not the algorithm itself. As a result, side-channel attacks are not general as cryptanalysis; however, they can be more serious as their effectiveness depends on how the design engineers are knowledgeable and invest time to implement countermeasures to protect their hardware.

Side-channel attacks can be classified into invasive and noninvasive attacks [2,21,29]. *Invasive* attacks need to depackage the chip to gain full access to the silicon die. By using different microscopy techniques, such as optical and electron microscopy, the attacker can have clear images for the chip layout [7,52,53]. Using this layout information, the attacker can extract different information about the used cryptographic algorithm and the actual places for storing keys and plain text (registers and memory). Further invasive attack can be performed by "microprobing" in which the attacker can eavesdrop on signals inside the chip and extract secret data. On the other hand, noninvasive attacks do not destructively interface to the chip; they use leaked information such as EMI, power consumption, and computation time. For example, crypto-processors are consuming different amount of power based on the current task they are performing. By observing the power consumption and correlating it to the processor tasks, attacker can know about the task in execution, which is known as power analysis attack. *Semi-invasive* attacks is another category in which it is required to depackage the chip but the die itself remains intact. Techniques in this category depend on optical imaging and optical probing to eavesdropping on secret keys and sensitive data [28]. The focus of this chapter is the noninvasive attacks.

Side-channel attacks can be classified based on the interference with the security device into active and passive attacks. In *active* attacks, the adversary manipulates the crypto-device input and/or environment to alter the device behavior. Therefore, by observing the change in the output, the secret key can be extracted [2]. On the other hand, *passive* attacks do not interfere with the device operation, the attacker tries to extract secret data by observing the physical properties of the device (power consumption, EMI, execution time, etc.).

9.2.1   *Power analysis attack*

Power consumption is an instantaneous physical property that depends on the data to be processed and the operation to be performed. In power analysis attack, the adversary tries to reveal secret data that are stored in the crypto-device by monitoring the device power consumption and correlate this consumption with the data or the process to be performed [12,14,16,17]. The attackers record the power traces, build a power model for the device, and make a guess on the secret information to be revealed. By comparing the measured power traces with the estimated ones from the power model, attackers accept or update their guess about secret information. Power analysis attacks are classified into simple power analysis (SPA) and differential power analysis (DPA).

SPA uses single (or very few) power traces to recover the secret keys by directly observing features of the power trace. Conditions for a successful SPA are hard to satisfy. For example, the crypto-device implementations must have significantly different power consumption depending on the secret key bits. In addition, the dependency in power traces should have a change in the absolute measured power that is considerably larger than any noise [15].

In contrast, DPA uses a large number of recorded power traces and statistically exploit the data dependency in the power traces to extract the secret key. Compared to SPA, DPA is independent of the details of the hardware implementation (how much absolute power is consumed to perform specific operations); on the contrary, it depends on how much the power traces will be different when the value of the data is changed (data dependency) [18,19,20,22,60,64].

The idea behind DPA is explained in Figure 9.5; large number of data is encrypted or decrypted using the target device and the power traces are recorded. The attacker constructs a power model for the device and chooses a hypothetical key. Using the power model, hypothetical power traces are constructed and compared with the measured traces. Using statistical analysis and divide-and-conquer algorithm, the hypothetical key is iteratively updated until the secret key is revealed [11,13,59].

9.2.1.1   Countermeasures

Power analysis generally is a passive attack; the adversary passively monitors the normal operation of the crypto-device and records the power traces. To avoid power attacks, the device must be engineered so that its power consumption does not leak information about the stored secret data. In other words, the task of power analysis countermeasure is to make the power consumption independent of the intermediate encryption values. There are many techniques to protect the crypto-device against the power analysis attacks [14,16,64]; we list the following.

> *Protocol*: Recording more power traces with the same secret key is the key point that gives the attacker a higher chance to guess the key. Changing the secret key frequently is one of the techniques that reduces the risk of power analysis attack. The lower the number of messages encrypted using the same key, the safer the device against power analysis attacks [10].

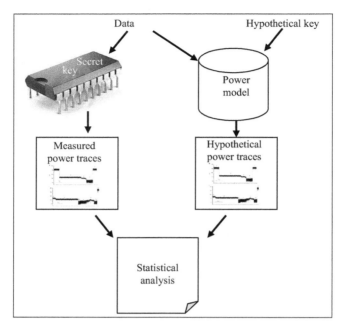

Figure 9.5   *DPA, measured power traces are compared with hypothetical power traces; the hypothetical key is iteratively updated until the secret key is revealed*

Hiding: The key idea behind power analysis is the dependency of the power on two parameters, the process to be executed and the input data (plain text and secret key). The target of hiding countermeasure is to remove these dependencies by making all the operations consume the same amount of power or making them consume random amount of power [10,12]. Viable technique for randomizing the power consumption is to randomly insert dummy operations before or after the encryption process. Equalizing the power consumption for all the operations can be achieved by two techniques, increasing the noise and reducing the signal. The simplest way to increase the noise for the operations is to perform different operations in parallel. In this way, the attacker is not able to identify the power consumption for specific operations. The second technique is to use special standard cell in which all logic cells are intentionally designed so that they use the same amount of power [10,12]. Another technique is to use emerging transistor technologies to reduce the power consumption and hide the power trances [22–25,68].

Masking: In this countermeasure, the objective is to randomize the intermediate results processed by the crypto-device [1]. This can be achieved on the algorithmic level (without removing the power/data dependency on the cell level) or by masking on the cell level [17]. Recently, masking on the cell level has gained attention [12]. Each intermediate value V is masked by a random value r. The hardware is processing the masked value Vr. The power needed to process the intermediate value V and the masked value Vr is different [10,12,17]. Dual-rail and asynchronous logic is one of the most efficient technique to realize these types of countermeasures. They will be discussed later in this chapter.

9.2.2 Fault analysis attack

In differential fault analysis (DFA) [26,27,29,30], the attacker injects faults into the crypto-device and analyzes the faulty ciphertext to extract the secret key; the same key is used to encrypt plaintext at least two times. The adversary provokes computational error during one of the encryption processes and records the output ciphertext in pairs, correct ciphertext and erroneous ciphertext. Both ciphertexts are encrypted identically to the point where the error is inserted. The attacker can guess the secret key by comparing the two ciphertexts and observing how the introduced error propagates in the encryption rounds after introducing the error [31–34]. The idea here is to introduce a known differential between the two encryptions and observe the propagation of this differential on a reduced number of rounds. Figure 9.6 illustrates how fault analysis is performed.

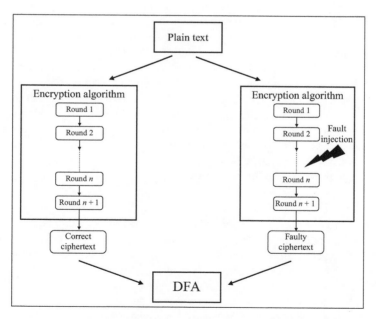

Figure 9.6 DFA, correct ciphertext and faulty ciphertext are compared; error is injected at the chosen phase of the encryption to introduce known differential between the two encryption in limited number of rounds

Choosing the right timing and target register in which the error is inserted are critical parameters for a successful DFA. These two parameters are strongly affected by the used method for the error injection. Since the error is injected repeatedly, the error injection method should be highly precise and very well controlled. Fault injection techniques can be classified according to their cost into high-cost- and low-cost techniques [26,27].

High-cost techniques: Techniques in this category are identified as the most powerful methods for side-channel attack. Using these techniques, the adversary gains access to the silicon die and he is able to inject errors in very specific part of the chip and at a very accurate timing. The first technique in this category is realized by targeting a flip-flop or memory cell by very concentrated light pulse to alter its contents (flip-up or flip-down); one successful example of this attack is using laser beam. The most effective method in this category is focused ion beam microsurgery; however, it can induce a permanent alteration to the circuit under attack [28].

Low-cost techniques: These techniques cannot achieve the same time and space accuracy reachable by high-cost techniques. On the other hand, their much lower cost and lighter experience requirements enable the attackers to collect massive numbers of erroneous ciphertext and select those best suitable for their fault model. The first technique in this category is underfeeding, in which the device under attack is powered by undervoltage power source [27]. Running the device on undervoltage supply, the adversary can insert errors to single/many bits, the lower the supply, the higher the number of errors. These errors appear first at the critical paths due to the setup-time violations. Decreasing the supply voltage gradually will increase the number of paths in which the error appears. The advantage with this method is its spatial accuracy since repeating the experiments with the same voltage scenarios is able to produce (most of the time) the same error scenario. The disadvantage of the underfeeding method is the loose control over the timing and the number of errors since this is dependent on the hardware architecture and the status of the critical paths. Overclocking is another viable method in the low-cost category. Operating the chip on a clock speed that is higher than its critical frequency will introduce an error to the data registers. The errors appear at the worst paths first and gradually will appear in other critical paths with the gradual increase in the clock speed.

9.2.2.1   Countermeasures

The concept of fault attacks is based on having two encryption outputs, one is correct and the other is erroneous due to an injected fault. Countermeasures for fault analysis are based on the concept of preventing the adversary from having correct encrypted message with its erroneous counterpart. To protect crypto-devices against fault attacks countermeasures based on error detection/correction and repeated computations are used [17,33]. In countermeasures based on error detection and correction, the protected device is equipped with error detection hardware to check for erroneous output, which should be masked to avoid the attack [35–37]. On the other hand, another technique is based on performing every encryption twice and compare the results; if any discrepancy is noticed, the system avoids producing the erroneous output and outs random bits instead [17,34].

9.2.3 Electromagnetic analysis

Integrated circuits (ICs) are composed of millions of transistors, which are communicating on chip using metal wires. All the data signal are transferred over these wires with their full speed. Metal wires inside the chip act as antennas and they can emit electromagnetic wave. The characteristics of this wave are determined by the electric current passing the wire, which is equivalent to a data bit traveling across the chip. Adversary can monitor the emitted EM radiation and analyze it to extract secret data, such as the encryption key; this attack is known as electromagnetic analysis (EMA) [38–41].

Like the DPA, EMA can be classified into two main categories, simple electromagnetic analysis (SEMA) and differential electromagnetic analysis (DEMA). In SEMA, the attacker derives the secret key from a single, or very few, EM trace. In this type of attacks, the attacker needs to know the details of the encryption algorithm and the architecture of the crypto-device. On the other hand, DEMA needs less information about the crypto system implementation but it requires much more EM traces and more complicated analysis [42].

One feature of EMA is the ability of recording the EMI traces without any contact with the device under attack; electric field and magnetic field probes can detect the radiation at distance from the chip. On the other hand, the setup of an EMA attack should be in an environment that has minimum electromagnetic noise to avoid interference with the emitted EMI from the chip. The attacker might need to use special setup like a Faraday cage.

9.2.3.1 Countermeasures

EMA countermeasures target to either reduce the electromagnetic emissions or randomize the EMI profile to make the adversary task harder [5,39]. To reduce the EM emanations, designers may use ultra-low-power design techniques [39,57], target transistor emerging technologies known by low-power consumption [22–25], or use strong shielding to isolate the crypto-device [44]. Randomization is an alternative technique to remove the correlation between the performed operation and its data on one side and the EM emanation on the other side. This can be implemented by randomizing the clock cycles, inserting dummy operations, and using shorter session keys [5,43,44].

9.2.4 Timing analysis attack

Timing attacks is based on the fact that execution differs according to the instruction to be executed. In addition, and for the same process, execution time may be different based on the input data. Execution time holds side-channel information that can reveal the type of the process in execution and the value of its input data. Adversary can analyze the execution time of crypto-device and extract the secret data from the timing side-channel information; this attack is known as timing attack [45].

Timing attacks can be classified based on the targeted system component [45,46]. The first category is based on the chosen execution path. Secret key affects the execution path; some paths are slower than others. When the execution path changes based on the secret key value, the execution time is changed in return. The attacker can guess the key values based on this side-channel leakage. Another attack category targets branch predictors. Most of the modern processors, even the dedicated crypto-processors, have branch predictors to reduce the branching overhead [47]. These predictors may change the execution time significantly based on branching decision. The most common timing attacks are based on cash memory access. Cash miss/hit may depend on the secret key values. The execution time is greatly affected by the status of the cash access (miss/hit); the attacker can guess the secret key values using this information [48].

9.2.4.1 Countermeasures

Countermeasures against timing analysis can be categorized into two main categories. The first category is based on noise insertion and the second category is based on branch equalization. Blinding can be used to insert random parameters into the input before performing the encryption. Inserting dummy operations and randomization to the clock can also be categorized in this type [5,45,49]. Branch equalization and constant time implementation (where the designers use special standard cell that implements the different encryption tasks in fixed time) can be used to hide the correlation between the encryption data and their execution time [5,12,45].

9.2.5 Other attacks

Acoustic attacks is one of the oldest side-channel attacks. In the era of electrome-chanical crypto-machines, scientists were able to eavesdrop sounds coming out of the "Hagelin" cipher machine and they could retrieve the secret key [51]. Keyboard strikes sound is used to retrieve what is entered on the keyboard including passwords and login information. The most interesting attack reported so far in this category is the attack by Shamir *et al.*, who used the vibration generated by electronic compo-nents in a computer (such as capacitors and inductors on the motherboard and power supply) to extract RSA-2048 key [50].

Optical attack – visible light emitted by computer displays, and activity LEDs in network cards and routers found to hold different information. Kuhn could reconstruct images on a computer screen from the reflection over the user face and shirt [52]. Loughry and Umphress used the activity LEDs to extract serial port data [53].

9.2.6 Asynchronous logic

Asynchronous circuits (also known as self-timed circuits) are a class of circuits that contain no global synchronization signal (such as the clock in synchronous circuits). Data flow in asynchronous circuits is based on local handshaking between registers, which distributes the switching activity over time producing a nicely shaped power and EMI distribution. This section discusses the architecture of asynchronous circuits and their potential benefits for securing hardware designs.

Asynchronous circuits are gradually attracting the interest of both research and industry due to their interesting characteristics. Figure 9.7 depicts a pipeline that is

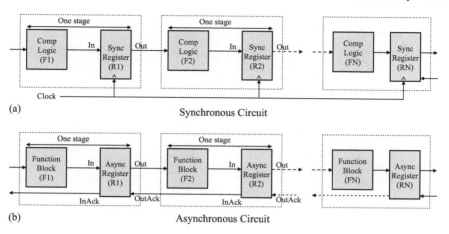

Figure 9.7 Synchronous circuits versus asynchronous circuits (basic view)

implemented in synchronous and asynchronous style. In synchronous design style, shown in Figure 9.7(a), circuit functionality is implemented by combinational function blocks; synchronous registers are sampling the output of these blocks based on the clock events that are controlling the sampling time of the registers. The clock period is fixed so that all function blocks correctly complete their operations and their data outputs are stable and ready to be sampled. That implies a global timing assumption that is applied to the whole circuit. In 40 nm and beyond, uncertainty about the delay is drastically increased. That makes the global timing assumption of the clock costly from performance point of view as more and more pessimism is added to compensate the delay uncertainty. In addition to this, clock trees in recent chips are huge and power hungry since they have transitions regardless of whether the circuit is computing or not. Consequently, designing a chip with no clock enhances the speed, and more importantly, the power consumption of the design.

In asynchronous circuit, shown in Figure 9.7(b), asynchronous registers have a local handshaking protocol that synchronize the register with the preceding and the following registers. By means of this local handshaking protocol, the register informs the preceding stage that the input data are latched (using the input acknowledgment signal); then the preceding stage can process a new data. On the output side, the stage register uses handshaking signals to inform the following stage that a new data are ready to be memorized (output request). This localization of the circuit synchronization avoids problems caused by the generic timing assumption presented by the clock in synchronous circuit style. Asynchronous circuits can be classified based on their architecture, timing assumptions, or their handshaking protocol [54,55]. There are different architecture styles for realizing asynchronous circuit; the main two styles are shown in Figure 9.8.

Asynchronous circuits can be implemented as bundled data (Figure 9.8(a)). In these circuits, there are two paths: the data path and the control path. In the data path, data are single rail and function blocks are normal combinational logic. The control

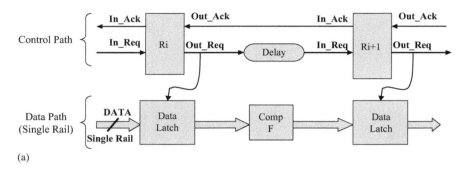

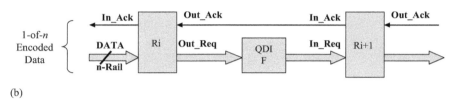

Figure 9.8   The most common implementation styles of asynchronous circuits:
(a) bundled data; (b) 1-of-n encoding

path contains the request and acknowledge signals for implementing the handshaking protocol. To maintain correct behavior, matching delays have to be inserted in the request signal paths to compensate the propagation delays of the function blocks in the data path. In this way, there are many local timing assumptions inside the circuit instead of a single timing assumption as in the case of clocked circuits. Indeed this enhances the circuit performance as it reduces the pessimism. The second asynchronous circuit style is called 1-of-n encoding style (Figure 9.8(b)). In this style, requests are encoded with the data, which implies more complex function blocks as they should be hazard-free circuits. In 1-of-n style, there are no timing assumptions on the function blocks.

The most common implementation of 1-of-n encoded circuits is the dual-rail asynchronous logic. In dual-rail logic, each data bit is encoded by two wires, D0 and D1. As shown in Figure 9.9, when $D0 = 1$ and $D1 = 0$ the dual-rail output is equal to logic-0. However, when $D0 = 0$ and $D1 = 1$ the dual-rail output is equal to logic-1. In dual-rail data encoding, the communication parties need to reset the wires to "00," which is known as the return-to-zero phase (RTZ). The communication protocol in this case is known as the "four-phase-protocol" [54].

Muller-gate (also known as C-element) is the basic component used to build asynchronous circuits. The idea of this gate is that the output is switched high whenever all the inputs are high, and the output is switched low whenever all the inputs are low; otherwise, the Mueller-gate holds its state (the truth table is shown in Figure 9.10). By using Muller-gates, designers can build complex functions. A simple asynchronous

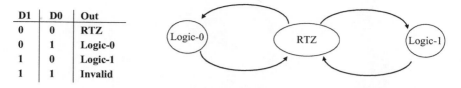

D1	D0	Out
0	0	RTZ
0	1	Logic-0
1	0	Logic-1
1	1	Invalid

Figure 9.9   Dual-rail encoding (truth table and state machine)

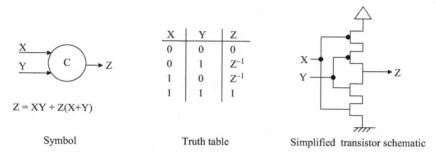

$$Z = XY + Z(X+Y)$$

X	Y	Z
0	0	0
0	1	Z^{-1}
1	0	Z^{-1}
1	1	1

Symbol   Truth table   Simplified transistor schematic

Figure 9.10   The Muller-gate (C-element)

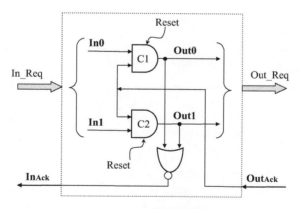

Figure 9.11   Dual-rail asynchronous register

register is shown in Figure 9.11, the input and output data of the register are encoded using two wires using the dual-rail encoding shown in Figure 9.9 [57,58]. The number of transitions needed to switch from RTZ to logic-0 is equal to the number of transitions needed to switch from RTZ to logic-1 and vice versa. This constant Hamming weight while transmitting or computing data makes the power consumption in asynchronous circuits balanced (between processing logic-0 or logic-1), which reduces the side-channel leakage and makes asynchronous circuits more secured compared to their synchronous counterparts [59–62].

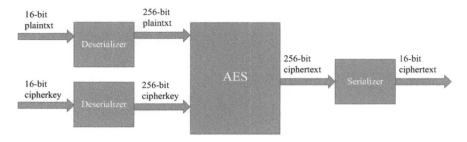

Figure 9.12   The AES core with deserializer and serializer

As discussed in the previous sections, lowering the power consumption of the circuits enhances the security due to harder power tracing and lower emitted EMI. In asynchronous circuits, data communication is based on local handshaking, which avoids the global clock. This gives asynchronous circuits two interesting features. The first is their lower power due to avoiding the clock tree, which consumes significant power due to continuous switching regardless of the block is processing data or not [63–65]. In addition to this, switching activity in asynchronous circuits is distributed in time (every block is locally synchronized with its adjacent blocks using local handshaking without any global synchronization). In this case, power consumption is distributed over time and it is much harder to trace the circuit activity using power or EMI traces [6,56,66–68].

9.2.7   Low-power asynchronous AES core

In this section, we introduce Application Specific Integrated Circuit (ASIC) design for advanced encryption standard (AES) cryptoprocessor that is implemented in fully Quasi Delay Insensitive (QDI) asynchronous style [73]. This design shows how asynchronous circuits can be used to reduce the power consumption to make the design more secure against power analysis attacks.

9.2.7.1   The chip architecture

The designed (AES) chip has 128-bit plain text (256-bit dual rail) and 128-bit cipherkey (256-bit dual rail). Since the number of pins in the fabricated chip is limited, we need to feed the AES core using deserializer block and out the cipher text by a serializer block. Deserializer block has 16-bit dual-rail data/key as input and produces 256-bit data/key as output. The deserializer is used to reduce the required number of input pins. In the same way, a serializer is used to reduce the number of output pins as shown in Figure 9.12.

The AES core implements the four main functions of the AES algorithm (AddRound, SubByte, ShiftRow, and MixColumn) as shown in Figure 9.13. The core takes plaintext and cipherkey as an input, and it produces ciphertext as an output after performing the four functions 10 times (10 rounds); as specified in the standard, the last round does not contain the MixColumn function.

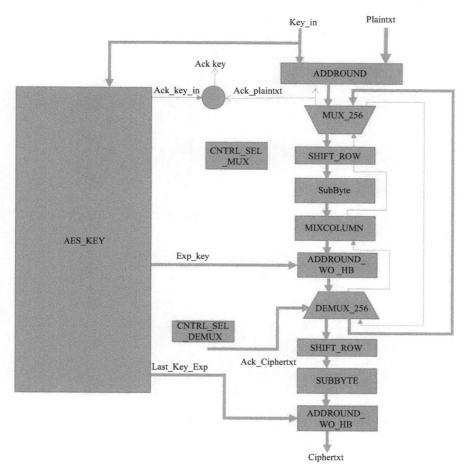

Figure 9.13 The architecture of the AES core

9.2.7.2 The fabricated chip

The presented architecture is modeled using Hardware Description Language (HDL) and synthesized targeting UMC 130 nm Faraday standard cells. Figure 9.14 shows the micrograph of the chip including the AES Core surrounded by the deserializer–serializer hardware.

Table 9.1 shows the area and speed of the fabricated chip. The area is $0.64 \, \text{mm}^2$ including I/O. The ciphering time (the time needed between starting the ciphering process until getting the ciphertext) is measured at the typical voltage (@ 1.2 V) and is equal to 300 ns. The fabricated core is able to encrypt 426 Mb/s under the typical conditions.

The fabricated core is tested under different supply voltage and guaranteed to work correctly while the supply voltage is reduced down to 0.7 V. By using the Dynamic

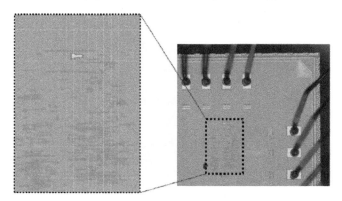

Figure 9.14   Micrograph of the chip including AES Core, deserializer–serializer hardware

Table 9.1   The fabricated AES area, power, and speed figures

Key length	Area	Power	Ciphering time	Technology
128	$0.64\,\text{mm}^2$	5.47 MW	300 ns	130 nm

Voltage Scaling (DVS), we could reduce the power consumption by 15% compared to operating the core on the typical voltage.

This chip is one of the lowest ASIC implementations of the AES in the literature [73]. It shows how asynchronous circuits can reduce the power of the cryptoprocessor, which implies lower current peaks with more security against power analysis attacks.

9.3   Malicious hardware: Trojans

Previous sections discussed different side-channel attacks and their countermeasures. Referring to Figure 9.4, protecting the hardware against side-channel attacks is an important step to avoid attackers retrieving secret information. However, during the long fabrication process, malicious hardware (such as HT) can be added to the hardware design, and hence compromise the whole system security. In this section, the definition of the HT is discussed and its threats to the system security are explained. The vulnerabilities in IC supply chain and the importance of trust in CAD tools are addressed. The section elaborates on different techniques to detect HT and protect the hardware design.

9.3.1   Hardware Trojan

HT is a malicious alteration of the hardware design to add a tiny module that tries to bypass security protocols, leak confidential information (such as secret keys or user certificates), or even completely disable the hardware functionality.

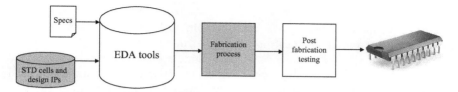

Figure 9.15 IC design life cycle: unshaded phases are trusted, shaded phases are untrusted

Most of the modern ICs are systems on chip (SoC), which contain different modules such as microprocessors, DSPs, ADCs, and communication peripherals (USB, I2C). To speed up the design process and the time to market the designed products, many of these blocks are inserted as design IPs. This creates a huge and complicated supply chain of design IP, which may contain some untrusted vendors. Figure 9.15 shows a simplified view of the IC design life cycle.

Any IC starts with the specification and front-end design files; since these steps are done inside the IC owner house, they should be trusted phases. Using the design specification files, EDA tools are used to automate the design compilation (most of the digital modules involve design automation). The EDA tools must be trusted to be sure they do not insert any malicious alteration to the original design. Industry vendors such as Cadence, Synopsys, and Mentor Graphics supply the design tools. In this case, these tools are considered as trusted design phase. For producing the IC design, EDA tools use standard cells and design IPs. These libraries are supplied by different design houses, which may be untrusted. Even IPs supplied by trusted vendors may contain malicious hardware if part of the IP is developed by untrusted third party. That makes the standard cell and IP libraries untrusted blocks in the design cycle. Fabrication process is also untrusted since it is completely performed out of the control of the IC owner. After finalizing the IC, the IC owner shall perform final design testing and characterization, which is supposed to be performed internally, which makes this step a trusted phase. As is clear from this simplified IC-fabrication life cycle, controlling all the steps is out of the question and we shall understand HT, classify them in a proper taxonomy, and provide efficient techniques to detect them [3,6].

9.3.2 Classification of HT

HT can have many different shapes and can affect the chip functionality in various ways. As a result, their classification can be viewed in many different ways; there is no common agreement about their classification. We will try here to list the most sounding classifications. For example in [72], the authors suggest a simple classification for the HT based on the triggering method. They classify them into two categories, "*combinational* Trojan" which is a combinational circuit that is activated by signal conditions. Their second category is the "*sequential* Trojan," which is a state machine that monitors some signal and activated upon the occurrence of specific sequence.

The authors in [71] classify HT based on *physical, activation,* and *action* characteristics. Trojan classification based on their physical characteristics divides them into many categories. The first category is the Trojan *type*; if it is *"functional* Trojan" or *"parametric* Trojan." *Functional* Trojans are this class implemented by altering the physical design (by adding or deleting transistors). *Parametric* Trojans are realized by modifying the design parameters (such as transistor sizing and wire thickness). Another physical classification is based on the Trojan *size* based on the size of the silicon area added/deleted or modified. Another category in the physical classification is the *distribution*; it describes the location of the Trojan inside the design (if the Trojan is located in one area or distributed among different areas in the layout). *Structural* alteration of the layout size is another physical category that determines whether the added Trojan changes the IC size or not. The second class streamed in this chapter is based on the activation method (how the Trojan is triggered to perform its malicious function). In this Trojan class, the authors mentioned two types, *"externally* activated,"* where the Trojan is activated from outside the chip; and *"internally* activated,"* which can be always active or activated based on internal conditions. The third class is based on the Trojan action. This class describes the action taken by the Trojan whenever it is activated and it is divided into three categories: *"modify function,"* *"modify specification,"* and *"transmit information."*

Another classification effort is conducted in [6], Chapter 14. The authors in this chapter classify the HT based on their *"phase of insertion"* into five categories: *specification* phase, *design* phase, *fabrication* phase, *assembly* phase, and *testing* phase. The Trojan *"level of abstraction"* is used in the same chapter to classify another six categories: *system* level, *development environment*, *RTL* level, *gate* level, *transistor* level, and *layout* level. *"Activation method"* is also used in the same chapter to describe two categories: *internally* and *externally* activated. The chapter adds other classification parameters such as *"Trojan effect"* and *"Trojan location"* [6].

9.3.3   HT detection

As described in the previous section, HT can take many different shapes in their shape, physical presence, and their stealthy nature (conditionally activated or always activated). Researchers developed different methods to detect HT. Narasimhan and Bhunia in [6] classify the Trojan detection methods into two categories, *destructive* and *nondestructive* approaches. The destructive approach involves demetallization of the chip to remove the metal layers and acquire detailed images by electron microscope. These images are used to reverse engineer the chip design and verify if the original design is altered during the fabrication process. This technique is not very efficient due to its complexity, high cost, and limitation to few samples of the manufactured chip. The nondestructive approaches can be executed during *run-time* and *test-time*.

Another classification is reported in [71], where the authors classify the detection methods into *side-channel analysis* and *Trojan activation*. In the first category, side-channel information (such as power consumption and execution time) is used to detect the presence of the Trojan by identifying an alteration in the power consumption traces and/or the execution time profile. In Trojan activation detection methods, we try to systematically activate any inserted Trojan and inspect the power consumption traces. If the Trojan is activated, its circuitry will use more power, which can be used to identify a Trojan free chip versus an infected one.

9.4   Summary

In this chapter, we try to highlight the importance of hardware security in modern systems. Increasingly we are connected to loosely controlled networking infrastructures such as IoT and intelligent transportation networks. In such networks, users are connected in an ad hoc style, which makes users' authentication and identity management a very complex problem. Modern security frameworks, especially in battery-based devices, rely on hardware security to protect confidential information and secret data. The ICs used in such systems must be protected against different hardware attacks, such as side-channel attacks and HT insertion.

In side-channel attacks, adversary tries to gain access to secret data through the side-channel leaked data, such as power consumption and EMI. In power analysis attacks, the adversary records power traces and analyzes them to correlate between the performed operation over the target hardware and its power consumption traces. By this way, the attackers can guess secret information such as encryption keys. There are different countermeasures for power attacks, most of them are trying to reduce the power consumption, decorrelate the power consumption traces from the processed data, and randomize the power consumption figure in time to make the task of the adversary as hard as possible. Another efficient method used by attackers is fault injection attacks. In this method, the adversary injects faults at specific stages of the encryption process and compares the erroneous ciphertext with the correct ones to fully or partially guess the secret key. Error detection and correction techniques can be embedded to the hardware to avoid this attack. EMA is another side-channel method that is used to compromise the chip security fences. Like power attacks, EMA is based on the correlation between the processed data and the current flow inside the chip. This current flow is transferred by metal wires, which work as tiny antennas, can emit electromagnetic waves, and might reveal the data processed by the hardware. In addition to reducing the power consumption to reduce the EM emanations, designers use different shielding methods to reduce the chance of attacking their designs. Attackers also can use timing analysis methods to reveal confidential information about the target IC. In this case, they exploit the execution time changes due to the instruction in execution and/or the logic value of the data processed. An effective countermeasure to this attack is to blind the data processed by adding random parameters in a way such that the output result is not changed. Asynchronous logic is a very important technique to implement hardware blocks that are immune against side-channel attacks. Data flow in asynchronous logic is based on local handshaking, which localizes the activity synchronization down to the adjacent blocks. Power consumption figures, consequently EMI traces, in this case are randomized in time, which protects the design against different side-channel attacks.

In modern SoCs, IC life cycle involves different service providers (ranging from design tools to complete design-IPs). With increasing design complexity and tighter time-to-market, in-house engineers are not able to verify design components which are developed by untrusted third party. This situation leads to potential security breaches such as Hardware Trojans. Trojans are alteration in the original design by adding/removing transistors or changing the physical design parameters. They can be always active or stealthy activated upon some specific conditions. After activation, Trojans can modify the circuit functionality, transmit secret data, or even completely deactivate security functions. This chapter elaborates on different taxonomies of HT and their detection methods.

References

[1]   Verbauwhede IMR. Secure Integrated Circuits and Systems. Boston, MA: Springer US; 2010.

[2]   Aldini A, Barthe G, and Gorrieri R. Foundations of Security Analysis and Design V: FOSAD 2007/2008/2009 Tutorial Lectures. Berlin: Springer; 2009.

[3]   Mishra P, Bhunia S, and Tehranipoor M. Hardware IP Security and Trust. Cham: Springer; 2017.

[4]   Da Rolt J, Das A, Di Natale G, Flottes M, Rouzeyre B, and Verbauwhede I. Test versus security: past and present. IEEE Transactions on Emerging Topics in Computing. 2014;2(1):50–62.

[5]   Zhou V, and Fen D. Side-Channel Attacks: Ten Years after Its Publication and the Impacts on Cryptographic Module Security Testing. [Internet]. 2016 [cited 14 August 2017]. Available from: http://csrc.nist.gov/groups/STM/cmvp/documents/fips140-3/physec/papers/physecpaper19.pdf

[6]   Tehranipoor M, and Wang C, editors. Introduction to Hardware Security and Trust. Springer-Verlag New York; 2014.

[7]   Goubin L, and Matsui M. Cryptographic Hardware and Embedded Systems – CHES 2006. New York: Springer-Verlag Berlin/Heidelberg; 2006.

[8]   Xie Y, Bao C, Serafy C, Lu T, Srivastava A, and Tehranipoor M. Security and vulnerability implications of 3D ICs. IEEE Transactions on Multi-Scale Computing Systems. 2016;2(2):108–122.

[9]   Ngo X, Danger J, Guilley S, *et al.* Cryptographically secure shield for security IPs protection. IEEE Transactions on Computers. 2016;1–1.

[10] Popp T, Mangard S, and Oswald E. Power analysis attacks and countermeasures. IEEE Design and Test of Computers. 2007;24(6):535–543.

[11] Kocher P, Jaffe J, and Jun B. Differential power analysis. Proceedings of the 19th Annual International Cryptology Conference on Advances in Cryptology. 2017; in CRYPTO'99: pp. 388–397.

[12] Mangard S, Oswald E, and Popp T. Power Analysis Attacks: Revealing the Secrets of Smart Cards. New York, NY: Springer; 2010.

[13] Tiri K, and Verbauwhede I. A digital design flow for secure integrated circuits. IEEE Transactions on Computer-Aided Design of Integrated Circuits and Systems. 2006;25(7):1197–1208.

[14] Weiwei Shan, Xingyuan Fu, and Zhipeng Xu. A secure reconfigurable crypto IC with countermeasures against SPA, DPA, and EMA. IEEE Transactions on Computer-Aided Design of Integrated Circuits and Systems. 2015;34(7):1201–1205.

[15] Giraud C. An RSA implementation resistant to fault attacks and to simple power analysis. IEEE Transactions on Computers. 2006;55(9):1116–1120.

[16] Ratanpal G, Williams R, and Blalock T. An on-chip signal suppression countermeasure to power analysis attacks. IEEE Transactions on Dependable and Secure Computing. 2004;1(3):179–189.

[17] Marzouqi H, Al-Qutayri M, and Salah K. Review of gate-level differential power analysis and fault analysis countermeasures. IET Information Security. 2014 Jan;8(1):51–66.

[18] Yu W, and Kose S. A voltage regulator-assisted lightweight AES implementation against DPA attacks. IEEE Transactions on Circuits and Systems I: Regular Papers. 2016;63(8):1152–1163.

[19] Mazumdar B, and Mukhopadhyay D. Construction of rotation symmetric S-boxes with high nonlinearity and improved DPA resistivity. IEEE Transactions on Computers. 2017 Jan;66(1):59–72.

[20] Golic JD. Techniques for random masking in hardware. IEEE Transactions on Circuits and Systems I: Regular Papers. 2007;54(2):291–300.

[21] Lumbiarres-Lopez R, Lopez-Garcia M, and Canto-Navarro E. Hardware architecture implemented on FPGA for protecting cryptographic keys against side-channel attacks. IEEE Transactions on Dependable and Secure Computing. 2016;1.

[22] Kumar SD, Thapliyal H, and Mohammad A. FinSAL: A novel FinFET based secure adiabatic logic for energy-efficient and DPA resistant IoT devices. 2016 IEEE International Conference on Rebooting Computing (ICRC). 2016.

[23] BI Y, Shamsi K, Yuan J, Standaert F, and Jin Y. Leverage emerging technologies for DPA-resilient block cipher design. 2016 Design, Automation and Test in Europe Conference and Exhibition (DATE), Dredsen. 2016;1538–1543.

[24] Bi Y, Shamsi K, Yuan J, Jin Y, Niemier M, and Hu X. Tunnel FET current mode logic for DPA-resilient circuit designs. IEEE Transactions on Emerging Topics in Computing. 2016;1–1.

[25] Morrison M, Ranganathan N, and Ligatti J. Design of adiabatic dynamic differential logic for DPA-resistant secure integrated circuits. IEEE Transactions on Very Large Scale Integration (VLSI) Systems. 2015;23(8):1381–1389.

[26] Kim C, and Quisquater J. Faults, injection methods, and fault attacks. IEEE Design and Test of Computers. 2007;24(6):544–545.

[27] Joye M, and Tunstall M, editors. Fault Analysis in Cryptography. Springer-Verlag Berlin Heidelberg; 2014.

[28] Musil C, Bartelt J, and Melngailis J. Focused ion beam microsurgery for electronics. IEEE Electron Device Letters. 1986;7(5):285–287.

[29] Li Y, Ohta K, and Sakiyama K. New fault-based side-channel attack using fault sensitivity. IEEE Transactions on Information Forensics and Security. 2012;7(1):88–97.

[30] Sarkar S, Banik S, and Maitra S. Differential fault attack against grain family with very few faults and minimal assumptions. IEEE Transactions on Computers. 2015 Jan;64(6):1647–1657.

[31] Zhao G, Sun B, Li R, Cheng L, and Li C. Differential fault analysis on LED using Super-Sbox. IET Information Security. 2015 Jan;9(4):209–218.

[32] Ghalaty NF, Yuce B, and Schaumont P. Analyzing the efficiency of biased-fault based attacks. IEEE Embedded Systems Letters. 2016;8(2):33–36.

[33] Malkin TG, Standaert F-X, and Yung M. A comparative cost/security analysis of fault attack countermeasures. Lecture Notes in Computer Science Fault Diagnosis and Tolerance in Cryptography. 2006;159–172.

[34] Boneh D, Demillo R, and Lipton R. On the importance of checking computations. Technical report 9/25/96, an extended version appears in the Proceedings of Eurocrypt 97.

[35] Endo S, Li Y, Homma N, *et al.* A silicon-level countermeasure against fault sensitivity analysis and its evaluation. IEEE Transactions on Very Large Scale Integration (VLSI) Systems. 2015;23(8):1429–1438.

[36] Patranabis S, Chakraborty A, Mukhopadhyay D, and Chakrabarti PP. Fault space transformation: a generic approach to counter differential fault analysis and differential fault intensity analysis on AES-like block ciphers. IEEE Transactions on Information Forensics and Security. 2017;12(5):1092–1102.

[37] Ma K, and Wu K. Error detection and recovery for ECC: a new approach against side-channel attacks. IEEE Transactions on Computer-Aided Design of Integrated Circuits and Systems. 2014;33(4):627–637.

[38] Hayashi Y, Homma N, Mizuki T, Aoki T, and Sone H. Transient IEMI threats for cryptographic devices. IEEE Transactions on Electromagnetic Compatibility. 2013;55(1):140–148.

[39] Hayashi Y, Homma N, Mizuki T, *et al.* Analysis of electromagnetic information leakage from cryptographic devices with different physical structures. IEEE Transactions on Electromagnetic Compatibility. 2013;55(3):571–580.

[40] Kaliski BS, Koç Çetin K., and Paar C. Cryptographic hardware and embedded systems—CHES 2002: 4th International Workshop, Redwood Shores, CA, USA, August 2002: revised papers. Berlin: Springer-Verlag; 2002.

[41] Hayashi Y-I, Homma N, Mizuki T, *et al.* Analysis of electromagnetic information leakage from cryptographic devices with different physical structures. IEEE Transactions on Electromagnetic Compatibility. 2013;55(3):571–580.

[42] Hayashi Y, Homma N, Mizuki T, *et al.* Efficient evaluation of EM radiation associated with information leakage from cryptographic devices. IEEE Transactions on Electromagnetic Compatibility. 2013;55(3):555–563.

[43] Masoumi M, and Rezayati M. Novel approach to protect advanced encryption standard algorithm implementation against differential electromagnetic and power analysis. IEEE Transactions on Information Forensics and Security. 2015;10(2):256–265.

[44]   Quisquater J, and Samyde D. Electromagnetic analysis (EMA): measures and counter-measures for smart cards. In: Attali I, Jensen T, editors. Smart Card Programming and Security. Lecture Notes in Computer Science. Berlin, Heidelberg: Springer; 2001. Vol. 2140.

[45]   Rebeiro C, Mukhopadhyay D, and Bhattacharya S. Timing Channels in Cryptography: A Micro-Architectural Perspective. Cham: Springer; 2015.

[46]   Moradi A, Mischke O, and Paar C. One attack to rule them all: collision timing attack versus 42 AES ASIC cores. IEEE Transactions on Computers. 2013;62(9):1786–1798.

[47]   Toth R, Faigl Z, Szalay M, and Imre S. An advanced timing attack scheme on RSA. Networks 2008 – The 13th International Telecommunications Network Strategy and Planning Symposium. 2008.

[48]   Jiang ZH, Fei Y, and Kaeli D. A complete key recovery timing attack on a GPU. 2016 IEEE International Symposium on High Performance Computer Architecture (HPCA). 2016.

[49]   Coron J-S, and Kizhvatov I. Analysis and improvement of the random delay countermeasure of CHES 2009. In: Mangard S, Standaert F-X, editors. CHES. Lecture Notes in Computer Science. Berlin: Springer; 2010. Pp. 95–109.

[50]   Genkin D, Shamir A, and Tromer E. RSA key extraction via low-bandwidth acoustic cryptanalysis. In: Garay JA, and Gennaro R, editors. Advances in Cryptology – CRYPTO 2014. CRYPTO 2014. Lecture Notes in Computer Science. Berlin, Heidelberg: Springer; 2014. Vol. 8616.

[51]   Anderson R. Security Engineering: A Guide to Building Dependable Distributed Systems. Indianapolis, IN: Wiley Pub.; 2008.

[52]   Kuhn M. Optical time-domain eavesdropping risks of CRT displays. Proceedings 2002 IEEE Symposium on Security and Privacy.

[53]   Loughry J, and Umphress D. Information leakage from optical emanations. ACM Transactions on Information and System Security. 2002;5(3):262–289.

[54]   Sparsø J. Principles of Asynchronous Circuit Design: A Systems Perspective. Boston: Kluwer; 2010.

[55]   Yahya E, and Fesquet L. Asynchronous design: a promising paradigm for electronic circuits and systems. 2009 16th IEEE International Conference on Electronics, Circuits and Systems (ICECS 2009). 2009.

[56]   Beigne E, Vivet P, Thonnart Y, Christmann J-F, and Clermidy F. Asynchronous circuit designs for the internet of everything: a methodology for ultralow-power circuits with GALS architecture. IEEE Solid-State Circuits Magazine. 2016;8(4):39–47.

[57]   Zakaria H, Yahya E, and Fesquet L. Self-adaptation in SoCs. In: Phan Cong-Vinh, editors. Autonomic Networking-on-Chip: Bio-Inspired Specification, Development, and Verification. Boca Raton, FL: CRC Press; 2012.

[58]   Yahya E, and Renaudin M. QDI latches characteristics and asynchronous linear-pipeline performance analysis. In: Vounckx J, Azemard N, Maurine P, editors. Integrated Circuit and System Design. Power and Timing Modeling, Optimization and Simulation. PATMOS 2006. Lecture Notes in Computer Science. Berlin, Heidelberg: Springer; 2006. Vol. 4148.

[59]   Kulikowski K, Su M, Smirnov A, Taubin A, Karpovsky M, and Macdonald D. Delay insensitive encoding and power analysis: a balancing act. 11th IEEE International Symposium on Asynchronous Circuits and Systems.

[60]   Bouesse GF, Renaudin M, Dumont S, and Germain F. DPA on quasi delay insensitive asynchronous circuits: formalization and improvement. Design, Automation and Test in Europe (DATE). 2005;1:424–429.

[61]   Soares R, Calazans N, Moraes F, Maurine P, and Torres L. A robust architectural approach for cryptographic algorithms using GALS pipelines. IEEE Design and Test of Computers. 2011;28(5):62–71.

[62]   Fan X, Peter S, and Krstic M. GALS design of ECC against side-channel attacks—a comparative study. 24th International Workshop on Power and Timing Modeling, Optimization and Simulation (PATMOS). 2014;1–6.

[63]   Akkaya NEC, Erbagci B, Carley R, and Mai K. A DPA-resistant self-timed three-phase dual-rail pre-charge logic family. 2015 IEEE International Symposium on Hardware Oriented Security and Trust (HOST). 2015;112–117.

[64]   Guilley S, Sauvage L, Flament F, Vong V-N, Hoogvorst P, and Pacalet R. Evaluation of power constant dual-rail logics countermeasures against DPA with design time security metrics. IEEE Transactions on Computers. 2010;59(9):1250–1263.

[65]   Zhu N-H, Zhou Y-J, and Liu H-M. Employing symmetric dual-rail logic to thwart LPA attack. IEEE Embedded Systems Letters. 2013;5(4):61–64.

[66]   Monnet Y, Renaudin M, and Leveugle R. Designing resistant circuits against malicious faults injection using asynchronous logic. IEEE Transactions on Computers. 2006;55(9):1104–1115.

[67]   Ou Q, Luo F, Li S, and Chen L. Circuit level defences against fault attacks in pipelined NCL circuits. IEEE Transactions on Very Large Scale Integration (VLSI) Systems. 2015;23(9):1903–1913.

[68]   Amr E, Maher M, Rashad A, *et al.* Presenting a synchronous – asynchronous standard cell library based on 7nm FinFET technology. International Conference on Microelectronics (ICM). 2016.

[69]   Liu Y, Jin Y, Nosratinia A, and Makris Y. Silicon demonstration of hardware Trojan design and detection in wireless cryptographic ICs. IEEE Transactions on Very Large Scale Integration (VLSI) Systems. 2017;25(4):1506–1519.

[70]   Tang M, Guo Z, Heuser A, Ren Y, Li J, and Danger J. PFD—a flexible higher-order masking scheme. IEEE Transactions on Computer-Aided Design of Integrated Circuits and Systems. 2017;36(8):1327–1339.

[71]   Tehranipoor M, and Koushanfar F. A survey of hardware Trojan taxonomy and detection. IEEE Design and Test of Computers. 2010;27(1):10–25.

[72]   Banga M, and Hsiao MS. A region based approach for the identification of hardware Trojans. 2008 IEEE International Workshop on Hardware-Oriented Security and Trust. 2008.

[73]   Elmeligy N, Amin M, Yahya E, and Ismail Y. 130 nm low power asynchronous AES core. IEEE International Symposium on Circuits and Systems (ISCAS). 2017.

Chapter 10
Cybersecurity: timeline malware analysis and classification

Rafiqul Islam[1]

In this chapter, we address the introduction to cybersecurity and problems associated with cybersecurity in particular malicious activities in cyber space. The proliferation and exponential increase of malware has continued to present a serious threat to the security of information systems. Furthermore, with the development of evermore sophisticated methods of evading detection, malware has posed serious challenges to combat it. Moreover, due to the continuous changes in malware design, antimalware (AM) strategy that has been successful in a given time period will not work at a much later date. In this chapter, we propose the challenges of malware in cyberspace and its detection approach called cumulative timeline analysis (CTA) that retains high accuracy over an extended time period. The effectiveness of the proposed approach is tested on malware executables collected over a span of 10 years with almost constant accuracy.

10.1 Introduction

With the emerging applications of computer and information technology, cybercrime has become a significant challenge all over the world. Thousands of cyber criminals attempt every day to attack against computer systems to illegally access them through the Internet. Hundreds of new computer viruses and spam are released every month in an attempt to damage computer systems or to steal or destroy data with them. Such threats are expensive not only in terms of quantity but also in terms of quality. In recent years, experts are becoming more concerned about protecting computer and communication systems from growing cyber-attacks including deliberate attempts to access the computer systems by unauthorized persons with the goal of stealing crucial data, to make illegal financial transfers, to disrupt, damage or manipulate data, or other unlawful actions [1]. Consequently, cybersecurity has been gaining importance in the cyber world due to the increasing reliance on computer systems, smart devices, wireless networks such as Bluetooth and Wi-Fi, and the growth of the Internet. Cybersecurity involves protecting the information and systems we rely on

[1]School of Computing and Mathematics, Charles Sturt University, Australia

every day—whether at home, office, or business. Cybersecurity includes different elements such as application security, information security, network security, and disaster recovery [2].

Cybersecurity refers to the technologies, processes, and practices designed to protect networks, computers, programs, and data from vulnerabilities, attacks, or unauthorized access by cybercriminals over the Internet [3]. Cybersecurity, also known as computer security or IT security, generally means the protection of computer systems from the theft or damage to the hardware, software, or the information on them, as well as from disruption of the services they provide [4]. Cybersecurity includes controlling physical access to the hardware, as well as protecting against the harm that may come via network access, data and code injection, and due to malpractice by operators, whether intentional, accidental, or due to them being tricked into deviating from secure procedures [5].

According to the International Telecommunications Union, cybersecurity is defined as

> the collection of tools, policies, guidelines, risk management approaches, actions, training, best practices, assurance and technologies that can be used to protect the cyber environment and organization and user's assets. Organization and user's assets include connected computing devices, users, applications, services, telecommunications systems, and the totality of transmitted and/or stored information in the cyber environment. Cybersecurity ensures the attainment and maintenance of the security properties of the organization and user's assets against relevant security risks in the cyber environment. The security properties include one or more of the following: availability, integrity and confidentiality. [6]

Availability, integrity, and confidentiality are three core principles of cybersecurity [7]. Availability means that the information and systems must be available to those who need it. By integrity, we mean that the information must retain its reliability and not be altered from its original state. And confidentiality means that the information that is sensitive or confidential must remain so and be shared only with appropriate users.

10.1.1   Significance

Cybersecurity is crucial for building confidence and security in the use of information technologies so as to ensure trust by the information society. Lack of security in cyberspace undermines confidence in the information society. This is especially the case with many intrusions around the globe resulting in the stealing of money, assets, and sensitive military, commercial, and economic information. With information flowing through boundaries of different legal systems connected to different networks around the globe, there is a growing need to protect personal information, funds, and assets, as well as national security. As a result, cybersecurity is gaining interest by both the public and the private sectors.

Cybersecurity includes different activities and operations aiming at the reduction and prevention of threat and vulnerabilities and having in place policies for protection, incident response, recovery, data assurance, law enforcement, and military and intelligence operations relating to cyberspace security. It defends the systems from hacking and virus attacks [8].

Cybersecurity touches practically all activities and all citizens around the globe; it provides tremendous opportunities for enhancing human development as well as achieving better integration in the information society. It also supports wider access to knowledge and education, as well as to the development of policies and strategies [9].

In legal and regulatory institutions that lack cyberspace, security undermines the realization of the full potential of the information technology revolution. Consequently, special attention is needed to prevent cyberspace from turning into a source of danger for states and citizens, and to prevent the appearance of a cybercrime haven. The prevention of cybercrime is a key objective of cybersecurity.

10.1.2 Problems

One of the most problematic elements of cybersecurity is the quickly and constantly evolving nature of security risks. The threat is advancing quicker than the experts can keep up with it. The traditional approach has been to focus most resources on the most crucial system components and protect against the biggest known threats, which necessitated leaving some less important system components undefended and some less dangerous risks not protected against. Such an approach is insufficient in the current environment. Moreover, it imposes new types of commercial, professional, and social paradigms, giving rise to a number of legal and technical problems that must be addressed on the basis of respecting its special nature and needs. Hence, a different approach and different methodologies than what has been adopted are needed.

There are many risks and pitfalls in cybersecurity incident that can seriously affect computer and network systems. It can be due to improper cybersecurity controls, manmade or natural disasters, or malicious users wreaking havoc including the following [7,10]:

Denial-of-service refers to an attack that successfully prevents or impairs the authorized functionality of networks, systems, or applications by exhausting resources.

Malware, worms, and Trojan horses: These spread by e-mail, instant messaging, malicious websites, and infected non-malicious websites. Some websites will automatically download the malware without the user's knowledge or intervention. Other methods will require the users to click on a link or button.

Botnets and zombies: A botnet, short for robot network, is an aggregation of compromised computers that are connected to a central "controller." The compromised computers are often referred to as "zombies." These threats will continue to proliferate as the attack techniques evolve and become available to a broader audience, with less technical knowledge required to launch successful attacks.

Botnets designed to steal data are improving their encryption capabilities and thus becoming more difficult to detect.

Scareware: Fake security software warnings. This type of scam can be particularly profitable for cyber criminals as many users believe the pop-up warnings telling them their system is infected and are lured into downloading and paying for the special software to "protect" their system.

Social network attacks: Social network attacks are major sources of attacks because of the volume of users and the amount of personal information that is posted. Users' inherent trust in their online friends is what makes these networks a prime target. For example, users may be prompted to follow a link on someone's page, which could bring users to a malicious website.

Cybersecurity has never been simple. And because attacks evolve every day as attackers become more inventive, it is critical to properly define cybersecurity and identify what constitutes a good cybersecurity.

10.2 Timeline malware analysis and classification

Malware is a malevolent software that either tries to disrupt the normal computer operation or gathers sensitive information from private computer systems. Antivirus (AV) vendors, according to Perry [11], see 5,000 distinct malware samples per day. The malware writers also apply various code obfuscation techniques on previous malware (while keeping their original functionalities unchanged) to evade detection. A malware detector is a system that attempts to determine whether a program has malicious intent and thereafter stops its execution if it is malicious. The standard signature-based malicious code detection technique in all commercial AV softwares can only achieve detection once the virus has already caused damage, and thereby fails to detect new malware. A fundamental limitation of signature-based techniques is that they need to keep the signature database up to date in order to provide protection against the latest threats [12,13]. In contrast, behavioral analysis-based methods exploit behavioral patterns of malware to distinguish them from benign programs [14,15] and therefore is promised to be more effective compared to the signature-based malware detection techniques.

In this chapter, we address the problem of developing a malware detection approach that will be able to detect future malware. While a substantial number of various malware detection techniques based on static and dynamic analysis has been studied [16,17], the recent malware proliferation technique with dynamic nature has attracted attention among the AM researchers and vendors. This malware capabilities render an AV strategy, which has been successful in a given time period not to work at a much later date [14,18–23,41]. Moreover, because malware evolves with time and eventually becomes unrecognizable from the original form or because completely new malware is designed, which is unlike any known malware and so would not be detected by AV software constructed to detect known types of malware.

It is obvious from the current literature that present malware detection methods will not easily detect future malware. In this chapter, we propose a malware detection approach called CTA that retains high accuracy over an extended time period. Our method provides strong support for the argument that both static and dynamic features are needed in malware detection and also that these features can be chosen in such a way that they leverage better results when they act independently and so complement each other. By extracting both static and dynamic features from executables, and by accumulating these features over intervals in the 10-year period, we construct a high-accuracy malware detection method that retains very close to the same accuracy along the entire timeline in our tests. The main contributions of this chapter are as follows:

1. *A robust malware detection method retaining accuracy over a 10-year period.*
   The data presented in Section 10.3 indicate that our method retains accuracy to within 3.8% over the 10-year period. While the trend is down, these results strongly support the hypothesis that it is possible to develop a malware detection strategy that will work well into the future.
2. *A novel approach to feature collection by accumulating the features over time segments.*
   In traditional approaches to malware versus cleanware detection, sets of features are derived from the executable files and compared against each other. In this chapter, we adapt this approach to the timeline analysis by beginning with our oldest malware and doing such a comparison. Then we progressively add later malware in batches and continue the comparison.

The rest of the chapter is organized as follows: Section 10.3 provides a review of the literature, and Section 10.4 describes the set-up for the testing. In Section 10.5, we provide a detailed discussion of the experiment and present the results, and in Section 10.6, we discuss the analysis and its implications for future work.

10.3 Related work

Malware authors use various obfuscation techniques to transform a malicious program into undetectable variants with the same core functionalities of the parent malware program. It has been shown that 75% of malware released in 2006 were a variant of previously known malware [21]. The study in [24] investigates malicious attacks on several websites by creating web honeypots and collecting website-based malware executables over a period of 5 months. In their study, they collect and analyze malware samples using six different AV programs and conduct the same experiment 4 months later using the updated versions of the six programs to determine their efficacy and found different performance. Additionally, the work of Rajab *et al.* [25] focuses on mitigating web-based malware. They studied a dataset collected over a period of 4 years and demonstrated that existing malware characteristic can aid in detecting future malware. Both aforementioned works demonstrate that, with training on older malware, some AV software can significantly improve detection rates.

The research conducted by Rosyid *et al.* [19] is focused on detecting malicious attack patterns in botnets attacking a honeypot during the year 2009. After extracting the log files of malware sequences, they then apply the PrefixSpan algorithm to discover subsequence patterns. The authors extend their work by identifying attack patterns based on IP address and timestamp. The authors argue that the signature of a single malware file is not enough to detect the complex variants of the attacks by botnets. In [14], the authors apply a dynamic method for classifying malware, considering the interactions between the operating system and malicious programs as behavioral features. In their study, they use three different evaluation techniques: completeness, conciseness, and consistency. The authors mention that one limitation of their methodology is the failure to "detect fine-grained characteristics of the observed behaviors."

Another group of researchers [26] build their malware detection and classification framework based on comparisons of extracted strings using static analysis. They claim that the similarity between two files can be determined by comparing the character strings, which in turn is used to identify and determine whether the two instances are variants. Lee *et al.* [27] present a three-step methodology of extraction, refinement, and comparison. The authors show that if a mutated instance of malware is detected it is reflected as a huge peak under the respective malware family.

The present authors use a combination of static and dynamic analysis to achieve a high level of accuracy over a 10-year time period. We are not the first to integrate dynamic with static features however (e.g., see [24,28]), though we are the first to use this method applied over a long time period. In order to understand the evolution of malware over a long period of time and its effects on future malware, we consider three types of analysis: static, dynamic, and combined in this chapter. The features collected from the three analyses ensure that we do not omit any characteristics of the malware that could have been left out by conducting one type of analysis only.

10.4   Malware sample collection

10.4.1   The methodology

Static analysis can analyze a wide spectrum of possible execution paths of an executable, thus providing a good global view of the whole executable and of the entire program logic without running it; on the other hand, static analysis is susceptible to inaccuracies due to obfuscation and polymorphic techniques. Dynamic analysis monitors the behavior of the binary executable file during its execution, which enables it to collect a profile of the operations performed by the binary and thus offers potentially greater insight into the code itself. The main limitation of the dynamic analysis is that analysis results are only based on malware behavior during a specific execution run. Since some of the malwares' behavior may be triggered only under specific conditions, such behavior would be easy to be missed with only a single execution. In our testing, we extract from each executable (i) static features: printable string information (PSI) and function length frequency (FLF) and (ii) dynamic features: API calls including their parameters. The WEKA database of data mining algorithms [27] is used to derive the detection results based on the integrated vector set as input.

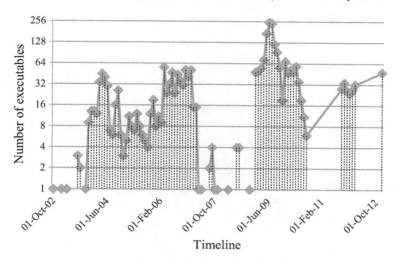

Figure 10.1 Collection of malware executables from 2002 to 2012

10.4.2 Data collection

The malware executables used in the experiment were collected from CA's VET Zoo (www.ca.com.au) over a span of 8 years (2002–2010) and we collect (2011–2012) manually from open sources (www.offensivecomputing.net, http://www.virussign. com); the cleanware executables were collected manually from various versions of Win32-based systems. Figure 10.1 indicates the dates at which malware files were collected.

The total numbers of malware and cleanware executables, used in our experiments, are 2,617 and 541, respectively. Table 10.1 shows the executables family by family.

10.5 Cumulative timeline analysis

This section provides our proposed malware detection method using CTA approach. First, we will present CTA data preparation method and then we will discuss CTA feature generation techniques both in static and in dynamic methods.

10.5.1 CTA data preprocessing

The date of a malware file was that associated with the file when the file was collected. We exported all files, along with their dates, into our Ida2DBMS schema and based on the dates broke the data into groups as described in Table 10.1.

To generate groups of malware for use in the testing, we begin with the earliest malware and add month by month across the timeline until all data are grouped. As the first data group, MG_1, we take the earliest dated 10% of the files. There are 262

Table 10.1   Experimental set of 3,158 files

Type		Family	Timeline collection	Samples	Instances
Malware	Trojan	Bambo	2003-07 ⇒ 2006-01	44	5,100
		Boxed	2004-06 ⇒ 2007-09	178	56,662
		Alureon	2005-05 ⇒ 2007-11	41	7,635
		Robknot	2005-10 ⇒ 2007-08	78	10,411
		Clagger	2005-11 ⇒ 2007-01	44	4,520
		Robzips	2006-03 ⇒ 2007-08	72	6,549
		Tracur	2011-08 ⇒ 2011-11	42	7,365
		Cridex	2011-10 ⇒ 2012-02	56	8,692
	Worms	SillyDl	2009-01 ⇒ 2010-08	439	56,933
		Vundo	2009-01 ⇒ 2010-08	80	1,660
		Lefgroo	2012-12 ⇒ 2012-12	121	35,421
		Frethog	2009-01 ⇒ 2010-08	174	28,042
		SillyAutorun	2009-01 ⇒ 2010-05	87	9,965
	Virus	Gamepass	2009-01 ⇒ 2010-07	179	23,730
		Bancos	2009-01 ⇒ 2010-07	446	89,554
		Adclicker	2009-01 ⇒ 2010-08	65	11,637
		Banker	2009-01 ⇒ 2010-06	47	12,112
		Agobot	2002-10 ⇒ 2006-04	283	216,430
		Looked	2003-07 ⇒ 2006-09	66	36,644
		Emerleox	2006-11 ⇒ 2008-11	75	61,242
Total of malware files			2002 ⇒ 2012	2,617	690,304
Cleanware				541	81,154
Total				3,158	771,458

executables in this group, which covers the period from October 2002 to December 2004. The second data group, MG_2, comprises the data collected during the period October 2002 to January 2005, and so on. When too few files appear in a subsequent month to justify including that month as a group, we jump to the following month. In all, this results in 65 malware data groups, which are labeled $MG_1 \ldots MG_{65}$.

The pseudocode in Algorithm 10.1 shows the CTA data preprocessing. The inputs to Algorithm 10.1 are the set of malware data group and cleanware data.

Algorithm 10.1 CTA data preprocessing

INPUT: CG=Cleanware data, M ={MG$_1$,MG$_2$,MG$_3$....,MG$_n$}
OUTPUT:Test and Train data set:
CG={CG$_1$,CG$_2$,...,CG$_{k+1}$}//Cumulative Timeline cleanware data group set
MG'={MG'$_1$,MG'$_2$,...,Mg'$_{k+1}$} // Cumulative timeline Malware data group set
BEGIN

1. i=1
2. **FOR EACH** ($MG_i \in M$) **DO**
3. Select CG // Select clean ware data

4. **IF size**(*CG*) > *size* (*MG*$_i$) **THEN**
5. $I \leftarrow \frac{|CG|}{|MG_i|}$ //Compute the integer part
6. $|CG| \leftarrow k|MG_i| + R$ //Compute reminder
7. Take k $\in |CG|$ of order $|MG i|$
8. **IF R>0 THEN**
9. $R \leftarrow k|MG_i| \parallel R$ // Pad reminder element
10. **ELSE**
11. $|MG_i| = \Phi$ // empty set and not used.
12. $CG = CG_1 \cup CG_2 \cup \ldots \cup CG_{k+1}$
13. Generate FV from CG_i
14. **ENDIF**
15. **ELSE** //malware group > cleanware group
16. $I \leftarrow \frac{|MG_i|}{|CG|}$ //Compute the integer part
17. $|MG_i| \leftarrow k|CG| + R$ //Compute reminder
18. Take k $\in |MG i|$ of order $|CG|$
19. **IF R>0 THEN**
20. $R \leftarrow k|MG_i| \parallel R$ // Pad reminder element
21. **ELSE**
22. $|MG_i| = \Phi$ // empty set and not used.
23. $MG = MG_1 \cup MG_2 \cup \ldots \cup MG_{k+1}$
24. Generate FV from MG_i
25. **ENDIF**
26. i=i+1 // until all the malware group done;
27. **ENDIF**
28. **ENDFOR**

END Algorithm

Figure 10.2 indicates the spread of malware across the 65 groups with each bar corresponding to a group. Throughout the test, the set of 541 WIN32 cleanware files is treated as a single group *CG*. However, when it is tested against a particular malware group, depending on the comparative size of the two groups, the cleanware group may be divided into subgroups.

10.5.2 CTA feature vector generation

To test our CTA classification, we fix the malware samples and cleanware samples by following the guidelines in [29]. We use an equal portion of malware and cleanware data. The selected malware group MG_i is compared with *CG*. If $|MG_i|$ is smaller than $|CG|$ then we compute the integer part of $|CG|/|MG_i|$ and the integer remainder $0 \le R < |MG_i|$ as in

$|CG| = k|MG_i| + R$, for some positive integer k.

We then divide *CG* into k disjoint groups of equal size. If $R > 0$, then the remaining elements must be padded out to a $(k + 1)$st group CG_{k+1}. However, if $R = 0$, this

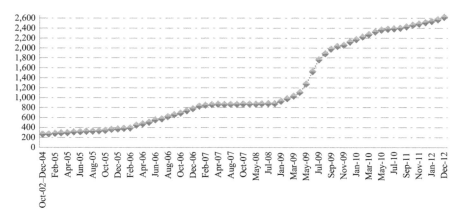

Figure 10.2   A number of malware executables accumulated by date

set is empty and is not used. If MG_i is bigger than $|CG|$ then we compute the integer part of $|MG_i|/|CG|$ and proceed in the same way. This procedure is repeated for every malware group. Algorithm 10.1 shows the data preparation process.

10.5.2.1   Static vector generation

Static analysis of malware is done based on features drawn from unpacked static versions of the executable files [21,30–33]. In [21], Tian *et al.* present a method for classifying Trojans based on function lengths and show that function length plays an important role in classifying malware and if combined with other features may result in a better method of malware classification. In [32], Lu *et al.* propose a hierarchical framework to classify the network traffic into different application communities based on payload signatures and a new cross-association clustering algorithm and then analyze the temporal-frequent characteristics of flows to distinguish malicious channels created by bots from normal traffic generated by human beings.

In [30], Tian *et al.* propose an approach to distinguish Trojan and virus families based on strings from library code. In [31], the authors use an automated tool running in an emulated environment to extract API call features from executables and apply pattern recognition algorithms and statistical methods to differentiate between malicious and benign files. In [33], Mohaisen and Alrawi show that artifacts like a file system, registry, and network features can be used to identify distinct malware families with high accuracy. One of the complaints about static analysis-based malware detection methods is that once they are made public, a malware writer need only to obfuscate the principal features used in the classification methods, for example, information about function calls or the strings present in the programs, in order to avoid the detection. Though the static analysis is not effective enough to detect unknown malware, it enables fast and safe analysis of malware. This is why many commercial AV products use static analysis to detect malware.

In our static analysis, the features are extracted from unpacked malware executables by means of a command line AV engine [16]. The AV engine identifies and

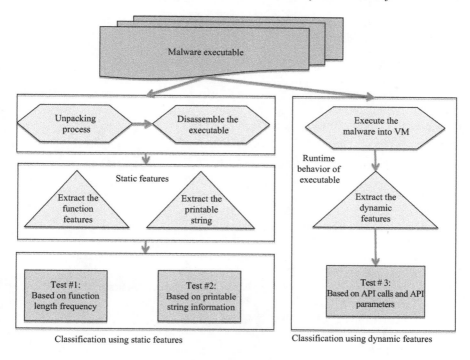

Figure 10.3 Our testing process

unpacks the packed executables in batch mode and identifies functions and printable strings. We extract two static features, from each of the executables, FLF and PSI, as shown in Figure 10.3.

FLF vector generation: To extract FLF features, we follow the methodology described in [21]. The FLF features are based on counting the number of functions in different length ranges or "bins." We derive a vector interpretation of an executable file based on the number of bins chosen and where the function lengths lie across the bins.

In our vector generation process, first, we introduce some standard notation. For instance, let $P = \{P_1, P_2, \ldots, P_N\}$ represent a general population of N function length vectors and $P' = \{P'_1, P'_2, \ldots, P'_N\}$ represent the set of all the standardized vectors. We use F for a set of n vectors from a specific data set having n samples. For any particular function vector P_k with m_k elements, we write $P_k = (p_{k1}, p_{k2}, \ldots, p_{kmk})$ and refer to m_k as the size of the function length vector.

Due to the order of magnitude of differences between function lengths, we increased the range covered by our bins exponentially. For example, we might count the number of functions of lengths between 1 and e bytes, the number between e and e^2 bytes, etc. However, in order to determine an appropriate number of intervals, that is, bins, we follow Sturges's well-established statistical formula [34], which recommends the use of approximately $1 + \log_2(k)$ bins, where k represents the number of instances in the experiment. Based on our value of $k = 771,458$ we use 20 bins.

Finally we count the frequency of the function length. Algorithm 10.2 represents the FLF vector generation process.

Algorithm 10.2 FLF vector generation

INPUT: MG' = {MG'$_1$,MG'$_2$,...,MG'$_{k+1}$}, CG={CG$_1$,CG$_2$,...,CG$_{k+1}$}/ / Data group both Malware and cleanware
Output FLF_V={CFV};//Cumulative feature vectors set.
BEGIN

1. FG = {{MG$_1$,MG$_2$,...,MG$_{k+1}$}{CG$_1$,CG$_2$,...,CG$_{k+1}$}} // Data group both Malware and cleanware
2. PFG ∈ MGi; //Positive data
3. NFG = CG$_i$; // Negative data
4. BN=1+log$_2$(k); //k-> number of malware instances.
5. **FOREACH** i=1...n **DO**;
6. **Cal_F** {ω,BN,FG$_i$,}; // calculate the frequency; ω -> Max Frequency
7.   **FOR EACH** k=1..i **DO**
8.   Read PFG **@param** r // r is the input stream containing the CSV
9.   Converts PFG -> { {}, {} }// 2D array
10. **RETURN** PFG'[{},{}] / the CSV data
11.   **ENDFOR**;
12. Count_Log_F {PFG'[{},{}], ω, BN};//mapping for log indexing scale
13.   Output FLF_V =OutputV + Write{outputV,CSVConverter};//2D Array
14. **ENDFOR**;
15.   **RETURN** FLF_V{PFG, NFG }//FLF Vectors.

END Algorithm;

Example

Consider an executable file with 22 functions that have the following lengths in bytes, presented in increasing order of size: 5, 6, 12, 12, 15, 18, 18, 50, 50, 130, 210, 360, 410, 448, 546, 544, 728, 848, 1344, 1538, 3138, 4632. For the purposes of illustration, we create 10 bins of function length ranges. The distribution of lengths across the bins is as shown in Table 10.2. This produces a vector of length 10 using the entries in the second column of Table 10.2 (0.0, 2.0, 5.0, 2.0, 1.0, 4.0, 4.0, 3.0, 1.0, 0.0), which corresponds to the FLF for the file chosen.

PSI vector generation: In extracting PSI features of a specific sample, we create a vector to represent which printable strings are present in that sample [16]. We first generate a global string ordered list of all the strings that occur in our data group. For instance, let $G = \{s_1, s_2, s_3, \ldots, s_{|G|}\}$, $|G|$ is the total number of distinct string, and s_i is a particular printable string. Each string is given an ordering according to its frequency in the list. For each data sample, we then test which of the strings in our global list it contains. This is computed efficiently by using a hash table to store the global list and by doing hash lookups on the strings contained in a given sample. The

Table 10.2 FLF bin distribution example

FLF bin distribution	
Length of functions	**FLF vectors**
1–2	0.0
3–8	2.0
9–21	5.0
22–59	2.0
60–166	1.0
167–464	4.0
465–1,291	4.0
1,292–3,593	3.0
3,594–9,999	1.0
$\geq 10,000$	0.0

results are recorded in a binary vector, where for each string in the global list, a *True* denotes that it is present and a *False* that it is not [30].

Let *FG* represent the CTA data group both malware and cleanware and each $FG_i = \{m_1, m_2, \ldots, m_n\}$ is a set of software modules m_i which is an executable file in the data group by its *moduleID* m_j^i. Thus, for any particular data group FG_i, we can write $\{m_1^i, m_2^i, \ldots, m_k^i\}$, where k is the number of executables in a particular data group FG_i. We can also view m_1^i as a binary vector capturing which of the strings in the global set *G* are present in the sample. Algorithm 10.3 demonstrates the PSI feature vector generation process.

Algorithm 10.3 PSI vector generation ();

INPUT: MG' = {MG'$_1$,MG'$_2$,...,MG'$_{k+1}$}, CG={CG$_1$,CG$_2$,...,CG$_{k+1}$}// Data group both Malware and cleanware
OUTPUT: PSI_V={CFV};//Cumulative feature vectors set.
BEGIN

1. FG = {{MG$_1$,MG$_2$,...,MG$_{k+1}$}{CG$_1$,CG$_2$,...,CG$_{k+1}$// Data group both Malware and cleanware
2. NFG =CG;
3. PFG ∈ MGi;
4. Generate the string list based on FG;
5. **G** = {s$_1$, s$_2$, s$_3$, ...s$_{|G|}$}// G be the order set of all string;
6. **FOREACH** i=1...n **DO**; // String vector generation.
7.   Call **Gen_String_Vector**(FGi);// Generate the string vector.
        PSI_V{}= PSI_V{}+SI_V{};
8. **ENDFOR;**
9. **RETURN** PSI_V{};

END Algorithm

Function:Gen_String_Vector ();

INPUT: FGi/ / specific data group
OUTPUT: PSI_V={CFV};//Cumulative feature vectors set.

1. **BEGIN**
2. $F=M_i=FG_i = \Phi$;
3. $F=FG_i$; /F represents the order set of FGi
4. $FG_i=\{M_1, M_2,...,Mn\}$// each FGi is a set of software moduesMi
5. $Mi=\{m_1^i, m_2^i, ..., m_k^i\}$ // where m_j^i is module ID and k is number of
6.   modules of FGi
7. **FOREACH** i=1...$|g|$ **DO**
8. $\Re$ = Calculate_String_Number(m_j^i //$\Re$ is string number.
9. **FOREACH** i= 1...$\Re$**DO**
10. **IF** $m_j^i \in G$ **THEN**
11.   Set $|v| = (b_{j1}^i, b_{j2}^i, ..., b_{j|G|}^i)$ //1 ifthe1thstringofGisinb$_j^i$,
12. **ELSE**
13.   Set $|v| = (b_{j1}^i, b_{j2}^i, ..., b_{j|G|}^i)$ //0 ifthe1thstringofGisinb$_j^i$,
14. **ENDIF**;
15. Create PFG' into { $\{m_j^i\}$, $\{ |v| \}$ } // a matrix representation
16.   **ENDFOR**;
17.   Generate SI_V {PFG'};
18.   **RETURNPSI_V**{};

END Algorithm

Example

Consider a global ordered string list containing 10 distinct strings:

{"LoadMemory","GetNextFileA", "FindLastFileA" "GetProcAddress", "RegQueryValueExW", "CreateFileW", "OpenFile", "FindFirstFileA", "FindNextFileA", "CopyMemory"}

Suppose that a particular executable has the following set of printable strings:

{"GetProcAddress","RegQueryValueExW","CreateFileW","GetProcAddress"}

The PSI vector for this executable file records, first of all, the total number of distinct strings in the file followed by a binary report on the presence of each string in the global list, where a "true" represents the fact that the string is present and a "false" that it is not. Table 10.3 presents the corresponding data for this executable file. The vector for this example becomes (4, false, false, false, true, true, true, false false, false, false).

10.5.2.2 Dynamic vector generation

Dynamic analysis of malware is done based on dynamic features of the (packed) executable file [14,15,35–39,42], which requires that malware be executed in a controlled

Table 10.3   Example of PSI vector generation

Printable string	PSI vector
String number	4
LoadMemory	False
GetNextFileA	False
FindLastFileA	False
GetProcAddress	True
RegQueryValueExW	True
CreateFileW	True
OpenFile	False
FindFirstFileA	False
FindNextFielA	False
CopyMemory	False

environment. In [14], Bailey *et al.* propose a method for automatically categorizing behavioral-patterns (e.g., files written, processes created) of malware into groups that reflect similar classes of behaviors and describe an effective way of classifying and analyzing Internet malware.

In [38], Willems *et al.* present an automated dynamic malware analysis technique using CWSand-box. In [15], Wagener *et al.* propose a flexible and automated approach for extracting malware behavior based on system function calls performed by programs in a virtualized execution environment. In [15], Ahmed *et al.* propose a technique by using statistical features that are extracted from both spatial (arguments) and temporal (sequences) information available in Windows API calls. In [39], Zhao *et al.* propose a behavior-based classification method by characterizing malware behavioral profile in a trace report. In [37], Sami *et al.* also propose an approach for detecting malware based on mining API calls from PE files. However, malware writers have developed anti-virtual machine (anti-VM) techniques to compete with dynamic analysis-based malware detection. Malware with anti-VM can recognize that they are in a simulated environment. There is also one observable difference between an emulated and a real system, for example, speed of execution. Dynamic analysis needs much time to determine the features to be used in detection and therefore, rarely used by commercial AV products.

In our feature vector generation process, we run all the executable files and then log the Windows API calls. We extract API features, comprising API function names and parameters, from the log files and again construct a global list that is similar to our existing process in [21]. We treat the functions and its parameters as separate entities as they may separately impact the ability to detect and identify the executable. The figure 10.4 describes the file in execution and API log generation process. The figure describes the file in execution. A vector representation of the log data is extracted after emulation is used in the classification. After running all the executable files in our sample set and logging the Windows API calls, we extract the strings from the log files and again construct a global string list, same method as our previous work [16]. The strings extracted include API function names and parameters passed to the functions.

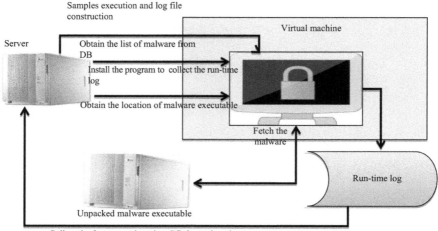

Figure 10.4   API log generation process

In our feature extraction process, we follow the methodology to generate dynamic logs, as described in [16]. For generating a normalized feature vector from dynamic log files, we construct a global feature list from all extracted API calls and API parameters. We treat the functions and parameters as separate entities as they may separately affect the ability to detect and identify the executable. Algorithm 10.4 illustrates the dynamic vector generation process.

Algorithm 10.4 Dynamic vector generation()

INPUT: MG' = {MG'$_1$,MG'$_2$,…,MG'$_{k+1}$} and
      CG={CG$_1$,CG$_2$,…,CG$_{k+1}$}// Data group both Malware and cleanware
OUTPUT: DYNAMIC_V={CFV};//Cumulative feature vectors set.
BEGIN

1. FG = {{MG$_1$,MG$_2$,…,MG$_{k+1}$}{CG$_1$,CG$_2$,…,CG$_{k+1}$// Data group both Malware and cleanware
2. NFG =CG$_i$; PFG ∈ MG$_i$;
3. RESULT {} ← Φ;;// empty buffer for string the unic API calls and API parameters.
4. Calculate_Unic_API_Calls(PFG∩NFG,δ, Θ)// δ is threshold and Θ are Boolean value.
5. K ← $ //Key variable.
6. Create H <$,ℤ>←Φ; // temporary hashtable and initialize the hash table;
7. **FOREACH** i= 1 …Size(PFG)**DO**
8. Create Buff_R←(FileR(PFG[i])); // read the samples the put into a buffer.
9. St ← StringTokenizer;
10. **DO**

11.　　　　K← st.nextToken(); //original string of API Calls and API parameters.
12.　　　　K← Encode. encodeBase64(K); // encode the string using bused 64.
13.　　　　**UNTIL** ((line = bufR.readLine()) != Φ)//for each of the API parameters line.
14.　　　　**DO**
15.　**IF** (H.containsKey(K)==T)**THEN**H ←(K,(H.Get(K))+1);
16.　**ELSEH**←(K, 1);
17.　**ENDIF**;
18.　**UNTIL** (st.H.moreToken()==T);//continue until there is more API calls and API parameters.
19.　**ENDFOR**;
20.　　Call Cal_API_Frequency(H); //calculate the API call and API parameter frequency
21.　$G = \{s_1, s_2, s_3, \ldots s_{|G|} \}$// Generate the string list based on FG; G be the order set of all string;
22.　**FOREACH** i=1…n **DO**; // String vector generation.
23.　　　Call **Gen_StringVector**(FGi);// Generate the string vector.
24.　　　DYNAMIC_V{}= DYNAMIC_V{}+RESULT{};
25.　**ENDFOR**;
26.　**RETURN** DYNAMIC_V{};

END Algorithm;

Function:Cal_API_Frequency()

INPUT : H;// hash table.
BEGIN

1.　Create e = Enumeration<$>;//order the hash table;
2.　　　Create H' <$,$\mathbb{Z}$>←Φ; //initialize the hash table;
3.　　　e ← H.K();
4.　**FOREACH** j= 1.. e.hasMoreElements()==T **DO**
5.　　　$ K'=($) e.nextElement(); //next API;
6.　**IF** (H'.Get(K')>δ) **THEN** // eliminate the duplicates APIs;
7.　**IF** (H'.containsK(K')) **THEN** H' ← (K',H'.Get(K')+1);
8.　**ELSE** H'←(K', H.G(K'));
9.　　　**ENDIF**;
10.　RESULT ← ($\mathbb{Z}$) [H'.size()]; // initialize the buffer;
11.　　**ENDIF**;
12.　**FOREACH** k ← 1.. H'.size() **DO**
13.　　RESULT[i]← i;
14.　**ENDFOR**;
15.　　**RETURN** RESULT;
16.　**ENDFOR**;

END Algorithm;

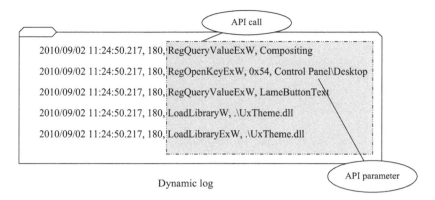

Figure 10.5   Example dynamic log for an executable

Example

For illustration, consider the following global API feature list:

> {"RegOpenKeyEx","RegQueryValueExW","Compositing","RegOpenKeyExW",
> "0x54","ControlPanel\Desktop","LameButtonText","LoadLibraryW",
> ".\UxTheme.dll","LoadLibraryExW","MessageBoxW"}.

Suppose a particular executable generates a log file as shown in Figure 10.5. The API calls and API parameters are highlighted in the figure. We now list the distinct features in the global list and generate a vector for the executable based on the frequency of these features. Table 10.4 shows the distinct global feature list with corresponding frequencies for this particular example and the corresponding feature vector is (0, 2, 1, 1, 1, 1, 1, 1, 2, 1, 0).

10.6   CTA malware detection method

In our classification process, we input the generated feature vectors into the WEKA classification system [23,43] for which we have written an interface. In all experiments, 10-fold cross-validation is applied to ensure a thorough mixing of the features. In this procedure, we first select one group of malware data from a particular data set and divide it into ten portions of equal size; then we select cleanware data of the same size as the group of malware data and also divide it into 10 portions. The portions are then tested against each other. The whole process is repeated for each group and we then calculate average classification results. In our test, we have multiple tests within each group. Figure 10.6 shows the number of tests within a period range.

To establish the training set, our detection engine takes nine portions from each of the malware and cleanware to set up the training set and the remaining portions from both malware and cleanware are used for the testing set. As is customary, the training set is used to establish the model and the testing set is used to validate it. The whole

Table 10.4   Example of dynamic feature vector generation.

Dynamic feature vector generation

Global feature	Frequency
RegOpenKeyEx	0
RegQueryValueExW	2
Compositing	1
RegOpenKeyExW	1
0x54	1
ControlPanel\Desktop	1
LameButtonText	1
LoadLibraryW	1
.\UxTheme.dll	2
LoadLibraryExW	2
MessageBoxW	0

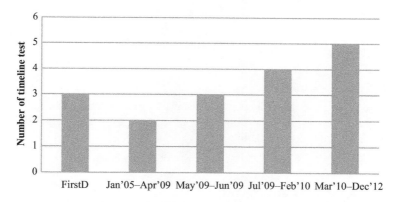

Figure 10.6   Number of tests within the group of data set

process is repeated so that every portion of both malware and cleanware is chosen as testing data. The results are then averaged. In order to ensure that the input vectors are trained and tested over a broad spectrum of classifiers, we chose the following four classifiers from WEKA as they represent differing approaches to statistical analysis of data: support vector machines (SVM), random forest (RF), decision table (DT), and IB1.

10.6.1   Environment

We have run our experiments using an Intel(R) Core(TM) Duo E8400 3.0 GHz Windows XP PC with 3.49 GB RAM. The refinement algorithms have been implemented in Java along with SQL server 5.1 and SDK is Eclipse 3.5. The tested classifiers are integrated into our framework from WEKA class library [40].

10.6.2   Evaluation process

We evaluate the effectiveness of our framework by three different measures. These are malware detection rate (MDR), false alarm rate (FAR), and accuracy (ACC). Let n_{tp} be the number of malware that are correctly classified as malware, n_{fp} be the number of benign programs that are incorrectly classified as malware, n_{tn} be the number of benign programs that are correctly classified as benign programs, and n_{fn} be the number of malware that are incorrectly classified as benign programs. Then MDR, FAR, and ACC are defined as follows:

$$MDR = \frac{n_{tp}}{n_{tp} + n_{fn}} \tag{10.1}$$

$$FAR = \frac{n_{fp}}{n_{tn} + n_{fp}} \tag{10.2}$$

$$ACC = \frac{n_{tp} + n_{tn}}{n_{tp} + n_{tn} + n_{fp} + n_{fn}} \tag{10.3}$$

The MDR measures the proportion of malware that are correctly labeled as malware by the system and the FAR measures the proportion of benign programs that are falsely labeled as malware. In contrast, the ACC measures the overall accuracy of the system to detect malware and benign files.

10.7   Experiments and results

We ran the entire experiment using each of the four base classifiers SVM, IB1, DT, and RF mentioned in Section 10.3. In addition, each test was run five times and the results averaged in order to ensure that any anomalies in the experimental set-up were discounted. The following sections present our empirical results.

10.7.1   Timeline classification results using FLF features

As mentioned in Section 10.3, the total number of FLF features used is fixed at 20 (bins) throughout the tests. Figure 10.7 shows the result over the ten year timeline. The X-axis shows the timeline data group and the Y-axis shows the detection ratio of malware. It is clear that we achieve better detection accuracy for early malware compared to that for later malware. IB1 and RF give consistently better results across the timeline. SVM gives the worst performance, likely due to the very small feature set used in the experiment given that it is designed to handle large feature spaces.

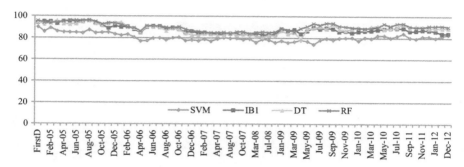

Figure 10.7   Cumulative timeline results based on FLF test

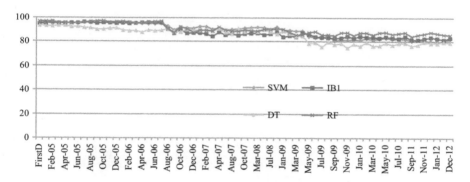

Figure 10.8   Timeline results based on PSI test

10.7.2   Timeline classification results using PSI features

The number of PSI features used for each data group grows across the timeline, varying from approximately 800 to 2,085. Figure 10.8 shows the detection results using the PSI feature set. Compared to FLF results, these are more consistent, varying less over the timeline for all classifiers.

10.7.3   Timeline classification results using dynamic features

The number of features used in this test increases from approximately 2,600 to 8,800 over the timeline. Figure 10.9 shows the detection accuracy of the dynamic feature set, which is based on API calls and API parameters.

For all but the IB1 classifier, the dynamic feature results give a consistent performance compared to either of the static feature methods. With a large feature set, IB1 is inclined to make errors when building the training sets, which is likely to account for the poor performance here.

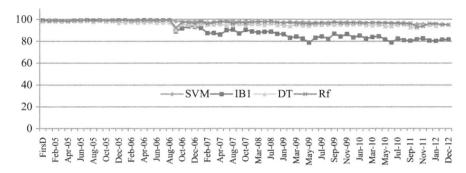

Figure 10.9   Timeline results based on dynamic test

Table 10.5   Comparison of the methods for the 65th group

Feature set	SVM			IB1			DT			RF		
	FP	FN	ACC	FP	FN	ACC	FP	FN	ACC	FP	FN	ACC
FLF	0.07	0.66	83.26	0.14	0.25	84.23	0.17	0.28	89.17	0.03	0.11	90.51
PSI	0.12	0.25	81.98	0.1	0.23	82.92	0.15	0.24	78.87	0.12	0.21	85.33
Dynamic	0.01	0.12	94.81	0.17	0.16	81.65	0.02	0.08	95.35	0.03	0.04	95.29

In Table 10.5, we have summarized the data for the last group, the 65th group of our dataset, which includes all of the executables, showing the false positive (FP) and false negative (FN) rates. Note the very poor accuracy of SVM with FLF while, with IB1, FLF has slightly better accuracy than the dynamic test, and with DT and RF, the results for FLF are not too far from those for the PSI test. It is thus difficult to argue that FLF should be deleted from the test altogether. Additionally, the FNs and FPs of all tests in the case of IB1 and DT are much higher than other two classifiers. However, the dynamic test gives better performance comparing all parameters.

10.8   Conclusions and future work

In this chapter, we have presented a cumulative timeline approach to identifying malware from cleanware and demonstrated that it retains high accuracy over 10-year period. The results presented in Section 10.4 indicate that our method retains fairly consistent accuracy over the 10-year period. Our approach to feature collection is novel in that we accumulate the features over time segments of a 10-year span. In progressively adding malware over the time period, we thereby strengthen the accuracy of the test. The implication for AV engines is that they are then able to use previously detected malware to provide features based on which to test new executables. The results presented in Section 10.4 indicate that no one feature type is the most significant over the 10-year span. In our experiment, the static (FLF and PSI) and dynamic features act independently. Therefore, it is expected that combining static and dynamic features in an integrated manner could give a better detection rate; we will explore this in our future work.

References

[1] Eric A.F. *Cybersecurity Issues and Challenges: In Brief*, Congressional Research Service (CRS) Report—R43831, August 12, 2016 (available at http://www.crs.gov).

[2] Wu C.H., and Irwin J.D. *Introduction to Computer Networks and Cybersecurity*. Boca Raton: CRC Press, 2013.

[3] Lee N. *Counterterrorism and Cybersecurity: Total Information Awareness* (2nd ed.). Springer International Publishing Switzerland, 2015.

[4] Singer P.W., and Friedman A. *Cybersecurity and Cyberwar: What Everyone Needs to Know*. P. W. Singer and Allan Friedman (P)2016 Tantor, 2014.

[5] Kim P. *The Hacker Playbook: Practical Guide to Penetration Testing*. Seattle: CreateSpace Independent Publishing Platform, 2014.

[6] ITU publication. *Understanding Cybercrime: Phenomena, Challenges and Legal Response*, September 2012 (available online at www.itu.int/ITU-D/cyb/cybersecurity/legislation.html).

[7] State of Alabama Information Services Division. *Why Cyber Security Is Important*. A report available at www.cybersecurity.alabama.gov (retrieved on 20 November 2016).

[8] Bishop M. *Introduction to Computer Security*. Addison-Wesley Professional; 1 edition, November 5, 2004.

[9] Rogers D. *Mobile Security: A Guide for Users*. Copper Horse Solutions Limited, 2013. ISBN 9781291533095.

[10] Nikola Z. *Computer Security and Mobile Security Challenges*, Research-Gate, 2015 (available online at https://www.researchgate.net/publication/298807979).

[11] Perry D. *Here comes the flood or end of the pattern file*. Virus Bulletin, 2008.

[12] Zhou Y., and Inge W.M. 'Malware detection using adaptive data compression', *AISec*, 2008; pp. 53–60.

[13] Aaraj N., Raghunathan A., and Jha N.K. 'Dynamic binary instrumentation-based framework for malware defense', *DIMVA*, 2008; pp. 64–87.

[14] Bailey M., Oberheide J., Andersen J., Mao Z., Jahanian F., and Nazario J. *Automated Classification and Analysis of Internet Malware*, In: Recent Advances in Intrusion Detection. 2007, pp. 178–197.

[15] Wagener G., State R., and Dulaunoy A. 'Malware behaviour analysis'. *Journal in Computer Virology*, vol. 4, 2008; pp. 279–287.

[16] Islam R., Tian R., Batten L.M., and Versteeg S. 'Classification of malware based on integrated static and dynamic features'. *Journal of Network and Computer Applications*, vol. 36, pp. 646–656.

[17]   Egele M., Scholte T., Kirda E., and Kruegel C. 'A survey on automated dynamic malware-analysis techniques and tools'. *ACM Computing Surveys*, 44(2), 2008; pp. 6:1–6:42.

[18]   Fossi M., Johnson E., Mack T., *et al. Symantec global internet security threat report trends for 2009*. Technical report, 2009.

[19]   Rosyid N.R., Ohrui M., Kikuchi H., Sooraksa P., and Terada M. 'A discovery of sequential attack patterns of malware in botnets'. *IEEE International Conference on Systems Man and Cybernetics*, IEEE, 2010, pp. 2564–2570.

[20]   Tang H., Zhu B., and Ren K. 'A new approach to malware detection'. *Advances in Information Security and Assurance*, 2009; pp. 229–238.

[21]   Tian R., Batten L.M., and Versteeg S.C. 'Function length as a tool for malware classification'. *Proceedings of the 3rd International Conference on Malicious and Unwanted Software: MALWARE 2008*, 2008; pp. 69–76.

[22]   You I., and Yim K. 'Malware obfuscation techniques: A brief survey'. *International Conference on Broadband, Wireless Computing, Communication and Applications (BWCCA 2010)*, IEEE, 2010; pp. 297–300.

[23]   Mark H., Eibe F., Geoffrey H., Bernhard P., Peter R., and Ian H.W. 'The WEKA Data Mining Software: An Update'. *SIGKDD Explorations*, vol. 11, 2009; pp. 10–18.

[24]   Yagi T., Tanimoto N., Hariu T., and Itoh M. 'Investigation and analysis of malware on websites'. *12th IEEE International Symposium Web Systems Evolution (WSE 2010)*, IEEE, 2010. pp. 73–81.

[25]   Rajab M., Ballard L., Jagpal N., *et al. Trends in circumventing web-malware detection*, Technical report, Google, July 2011.

[26]   Marcus D., Greve P., Masiello S., and Scharoun D. *Mcafee threats report: Third quarter 2009*. Technical report, 2009.

[27]   Lee J., Im C., and Jeong H. 'A study of malware detection and classification by comparing extracted strings'. *Proceedings of the 5th International Conference on Ubiquitous Information Management and Communication*, ACM, 2011; p. 75.

[28]   Soltani S., Ali K.S., and Radha H. 'Detecting malware outbreaks using a statistical model of blackhole traffic'. *IEEE International Conference Communications* (ICC 2008). IEEE, 2008; pp. 1593–1597.

[29]   Nair V.P., Jain H., Golecha Y.K., Gaur M.S., and Laxmi V. 'Medusa: Metamorphic malware dynamic analysis using signature from API'. *Proceedings of the 3rd International Conference on Security of Information and Networks*, ACM, 2010; pp. 263–269.

[30]   Tian R., Batten L., Islam R., and Versteeg S. 'An automated classification system based on the strings of Trojan and virus families'. *Proceedings of the 4rd International Conference on Malicious and Unwanted Software: MALWARE 2009*, 2009; pp. 23–30.

[31]   Tian R., Islam R., Batten L., and Versteeg S. 'Differentiating malware from cleanware using behavioural analysis'. *5th International Conference on Malicious and Unwanted Software (MALWARE 2010)*, 2010. pp. 23 –30.

[32]   Lu W., Tavallaee M., and Ghorbani A.A. 'Automatic discovery of botnet communities on large-scale communication networks'. *Proceedings of the 4th International Symposium on Information, Computer, and Communications Security*, ACM, NY, USA. pp. 1–10.

[33]   Mohaisen A., and Alrawi O., 'Unveiling zeus, automated classification of malware samples'. In: *WWW (Companion volume)*, 2013, pp. 829–832.

[34]   Sturges H.A. 'The choice of a class interval'. *Journal of the American Statistical Association*, vol. 21, 1926; pp. 65–66.

[35]   Ahmed F., Hameed H., Shafiq M.Z., and Farooq M. 'Using spatio-temporal information in api calls with machine learning algorithms for malware detection', *Proceedings of the 2nd ACM Workshop on Security and Artificial Intelligence*, ACM, New York, USA. 2009; pp. 55–62.

[36]   Cesare S., and Xiang Y. 'A fast flowgraph based classification system for packed and polymorphic malware on the endhost'. *AINA*, 2010; pp. 721–728.

[37]   Sami A., Yadegari B., Rahimi H., Peiravian N., Hashemi S., and Hamze A. 'Malware detection based on mining api calls'. *Proceedings of the ACM Symposium on Applied Computing*, ACM, New York, USA, 2010. pp. 1020–1025.

[38]   Willems C., Holz T., and Freiling F. 'Toward automated dynamic malware analysis using cwsandbox'. *IEEE Security and Privacy*, 2007; vol 5, pp. 32–39.

[39]   Zhao H., Xu M., Zheng N., Yao J., and Ho Q. 'Malicious executables classification based on behavioral factor analysis'. *Proceedings of the 2010 International Conference on e-Education, e-Business, e-Management and e-Learning, IEEE Computer Society*, 2010, Washington, DC, USA. pp. 502–506.

[40]   Hall M., Frank E., Holmes G., Pfahringer B., Reutemann P., and Witten I.H., 'The weka data mining software: An update'. *SIGKDD Explorations*, 11, 2009; pp. 10–18.

[41]   Braverman M., Williams J., and Mador Z. *Microsoft security intelligence report*, May 2011.

[42]   Roundy K., and Miller B. 'Hybrid analysis and control of malware'. Jha S., Sommer R., Kreibich C. (eds.) *Recent Advances in Intrusion Detection*, volume 6307 of Lecture Notes in Computer Science, Springer Berlin/Heidelberg, 2010; pp. 317–338.

[43]   Myers, B.A., Weitzman, D.A., Ko A.J., and Chau D.H. 2006. Answering why and why not questions in user interfaces. In: *CHI*, 2013, pp. 397–406. PE-Explorer.

Chapter 11

Recent trends in the cryptanalysis of block ciphers

Ahmed Abdelkhalek[1], Mohamed Tolba[1], and Amr M. Youssef[1]

11.1   Introduction and overview

Cryptology is a science that consists of two complementary fields [1]: cryptography and cryptanalysis. On the one hand, cryptography encompasses the design of algorithms that are used to achieve specific security goals. On the other hand, cryptanalysis studies techniques with the aim of violating the security goals of these cryptographic algorithms. The security goals considered in modern cryptography vary according to its application and include confidentiality, integrity, authenticity, anonymity, and nonrepudiation [2]. The basic primitives in a security system that are used to provide such security goals are called cryptographic primitives.

Basic cryptographic primitives comprise symmetric primitives, also known as secret-key primitives and asymmetric or public-key primitives. The former uses a shared key that has to be kept secret within a restricted group, while in the latter, each user has a pair of keys; one is kept private and never shared and the other is public. After the invention of public-key cryptography in the mid-1970s, there was a misconception that symmetric primitives would become obsolete. However, symmetric primitives are still extensively used as they achieve high-throughput performance or low-cost encryption, fast authentication, and efficient hashing. Nowadays, symmetric primitives are used in securing wireless communications, Internet online transactions, and WLAN connections and symmetric cryptology is an active research area as it has always been. In fact, there is still a compelling need to further advance the symmetric cryptology research. On the one hand, the huge demand for deploying resource-constrained, yet cryptographically secure, devices such as RFID (Radio Frequency IDentification) tags and wireless sensor nodes dictates the demand for low-cost primitives. On the other hand, the development of the state-of-the-art of cryptanalysis may threaten the security of some existing and widely used primitives. Therefore, the problem of studying new cryptographic techniques remains necessary to evaluate the existing cryptographic primitives and design new efficient and more secure ones.

[1]Concordia Institute for Information Systems Engineering, Concordia University, Canada

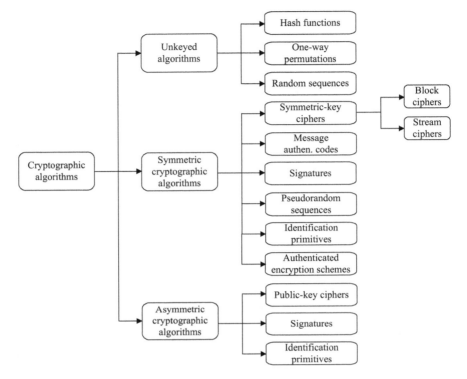

Figure 11.1   A classification of cryptographic primitives [2]

Figure 11.1 presents a classification of cryptographic primitives. In this chapter, we focus on symmetric cryptographic primitives in general and, in particular, block ciphers which are crucial primitives that can be used to build other symmetric cryptographic primitives.

11.1.1   Symmetric cryptographic primitives

A symmetric cryptographic primitive is a transformation that takes, at least, two inputs (data and a secret key) and maps them into one or two output(s). Three basic types that are of interest are ciphers (either block or stream ciphers), message authentication codes (MAC), and authenticated encryption (AE) schemes. Strictly speaking, cryptographic hash functions are not symmetric cryptographic primitives, since they do not use a secret key. However, a MAC primitive or a MAC scheme can be constructed using hash functions. Moreover, hash functions can be built using block ciphers. Therefore, the properties of hash functions are closely related to those of symmetric cryptographic primitives. Usually, only data confidentiality, integrity, and authenticity can be directly attained by symmetric cryptographic primitives. Cryptographic protocols based on symmetric cryptographic primitives achieve other security goals.

Block ciphers and stream ciphers provide data confidentiality by encrypting a plaintext (the input message) to a ciphertext (the transformed output message). For a fixed key, block ciphers and stream ciphers become invertible mappings. On the one hand, a block cipher [3] can be thought of as a class of permutations on blocks of bits. When a particular key is selected, a specific permutation is chosen out of this class. The encryption process is done by applying this permutation to the plaintext yielding the ciphertext. The plaintext is restored via the decryption process by applying the inverse permutation to the ciphertext. On the other hand, a stream cipher [4] generates a stream of pseudorandom digits (keystream) which is combined (e.g., through an XOR operation) with the plaintext (ciphertext) to produce the ciphertext (plaintext).

A MAC [5] scheme provides data integrity and authenticity. A MAC primitive takes an input message and a secret key and computes an authentication tag which is then sent along with the message. The receiver of the message then uses the shared secret key to compute the authentication tag corresponding to the received message. If the calculated authentication tag matches the received one, then the sender is authenticated and the message integrity is verified. It is worth mentioning that, unlike block ciphers and stream ciphers, MAC primitives do not have to be invertible, as both users perform the same operation to compute or verify the authentication tag.

A hash function [6] is a primitive that transforms a message of any arbitrary, but usually limited, length into a hash value of fixed length. In other words, a hash function compresses a message and generates a digest that depends on all the bits of the message. Therefore, hash functions, similar to MAC primitives, can be used to provide data integrity. However, they do not use a secret key and thus anyone can generate the hash value for a given message. The cryptographic properties of hash functions vary according to the application that embodies them and include preimage resistance, second preimage resistance, and collision resistance [2].

AE schemes [7] are symmetric cryptographic primitives that provide data confidentiality, integrity, and authenticity at the same time. An extension of AE schemes is Authenticated Encryption with Associated Data (AEAD) schemes. AEAD schemes take an input called Associated Data (AD) whose integrity and authenticity has to be ensured while being sent in the clear without encryption. For example, routing information in headers of datagram packets which has to remain unencrypted for routing purposes and at the same time has to be authenticated to detect any tampering. A very common approach to construct AE(AD) schemes is the generic composition which combines a symmetric encryption scheme such as a block cipher or a stream cipher and a MAC primitive. Usually, each primitive uses its own secret key. Encrypt-and-MAC, MAC-then-Encrypt, and Encrypt-then-MAC are three well-known generic composition approaches. Another approach to build AE(AD) schemes is through the use of specific AE(AD) block cipher modes of operation, such as Galois Counter Mode (GCM) [8], Offset Codebook (OCB) Mode [9], Counter with CBC-MAC [10], and EAX Mode [11]. AE(AD) modes of operation transform an arbitrary block cipher into an AE scheme usually supporting AD as well. A third approach is to construct dedicated AE(AD) schemes using one secret key either employing a permutation in sponge construction such as FIDES [12] and APE [13], or using the components of block ciphers such as the AES (Advanced Encryption Standard) [14] round function in the AES-based Lightweight authenticated Encryption [15], AEGIS [16], and PAES (Parallelizable Authenticated Encryption Schemes) [17]. The design and cryptanalysis of AE(AD) primitives have found renewed interest driven by the NIST-funded competition: competition for authenticated encryption, security, applicability, and robustness (CAESAR) [18]. CAESAR was announced in 2013, and "will identify a portfolio of authenticated ciphers that (1) offer advantages over AES-GCM and (2) are suitable for widespread adoption" [18].

11.2 Introduction to block ciphers

11.2.1 Block ciphers definition

A block cipher is a symmetric primitive with the purpose of protecting the secrecy of messages sent over an insecure channel. It is defined as follows:

Definition 11.1. (Block cipher [2, Definition 7.1]). *An n-bit block cipher is a function* $E : V_n \times \mathcal{K} \rightarrow V_n$, *such that for each key* $K \in \mathcal{K}$, $E(P,K)$ *is an invertible mapping (the encryption function for K) from* V_n *to* V_n, *written* $E_K(P)$. *The inverse mapping is the decryption function, denoted* $D_K(C)$. $C = E_K(P)$ *denotes the ciphertext C resulting from encrypting plaintext P under K.*

A block cipher can be thought of as 2^k permutations on $\mathbb{F}_2^n$ out of its $2^n!$ distinct permutations, where n is the block size and k is the key size. Hence, for a block cipher to be ideal, its 2^k permutations have to be chosen randomly out of all the $2^n!$ possible permutations.

Definition 11.2. (Ideal block cipher [19]). *An n-bit block cipher E is called ideal, if the family of* 2^k *permutations on* $\mathbb{F}_2^n$ *specified by E is selected uniformly at random from of all* $2^n!$ *distinct permutation on* $\mathbb{F}_2^n$.

An ideal block cipher as defined above is impractical to implement as it requires storing 2^k truly random selected permutations on $\mathbb{F}_2^n$ which is practically infeasible for typical secure values of n and k. Therefore, the design of block ciphers is inevitably highly structured as discussed in the next section.

11.2.2 Block ciphers' design

In 1949, Shannon set the basis of the field of block ciphers' design by putting forward the concepts of confusion and diffusion [20] that are still considered while designing new block ciphers nowadays. In simple terms, confusion means that each bit of the ciphertext should depend on as many bits as possible of the plaintext and the secret key. It is achieved by using nonlinear components in the block cipher such as substitution boxes (Sboxes) and/or modular addition. On the other hand, diffusion captures the influence of each plaintext bit and each key bit on the ciphertext bits. Ideally, flipping one bit of the plaintext/ciphertext should result in flipping each ciphertext/plaintext

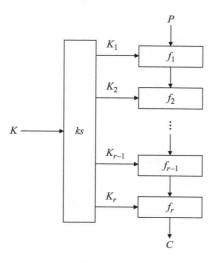

Figure 11.2   An iterative block cipher

bit with probability 0.5. To achieve diffusion, a block cipher designer usually uses linear transformations or permutations working at the bit or the byte level.

Today, the most efficient block ciphers are built by iterating a rather simple key-dependent round function. Such a simple key-dependent round function acts individually as a weak block cipher but iterating it several times achieves a high degree of confusion and diffusion and thus may yield a strong block cipher. Figure 11.2 gives a schematic view of an iterative block cipher. More formally, an iterative block cipher is defined as follows:

Definition 11.3. (Iterative block cipher [21, Definition 4]). *An n-bit block cipher E is called an iterative block cipher with r rounds if for each key it can be represented as a composition of keyed round permutations, that is, if for each $K \in \mathbb{F}_2^k$:*

$$E(K, .) = f_r(K_r, .) \circ f_{r-1}(K_{r-1}, .) \circ \cdots \circ f_2(K_2, .) \circ f_1(K_1, .), \tag{11.1}$$

where $\circ$ denotes the superposition of permutations, $f_i(K_i, .) : \mathbb{F}_2^n \to \mathbb{F}_2^n$ are key-dependent round permutations, K_i are round subkeys derived from the secret key K using a key schedule algorithm:

$$ks : K \to (K_1, K_2, \ldots, K_{r-1}, K_r). \tag{11.2}$$

If all the round permutations of an iterative block cipher are identical, i.e., $f_i = f$, then it is called an iterated block cipher. Typically, we still talk about an iterated block cipher even if the first and/or the last round are slightly different than the other rounds. Another distinguished class of iterative block ciphers is the key-alternating block ciphers. In such a block cipher, the input I to the key-dependent permutation f_i is first XORed with the key K_i and then a key-independent permutation f_i' is applied,

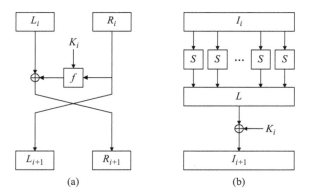

Figure 11.3   Round function of (a) Balanced Feistel Network and (b) Substitution–Permutation Network

i.e., $f_i(K_i, I) = f_i'(K_i \oplus I)$. A key-alternating block cipher that uses identical key-independent permutations is called a key-iterated block cipher.

There are so many constructions to build an iterative block cipher. Figure 11.3 shows the round functions of the two most widely adopted ones: Balanced Feistel Network (BFN) and Substitution–Permutation Network (SPN). In a BFN, the round function input is divided into two halves, i.e., L_i and R_i and the outputs L_{i+1} and R_{i+1} are computed as follows:

$$L_{i+1} = R_i, \tag{11.3}$$

$$R_{i+1} = L_i \oplus f(K_i, R_i), \tag{11.4}$$

where K_i is the ith round subkey and f is the round function. A BFN has the advantage of reusing the implementation of the encryption function to implement the decryption one where the round subkeys are used in reverse. The former US encryption standard DES (Data Encryption Standard) [22], which is an iterated non-key-alternating block cipher, follows the BFN construction. The round function of an SPN block cipher consists of three layers (not necessarily in the following order): the parallel execution of Sboxes, linear permutation, and round subkey addition layer. The decryption function in SPN block ciphers is performed by inverting the encryption process while taking the round subkeys in reversed order. The advantage of SPN block ciphers lies in the fact that they tend to have good diffusion properties. The current US encryption standard AES [14], which is a key-iterated block cipher, employs the SPN construction. Other constructions used to build iterative block ciphers include the Lai–Massey scheme followed by the IDEA block cipher [23] and Generalized Feistel Network exemplified by the TWINE block cipher [24].

Another type of block ciphers is the so-called tweakable block ciphers. In addition to the usual two inputs, the plaintext and the key, tweakable block ciphers accept a third input called the tweak which can be publicly known. The choice of a specific key along with a particular tweak selects one of the possible $2^n!$ permutations of an n-bit block cipher. Tweakable block ciphers are usually used when it is required to generate a different ciphertext each time the same message is encrypted using the same key. For example, if two identical sectors of a hard disk drive are encrypted using a particular key, they will yield the same ciphertext, then an adversary can copy an encrypted sector to an unused one and request its decryption. Therefore, in order to circumvent such attack, each sector should generate a different ciphertext even if it is encrypted under the same key and this is where the tweak comes to be handy. In such a case, the tweak can be chosen to be the sector number that would instantiate a different permutation of the employed block cipher and thus produce a different ciphertext for each sector given a specific key. Tweakable block ciphers should satisfy the following properties: they should be efficient, more specifically, changing the tweak should be more efficient than changing the key; and they should be secure considering that the tweak is publicly known. Recently, a large set of tweakable block ciphers were proposed, including Deoxys-BC [25], Joltik-BC [25], Kiasu-BC [25], and the SKINNY family [26].

11.3   Block ciphers' security

The highest level of security, perfect security, was introduced by Shannon [20] and is achieved when the ciphertext does not reveal any information about the plaintext, or in other words, if the plaintext and the ciphertext are statistically independent.

It was proved by Shannon that the entropy of the key in perfectly secure ciphers has to be at least as high as the entropy of the plaintext. This means that the length of the key in such ciphers must, at least, equal the length of the plaintext and, moreover, it cannot be reused again. As large amounts of data need to be encrypted, perfectly secure block ciphers are impractical. Instead, practical block ciphers can achieve at most computational security defined as follows:

Definition 11.4. (Computational security [27, Definition 7]). *A block cipher E using a k-bit secret key is called computationally secure if there exist no attacks on E with a complexity less than the one of an exhaustive key search, i.e., 2^k, where the complexity of the attack comprises the time (work factor), memory (storage requirement), and data (type and amount of data) complexities required to perform the attack.*

As the above definition implies, it is difficult to evaluate and/or prove that a block cipher is computationally (in)secure. Thus, the security of block ciphers is typically evaluated by considering their resistance against a large set of predefined cryptanalytic attacks and depends on two factors: the goal of the adversary and the assumed attack model, i.e., what the attacker is allowed to do to launch a certain attack.

11.3.1   Adversary's goal

The goal of the adversary differs greatly with the application in which the block cipher is deployed. Below, we give a hierarchical classification of these goals, following

Knudsen [28, p. 7–8], starting with the most powerful attack while assuming that the block cipher is used for encryption only:

- Total break: The adversary recovers the secret key K.
- Global deduction: The adversary can construct an algorithm that is functionally equivalent to E_K or D_K without knowing K.
- Local deduction: The adversary can decrypt (encrypt) a previously unseen ciphertext (plaintext) without knowing K.
- Distinguishing algorithm: The adversary can distinguish between the block cipher instantiated with a randomly chosen key and a randomly chosen permutation.

For other primitives, the adversary might seek additional goals. For example, in MAC primitives, the attacker may additionally attempt to generate a valid authentication tag for a given or a chosen message without the knowledge of the secret key. In hash functions, the attacker may try to find two distinct messages that yield the same hash value (a collision) or a (second) preimage for a given message. In AE(AD) schemes, the goals of the attacker combine the goals achieved while attacking an encryption scheme and a MAC primitive.

11.3.2   Attack models

The attack models specify the capabilities of the adversary while trying to violate the security claims of a block cipher. A common model assumed in conventional cryptography is so-called the black-box model where the end-users of the communication channel are assumed trusted. The black-box attack model, which is the focus of our cryptanalytic techniques in this chapter, can be classified into the following types according to the operations which the adversary is allowed to perform on the input and/or output of the block cipher:

- Ciphertext-only: The attacker can observe ciphertexts without any access to plaintexts. This is the weakest attack scenario and if a block cipher is vulnerable to such an attack, it is considered completely useless.
- Known-plaintext: The attacker observes a number of plaintexts and their corresponding ciphertexts.
- Chosen-plaintext (ciphertext): The attacker can choose plaintexts (ciphertexts) to be encrypted (decrypted) before the attack and observes their corresponding ciphertexts (plaintexts) during the attack.
- Adaptively chosen-plaintext (ciphertext): On top of the chosen-plaintext (ciphertext) capabilities mentioned above, the attacker can choose plaintexts (ciphertexts) during the attack based on some intermediate results obtained during the attack.
- Related-key: The attacker can encrypt (decrypt) plaintexts (ciphertexts) with the attacked key and other keys related to it, where such relation is known or even chosen by the attacker [29].

It is to be noted that the above classification is not comprehensive, for example, we can mix attacks from these classes yielding a, usually, more efficient one. In addition, in hash functions that are built using block ciphers the key of the block cipher is

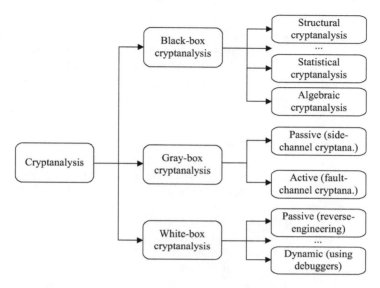

Figure 11.4   A classification of cryptanalytic attack models

known or even under the control of the attacker and thus other attack scenarios, such as the known key and the chosen key setting [30] can be relevant in this case.

Recently, with the proliferation of computers and communication systems, cryptographic applications implemented either in hardware or in software were brought closer to a very broad audience of end-users. Thus, the assumption that the end-users of the communication channel are trusted is no longer realistic leading to a need for more practical attack models incorporating more powerful adversaries. One such attack model is called the gray-box attack model. In this model, the attacks can be split into two main types: passive (side-channel cryptanalysis [31]) and active (fault cryptanalysis [32]). In side-channel cryptanalysis, the cryptanalyst exploits unintentionally leaked information from the implementation of the primitive such as its execution time, electromagnetic radiation, or power consumption. Fault cryptanalysis exploits faults intentionally induced during the computation of the cryptographic primitive.

Another more recent attack model incorporating the capabilities of an even more powerful attacker is the white-box attack model. This model focuses on the software implementations of cryptographic primitives. In such a model, the attacker has not only full access to the software implementation of a given cryptographic primitive but also full control over its execution environment. In other words, the attacker can use debuggers with breakpoint functionality to observe and manipulate intermediate results of the implementation or even search the memory for stored cryptographic keys. These techniques are often referred to as dynamic analysis. In what is called static analysis, the attacker is allowed to reverse-engineer the software implementation with the help of disassemblers or decompilers. Figure 11.4 gives a simple taxonomy of the cryptanalytic techniques.

In this chapter, our main focus is block ciphers and block cipher based constructions using the black-box attack model. Therefore, in the next section, we provide an introduction to the conventional cryptanalysis techniques including, but not limited to, differential cryptanalysis, linear cryptanalysis, and Meet-in-the-Middle (MitM) cryptanalysis. We also discuss some of the cryptanalytic techniques that emerged recently such as the invariant subspace attack.

11.4   Attacks on block ciphers

The attacks on block ciphers can be classified into generic and nongeneric attacks. Generic attacks exploit the core parameters of the block cipher, e.g., the block size and key length. These attacks include the exhaustive key search (brute-force) attack where all the possible values of the secret key are tested against known plaintext/ciphertext pair(s) and as such the time complexity of this attack to recover a k-bit secret key is about 2^k encryptions. Ciphertext collision attack, Time-memory trade-off attack [33, 34], Key-collision attack [35], and Related-key cube-based attack [36] are other examples of generic attacks. As the generic attacks are entirely independent on the block cipher design or its specification, the only countermeasure against these attacks is to increase the key and plaintext spaces. Currently, the set $\{80, 112, 128, 192, 256\}$ is the key length, specified in bits, recommended by NIST noting that an 80-bit key is no longer considered sufficiently secure [37].

This said, the tremendous advancement of building powerful and still cheap multicore processors, particularly, the Graphical Processing Units (GPUs) has given rise to a novel line of research to exploit their capabilities in speeding up exhaustive key search or in cryptanalysis in general. Indeed, a 64-GPU cluster was recently used to provide the first practical break of the full-step compression function of the SHA-1 hash function [38]. It needed 10 days of computation to generate a freestart colliding pair. In addition, GPU-like special-purpose hardware, i.e., multicore AES processors that can reach a throughput of up to 10^{12} AES operations per second were designed to evaluate the cost of cryptanalytic attacks on the full AES [39]. It was estimated that with one trillion US\$, a supercomputer built on such multicore processors could theoretically break the full AES within 1 year using related-key cryptanalysis [40] or in just a month when performing attacks exploiting Time-Memory-Key trade-offs [41].

When it comes to nongeneric attacks, these attacks exploit particular properties of the block cipher design, i.e., its structure and internal components. Usually, in the nongeneric attacks, the adversary first attempts to construct a distinguisher that covers as many rounds of the block cipher as possible and holds with a relatively high probability. Then, this distinguisher is then extended to a key-recovery attack on a few additional rounds using partial decryption and/or encryption. First, the involved bits of the subkeys of the appended rounds are guessed. Then, the ciphertext and/or the plaintext is partially decrypted/encrypted using these guessed subkeys to calculate the intermediate state values at the ends of the distinguisher. If the subkeys are correctly guessed then the distinguisher should hold and fail, otherwise.

As mentioned in Section 11.1, the spread of RFID tags in all our life aspects urged the need to design efficient lightweight primitives in general and lightweight block ciphers in particular. Designing an efficient lightweight block cipher is a challenging task where the design and the implementation of the block cipher go hand in hand. For example, while some designers opt for using a very simple key schedule, others choose using the same key and rely on using round constants to break the symmetry between the rounds. Another design strategy is to replace some of the Sboxes by unity mappings in some rounds [42,43]. A third design approach is to mix the tweak and/or the key with parts of the internal state and not with the whole internal state as in traditional block ciphers [44]. These oversimplifications of the design of block ciphers have opened the door for a number of new attacks [45,46]. Here below, we discuss some of the most important conventional nongeneric attacks along with the newly emerged ones.

11.4.1 Differential cryptanalysis

Differential cryptanalysis is a chosen plaintext attack that was published in the academic literature by Biham and Shamir in 1990 with applications on DES [47]. In differential cryptanalysis, the adversary looks at the input difference and at an intermediate difference after a few rounds. In other words, the distinguisher that differential cryptanalysis exploits is a differential [48], i.e., a pair of differences $(\Delta I_1, \Delta I_{r+1})$ that holds with a probability p significantly higher than 2^{-n}, where ΔI_1 is the input difference and ΔI_{r+1} is the output difference after r rounds and n is the block size in bits.

The data complexity, in terms of the number of chosen plaintext pairs, of a differential cryptanalysis is inversely proportional to the probability of the differential, i.e., the attacks that exploit differentials that hold with high probability require small number of chosen plaintext pairs. However, in many ciphers, finding differentials that hold with high probability is not an easy task. Instead, one searches for differential trails where an r-round differential trail is a sequence of $r + 1$ differences $(\Delta I_1, \Delta I_2, \ldots, \Delta I_r, \Delta I_{r+1})$, where ΔI_i is the input difference at round i. That is, while a differential cares about the input and output differences, a differential trail cares about the difference propagation throughout the block cipher different components. Through nonlinear components, the difference propagates with some probability, while it propagates deterministically through linear ones. Then, the probability of an r-round differential trail is approximated by $\prod_{i=1}^{r} p_i$, where p_i is the probability of this differential trail in round i. As an r-round differential $(\Delta I_1, \Delta I_{r+1})$ can be thought of as the set of all possible differential trails $(\Delta I_1, \ldots, \Delta I_{r+1})$ that have the same input and output differences, the probability of a differential is the sum of the probabilities of all its constituent differential trails. In general, the probability of a differential can depend on the values of the key, its input, and its output. Practically, for most ciphers, these dependencies are assumed negligible based on the Markov cipher assumption, hypothesis of stochastic equivalence, and hypothesis of independent round subkeys [48].

Many approaches and tools have been developed to facilitate the cryptanalysis of block ciphers. In [49], Mouha *et al.* proposed an Mixed Integer Linear Programming (MILP) based approach for finding the lower bound on the number of active nonlinear components, in particular the Sboxes that involve a nonzero difference, and used the maximum differential probability of the Sboxes to drive an upper bound on the differential probability of the best differential trail. However, several block ciphers use modular addition as a source of nonlinearity instead of Sboxes. Thus, for such ciphers, one needs to calculate the differential probability of modular addition to prove their security against differential cryptanalysis and its variations. In the former case of block ciphers employing usually small-sized Sboxes, it is a simple task to calculate the differential probability of a given Sbox by constructing its difference distribution table. Building a difference distribution table becomes impractical for block ciphers that employ addition modulo 2^{64} or even modulo 2^{32}. To address this problem, Mouha *et al.* [50] proposed using a graph theory approach to calculate the differential probability xdp^+ of addition modulo 2^n when differences are expressed using XOR and the differential probability $adp^\oplus$ of XOR when differences are expressed using addition modulo 2^n with a linear time in the word length. Recently, Biryukov and Velichkov [51] developed a new framework to automatically find differential trails in ARX (Addition, Rotation, and XOR)-based block ciphers by constructing a partial difference distribution table containing differentials whose probabilities are greater than a fixed threshold. Currently, there is a lot of research toward finding the best differential (trail) that can be exploited to launch an attack against block ciphers as exemplified by the work done by Song *et al.* [52], Biryukov *et al.* [53], and Bannier *et al.* [54].

11.4.2   Linear cryptanalysis

Linear cryptanalysis is one of the major cryptanalysis techniques used against symmetric primitives. It was first applied to FEAL [55] and then to DES by Matsui [56]. In linear cryptanalysis, which is a known plaintext attack, the r-round distinguisher exploited is a linear approximation that holds with probability p:

$$\Gamma_1 \bullet I_1 \oplus \Gamma_{r+1} \bullet I_{r+1} = 0, \tag{11.5}$$

where $\bullet$ denotes the scalar product over $\mathbb{F}_2$, I_1, I_{r+1} are the input at round 1 and output at round r, respectively, and Γ_1, Γ_{r+1} are called the input and output linear masks. In an ideal block cipher, the above linear approximation holds with probability 0.5. Therefore, the higher the bias $\varepsilon = |p - 1/2|$ of this linear approximation is, the more the block cipher deviates from an ideal block cipher.

In linear cryptanalysis, the number of known plaintext/ciphertext pairs is inversely proportional to the squared bias, i.e., ε^2, of the linear approximation. Similar to differentials, efficient linear approximations are found by searching for linear trails where an r-round linear trail is a sequence of $r + 1$ linear masks $(\Gamma_1, \Gamma_2, \ldots, \Gamma_r, \Gamma_{r+1})$. For the full linear trail to hold, each round linear approximation $\Gamma_i \bullet I_i \oplus \Gamma_{i+1} \bullet I_{i+1} = 0$ has to hold with bias ε_i. The propagation of the linear approximations are probabilistic through nonlinear components and deterministic through linear ones. The bias of an r-round linear trail can be computed as $2^{r-1} \prod_{i=1}^{r} \varepsilon_i$, according to the piling-up lemma [56] and under the same Markov cipher, hypothesis of stochastic equivalence and hypothesis of independent round subkeys assumptions mentioned above in the differential cryptanalysis, where ε_i is the bias of the linear approximation at round i. The pair (Γ_1, Γ_{r+1}) defines the so-called linear hull consisting of all linear trails that have the same input and output linear masks. Nyberg showed that the expected squared bias of a linear approximation averaged over all round keys is the sum of the expected squared biases of all relevant linear trails averaged over all round keys [57]. Later, it was proved that for key-alternating ciphers, the expected squared bias of a linear approximation averaged over all round keys is the sum of the squared biases of all relevant linear trails which are then independent of the key [58].

Analogous to differential cryptanalysis, many automated tools were developed in order to facilitate the work of the cryptanalyst. The same MILP-based approach developed by Mouha *et al.* [49] can be used to obtain bounds on the minimum number of active Sboxes and thus on the maximum linear bias. Sun *et al.* utilized the MILP technique [59] to build a tool that finds the best linear trail which holds with a high probability. Later, Liu *et al.* used a SAT solver to automatically search for linear trails in ARX-based block ciphers and applied this technique to the SPECK block cipher and the lightweight MAC primitive Chaskey, which is being considered for standardization by ISO/IEC and ITU-T [60].

11.4.3   *Differential-linear cryptanalysis*

The differential and linear attacks have been used jointly for the first time by Langford and Hellman [61]. In the differential-linear cryptanalysis, the block cipher is split into two parts such that for the first part of the block cipher, a high-probability truncated differential exists and for the second part, a high-bias linear approximation is found. Langford and Hellman introduced a specific case with a probability-one differential. Following that, Biham *et al.* [62] generalized the differential-linear cryptanalysis by using a probabilistic truncated differential. Under some assumptions, the resulting linear approximation is estimated to have a bias $\varepsilon' = 2p\varepsilon^2$, where p is the probability of the differential and ε is the bias of the linear approximation. Blondeau *et al.* [63] have revisited the differential-linear cryptanalysis to apply the theoretical link between linear and differential cryptanalysis [64]. They were able to use a closed form expression to accurately express the bias of a differential-linear approximation, with just one assumption, that is, the two parts of the block cipher are independent. They further introduced a multidimensional generalization of differential-linear cryptanalysis that includes multiple input differences and multidimensional linear output masks. Recently differential-linear cryptanalysis was successfully used to attack 7-round Chaskey [65].

11.4.4   *Higher order differential cryptanalysis*

Higher order differential cryptanalysis, proposed by Lai [66] in 1994, is a generalization of the differential cryptanalysis. While in differential cryptanalysis, the propagation of a specific difference, namely, the difference between two plaintexts, is studied in order to find highly correlated input and output differences, in higher order differential cryptanalysis the propagation of differences between a large set of plaintexts is studied. In the same year, Knudsen [67] indicated that there are block ciphers that are resistant against differential cryptanalysis, but not immune to higher order differential cryptanalysis. As an example, for the round function $f(X,k) = (X+k)^2$ mod q with block length $2 \times \log_2 q$, where q is a prime number, the non-trivial one round differential probability of this function is $1/q$ while its second-order differential is constant, i.e., it holds with probability one. Later, another block cipher, proposed by Nyberg and Knudsen, which was shown to be immune to differential cryptanalysis [57], was attacked by Jakobsen and Knudsen [68] utilizing the higher order differential cryptanalysis.

In general, the higher order differential cryptanalysis is more powerful than its special variant, i.e., the differential cryptanalysis, especially when applied to round functions employing low algebraic degree non-linear components. However, extending higher order differential to more than two rounds is not as simple as it is in differential cryptanalysis.

11.4.5   Truncated differential cryptanalysis

Truncated differential cryptanalysis was proposed by Knudsen in 1994 [67]. While in differential cryptanalysis, each bit of the input and output differences is specified, truncated differential cryptanalysis is more concerned whether there is a difference or not. To illustrate this point, let's take an example of a truncated differential for a 4-byte word represented as 0110, where 0 here indicates that the corresponding byte is inactive, or has a zero difference, and 1 indicates that the corresponding byte is active, or has any nonzero difference. This implies that a truncated differential can be considered as multiple differentials that have zero difference in the inactive bytes and have all the possible differences in the active ones.

The truncated differential cryptanalysis was first applied to attack 6-round DES using a small number of chosen plaintexts and very modest time complexity [67]. Afterwards, in 1999, Knudsen, Robshaw, and Wagner, using the truncated differential cryptanalysis, proposed a set of attacks on reduced-round Skipjack block cipher [69]. First, they launched an efficient key recovery attack against the first 16-round using practical data complexity. Second, the key of the middle 16-round was efficiently retrieved using two chosen plaintexts. Finally, they showed the existence of a 24-round truncated differential that holds with probability one. Since then, truncated differential cryptanalysis has been applied widely on many block ciphers such as SAFER [70], IDEA [71], E2 [72], Camellia [73], CRYPTON [74], and KLEIN [75], to name a few. Moreover, it has been used to launch the best known attacks on 3D [76] and Midori128 [77] block ciphers.

In addition, truncated differential cryptanalysis is used in other cryptanalysis techniques such as the MitM with differential enumeration attack that was proposed by Dunkelman, Keller, and Shamir [78]. It is also used in the MitM attacks on hash functions to launch preimage attacks and in the rebound attack to launch collision attacks.

11.4.6   Integral cryptanalysis

Integral cryptanalysis was proposed by Daemen, Knudsen, and Rijmen in 1997 [79] to study and analyze the security of the SQUARE block cipher. Then, it was unified and formalized by Knudsen and Wagner [80]. In integral cryptanalysis, we examine the propagation of the sum (XOR) of many plaintexts, not just two as in the differential cryptanalysis. Therefore, we can consider integral cryptanalysis as a dual technique of differential cryptanalysis as well. Integral cryptanalysis is quite useful especially in the analysis of block ciphers with only bijective components.

In 2012, Lu *et al.* [81] proposed combining the integral attack with the MitM attack in what they called the higher order MitM attack. They used this technique to launch 10/11/12-round attacks on Camellia-128/192/256 with FL/FL^{-1} functions and 14/16-round attacks on Camellia-192/256 without FL/FL^{-1}.

In Eurocrypt 2015, Todo proposed a new property which he named the division property [82]. The division property can be considered as a generalization of the integral property which, unlike the integral property, can exploit the algebraic degree of the block cipher. Moreover, it can be applied against bit-oriented block ciphers and block ciphers that use nonbijective components. In Crypto 2015, the division property was used to break the full-round MISTY1 block cipher based on a 6-round integral distinguisher [82] which was further enhanced in Crypto 2016 [83]. In FSE 2016, Todo and Morii introduced the bit-based division property which studies each bit independently and applied it to SIMON32 [84]. However, they pointed out that the search for an integral distinguisher by the bit-based division property is quite expensive in terms of both time and memory complexities. In particular, for an n-bit block cipher, the time and memory complexities are upper bounded by 2^n which makes it impractical for modern block ciphers. In ASIACRYPT 2016, Xiang *et al.* tackled this problem by applying MILP methodology to search for integral distinguishers based on the division property [85] and applied this technique to six lightweight block ciphers that employ a bit permutation linear layer. Finally, Sun *et al.* extended this approach to be applied to any linear layer by transforming it into its primitive representation [86].

11.4.7 Impossible differential cryptanalysis

The impossible differential cryptanalysis was introduced independently by Knudsen [87] and Biham *et al.* [88]. Impossible differential cryptanalysis exploits differentials with zero probability. So in these attacks, the distinguisher is a differential that holds with probability 0. Then, in the key recovery phase of the attack, the key guesses that result in the impossible differential are excluded. Once all wrong key candidates are eliminated, only the right key is left. To efficiently find the best impossible differential trail in an automated way for any given block cipher with a bijective round function, Kim *et al.* [89] proposed using what they called the matrix method. In this method, the internal state is divided into m words. Then, $2m \times m$ matrices are generated to represent the encryption and decryption operations of a single round of the targeted block cipher where the entry (i, j) of these matrices denotes if the input difference i and the output difference j are not related, linearly related, or related through the nonlinear component of the round function. Afterward, with the help of these matrices, we search for the longest two truncated differentials that hold with probability 1, one from the encryption side, the other from the decryption side and contradict in the middle. Combining these two deterministic truncated differential forms an impossible differential that can be exploited in an impossible differential attack.

Recently, in Crypto 2016, Derbez and Fouque presented an algorithm to exhaustively search for the best impossible differential attack on a wide range of block ciphers [90]. Their tool, which they published online, does not just find the best impossible differential trail and then leave it up to the cryptanalyst to find the best attack utilizing that impossible differential trail. Instead, it finds the best possible attack by taking both the block cipher and the key schedule algorithms into consideration. The tool takes as an input a system of equations describing the block cipher and whether each variable is a plaintext, ciphertext, key, or internal state. They have applied their tool to automatically find in a matter of seconds many of the best impossible differential attacks on bit and byte oriented block ciphers such as Crypton, mCrypton, AES, SIMON, IDEA, and XTEA.

11.4.8 Zero-correlation cryptanalysis

Analogous to the impossible differential cryptanalysis, Bogdanov and Rijmen proposed a new technique called zero-correlation cryptanalysis that uses a linear trail of probability exactly $1/2$, i.e., zero correlation, to exclude the wrong keys [91]. Since its inception, it is one of the most widely used cryptanalysis techniques against block ciphers. For example, it was used to study the security of the ISO standards Camellia and CLEFIA [92], LBlock [93], and TWINE [93].

The bottleneck of the zero-correlation cryptanalysis is the high data complexity requirement. Therefore, Bogdanov *et al.* [94] proposed the multidimensional zero-correlation cryptanalysis, where in this technique, we have m zero-correlation linear approximations such that all the $l = 2^m - 1$ nonzero linear approximations, which result from spanning the m zero-correlation linear approximations, have zero-correlation. This multidimensional zero-correlation approximation can act as a distinguisher. Moreover, this distinguisher can be employed in a key-recovery attack by prepending/appending additional rounds, usually referred to as the analysis rounds. The key recovery attack proceeds by, first, gathering N plaintext/ciphertext pairs and then initializing an array of counters $V[z]$ to zero, where $|z| = m$ bits. The attacker computes the corresponding bits needed to apply the m linear approximations by guessing the round keys involved in the analysis rounds, and partially decrypting the N plaintext/ciphertext pairs. Then, z is computed and the corresponding counter is incremented by one. Afterward, the attacker computes the statistic T [94]:

$$T = \sum_{z=0}^{2^m-1} \frac{(V[z] - N2^{-m})^2}{N2^{-m}(1 - 2^{-m})} = \frac{N2^m}{(1 - 2^{-m})} \sum_{z=0}^{2^m-1} \left(\frac{V[z]}{N} - \frac{1}{2^m} \right)^2. \tag{11.6}$$

The statistic T of the right key follows χ^2-distribution, its mean $\mu_0 = l\frac{2^n-N}{2^n-1}$, and its variance $\sigma_0^2 = 2l\left(\frac{2^n-N}{2^n-1}\right)^2$, while T of the wrong key follows χ^2-distribution with mean $\mu_1 = l$ and variance $\sigma_1^2 = 2l$ [94]. Equation (11.7) determines the required number of known plaintexts to launch the attack:

$$N = \frac{2^n(Z_{1-\gamma} + Z_{1-\zeta})}{\sqrt{l/2} - Z_{1-\zeta}}, \tag{11.7}$$

where γ (resp. ζ) denotes the probability to incorrectly discard the right key (resp. the probability to incorrectly accept a random key as the right key) and $Z_p = \phi^{-1}(p)$ $(0 < P < 1)$, ϕ is the standard normal distribution cumulative function. The decision threshold, according to the required success probabilities, is set to $\tau = \mu_0 + \sigma_0 Z_{1-\gamma} = \mu_1 - \sigma_1 Z_{1-\zeta}$.

11.4.9 Basic Meet-in-the-Middle cryptanalysis

MitM attacks can be viewed as enhanced/generalized exhaustive search techniques. These attacks try to split the block cipher into two parts: one is used in the encryption direction and the other is used in the decryption direction. Then, the attacker partially guesses key bits from both ends and propagates the knowledge of the internal state of the block cipher until the information propagated in both directions meet in the middle for matching. The key bits are considered wrong if no match is found, otherwise it is a key candidate. This technique was first introduced by Diffie and Hellman [95]. Later, it was applied to reduced-round DES by Chaum and Evertse [96].

Suppose we have an r-round cipher $E_K : \{0, 1\}^n \longrightarrow \{0, 1\}^n$, where K is the key that is used in the block cipher and n is the block length in bits. If this cipher can be split into two subciphers F_{K_f} and G_{K_b} such that $E_K = G_{K_b} \circ F_{K_f}$ and K_f *and* K_b are independent subkey bits, then the attack can be launched as shown in Algorithms 1 and 2.

Algorithm 1: MitM attack with low space complexity

Data: P_i/C_i pairs, where P_i/C_i denotes the plaintext/ciphertext pairs,
  $i = 1, 2, \ldots, N$ and N is determined by the unicity distance
Result: Right key k_f and k_b
foreach $k_f \in K_f$ **do**
  foreach $k_b \in K_b$ **do**
    compute $v = F_{k_f}(P_1)$;
    compute $u = G_{k_b}^{-1}(C_1)$;
    if $v = u$ **then**
      Test k_f and k_b using N plaintext/ciphertext pairs and return k_f
      and k_b if the test succeeds;

It is clear from Algorithms 1 and 2 that MitM attacks have the advantage of being able to offer some time-memory trade-off. The computational complexity of Algorithms 1 and 2 are $2^{|K_f|+|K_b|}$ and $2^{|K_f|} + 2^{|K_b|}$, respectively, and the memory complexity of Algorithms 1 and 2 are $\mathcal{O}(1)$ and $\mathcal{O}(2^{|K_f|})$, respectively. Algorithm 2 can

---

Algorithm 2: MitM attack with low time complexity

Data: P_i/C_i pairs, where P_i/C_i denotes the plaintext/ciphertext pairs,
  $i = 1, 2, \ldots, N$ and N is determined by the unicity distance
Result: Right key k_f and k_b
foreach $k_f \in K_f$ **do**
  $\llcorner$ compute $v = F_{k_f}(P_1)$ and store v with the corresponding k_f in table T_1;
foreach $k_b \in K_b$ **do**
  compute $u = G_{k_b}^{-1}(C_1)$;
  if *u has a match in table T_1* **then**
    $\llcorner$ Test k_f and k_b using N plaintext/ciphertext pairs and return k_f and k_b
      if the test succeeds;

---

be modified, by computing T_1 for the smaller key subset out of k_f, k_b and matching using the other key subset, to reduce its memory complexity to $\mathcal{O}(2^{\min(|K_f|,|K_b|)})$. The data complexity of the two algorithms is the same and equals the unicity distance of the block cipher, i.e., $\lceil \frac{k}{n} \rceil$.

In spite of the fact that this technique has a low data complexity, the unicity distance, it got less attention than the linear and differential cryptanalysis. The reason for this is that it needs to partition the block cipher into two parts that use independent subkey bits. For modern block ciphers, this is not easy to achieve since their key schedules usually contain nonlinear components such as Sboxes and/or addition modulo 2^n. Therefore, the number of rounds that can be attacked by this technique is very limited. Recently, new modifications of this basic MitM attack were proposed allowing attackers to penetrate more rounds or even the whole cipher as we discuss in the following subsections.

11.4.10   3-Subset MitM technique

Bogdanov and Rechberger proposed a new variation of the basic MitM attack [97] and used it to attack the full-round KTANTAN cipher. This technique relaxes the constraint of the two keys K_f and K_b to be fully independent by splitting the key into three subsets instead of two. This approach is divided into two main stages. The *MitM stage* in which the key space is filtered depending on the matching criteria and the *key testing stage* in which the reduced key space is tested exhaustively until the right key is found.

Let $E_K : \{0, 1\}^n \longrightarrow \{0, 1\}^n$ be an n-bit block cipher of r rounds that uses a k-bit key K. Suppose this cipher can be split into two subciphers F_{K_f} and G_{K_b} such that $E_K = G_{K_b} \circ F_{K_f}$. In this approach, K_f and K_b do not need to be fully distinct. Let $A_0 = K_f \cap K_b$ be the common key bits used in F_{K_f} and G_{K_b}, and let $A_1 = K_f \setminus A_0$ and $A_2 = K_b \setminus A_0$ denote the set of key bits that are used only in F_{K_f} and G_{K_b}, respectively. Then, the attack can be launched as shown in Algorithm 3. The computational

---

Algorithm 3: Three-subset MitM attack [97]

> **Data:** P_i/C_i pairs, where P_i/C_i denotes the plaintext/ciphertext pairs,
> $\quad\quad i = 1, 2, \ldots, N$ and N is determined by the unicity distance
>
> **Result:** Right key k_f and k_b
>
> //**MitM stage**
>
> **foreach** $a_0 \in A_0$ **do**
> > **foreach** $a_1 \in A_1$ **do**
> > > compute $v = F_{a_0,a_1}(P_1)$;
> >
> > **foreach** $a_2 \in A_2$ **do**
> > > compute $u = G^{-1}_{a_0,a_2}(C_1)$;
> >
> > perform the matching between v and u, let $|v| = |u| = n$-bit, where $|v|$
> > denotes the length of v in bits, then we will have 2^{k-n} remaining
> > candidates;
>
> //**key testing stage**
>
> the remaining candidates are exhaustively searched until the right key is
> found

---

complexity of the two stages, MitM stage and key testing stage, can be determined as
follows:

$$\overbrace{2^{|A_0|}(2^{|A_1|} + 2^{|A_2|})}^{\text{MitM stage}} + \overbrace{(2^{k-n} + 2^{k-2n} + \cdots)}^{\text{Key testing stage}} \quad\quad (11.8)$$

The data complexity of this approach is dominated by the data needed in order
to accomplish the key testing stage and is determined by the unicity distance of the
block cipher, i.e., $\lceil \frac{k}{n} \rceil$. The memory required by this approach is used to save one of
the lists A_1 or A_2. Therefore, the memory complexity is $\min(2^{|A_1|}, 2^{|A_2|})$. Clearly, this
approach has an advantage over exhaustive search when both sets A_1 and A_2 are not
empty.

11.4.11 Splice-and-cut technique

Aoki and Sasaki proposed another variant of the 3-subset MitM attack to perform a
preimage attack on SHA-0 and SHA-1 hash functions [98]. This approach relaxed
the constraint of the MitM stage that should begin from the plaintext P and the
ciphertext C to compute the intermediate state values v and u, respectively. Instead,
the attack begins from an intermediate state X as shown in Figure 11.5. Then, by
partially decrypting (encrypting) X to obtain plaintext (ciphertext) and using the
encryption (decryption) oracle, the attacker can obtain the corresponding ciphertext
(plaintext). After that, v and u can be computed from X and C (or P), respectively.
This approach changes the data requirement to chosen plaintext instead of known
plaintext as the previous variants. Moreover, its data complexity is higher than the
3-subset MitM variant and determined by the plaintext (ciphertext) bits that are

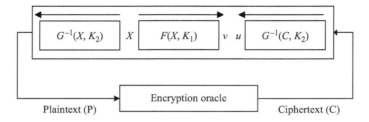

Figure 11.5   Meet-in-the-middle with a splice-and-cut technique

affected by the guessed key bits, the computational complexity may be enhanced, however.

11.4.12   Multidimensional MitM and generalized MitM cryptanalysis technique

Two more variants of the MitM cryptanalysis are the multidimensional MitM (MD-MitM) and the generalized MitM cryptanalysis technique. The first one was proposed by Zhu and Gong [99]. In this approach, the block cipher is divided into multiple subciphers where the number of these subciphers determines the dimension of the attack, e.g., if the block cipher is divided into two subciphers then the attack is called 2D-MitM attack. Then, by guessing the intermediate states, a MitM attack can be launched on each subcipher. Finally, the correct key is derived from the matching of the multiple MitM attacks. The basic MitM attack can be considered as a special case of MD-MitM cryptanalysis and would be denoted as 1D-MitM cryptanalysis.

The second variant, i.e., the generalized MitM cryptanalysis technique, was proposed by Tolba and Youssef [100]. While in the 3-subset MitM attack, the key space is partitioned, as mentioned above, into 3 subsets, namely, A_0, A_1, and A_2 with the two subsets A_1 and A_2 are restricted to be independent. In the generalized MitM approach, the restrictions of the 3-subset MitM attack are elevated by allowing the key space to be partitioned into $n \geq 3$ subsets and these subsets are allowed to be dependent. Using dependent subsets raises a new problem of how to efficiently compute the internal states that are dependent on two or more key subsets. To tackle this problem, the recomputation technique exploited in the biclique cryptanalysis [101], discussed later in this chapter, is utilized.

11.4.13   MitM with differential enumeration cryptanalysis

Demirci and Selçuk were the first to apply the MitM approach on AES [102] triggering a new line of research. They have shown that if the input of four AES rounds has just one active (nonzero difference) byte then the value of each byte of the output can be described as a parameterized function of that active byte. The number of parameters was deduced to be 25 eight-bit parameters in [102] and then reduced to 24 eight-bit parameters in [103]. The reduction in the number of parameters was possible by noticing that any of the 25 parameters can be taken as a reference for the others. Therefore, by considering the differences of the functions rather than the mere values, only 24 parameters are needed. The main disadvantage of this MitM attack, even with the reduced number of parameters, is the high memory requirement to store a precomputation table of all the sequences resulting from all the possible combinations of these parameters. As such, this attack only works for AES-256 and then a time-memory trade-off is used to extend the attack to AES-192.

At ASIACRYPT 2010, Dunkelman, Keller, and Shamir [78] proposed a couple of new ideas to address the high memory requirement of this MitM attack. First, they showed that the precomputation table does not need to have the whole sequence, just its associated multiset, i.e., the unordered sequence with multiplicity rather than the ordered one. The introduction of the multiset concept reduced the size of the precomputation table by a factor of four. However, the more significant reduction in the size of the precomputation table was due to the second and main idea which they called the differential enumeration. Differential enumeration reduced the number of parameters that describe the sequence or rather the multiset from 24 to 16 bytes. This is achievable by relying on a low probability truncated differential characteristic where the generated sequence or multiset at its output can only take a restricted number of values. Consequently, the memory requirement has been reduced from 2^{192} to 2^{128}. However, the use of this truncated differential characteristic increases the data complexity as now we have to search through a large amount of input data pairs to find one pair that conforms to the used truncated differential characteristic.

Later, in Eurocrypt 2013, Derbez, Fouque, and Jean showed that it is possible, by borrowing ideas from the rebound attack [104], to enumerate the whole set of sequences more efficiently [105]. In particular, they showed that using their technique, which they called efficient enumeration, the whole set can take only 2^{80} values instead of 2^{128}. This means that the number of parameters is further reduced to 10 parameters only. The consequences of using the efficient enumeration technique were numerous. First, the attack became feasible on AES-128 and in fact, their attack is considered the most efficient attack on 7-round reduced AES-128. Second, the use of a 5-round truncated differential characteristic is feasible which mounts to attacking 9-round reduced AES-256. Third, the memory complexity is no longer the bottleneck of the attack.

Afterwards, Li, Jia, and Wang [106] employed a key-dependent sieve to further reduce the memory complexity of Derbez's attack. This technique helped them present an attack on 9-round reduced AES-192 using a 5-round truncated differential characteristic and an attack on 8-round reduced PRINCE. The key-dependent sieve was recently used to mount an attack on 10-round reduced AES-256 [107]. Finally, it is worth noting that the MitM attacks that found success in attacking SPN based block ciphers [108–110] were also proven to be equally powerful on Feistel constructions [111–113].

11.4.14 Biclique cryptanalysis

The biclique cryptanalysis was proposed by Bogdanov *et al.* [101] where they succeeded in theoretically attacking the full-round AES block cipher. This technique consists of two parts: building a biclique for some rounds of the block cipher at

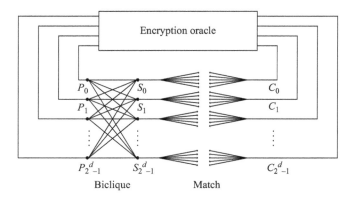

Figure 11.6   General structure of the biclique cryptanalysis

its beginning or end and applying the MitM with recomputation technique on the remaining part of the block cipher. The technique was inspired by the splice-and-cut technique and biclique cryptanalysis' general structure is depicted in Figure 11.6. The attack works in the single-key setting and has two main parameters: the *length* which denotes the number of rounds covered by the biclique and the *dimension* which denotes the length of the biclique elements.

Here, we give a brief definition of bicliques as applied to this class of attacks. Suppose we have a subcipher F_K which maps a plaintext P to intermediate state S in which we have 2^d plaintexts P_i and 2^d intermediate states S_j connected by 2^{2d} keys $K[i,j]$ as shown in Figure 11.7. A d-dimensional biclique is the tuple $(P_i, S_j, K[i,j])$ where the following relation holds:

$$S_j = F_{K[i,j]}(P_i); \forall i,j \in 0, \ldots, 2^{d-1} \tag{11.9}$$

This technique succeeds with probability 1 since all the key space is exhaustively tested. The time complexity of this technique is given by:

$$2^{n-2d}(C_{\text{biclique}} + C_{\text{precomp}} + C_{\text{recomp}} + C_{\text{falsepos}}) \tag{11.10}$$

where C_{biclique} is the time needed to construct the biclique, C_{precomp} is the time required to compute the elements affected by K_1 or K_2, C_{recomp} is the time required to compute the elements affected by both K_1 and K_2, and C_{falsepos} is the time needed to check the remaining candidates after the matching.

11.4.15   Unbalanced biclique cryptanalysis

The original biclique attack succeeded in attacking the full-round versions of AES; AES-128/192/256 [101]. However, its data complexity is very high not only for AES but also when the attack is applied on other lightweight block ciphers such as LBlock [114] and TWINE [115]. To address this issue, some ideas were proposed [116–118]. All these ideas focused on changing the structure of the biclique from balanced where the two sets P_i and S_j of the biclique have the same cardinality

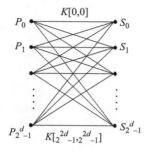

Figure 11.7   d-Dimensional biclique

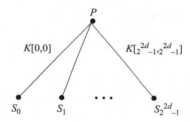

Figure 11.8   Star biclique

2^d, to unbalanced biclique where the two sets have different cardinality. An example of the unbalanced biclique is the star biclique in which one of the sets has cardinality one. The star biclique was first proposed by Canteaut *et al.* [116]. They used the star biclique with the MitM attack to reduce the data complexity of the MitM stage to a single plaintext/ciphertext pair [116].

The star biclique can be placed at the beginning or the end of the block cipher. For simplicity and without loss of generality, we place it at the beginning of the block cipher. As seen in Figure 11.8, we have only one plaintext P mapped to intermediate states S_l, where $l = 0, 1, \ldots, 2^{2d} - 1$ and each l is equivalent to a unique i,j pair, where i,j take values from 0 to $2^d - 1$. Each $S_l \equiv S_{i,j}$ is obtained by partially encrypting P using key $K[i,j]$. Such structure is called a star biclique with dimension d.

11.4.16   Invariant subspace cryptanalysis

Invariant subspace attack was first proposed by Leander *et al.* [119] at Crypto 2011 to cryptanalyze the PRINTCIPHER block cipher. For simplicity and without loss of generality, assume that we have an n-bit block cipher whose round function E_K consists of a key addition followed by an SP-layer E, such that $E_k(x) = E(x + k)$; and E has the following property:

$$E(U + c) = U + d, \tag{11.11}$$

where U is a subspace such that $U \subseteq \mathbb{F}_2^n$ and $c, d \in \mathbb{F}_2^n$ are two constants. Then, for the round keys of the form $k = u + c + d$ and $u \in U$, the following holds:

$$E_k(U + d) = E((U + d) + (u + c + d)) = E(U + c) = U + d, \qquad (11.12)$$

i.e., the round function maps the affine subspace $U + d$ onto itself. Consequently, if all the round keys belong to the subspace $U + c + d$, then there exists a very efficient distinguisher for a fraction of keys over any number of rounds. Consequently, for PRINTCIPHER-48 (resp. PRINTCIPHER-96) there exist 2^{52} weak keys out of 2^{80} (resp. 2^{102} out of 2^{160} weak keys). This attack requires 5 chosen plaintexts if the key belongs to the weak keys class which is considered as a low data complexity attack.

Afterward, a complete study of the attack against PRINTCIPHER was done by Bulygin *et al.* [120]. Later, in Eurocrypt 2015, Leander *et al.* [121] proposed a generic algorithm to detect the invariant subspaces and applied it on iSCREAM (one of the CAESAR competition candidates), Robin (LS-design), and Zorro (a lightweight block cipher). Then, it was used by Guo *et al.* [122] to present a full-round attack against Midori64. Finally, Grassi *et al.* [123] proposed the subspace trail cryptanalysis which can be considered as a generalization to the invariant subspace attack in which they do no longer rely on specific choices of round constants or subkeys, and applied this technique on AES to present a 5-round distinguisher in the single-key setting.

11.5 Summary

In this chapter, we have tried to provide a summary of the recent trends of block ciphers' design and cryptanalysis. We started by establishing the importance of symmetric key cryptographic primitives in our daily life. Then, we briefly introduced the different primitives starting from stream/block ciphers, ending with AE schemes and passing by MAC and hash functions. Afterward, we focused on block ciphers, which is, arguably, considered the most widely deployed symmetric key cryptographic primitive. We formally defined what a block cipher is, discussed the two most common ways to build a block cipher, and explained what it means for a block cipher to be secure. Finally, we have presented the new developments in the conventional attacks along with the newly surfaced ones as a result of adapting new design strategies targeting resource-constrained devices. In conclusion, we would like to highlight that the research literature on block ciphers is still advancing and is as active as it has always been.

References

[1]   Tilborg HCAV. Fundamentals of Cryptology: A Professional Reference and Interactive Tutorial. 1st ed. Kluwer Academic Publishers; 1999.
[2]   Menezes AJ, Vanstone SA, and Oorschot PCV. Handbook of Applied Cryptography. 1st ed. CRC Press, Inc.; 1996.

[3]   Knudsen LR. Block Ciphers. In: Tilborg HCAV, Jajodia S, editors. Encyclopedia of Cryptography and Security. Springer US; 2011. p. 152–157. Available from: http://dx.doi.org/10.1007/978-1-4419-5906-5_549.

[4]   Canteaut A. Stream Cipher. In: Tilborg HCAV, Jajodia S, editors. Encyclopedia of Cryptography and Security. Springer US; 2011. p. 1263–1265. Available from: http://dx.doi.org/10.1007/978-1-4419-5906-5_374.

[5]   Preneel B. MAC Algorithms. In: Tilborg HCAV, Jajodia S, editors. Encyclopedia of Cryptography and Security. Springer US; 2011. p. 742–748. Available from: http://dx.doi.org/10.1007/978-1-4419-5906-5_592.

[6]   Preneel B. Hash Functions. In: Tilborg HCAV, Jajodia S, editors. Encyclopedia of Cryptography and Security. Springer US; 2011. p. 543–553. Available from: http://dx.doi.org/10.1007/978-1-4419-5906-5_580.

[7]   Black J. Authenticated Encryption. In: Tilborg HCAV, Jajodia S, editors. Encyclopedia of Cryptography and Security. Springer US; 2011. p. 52–61. Available from: http://dx.doi.org/10.1007/978-1-4419-5906-5_548.

[8]   National Institute of Standards and Technology. Recommendation for Block Cipher Modes of Operation: Galois/Counter Mode (GCM) and GMAC; 2007. http://csrc.nist.gov/publications/nistpubs/800-38D/SP-800-38D.pdf.

[9]   Rogaway P, Bellare M, and Black J. OCB: A Block-Cipher Mode of Operation for Efficient Authenticated Encryption. ACM Transactions on Information and System Security. 2003 August;6(3):365–403. Available from: http://doi.acm.org/10.1145/937527.937529.

[10] Whiting D, Housley R, and Ferguson N. Counter with CBC-MAC (CCM). IETF; 2003. RFC 3610 (Informational). Available from: http://www.ietf.org/rfc/rfc3610.txt.

[11] Bellare M, Rogaway P, and Wagner D. The EAX Mode of Operation. In: Roy B, Meier W, editors. Fast Software Encryption: 11th International Workshop, FSE 2004, Delhi, India, February 5–7, 2004. Revised Papers. Springer Berlin Heidelberg; 2004. p. 389–407. Available from: http://dx.doi.org/10.1007/978-3-540-25937-4_25.

[12] Bilgin B, Bogdanov A, Kneevi M, Mendel F, and Wang Q. FIDES: Lightweight Authenticated Cipher with Side-Channel Resistance for Constrained Hardware. In: Bertoni G, and Coron J-S, editors. Cryptographic Hardware and Embedded Systems – CHES 2013: 15th International Workshop, Santa Barbara, CA, USA, August 20–23, 2013. Proceedings. vol. 8086 of Lecture Notes in Computer Science. Springer Berlin Heidelberg; 2013. p. 142–158. Available from: http://dx.doi.org/10.1007/978-3-642-40349-1_9.

[13] Andreeva E, Bilgin B, Bogdanov A, et al. APE: Authenticated Permutation-Based Encryption for Lightweight Cryptography. In: Cid C, Rechberger C, editors. Fast Software Encryption: 21st International Workshop, FSE 2014, London, UK, March 3–5, 2014. Revised Selected Papers. Springer Berlin Heidelberg; 2015. p. 168–186. Available from: http://dx.doi.org/10.1007/978-3-662-46706-0_9.

[14]   National Bureau of Standards, U.S. Department of Commerce. Advanced Encryption Standard. FIPS. Publication 197. National Bureau of Standards, U.S. Department of Commerce; 2001.

[15]   Bogdanov A, Mendel F, Regazzoni F, Rijmen V, and Tischhauser E. ALE: AES-Based Lightweight Authenticated Encryption. In: Moriai S, editor. Fast Software Encryption: 20th International Workshop, FSE 2013, Singapore, March 11–13, 2013. Revised Selected Papers. Lecture Notes in Computer Science. Springer Berlin Heidelberg; 2014. p. 447–466. Available from: http://dx.doi.org/10.1007/978-3-662-43933-3_23.

[16]   Wu H, and Preneel B. AEGIS: A Fast Authenticated Encryption Algorithm. In: Lange T, Lauter K, Lisoněk P, editors. Selected Areas in Cryptography: 20th International Conference, SAC 2013, Burnaby, BC, Canada, August 14–16. 2013. Revised Selected Papers. Springer Berlin Heidelberg; 2014. p. 185–201. Available from: http://dx.doi.org/10.1007/978-3-662-43414-7_10.

[17]   Ye D, Wang P, Hu L, *et al.* PAES v1: Parallelizable Authenticated Encryption Schemes based on AES Round Function, First round submission to the CAESAR Competition, March 2014. http://competitions.cr.yp.to/round1/paesv1.pdf.

[18]   CAESAR. Competition for Authenticated Encryption: Security, Applicability, and Robustness; 2013–2017. http://competitions.cr.yp.to/caesar.html.

[19]   Black J. The Ideal-Cipher Model, Revisited: An Uninstantiable Blockcipher-Based Hash Function. In: Robshaw M, editor. Fast Software Encryption: 13th International Workshop, FSE 2006, Graz, Austria, March 15–17, 2006. Revised Selected Papers. Springer Berlin Heidelberg; 2006. p. 328–340. Available from: http://dx.doi.org/10.1007/11799313_21.

[20]   Shannon EC. Communication Theory of Secrecy Systems. Bell System Technical Journal. 1949;28(4):656–715. Available from: http://dx.doi.org/10.1002/j.1538-7305.1949.tb00928.x.

[21]   Bogdanov A. Analysis and Design of Block Cipher Constructions [Ph.D. Dissertation]. Ruhr University; 2009.

[22]   National Bureau of Standards, U.S. Department of Commerce. Data Encryption Standard: FIPS. National Bureau of Standards, U.S. Department of Commerce; 1977.

[23]   Lai X, Massey JL. A Proposal for a New Block Encryption Standard. In: Damgård IB, editor. Advances in Cryptology—EUROCRYPT '90: Workshop on the Theory and Application of Cryptographic Techniques, Aarhus, Denmark, May 21–24, 1990. Proceedings. Springer Berlin Heidelberg; 1991. p. 389–404. Available from: http://dx.doi.org/10.1007/3-540-46877-3_35.

[24]   Suzaki T, Minematsu K, Morioka S, and Kobayashi E. TWINE: A Lightweight, Versatile Block Cipher. In: Proceedings of ECRYPT Workshop on Lightweight Cryptography (2011); 2011. Available from: http://www.uclouvain.be/.

[25]   Jean J, Nikolić I, and Peyrin T. Tweaks and Keys for Block Ciphers: The TWEAKEY Framework. In: Sarkar P, Iwata T, editors. Advances in Cryptology – ASIACRYPT 2014: 20th International Conference on the Theory and Application of Cryptology and Information Security, Kaoshiung,

Taiwan, R.O.C., December 7–11, 2014. Proceedings, Part II. Springer Berlin Heidelberg; 2014. p. 274–288. Available from: http://dx.doi.org/10.1007/978-3-662-45608-8_15.

[26]   Beierle C, Jean J, Kölbl S, *et al.* The SKINNY Family of Block Ciphers and Its Low-Latency Variant MANTIS; 2016. https://eprint.iacr.org/2016/660.pdf. IACR Cryptology ePrint Archive, Report 2016/660.

[27]   De Mulder Y. White-Box Cryptography [Ph.D. Dissertation]. Katholieke Universiteit, Leuven, Belgium 2014.

[28]   Knudsen LR, and Robshaw M. The Block Cipher Companion. Information Security and Cryptography. Springer; 2011. Available from: http://opac.inria.fr/ record=b1133847.

[29]   Biham E. New Types of Cryptanalytic Attacks Using Related Keys. In: Helleseth T, editor. Advances in Cryptology—EUROCRYPT '93: Workshop on the Theory and Application of Cryptographic Techniques Lofthus, Norway, May 23–27, 1993. Proceedings. Springer Berlin Heidelberg; 1994. p. 398–409. Available from: http://dx.doi.org/10.1007/3-540-48285-7_34.

[30]   Knudsen LR, and Rijmen V. Known-Key Distinguishers for Some Block Ciphers. In: Kurosawa K, editor. Advances in Cryptology – ASIACRYPT 2007: 13th International Conference on the Theory and Application of Cryptology and Information Security, Kuching, Malaysia, December 2–6, 2007. Proceedings. Springer Berlin Heidelberg; 2007. p. 315–324. Available from: http://dx.doi.org/10.1007/978-3-540-76900-2_19.

[31]   Peeters E. Side-Channel Cryptanalysis: A Brief Survey. In: Advanced DPA Theory and Practice: Towards the Security Limits of Secure Embedded Circuits. Springer New York; 2013. p. 11–19. Available from: http://dx.doi.org/10.1007/978-1-4614-6783-0_2.

[32]   Sakiyama K, Sasaki Y, and Li Y. Security of Block Ciphers: From Algorithm Design to Hardware Implementation. 1st ed. Wiley; 2016.

[33]   Hellman ME. A Cryptanalytic Time-Memory Trade-Off. IEEE Transactions on Information Theory. 1980 July;26(4):401–406.

[34]   Oechslin P. Making a Faster Cryptanalytic Time-Memory Trade-Off. In: Boneh D, editor. Advances in Cryptology – CRYPTO 2003: 23rd Annual International Cryptology Conference, Santa Barbara, California, USA, August 17–21, 2003. Proceedings. Springer Berlin Heidelberg; 2003. p. 617–630. Available from: http://dx.doi.org/10.1007/978-3-540-45146-4_36.

[35]   Biham E. How to Decrypt or Even Substitute DES-Encrypted Messages in 2^{28} Steps. Information Processing Letters. 2002 November;84(3):117–124. Available from: http://dx.doi.org/10.1016/S0020-0190(02)00269-7.

[36]   De Cannière C, Dinur I, and Shamir A. New Generic Attacks Which Are Faster Than Exhaustive Search. Presented at the Rump Session of FSE 2009; 2009.

[37]   NIST Special Publication 800-57 Part 1 Revision 4. Recommendation for Key Management Part 1: General; 2016. http://dx.doi.org/10.6028/NIST.SP.800-57pt1r4.

[38]   Stevens M, Karpman P, and Peyrin T. Freestart Collision for Full SHA-1. In: Fischlin M, Coron J-S, editors. Advances in Cryptology – EUROCRYPT 2016: 35th Annual International Conference on the Theory and Applications

of Cryptographic Techniques, Vienna, Austria, May 8–12, 2016. Proceedings, Part I. Springer Berlin Heidelberg; 2016. p. 459–483. Available from: http://dx.doi.org/10.1007/978-3-662-49890-3_18.

[39]   Biryukov A, and Großschädl J. Cryptanalysis of the Full AES Using GPU-Like Special-Purpose Hardware; 2011. http://eprint.iacr.org/2011/710. Cryptology ePrint Archive, Report 2011/710.

[40]   Biryukov A, Khovratovich D, and Nikolić I. Distinguisher and Related-Key Attack on the Full AES-256. In: Halevi S, editor. Advances in Cryptology – CRYPTO 2009: 29th Annual International Cryptology Conference, Santa Barbara, CA, USA, August 16–20, 2009. Proceedings. Springer Berlin Heidelberg; 2009. p. 231–249. Available from: http://dx.doi.org/10.1007/978-3-642-03356-8_14.

[41]   Biryukov A, Mukhopadhyay S, and Sarkar P. Improved Time-Memory Trade-Offs with Multiple Data. In: Preneel B, Tavares S, editors. Selected Areas in Cryptography: 12th International Workshop, SAC 2005, Kingston, ON, Canada, August 11–12, 2005. Revised Selected Papers. Springer Berlin Heidelberg; 2006. p. 110–127. Available from: http://dx.doi.org/10.1007/11693383_8.

[42]   Albrecht MR, Rechberger C, Schneider T, Tiessen T, and Zohner M. Ciphers for MPC and FHE. In: Oswald E, and Fischlin M, editors. Advances in Cryptology – EUROCRYPT 2015: 34th Annual International Conference on the Theory and Applications of Cryptographic Techniques, Sofia, Bulgaria, April 26–30, 2015. Proceedings, Part I. Springer Berlin Heidelberg; 2015. p. 430–454. Available from: http://dx.doi.org/10.1007/978-3-662-46800-5_17.

[43]   Gérard B, Grosso V, Naya-Plasencia M, and Standaert F-X. Block Ciphers That Are Easier to Mask: How Far Can We Go? In: Bertoni G, and Coron J-S, editors. Cryptographic Hardware and Embedded Systems – CHES 2013: 15th International Workshop, Santa Barbara, CA, USA, August 20–23, 2013. Proceedings. Springer Berlin Heidelberg; 2013. p. 383–399. Available from: http://dx.doi.org/10.1007/978-3-642-40349-1_22.

[44]   Beierle C, Jean J, Kölbl S, *et al.* The SKINNY Family of Block Ciphers and Its Low-Latency Variant MANTIS. In: Robshaw M, and Katz J, editors. Advances in Cryptology – CRYPTO 2016: 36th Annual International Cryptology Conference, Santa Barbara, CA, USA, August 14–18, 2016. Proceedings, Part II. Springer Berlin Heidelberg; 2016. p. 123–153. Available from: http://dx.doi.org/10.1007/978-3-662-53008-5_5.

[45]   Dobraunig C, Eichlseder M, and Mendel F. Square Attack on 7-Round Kiasu-BC. In: Manulis M, Sadeghi AR, Schneider S, editors. Applied Cryptography and Network Security: 14th International Conference, ACNS 2016, Guildford, UK, June 19–22, 2016. Proceedings. Springer International Publishing; 2016. p. 500–517. Available from: http://dx.doi.org/10.1007/978-3-319-39555-5_27.

[46]   Tolba M, Abdelkhalek A, and Youssef AM. A Meet in the Middle Attack on Reduced Round Kiasu-BC. IEICE Transactions on Fundamentals of Electronics, Communications and Computer Sciences. 2016;E99-A(10):1888–1890.

[47] Biham E, and Shamir A. Differential Cryptanalysis of DES-Like Cryptosystems. In: Menezes AJ, Vanstone SA, editors. Advances in Cryptology-CRYPT0 '90. Proceedings. Springer Berlin Heidelberg; 1991. p. 2–21. Available from: http://dx.doi.org/10.1007/3-540-38424-3_1.

[48] Lai X, Massey JL, and Murphy S. Markov Ciphers and Differential Cryptanalysis. In: Davies DW, editor. Advances in Cryptology—EUROCRYPT '91: Workshop on the Theory and Application of Cryptographic Techniques, Brighton, UK, April 8–11, 1991. Proceedings. Springer Berlin Heidelberg; 1991. p. 17–38. Available from: http://dx.doi.org/10.1007/3-540-46416-6_2.

[49] Mouha N, Wang Q, Gu D, and Preneel B. Differential and Linear Cryptanalysis Using Mixed-Integer Linear Programming. In: Wu C-K, Yung M, and Lin D, editors. Information Security and Cryptology: 7th International Conference, Inscrypt 2011, Beijing, China, November 30–December 3, 2011. Revised Selected Papers. vol. 7537 of Lecture Notes in Computer Science. Springer Berlin Heidelberg; 2012. p. 57–76. Available from: http://dx.doi.org/10.1007/978-3-642-34704-7_5.

[50] Mouha N, Velichkov V, De Cannière C, and Preneel B. The Differential Analysis of S-Functions. In: Biryukov A, Gong G, and Stinson DR, editors. Selected Areas in Cryptography: 17th International Workshop, SAC 2010, Waterloo, Ontario, Canada, August 12–13, 2010. Revised Selected Papers. Springer Berlin Heidelberg; 2011. p. 36–56. Available from: http://dx.doi.org/10.1007/978-3-642-19574-7_3.

[51] Biryukov A, and Velichkov V. Automatic Search for Differential Trails in ARX Ciphers. In: Benaloh J, editor. Topics in Cryptology – CT-RSA 2014: The Cryptographer's Track at the RSA Conference 2014, San Francisco, CA, USA, February 25–28, 2014. Proceedings. Springer International Publishing; 2014. p. 227–250. Available from: http://dx.doi.org/10.1007/978-3-319-04852-9_12.

[52] Song L, Huang Z, and Yang Q. Automatic Differential Analysis of ARX Block Ciphers with Application to SPECK and LEA. In: Liu KJ, and Steinfeld R, editors. Information Security and Privacy: 21st Australasian Conference, ACISP 2016, Melbourne, VIC, Australia, July 4–6, 2016. Proceedings, Part II. Springer International Publishing; 2016. p. 379–394. Available from: http://dx.doi.org/10.1007/978-3-319-40367-0_24.

[53] Biryukov A, Vesselin V, and Yann Le C. Automatic Search for the Best Trails in ARX: Application to Block Cipher SPECK; 2016. http://eprint.iacr.org/2016/409. Cryptology ePrint Archive, Report 2016/409.

[54] Bannier A, Bodin N, and Filiol E. Automatic Search for a Maximum Probability Differential Characteristic in a Substitution-Permutation Network; 2016. http://eprint.iacr.org/2016/652. Cryptology ePrint Archive, Report 2016/652.

[55] Matsui M, and Yamagishi A. A New Method for Known Plaintext Attack of FEAL Cipher. In: Rueppel RA, editor. Advances in Cryptology—EUROCRYPT '92: Workshop on the Theory and Application of Cryptographic Techniques, Balatonfüred, Hungary, May 24–28, 1992. Proceedings.

vol. 658 of Lecture Notes in Computer Science. Springer Berlin Heidelberg; 1993. p. 81–91. Available from: http://dx.doi.org/10.1007/3-540-47555-9_7.

[56] Matsui M. Linear Cryptanalysis Method for DES Cipher. In: Helleseth T, editor. Advances in Cryptology—EUROCRYPT '93: Workshop on the Theory and Application of Cryptographic Techniques, Lofthus, Norway, May 23–27, 1993. Proceedings. Springer Berlin Heidelberg; 1994. p. 386–397. Available from: http://dx.doi.org/10.1007/3-540-48285-7_33.

[57] Nyberg K. Linear Approximation of Block Ciphers. In: De Santis A, editor. Advances in Cryptology—EUROCRYPT '94: Workshop on the Theory and Application of Cryptographic Techniques, Perugia, Italy, May 9–12, 1994. Proceedings. Springer Berlin Heidelberg; 1995. p. 439–444. Available from: http://dx.doi.org/10.1007/BFb0053460.

[58] Daemen J, and Rijmen V. The Design of Rijndael. The Advanced Encryption Standard. Information Security and Cryptography. Springer, New York; 2002.

[59] Sun S, Hu L, Wang M, *et al.* Towards Finding the Best Characteristics of Some Bit-Oriented Block Ciphers and Automatic Enumeration of (Related-Key) Differential and Linear Characteristics with Predefined Properties; 2014. https://eprint.iacr.org/2014/747.pdf. IACR Cryptology ePrint Archive, Report 2014/747.

[60] Liu Y, Wang Q, and Rijmen V. Automatic Search of Linear Trails in ARX with Applications to SPECK and Chaskey. In: Manulis M, Sadeghi A-R, and Schneider S, editors. Applied Cryptography and Network Security: 14th International Conference, ACNS 2016, Guildford, UK, June 19–22, 2016. Proceedings. Springer International Publishing; 2016. p. 485–499. Available from: http://dx.doi.org/10.1007/978-3-319-39555-5_26.

[61] Langford SK, and Hellman ME. Differential-Linear Cryptanalysis. In: Desmedt YG, editor. Advances in Cryptology—CRYPTO '94: 14th Annual International Cryptology Conference, Santa Barbara, California, USA, August 21–25, 1994. Proceedings. Springer Berlin Heidelberg; 1994. p. 17–25. Available from: http://dx.doi.org/10.1007/3-540-48658-5_3.

[62] Biham E, Dunkelman O, and Keller N. Enhancing Differential-Linear Cryptanalysis. In: Zheng Y, editor. Advances in Cryptology—ASIACRYPT 2002: 8th International Conference on the Theory and Application of Cryptology and Information Security, Queenstown, New Zealand, December 1–5, 2002. Proceedings. Springer Berlin Heidelberg; 2002. p. 254–266. Available from: http://dx.doi.org/10.1007/3-540-36178-2_16.

[63] Blondeau C, Leander G, and Nyberg K. Differential-Linear Cryptanalysis Revisited. In: Cid C, and Rechberger C, editors. Fast Software Encryption: 21st International Workshop, FSE 2014, London, UK, March 3–5, 2014. Revised Selected Papers. Springer Berlin Heidelberg; 2015. p. 411–430. Available from: http://dx.doi.org/10.1007/978-3-662-46706-0_21.

[64] Chabaud F, and Vaudenay S. Links Between Differential and Linear Cryptanalysis. In: De Santis A, editor. Advances in Cryptology—EUROCRYPT '94: Workshop on the Theory and Application of Cryptographic Techniques, Perugia, Italy, May 9–12, 1994. Proceedings. vol. 950 of Lecture Notes in

Computer Science. Springer Berlin Heidelberg; 1995. p. 356–365. Available from: http://dx.doi.org/10.1007/BFb0053450.

[65] Leurent G. Improved Differential-Linear Cryptanalysis of 7-Round Chaskey with Partitioning. In: Fischlin M, and Coron J-S, editors. Advances in Cryptology – EUROCRYPT 2016: 35th Annual International Conference on the Theory and Applications of Cryptographic Techniques, Vienna, Austria, May 8–12, 2016. Proceedings, Part I. Springer Berlin Heidelberg; 2016. p. 344–371. Available from: http://dx.doi.org/10.1007/978-3-662-49890-3_14.

[66] Lai X. Higher Order Derivatives and Differential Cryptanalysis. In: Blahut RE, Costello DJ, Maurer U, and Mittelholzer T, editors. Communications and Cryptography: Two Sides of One Tapestry. Springer US; 1994. p. 227–233. Available from: http://dx.doi.org/10.1007/978-1-4615-2694-0_23.

[67] Knudsen L. R. Truncated and Higher Order Differentials. In: Preneel B, editor. Fast Software Encryption: Second International Workshop Leuven, FSE '94, Belgium, December 14–16, 1994. Proceedings. Springer Berlin Heidelberg; 1995. p. 196–211. Available from: http://dx.doi.org/10.1007/3-540-60590-8_16.

[68] Jakobsen T, and Knudsen LR. The Interpolation Attack on Block Ciphers. In: Biham E, editor. Fast Software Encryption: 4th International Workshop, FSE '97, Haifa, Israel, January 20–22 1997. Proceedings. Springer Berlin Heidelberg; 1997. p. 28–40. Available from: http://dx.doi.org/10.1007/BFb0052332.

[69] Knudsen LR, Robshaw MJB, and Wagner D. Truncated Differentials and Skipjack. In: Wiener M, editor. Advances in Cryptology—CRYPTO '99: 19th Annual International Cryptology Conference, Santa Barbara, California, USA, August 15–19, 1999. Proceedings. Springer Berlin Heidelberg; 1999. p. 165–180. Available from: http://dx.doi.org/10.1007/3-540-48405-1_11.

[70] Wu H, Bao F, Deng RH, and Ye QZ. Improved Truncated Differential Attacks on SAFER. In: Ohta K, and Pei D, editors. Advances in Cryptology—ASIACRYPT '98: International Conference on the Theory and Application of Cryptology and Information Security, Beijing, China, October 18–22, 1998. Proceedings. Springer Berlin Heidelberg; 1998. p. 133–147. Available from: http://dx.doi.org/10.1007/3-540-49649-1_12.

[71] Borst J, Knudsen LR, and Rijmen V. Two Attacks on Reduced IDEA. In: Fumy W, editor. Advances in Cryptology—EUROCRYPT '97: International Conference on the Theory and Application of Cryptographic Techniques Konstanz, Germany, May 11–15, 1997. Proceedings. Springer Berlin Heidelberg; 1997. p. 1–13. Available from: http://dx.doi.org/10.1007/3-540-69053-0_1.

[72] Moriai S, Sugita M, Aoki K, and Kanda M. Security of E2 against Truncated Differential Cryptanalysis. In: Heys H, Adams C, editors. Selected Areas in Cryptography: 6th Annual International Workshop, SAC '99, Kingston, Ontario, Canada, August 9–10, 1999. Proceedings. Springer Berlin Heidelberg; 2000. p. 106–117. Available from: http://dx.doi.org/10.1007/3-540-46513-8_8.

[73] Lee S, Hong S, Lee S, Lim J, and Yoon S. Truncated Differential Cryptanalysis of Camellia. In: Kim K, editor. Information Security and Cryptology—ICISC 2001: 4th International Conference, Seoul, Korea, December 6–7, 2001. Proceedings. Springer Berlin Heidelberg; 2002. p. 32–38. Available from: http://dx.doi.org/10.1007/3-540-45861-1_3.

[74] Kim J, Hong S, Lee S, Song J, and Yang H. Truncated Differential Attacks on 8-Round CRYPTON. In: Lim J-I, Lee D-H, editors. Information Security and Cryptology – ICISC 2003: 6th International Conference, Seoul, Korea, November 27–28, 2003. Revised Papers. Springer Berlin Heidelberg; 2004. p. 446–456. Available from: http://dx.doi.org/10.1007/978-3-540-24691-6_33.

[75] Rasoolzadeh S, Ahmadian Z, Salmasizadeh M, and Aref MR. An Improved Truncated Differential Cryptanalysis of KLEIN; 2014. https://eprint. iacr.org/2014/485.pdf. IACR Cryptology ePrint Archive, Report 2014/485.

[76] Koyama T, Wang L, Sasaki Y, Sakiyama K, and Ohta K. New Truncated Differential Cryptanalysis on 3D Block Cipher. In: Ryan MD, Smyth B, and Wang G, editors. Information Security Practice and Experience: 8th International Conference, ISPEC 2012, Hangzhou, China, April 9–12, 2012. Proceedings. Springer Berlin Heidelberg; 2012. p. 109–125. Available from: http://dx.doi.org/10.1007/978-3-642-29101-2_8.

[77] Tolba M, Abdelkhalek A, and Youssef AM. Truncated and Multiple Differential Cryptanalysis of Reduced Round Midori128. In: Bishop M, and Nascimento ACA, editors. Information Security: 19th International Conference, ISC 2016, Honolulu, HI, USA, September 3–6, 2016. Proceedings. Springer International Publishing; 2016. p. 3–17. Available from: http://dx.doi.org/ 10.1007/978-3-319-45871-7_1.

[78] Dunkelman O, Keller N, and Shamir A. Improved Single-Key Attacks on 8-Round AES-192 and AES-256. In: Abe M, editor. Advances in Cryptology – ASIACRYPT 2010: 16th International Conference on the Theory and Application of Cryptology and Information Security, Singapore, December 5–9, 2010. Proceedings. Springer Berlin Heidelberg; 2010. p. 158–176. Available from: http://dx.doi.org/10.1007/978-3-642-17373-8_10.

[79] Daemen J, Knudsen LR, and Rijmen V. The Block Cipher SQUARE. In: Biham E, editor. Fast Software Encryption: 4th International Workshop, FSE '97, Haifa, Israel, January 20–22, 1997. Proceedings. Springer Berlin Heidelberg; 1997. p. 149–165. Available from: http://dx.doi.org/10.1007/BFb0052343.

[80] Knudsen LR, and Wagner D. Integral Cryptanalysis. In: Daemen J and Rijmen V, editors. Fast Software Encryption: 9th International Workshop, FSE 2002, Leuven, Belgium, February 4–6, 2002. Revised Papers. Springer Berlin Heidelberg; 2002. p. 112–127. Available from: http://dx.doi.org/10.1007/3-540-45661-9_9.

[81] Lu J, Wei Y, Kim J, and Pasalic E. The Higher-Order Meet-in-the-Middle Attack and Its Application to the Camellia Block Cipher. In: Galbraith S, and Nandi M, editors. Progress in Cryptology – INDOCRYPT 2012: 13th

International Conference on Cryptology in India, Kolkata, India, December 9–12, 2012. Proceedings. Springer Berlin Heidelberg; 2012. p. 244–264. Available from: http://dx.doi.org/10.1007/978-3-642-34931-7_15.

[82] Todo Y. Integral Cryptanalysis on Full MISTY1. In: Gennaro R and Robshaw M, editors. Advances in Cryptology – CRYPTO 2015: 35th Annual Cryptology Conference, Santa Barbara, CA, USA, August 16–20, 2015. Proceedings, Part I. Springer Berlin Heidelberg; 2015. p. 413–432. Available from: http://dx.doi.org/10.1007/978-3-662-47989-6_20.

[83] Bar-On A, Keller N. A 2^{70} Attack on the Full MISTY1. In: Robshaw M, and Katz J, editors. Advances in Cryptology – CRYPTO 2016: 36th Annual International Cryptology Conference, Santa Barbara, CA, USA, August 14–18, 2016. Proceedings, Part I. Springer Berlin Heidelberg; 2016. p. 435–456. Available from: http://dx.doi.org/10.1007/978-3-662-53018-4_16.

[84] Todo Y, and Morii M. Bit-Based Division Property and Application to Simon Family. In: Peyrin T, editor. Fast Software Encryption: 23rd International Conference, FSE 2016, Bochum, Germany, March 20–23, 2016. Revised Selected Papers. Springer Berlin Heidelberg; 2016. p. 357–377. Available from: http://dx.doi.org/10.1007/978-3-662-52993-5_18.

[85] Xiang Z, Zhang W, Bao Z, and Lin D. Applying MILP Method to Searching Integral Distinguishers Based on Division Property for 6 Lightweight Block Ciphers. In: Cheon JH, and Takagi T, editors. Advances in Cryptology – ASIACRYPT 2016: 22nd International Conference on the Theory and Application of Cryptology and Information Security, Hanoi, Vietnam, December 4–8, 2016. Proceedings, Part I. Springer Berlin Heidelberg; 2016. p. 648–678. Available from: http://dx.doi.org/10.1007/978-3-662-53887-6_24.

[86] Sun L, Wang W, and Wang M. MILP-Aided Bit-Based Division Property for Primitives with Non-Bit-Permutation Linear Layers; 2016. http://eprint.iacr.org/2016/811. Cryptology ePrint Archive, Report 2016/811.

[87] Knudsen LR. DEAL: A 128-bit Block Cipher. Complexity. 1998;258(2). NIST AES Proposal.

[88] Biham E, Biryukov A, and Shamir A. Cryptanalysis of Skipjack Reduced to 31 Rounds Using Impossible Differentials. In: Stern J, editor. Advances in Cryptology—EUROCRYPT '99: International Conference on the Theory and Application of Cryptographic Techniques Prague, Czech Republic, May 2–6, 1999. Proceedings. vol. 1592 of Lecture Notes in Computer Science. Springer Berlin Heidelberg; 1999. p. 12–23. Available from: http://dx.doi.org/10.1007/3-540-48910-X_2.

[89] Kim J, Hong S, and Lim J. Impossible Differential Cryptanalysis Using Matrix Method. Discrete Mathematics. 2010;310(5):988–1002.

[90] Derbez P, and Fouque P-A. Automatic Search of Meet-in-the-Middle and Impossible Differential Attacks. In: Robshaw M, Katz J, editors. Advances in Cryptology – CRYPTO 2016: 36th Annual International Cryptology Conference, Santa Barbara, CA, USA, August 14–18, 2016. Proceedings, Part II. Springer Berlin Heidelberg; 2016. p. 157–184. Available from: http://dx.doi. org/10.1007/978-3-662-53008-5_6.

[91]   Bogdanov A, and Rijmen V. Linear Hulls with Correlation Zero and Linear Cryptanalysis of Block Ciphers; 2011. http://eprint.iacr.org/2011/123.pdf. IACR Cryptology ePrint Archive, Report 2011/123.

[92]   Bogdanov A, Geng H, Wang M, Wen L, and Collard B. Zero-Correlation Linear Cryptanalysis with FFT and Improved Attacks on ISO Standards Camellia and CLEFIA. In: Lange T, Lauter K, and Lisoněk P, editors. Selected Areas in Cryptography: 20th International Conference, SAC 2013, Burnaby, BC, Canada, August 14–16, 2013. Revised Selected Papers. Springer Berlin Heidelberg; 2014. p. 306–323. Available from: http://dx.doi.org/10.1007/978-3-662-43414-7_16.

[93]   Wang Y, and Wu W. Improved Multidimensional Zero-Correlation Linear Cryptanalysis and Applications to LBlock and TWINE. In: Susilo W, Mu Y, editors. Information Security and Privacy: 19th Australasian Conference, ACISP 2014, Wollongong, NSW, Australia, July 7–9, 2014. Proceedings. Springer International Publishing; 2014. p. 1–16. Available from: http://dx.doi.org/ 10.1007/978-3-319-08344-5_1.

[94]   Bogdanov A, Leander G, Nyberg K, and Wang M. Integral and Multi-dimensional Linear Distinguishers with Correlation Zero. In: Wang X, and Sako K, editors. Advances in Cryptology – ASIACRYPT 2012: 18th International Conference on the Theory and Application of Cryptology and Information Security, Beijing, China, December 2–6, 2012. Proceedings. Springer Berlin Heidelberg; 2012. p. 244–261. Available from: http://dx.doi.org/10.1007/978-3-642-34961-4_16.

[95]   Diffie W, and Hellman ME. Special Feature Exhaustive Cryptanalysis of the NBS Data Encryption Standard. Computer. 1977 June;10(6):74–84. Available from: http://dx.doi.org/10.1109/C-M.1977.217750.

[96]   Chaum D, and Evertse J-H. Cryptanalysis of DES with a Reduced Number of Rounds. In: Williams HC, editor. Advances in Cryptology—CRYPTO '85. Proceedings. Springer Berlin Heidelberg; 1986. p. 192–211. Available from: http://dx.doi.org/10.1007/3-540-39799-X_16.

[97]   Bogdanov A, and Rechberger C. A 3-Subset Meet-in-the-Middle Attack: Cryptanalysis of the Lightweight Block Cipher KTANTAN. In: Biryukov A, Gong G, and Stinson DR, editors. Selected Areas in Cryptography: 17th International Workshop, SAC 2010, Waterloo, Ontario, Canada, August 12–13, 2010. Revised Selected Papers. Springer Berlin Heidelberg; 2011. p. 229–240. Available from: http://dx.doi.org/10.1007/978-3-642-19574-7_16.

[98]   Aoki K, and Sasaki Y. Meet-in-the-Middle Preimage Attacks against Reduced SHA-0 and SHA-1. In: Halevi S, editor. Advances in Cryptology – CRYPTO 2009: 29th Annual International Cryptology Conference, Santa Barbara, CA, USA, August 16–20, 2009. Proceedings. Springer Berlin Heidelberg; 2009. p. 70–89. Available from: http://dx.doi.org/10.1007/978-3-642-03356-8_5.

[99]   Zhu B, and Gong G. Multidimensional Meet-in-the-Middle Attack and Its Applications to KATAN32/48/64; 2011. https://eprint.iacr.org/2011/619.pdf. IACR Cryptology ePrint Archive, 2011/619.

[100]   Tolba M, and Youssef AM. Generalized MitM Attacks on Full TWINE. Information Processing Letters. 2016;116(2):128–135. Available from: http://www.sciencedirect.com/science/article/pii/S0020019015001660.

[101]   Bogdanov A, Khovratovich D, and Rechberger C. Biclique Cryptanalysis of the Full AES. In: Lee D, and Wang X, editors. Advances in Cryptology – ASIACRYPT 2011: 17th International Conference on the Theory and Application of Cryptology and Information Security, Seoul, South Korea, December 4–8, 2011. Proceedings. vol. 7073 of Lecture Notes in Computer Science. Springer Berlin Heidelberg; 2011. p. 344–371. Available from: http://dx.doi.org/ 10.1007/978-3-642-25385-0_19.

[102]   Demirci H, and Selçuk AA. A Meet-in-the-Middle Attack on 8-Round AES. In: Nyberg K, editor. Fast Software Encryption: 15th International Workshop, FSE 2008, Lausanne, Switzerland, February 10–13, 2008. Revised Selected Papers. vol. 5086 of Lecture Notes in Computer Science. Springer Berlin Heidelberg; 2008. p. 116–126. Available from: http://dx.doi.org/10.1007/978-3-540-71039-4_7.

[103]   Demirci H, Taşkın İ, Çoban M, and Baysal A. Improved Meet-in-the-Middle Attacks on AES. In: Roy B, and Sendrier N, editors. Progress in Cryptology – INDOCRYPT 2009: 10th International Conference on Cryptology in India, New Delhi, India, December 13–16, 2009. Proceedings. Springer Berlin Heidelberg; 2009. p. 144–156. Available from: http://dx.doi.org/10.1007/978-3-642-10628-6_10.

[104]   Mendel F, Rechberger C, Schläffer M, and Thomsen, SS. The Rebound Attack: Cryptanalysis of Reduced Whirlpool and Grøstl. In: Dunkelman O, editor. Fast Software Encryption: 16th International Workshop, FSE 2009 Leuven, Belgium, February 22–25, 2009. Revised Selected Papers. Springer Berlin Heidelberg; 2009. p. 260–276. Available from: http://dx.doi.org/ 10.1007/978-3-642-03317-9_16.

[105]   Derbez P, Fouque P-A, and Jean J. Improved Key Recovery Attacks on Reduced-Round AES in the Single-Key Setting. In: Johansson T, Nguyen PQ, editors. Advances in Cryptology – EUROCRYPT 2013: 32nd Annual International Conference on the Theory and Applications of Cryptographic Techniques, Athens, Greece, May 26–30, 2013. Proceedings. Berlin, Heidelberg: Springer Berlin Heidelberg; 2013. p. 371–387. Available from: http://dx.doi.org/ 10.1007/978-3-642-38348-9_23.

[106]   Li L, Jia K, and Wang X. Improved Meet-in-the-Middle Attacks on AES-192 and PRINCE; 2013. http://eprint.iacr.org/. Cryptology ePrint Archive, Report 2013/573.

[107]   Li R, and Jin C. Meet-in-the-Middle Attacks on 10-Round AES-256. Designs, Codes and Cryptography. 2016;80(3):459–471. Available from: http://dx.doi. org/10.1007/s10623-015-0113-3.

[108]   Abdelkhalek A, AlTawy R, Tolba M, and Youssef AM. Meet-in-the-Middle Attacks on Reduced-Round Hierocrypt-3. In: Lauter K, and Rodríguez-Henríquez F, editors. Progress in Cryptology – LATINCRYPT 2015: 4th International Conference on Cryptology and Information Security in

Latin America, Guadalajara, Mexico, August 23–26, 2015. Proceedings. Springer International Publishing; 2015. p. 187–203. Available from: http://dx.doi.org/10.1007/978-3-319-22174-8_11.

[109] Abdelkhalek A, Tolba M, and Youssef AM. Improved Key Recovery Attack on Round-Reduced Hierocrypt-L1 in the Single-Key Setting. In: Chakraborty RS, Schwabe P, and Solworth J, editors. Security, Privacy, and Applied Cryptography Engineering: 5th International Conference, SPACE 2015, Jaipur, India, October 3–7, 2015. Proceedings. Springer International Publishing; 2015. p. 139–150. Available from: http://dx.doi.org/10.1007/978-3-319-24126-5_9.

[110] Hao Y, Bai D, and Li L. A Meet-in-the-Middle Attack on Round-Reduced mCrypton Using the Differential Enumeration Technique. In: Au M, Carminati B, and Kuo C-C J, editors. Network and System Security: 8th International Conference, NSS 2014, Xi'an, China, October 15–17, 2014. Proceedings. vol. 8792 of Lecture Notes in Computer Science. Springer International Publishing; 2014. p. 166–183. Available from: http://dx.doi.org/10.1007/978-3-319-11698-3_13.

[111] Guo J, Jean J, Nikolić I, and Sasaki Y. Meet-in-the-Middle Attacks on Generic Feistel Constructions. In: Sarkar P, and Iwata T, editors. Advances in Cryptology – ASIACRYPT 2014: 20th International Conference on the Theory and Application of Cryptology and Information Security, Kaoshiung, Taiwan, R.O.C., December 7–11, 2014. Proceedings, Part I. Springer Berlin Heidelberg; 2014. p. 458–477. Available from: http://dx.doi.org/10.1007/978-3-662-45611-8_24.

[112] Tolba M, Abdelkhalek A, and Youssef AM. Meet-in-the-Middle Attacks on Round-Reduced Khudra. In: Chakraborty RS, Schwabe P, and Solworth J, editors. Security, Privacy, and Applied Cryptography Engineering: 5th International Conference, SPACE 2015, Jaipur, India, October 3–7, 2015. Proceedings. Springer International Publishing; 2015. p. 127–138. Available from: http://dx.doi.org/10.1007/978-3-319-24126-5_8.

[113] Tolba M, Abdelkhalek A, and Youssef AM. Meet-in-the-Middle Attacks on Reduced Round Piccolo. In: Güneysu T, Leander G, and Moradi A, editors. Lightweight Cryptography for Security and Privacy: 4th International Workshop, LightSec 2015, Bochum, Germany, September 10–11, 2015. Revised Selected Papers. Springer International Publishing; 2016. p. 3–20. Available from: http://dx.doi.org/10.1007/978-3-319-29078-2_1.

[114] Wang Y, Wu W, Yu X, and Zhang L. Security on LBlock against Biclique Cryptanalysis. In: Lee DH, and Yung M, editors. Information Security Applications: 13th International Workshop, WISA 2012, Jeju Island, Korea, August 16–18, 2012. Revised Selected Papers. Springer Berlin Heidelberg; 2012. p. 1–14. Available from: http://dx.doi.org/10.1007/978-3-642-35416-8_1.

[115] Çoban M, Karakoç F, and Özkan B. Biclique Cryptanalysis of TWINE. In: Pieprzyk J, Sadeghi A-R, and Manulis M, editors. Cryptology and Network Security: 11th International Conference, CANS 2012, Darmstadt, Germany, December 12–14, 2012. Proceedings. vol. 7712 of Lecture Notes

in Computer Science. Springer Berlin Heidelberg; 2012. p. 43–55. Available from: http://dx.doi.org/10.1007/978-3-642-35404-5_5.

[116] Canteaut A, Naya-Plasencia M, and Vayssière B. Sieve-in-the-Middle: Improved MITM Attacks. In: Canetti R, and Garay JA, editors. Advances in Cryptology – CRYPTO 2013: 33rd Annual Cryptology Conference, Santa Barbara, CA, USA, August 18–22, 2013. Proceedings, Part I. Springer Berlin Heidelberg; 2013. p. 222–240. Available from: http://dx.doi.org/10.1007/978-3-642-40041-4_13.

[117] Ahmadi S, Ahmadian Z, Mohajeri J, and Aref MR. Low-Data Complexity Biclique Cryptanalysis of Block Ciphers with Application to Piccolo and HIGHT. IEEE Transactions on Information Forensics and Security. 2014;9:1641–1652.

[118] Bogdanov A, Chang D, Ghosh M, and Sanadhya S. Bicliques with Minimal Data and Time Complexity for AES. In: Lee J, and Kim J, editors. Information Security and Cryptology – ICISC 2014: 17th International Conference, Seoul, South Korea, December 3–5, 2014. Revised Selected Papers. vol. 8949 of Lecture Notes in Computer Science. Springer International Publishing; 2015. p. 160–174. Available from: http://dx.doi.org/10.1007/978-3-319-15943-0_10.

[119] Leander G, Abdelraheem MA, AlKhzaimi H, and Zenner E. A Cryptanalysis of PRINTcipher: The Invariant Subspace Attack. In: Rogaway P, editor. Advances in Cryptology – CRYPTO 2011: 31st Annual Cryptology Conference, Santa Barbara, CA, USA, August 14–18, 2011. Proceedings. Springer Berlin Heidelberg; 2011. p. 206–221. Available from: http://dx.doi.org/10.1007/978-3-642-22792-9_12.

[120] Bulygin S, Walter M, and Buchmann J. Full Analysis of PRINTcipher with Respect to Invariant Subspace Attack: Efficient Key Recovery and Countermeasures. Designs, Codes and Cryptography. 2014;73(3):997–1022. Available from: http://dx.doi.org/10.1007/s10623-013-9840-5.

[121] Leander G, Minaud B, and Rønjom S. A Generic Approach to Invariant Subspace Attacks: Cryptanalysis of Robin, iSCREAM and Zorro. In: Oswald E, and Fischlin M, editors. Advances in Cryptology – EUROCRYPT 2015: 34th Annual International Conference on the Theory and Applications of Cryptographic Techniques, Sofia, Bulgaria, April 26–30, 2015. Proceedings, Part I. Springer Berlin Heidelberg; 2015. p. 254–283. Available from: http://dx.doi. org/10.1007/978-3-662-46800-5_11.

[122] Guo J, Jean J, Nikolić I, Qiao K, Sasaki Y, and Sim SM. Invariant Subspace Attack against Full Midori64; 2015. http://eprint.iacr.org/2015/1189. Cryptology ePrint Archive, Report 2015/1189.

[123] Grassi L, Rechberger C, and Rnjom S. Subspace Trail Cryptanalysis and Its Applications to AES; 2016. http://eprint.iacr.org/2016/592. Cryptology ePrint Archive, Report 2016/592.

Chapter 12

Image provenance inference through content-based device fingerprint analysis

Xufeng Lin[1] and Chang-Tsun Li[1]

12.1 Introduction

The last few decades have witnessed the increasing popularity of low-cost and high-quality digital imaging devices ranging from digital cameras to cell phones with built-in cameras, which make the acquisition of digital images easier than ever before. Meanwhile, the ever-increasing convenience of image acquisition has bred the pervasiveness of powerful image-editing tools, which allow even unskilled persons to easily manipulate digital images. As a consequence, the credibility of digital images has been questioned and challenged. Under the circumstance where digital images serve as the critical evidence, e.g., presented as evidence in courts, being able to infer the provenance of an image becomes essential for recovering truth and ensuring justice.

As an important branch of digital forensics, image provenance inference aims to determine the original source of a digital image. The provenance of an image provides forensic investigators with rich information about the originality and integrity of the image. It does not only look for answers to the question of which device has been used to acquire a given image but also convey other implications of the credibility of an image. For example, the inconsistent provenance information from different regions of an image indicates that the image may have been tampered with. This chapter mainly introduces and discusses several intrinsic *device fingerprints* and their applications in image provenance inference. These fingerprints arise from either the hardware or software processing components in the image acquisition pipeline and exhibit themselves as specific patterns or traces in the image. Analyses of these fingerprints provide useful information for inferring the image provenance and uncovering underlying facts about the image.

In the remainder of this chapter, we will first discuss why the techniques that are based on digital watermark and metadata are impractical or unreliable for image provenance inference in Sections 12.2 and 12.3, respectively. In Section 12.4, we will introduce several intrinsic device fingerprints arising from different processing

---

[1]School of Computing and Mathematics, Charles Sturt University, Australia

components in the imaging pipeline of a device. In Section 12.5, we will concentrate on sensor pattern noise (SPN) and discuss in detail its applications in image provenance inference. Section 12.6 concludes this chapter and points out several directions of future research.

12.2 Why not digital watermark?

Digital watermark is an extra message that is embedded, usually in an invisible way, to digital contents like images, audio, and video, for the purpose of protecting the ownership of digital contents. It offers an imperceptible way to insert digital object identifier, serial number, or other image source information in host images, and thus provides a promising approach for inferring the provenance of an image. The *robust* watermark, which is able to survive a variety of image processing operations such as image compression, image filtering, and geometric modifications, can be used to verify the provenance of an image that has been redistributed over untrusted networks. The *fragile* or *semi-fragile* watermark [1–9], which is readily altered or destroyed when the host image is modified, has been intensively used to determine whether the image has been altered since its original recording.

In spite of the effectiveness of the techniques based on digital watermark, they can only be applied when the image is protected at the origin. Nowadays, the majority of images do not contain a digital watermark mainly due to the following reasons:

- Camera manufacturers have to devise extra digital watermark embedding components in the camera, so only some high-end cameras have watermark embedding features.
- The embedded watermark may degrade the image quality and significantly reduce the market value of cameras equipped with a watermark embedding component.
- The successful implementation of watermark-based protection requires close collaborations among publishers/manufacturers, investigators, and potentially trusted third-party organizations. This restricts the wide adoption of digital watermark in digital devices.

12.3 Why not metadata?

Another way to determine the provenance of an image is through the use of metadata created by the source device. In particular, the exchangeable image file format (EXIF) is the most ubiquitous metadata standard supported by many digital camera manufacturers. Part of the information retrieved from the EXIF header of an image is shown in Figure 12.1. By accessing the EXIF header, some information, such as the "Make" and "Model" of the camera that has been used to take the image, can be retrieved. Other information, such as the "Create Date" and "Modify Date", can serve as useful clues to determine whether the image has been modified since its original recording. A few attempts [10,11] have been made to exploit the EXIF information for forensic purposes.

Make	CASIO COMPUTER CO., LTD.
Model	EX-Z150
Orientation	Horizontal (normal)
XResolution	72
YResolution	72
ResolutionUnit	inches
Software	1.00
ModifyDate	2009:01:06 12:39:41
YCbCrPositioning	Co-sited
---- ExifIFD ----	
ExposureTime	1/80
FNumber	10.0
ExposureProgram	Program AE
ISO	64
ExifVersion	0221
DateTimeOriginal	2009:01:06 12:39:41
CreateDate	2009:01:06 12:39:41
ComponentsConfiguration	Y, Cb, Cr, -
CompressedBitsPerPixel	4.098876437
ApertureValue	10.0

Figure 12.1   Part of the EXIF information retrieved from an image with an EXIF editing tool [12]

However, EXIF metadata is not always available. On the one hand, not all imaging devices and image file formats support EXIF standard, especially the older versions of devices and image formats. As a result, images taken with such devices or stored in such formats may not contain EXIF information. Early versions of image editing software, such as Adobe Photoshop 5.0, do not recognize the EXIF standard and strip the EXIF metadata when they resave the images. On the other hand, with the rise of photo sharing on social networks like Facebook, Instagram, and Twitter, there has been increasing concern and fear about the personal information embedded in the photos shared online. At the same time, the latest generation of cameras and phones is able to add location information or Global Positioning System (GPS) coordinates to the EXIF metadata, which makes photo sharing a privacy hazard. For this reason, the EXIF metadata is stripped out by almost all the major social networks when the images are being uploaded.

Moreover, the EXIF metadata is easily removable or replaceable. Anyone who wishes to remove or edit EXIF metadata will find a range of tools at their disposal on the Internet. With these EXIF editing tools at hand, experienced photographers can even develop their own techniques to edit EXIF metadata. Therefore, even if EXIF metadata is present, it is not a reliable or trustworthy indicator of the image source.

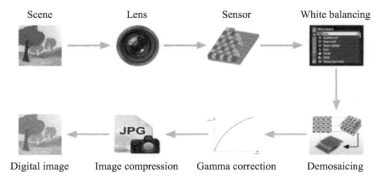

Scene	Lens	Sensor	White balancing
Digital image	Image compression	Gamma correction	Demosaicing

Figure 12.2   A simplified image acquisition pipeline in typical cameras

12.4   Device fingerprints

Illustrated in Figure 12.2 is a simplified image acquisition pipeline in typical cameras. The light from the scene goes through the lens [usually covered by an associated color filter array (CFA)] and projects on the surface of the sensor, which converts the optical signal into the raw image signal. Sequentially undergoing different processing components such as CFA interpolation, white balancing, camera response function (CRF) and Joint Photographic Experts Group (JPEG) compression, the raw image signal finally forms the image data suitable for visualization or display purpose. The final image carries specific patterns or traces left by each processing component in the image acquisition pipeline. Such patterns or traces are intrinsic to the imaging pipeline, so they can be considered as some sort of fingerprints of the source device and used for image provenance inference. It is similar to bullet scratches allowing forensic investigators to match a bullet to a particular barrel. In the following subsections, we will introduce different device fingerprints arising from different processing components in the image acquisition pipeline.

12.4.1   Optical aberrations

Each camera is equipped with a complex optical system. In an ideal imaging system, the light rays from a point of an object pass through the lens and converge to a corresponding point on the sensor. However, realistic optical systems deviate from such an ideal model and introduce optical aberrations in the captured images. It should be noted that optical aberrations are caused by the optical specifications designed by device manufacturers (due to the wave nature of light) rather than any flaws in the optical elements. Different camera models are typically equipped with different optical systems, which have their own aberration characteristics. Therefore, the optical aberrations appear in an image can be used for inferring the provenance of the image or even verifying the content of the image. Optical aberrations can be categorized into different types, such as chromatic aberrations, spherical aberrations, coma, and radial lens distortion. We refer readers to Chapter 3 of [13] for a detailed description of each type of aberrations. Some of the optical aberrations have been exploited for image provenance inference. Johnson and Farid [14] modeled the lateral chromatic aberration, which occurs when different wavelengths of light do not converge to the same point on the sensor, as the expansion/contraction of the coordinates of the red and blue channel with respect to the coordinate of the green channel:

$$\begin{pmatrix} x_r \\ y_r \end{pmatrix} = \begin{pmatrix} x_g - x_1 \\ y_g - y_1 \end{pmatrix} \alpha_1 + \begin{pmatrix} x_1 \\ y_1 \end{pmatrix} \tag{12.1}$$

$$\begin{pmatrix} x_b \\ y_b \end{pmatrix} = \begin{pmatrix} x_g - x_2 \\ y_g - y_2 \end{pmatrix} \alpha_2 + \begin{pmatrix} x_2 \\ y_2 \end{pmatrix},$$

where $(x_c, y_c), c \in \{r, g, b\}$ is the coordinate of channel c, and $(x_i, y_i), i \in \{1, 2\}$ and $\alpha_i, i \in \{1, 2\}$ are the coordinates of the center and the magnitude of distortion, respectively. In such a way, the red-to-green channel and blue-to-green channel distortions are characterized by the parameters (x_1, y_1, α_1) and (x_2, y_2, α_2), respectively. By maximizing the mutual information between each pair of color channels (i.e., the red and green channel, or the blue and green channel), the parameters can be globally estimated from the entire image. Any inconsistency between the globally estimated parameters and the parameters estimated locally from a suspect image region can be used as evidence of image forgery [14]. In [15], these six parameters estimated from images captured by four cell phones (two of them are of the same model) are used as features to train a support vector machine (SVM) classifier, which will be used for classifying images of unknown provenance. Testing on 180 images taken by three cell phones of different models shows an average classification accuracy of 92.2%. But the accuracy of differentiating the two cameras of the same model is as low as 50%, which is akin to a random guess.

Another pronounced and visually distinct aberration is the radial lens distortion, which arises from the fact that the magnification of an image is nonuniformly across the image plane but depends on the radial distance, r, from the optical center. When the magnification increases with r, the distortion is known as the "barrel distortion" (Figure 12.3(b)). Conversely, it is known as the "pincushion distortion" (Figure 12.3(c)), if the magnification decreases with r. Choi *et al.* [16,17] adopted a simple polynomial model [18] to formulate the relationship between the distorted image coordinate (x_d, y_d) and undistorted image coordinate (x_u, y_u):

$$r_u = r_d + k_1 r_d^3 + k_2 r_d^5, \tag{12.2}$$

where $r_d = \sqrt{(x_d - x_0)^2 + (y_d - y_0)^2}$ and $r_u = \sqrt{(x_u - x_0)^2 + (y_u - y_0)^2}$ are the radius from the optical center (x_0, y_0) in the distorted and undistorted image, respectively. The parameters (k_1, k_2) characterizing the radial distortions can be estimated using the algorithm proposed in [18]. Similar to the work in [15], Choi *et al.* trained an SVM classifier using the distortion parameters estimated from images of different cameras and classified images of unknown provenance. On a small dataset consisting

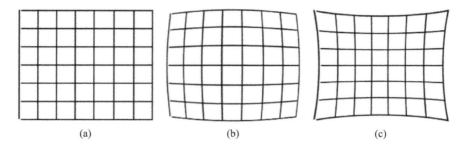

(a)   (b)   (c)

Figure 12.3   Radial lens distortion of a rectangular grid: (a) Undistorted grid, (b)
Barrel distortion, (c) Pincushion distortion

of 180 images taken by three cameras of different models, they reported an average accuracy of 91.5% [16]. The accuracy decreases to 89.1% on a larger dataset consisting of images from five cameras [17].

The results on small datasets show that the optical aberrations are promising in image provenance inference but their limitations are apparent:

- Cameras of the same model are equipped with the same optical specification; therefore, the optical aberrations are insufficient for identifying individual source cameras of the same model [15].
- The optical aberrations are closely related with camera settings, such as focal length [16,17,19], focal distance, and even aperture size [20]. Different camera settings may introduce considerable intramodel variations and make the classification over a range of camera settings more problematic.
- The estimation of aberration parameters is influenced by JPEG compression, random noise, and image cropping. Van *et al.* [15] showed that the classification accuracy declines when testing on images processed by some common image operations.

The above limitations of optical aberrations restrict their applicability to more diverse datasets in the sense of camera models, camera settings, and image processing operations.

12.4.2   CFA and demosaicing

In consequence of cost considerations, most consumer digital cameras are equipped with only one imaging sensor and an associated CFA. Only one color component that passes through CFA is captured at each pixel and consequently forms a mosaic-like monochrome image, as shown in Figure 12.4. The missing components have to be interpolated based on the captured components to recover the full-color image. The process of CFA interpolation is also known as demosaicing (Figure 12.4), which will introduce specific interpixel and interchannel correlations in the recovered full-color image. Therefore, by detecting the specific patterns introduced by demosaicing, we are able to infer the provenance of images.

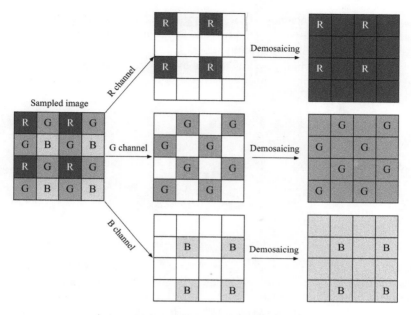

Figure 12.4 The process of CFA interpolation (demosaicing)

Demosaicing has been extensively exploited for forensic purposes. Popescu and Farid [21] modeled the correlation between each pixel $I(x,y)$ and its neighboring pixels using a linear model

$$I(x,y) = \sum_{i=-N}^{N} \alpha_i I(x + \Delta x_i, y + \Delta y_i) + n(x,y), \qquad (12.3)$$

where $n(x,y)$ is the modeling error, $(2N + 1) \times (2N + 1)$ is the size of the neighborhood, $\{\alpha_i| - N \leq i \leq N\}$ are the interpolation coefficients, and $(\Delta x_i, \Delta y_i)$ is the offset of the ith pixel within the neighborhood. They assumed that image tampering will likely destroy the interpixel correlations or produce inconsistent correlations. To reveal the potential tampering, they employed the expectation/maximization algorithm to simultaneously estimate the interpolation coefficients α_i and the probability map p indicating how likely one pixel conforms to the neighboring correlation characterized by (12.3). An image region without the presence of periodic pattern in the probability map p is considered as tampered, otherwise it is nontampered. They also observed that the magnitude spectrum of the probability map p varies from one demosaicing algorithm to another. Motivated by this observation, Bayram *et al.* [22] used the peak locations and magnitudes in the Discrete Fourier Transform (DFT) spectrum of the probability map p, along with the interpolation coefficients α, as features to differentiate camera models. With the LibSVM classifier [23] and the sequential forward floating search (SFFS) algorithm [24] for feature selection, they reported an average classification accuracy of 83.3% on three cameras of different brands. The accuracy on the same dataset was improved to 96% when the smooth and nonsmooth image regions were handled differently [25].

In [26], Long and Huang formulated the mean square error of $n(x, y)$ across the entire image in a quadratic form

$$\frac{1}{WH} \sum_{x=1}^{W} \sum_{y=1}^{H} |n(x,y)|^2 = X^T A X, \tag{12.4}$$

where $X = \{\alpha_{-N}, \dots, \alpha_N, \alpha_{N+1}\}^T$ and

$$A(i,j) = \frac{1}{WH} \sum_{x=1}^{W} \sum_{y=1}^{H} I(x + \Delta x_i, y + \Delta y_i) I(x + \Delta x_j, y + \Delta y_j), -N \le i,j \le N,$$

$$\tag{12.5}$$

with $\alpha_{N+1} = -1$ and $\Delta x_{N+1} = \Delta y_{N+1} = 0$. Instead of using the interpolation coefficients, they represented A in a 13×13 neighborhood as a 169-dimensional feature, the dimension of which will be reduced to 15 using the principal component analysis [27]. Instead of using the SVM classifier like in [22,25], a three-layer feed-forward neural network was trained using the 15-dimensional features for classifying different camera models. Almost perfect results were reported on the uncompressed images produced by digital cameras (four cameras and one class of cartoon images). But their algorithm tends to be sensitive to JPEG compression and median filtering.

Considering that the demosaicing algorithm may handle different image regions differently, Swaminathan *et al.* [28,29] first divided the image regions into three categories:

- Region containing pixels with a significant horizontal gradient,
- Region containing pixels with a significant vertical gradient,
- Region that is mostly smooth.

Then, they estimated the interpolation coefficients in each of the three regions by minimizing the approximation error over 36 CFA configurations. The estimation was performed in a 7×7 neighborhood in each of the three color channels (red, green, and blue), and thus results in $7 \times 7 \times 3 \times 3 = 441$ coefficients per image. These coefficients serve as 441-dimensional features that are fed into a probabilistic SVM classifier for training and classifying images of unknown provenance. An average classification rate of 90% was reported for nine cameras of different brands, but it drops to 86% on a larger dataset consisting 19 cameras of different models [29]. In the latter case, the classification errors were largely attributed to the ambiguities among cameras of the same brand.

Most advanced demosaicing algorithms often exploit the color difference and inevitably introduce strong interchannel dependencies. However, the aforementioned algorithms only consider the interpixel correlations in the same color channel but ignore the interchannel correlations. Cao and Kot [30] found that demosaicing is equivalent to estimating the second-order derivatives of neighboring pixels. Thus, they modeled the pixel dependencies using a partial second-order derivative correlation formula, which takes both the intrachannel and interchannel correlations into consideration. Additionally, they proposed an expectation/maximization reverse classification (EMRC) algorithm to simultaneously classify the pixels demosaiced by the same formula into 1 of 16 demosaicing categories and estimated the interpolation coefficients representing the underlying demosaicing formulas. Based on the outcomes of the EMRC algorithm, a total of 1,536 features were computed for each image. Similar to the work in [22,25], the SFFS algorithm and the LibSVM classifier were jointly used to classify the images of unknown source. With 250 features selected by SFFS, an average accuracy of 97.5% was achieved over a dataset of 14 cameras, some of which are of the same brand. The leading-edge performance was also confirmed by the results on a dataset of 15 mobile cameras [31]. But as expected, the algorithm tends to confuse the cameras of the same model due to the identical in-camera demosaicing algorithm [31].

12.4.3   Camera response function

In digital cameras, the CRF, which is generally a nonlinear mapping, is used to transform the wide-ranging *irradiance* (i.e., the output of demosaicing) to a limited range of measurable image intensities. The principle of using CRF for image provenance inference is that cameras of the same model are expected to employ the same CRF. By adopting the CRF estimation algorithm in [32], Lin *et al.* [33] defined three features to measure the properties and consistencies of the CRFs recovered from the CRFs of different color channels. Positive samples (i.e., the normal CRFs collected from a database of response functions [34]) and negative samples (i.e., the abnormal CRFs estimated from forged images) are used to train an SVM predictor, which will be used to predict a confidence indicating the normality of the CRFs estimated from an image in question. The effectiveness of the algorithms was validated via comparison experiments on a few forged and nonforged images.

Hsu and Chang [35–37] proposed a CRF-based image splicing detection algorithm. They modeled the CRF using the generalized gamma curve model (CGCM) and estimated the parameters of CGCM using geometry invariants (GIs) calculated from locally planar irradiance points in an image [38]. By automatically segmenting an image, they first obtained the suspect spliced regions and the boundary segments between neighboring regions. If the image is authentic, the GIs in the region on one side of a boundary segment is expected to fit well to the CRF estimated from the region on the other side of the boundary segment. Otherwise, if the regions on two sides of a boundary segment are from different cameras, it is expected to see large cross fitting errors. Therefore, they calculated 20-dimensional features for each boundary segment to measure the cross fitting errors as well as the fitness of CRF estimation and classified the segments as authentic or spliced using an SVM classifier. They reported an image-level classification accuracy of 70% precision and 70% recall rate, on a dataset consisting of 180 spliced and 183 authentic images taken by 4 cameras.

While early works focused on exploiting the abnormality or inconsistency of CRFs from different sources for detecting image manipulations, the concept of camera

CRF signature for distinguishing different camera models was introduced later in [39,40]. The authors extended their CRF estimation algorithm [38] and defined a CRF signature as the histogram of the fitness scores of selected points with regard to the estimated CRF. Visual examination on the CRF signatures of four different camera models shows that cameras of different models are prone to have CRF signatures of different shapes, and the CRF signatures extracted from images with the same CRF tend to be consistent. However, the abovementioned experiments related to CRF, for either image manipulation detection or image source identification, were conducted on datasets involving only a few cameras. Further studies on the distinctiveness of CRF over a large set of different camera models are yet to be conducted.

12.4.4   Quantization table

In the last step of the imaging pipeline, most digital cameras export images in JPEG format. This lossy compression standard employs quantization tables to control the desired amount of compression. Although the Independent JPEG Group recommended using the standard quantization tables, the JPEG users (e.g., camera manufacturers and computer programs) are free to specify their own quantization tables. In fact, the majority of cameras employ a different set of quantization tables. Therefore, comparing the quantization tables of different images offers a simple way to distinguish different image sources.

The idea of using JPEG quantization tables for camera ballistics was first proposed by Farid in [41], where an initial investigation on 204 cameras revealed that 62 (30.4%) out of the 204 cameras had a unique quantization table. While in the remaining cameras, not only the cameras from the same manufacturer may share the same quantization table but even different makes and models are likely to have identical quantization tables. His follow-up study on a larger database [42] shows that the distinctiveness of quantization table can be even lower, with only 517 (5.1%) out of 10,153 entries having a unique table. But an independent investigation carried out by Sorell [43] leads to a different interpretation. He found that, among the 330 distinct quantization tables extracted from 5,485 images, over 92% of them are unique to 1 camera series. Furthermore, even after recompression of an image, residual artifacts of double compression continue to provide useful information for source camera identification.

Given the above attempts to discriminate image source via quantization tables, there is no denying that the quantization table is a reasonable discriminator between model series and effective at narrowing down the source of an image to a smaller set of possible cameras, but apparently it is insufficient to uniquely identify the image source. Besides, as pointed out in [43], the distinctiveness of quantization tables can be obscured by the smaller valued quantization tables adopted in high-quality cameras for acquiring higher quality images.

12.4.5   Image thumbnail

Another in-camera operation is the generation of an image thumbnail, which is a thumbnail-sized version of the full resolution image and typically stored in the header of a JPEG image. A thumbnail is used to quickly preview the image without loading and displaying the full-sized image. The creation of a thumbnail involves a series of operations including cropping, blurring, downsampling, sharpening contrast and brightness adjustment, and JPEG compression. The parameters of these operations vary across camera brands or even models, and thus can be used to identify the source device of an image. Experimental results on 1,514 images covering 142 cameras of different makes and models show that 40.8% of the cameras can be uniquely identified by using the thumbnail parameters [44].

To increase the accuracy of camera identification, one can simply incorporate more information. For example, by jointly using quantization tables, thumbnail parameters, and full resolution image size, the percentage of cameras that can be uniquely identified increases from 40.8% to 72.2% [11]. The results on a much larger database [11] show that a 576-valued camera signature, consisting of the information from quantization tables, Huffman codes, thumbnail parameters, and EXIF metadata parameters, is capable of uniquely identifying 69.1% of 9,163 camera configurations. It should be noted that the percentage of cameras that can be uniquely identified varies from one database to another and also depends on what "fingerprints" are used for identification. But any of the device fingerprints we have discussed so far is only sufficient for brand-level or model-level image provenance inference. So even after involving all of the aforementioned fingerprints, ambiguities still abound in identifying the individual devices of the same brand or model.

12.5 Sensor pattern noise

A promising method for uniquely distinguishing individual devices is based on SPN [45]. As shown in Figure 12.5, pattern noise consists of two main components. One is the fixed pattern noise (FPN) (or dark current noise as it is more commonly referred to as), which is the pixel-to-pixel differences when the sensor array is not exposed to light. The dominant component in SPN is the photo response nonuniformity (PRNU) noise. It is primarily resulted from the variation among pixels in their sensitivity to light, which is caused by the manufacturing imperfections and the inhomogeneity of silicon wafers during the sensor manufacturing process [45]. It has attracted much

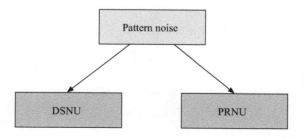

Figure 12.5   Pattern noise of imaging sensors

attention from researchers in the past decade because of its desired characteristics:

1. **Universality**. Every imaging sensor exhibits SPN; therefore, the methods based on SPN are widely applicable to any device equipped with an imaging sensor.
2. **Stability**. SPN is not subject to the influence of environmental conditions, such as temperature and humidity, and essentially time-independent.
3. **Robustness**. SPN is robust to common image processing operations, such as JPEG compression, gamma correction, and image filtering.
4. **Uniqueness**. SPN can be considered as unique to each sensor because of the large number of pixels of the sensor and the randomness of SPN.

Therefore, SPN is considered as the fingerprint of imaging devices and has been widely and successfully applied image provenance inference. In the following subsections, we will introduce the estimation of SPN, and its use in source camera identification, device linking, source-oriented image clustering, and image forgery detection.

12.5.1 Estimation of SPN

The SPN of a device can be estimated from the noise residuals extracted from a collection of images acquired by the device. The noise residue is defined as the difference between the original image $\mathbf{I}$ and its denoised version $\hat{\mathbf{I}}^{(0)}$ [46]:

$$
\begin{aligned}
\mathbf{W} &= \mathbf{I} - \hat{\mathbf{I}}^{(0)} \\
&= (1 + \mathbf{K})\mathbf{I}^{(0)} + \mathbf{\Theta} - \hat{\mathbf{I}}^{(0)} \\
&= \mathbf{I}\mathbf{K} + \mathbf{I}^{(0)} - \hat{\mathbf{I}}^{(0)} + (\mathbf{I}^{(0)} - \mathbf{I})\mathbf{K} + \mathbf{\Theta} \\
&= \mathbf{I}\mathbf{K} + \mathbf{\Xi},
\end{aligned}
\tag{12.6}
$$

where $\hat{\mathbf{I}}^{(0)}$ is the estimation of the noise-free image $\mathbf{I}^{(0)}$ and can be obtained by applying a denoising filter $F(\,\cdot\,)$ to $\mathbf{I}$, i.e., $\hat{\mathbf{I}}^{(0)} = F(\mathbf{I})$, $\mathbf{K}$ is the noise-like multiplicative factor responsible for PRNU noise, $\mathbf{\Theta}$ stands for a complex of independent random noise components containing the interferences from image content and other noises, and $\mathbf{\Xi}$ is the sum of $\mathbf{\Theta}$ and the two additional terms $\mathbf{I}^{(0)} - \hat{\mathbf{I}}^{(0)}$ and $(\mathbf{I}^{(0)} - \mathbf{I})\mathbf{K}$. $\mathbf{I}\mathbf{K}$ can be reasonably assumed to be independent of $\mathbf{\Xi}$ as the term $(\mathbf{I}^{(0)} - \mathbf{I})\mathbf{K}$ in $\mathbf{\Xi}$ is very weak [46].

The estimation of SPN is usually referred to as the *reference* SPN (RSPN), which is considered as the unique fingerprint of a source device. It can be obtained by averaging the noise residuals of N images taken by the source device:

$$
\mathbf{R} = \frac{1}{N} \sum_{k=1}^{N} \mathbf{W}_k,
\tag{12.7}
$$

where $\mathbf{W}_k$ represents the noise residual of the kth image. Alternatively, the PRNU term $\mathbf{K}$ can be explicitly estimated through a maximum likelihood estimate (MLE) method [46]:

$$\hat{\mathbf{K}} = \frac{\sum_{k=1}^{N} \mathbf{W}_k \mathbf{I}_k}{\sum_{k=1}^{N} \mathbf{I}_k^2}. \tag{12.8}$$

By comparison, (12.7) not only considers the PRNU noise but also implicitly includes the FPN in $\mathbf{R}$. It is worth mentioning that the FPN is not as stable as PRNU and may have been removed by dark-frame subtraction in device, but it facilitates the image provenance inference if it remains in the image. To better estimate the SPN, the image intensity I_k should be as high as possible but not saturated because of the multiplicative nature of the PRNU noise IK [46]. Also note that in (12.6) the smaller the variance of undesired signal Ξ, the more accurate the estimation in (12.7) and (12.8). Therefore, images of bright and smooth scenes, such as blue sky and flat-field (i.e., intensities are approximately constant) images, are commonly used for SPN estimation. In the case of flat-field images, there is not much difference between the simple averaging method in (12.7) and the MLE method in (12.8). Unless otherwise stated in the rest of this chapter, RSPN refers to the estimation of SPN using the simple averaging method in (12.7).

12.5.2   Source device identification

As shown in Figure 12.6, to identify the source device among a set of candidate devices $\mathscr{C}$ for a *test* image of unknown source, the typical process is to calculate the normalized cross-correlation (NCC) between the noise residual $\mathbf{W}$ of the test image and the RSPN $\mathbf{R}_c$ of each device $c \in \mathscr{C}$ [45]:

$$\rho(\mathbf{R}_c, \mathbf{W}) = \frac{\sum_{k,l} (\mathbf{W}(k,l) - \overline{\mathbf{W}}(k,l))(\mathbf{R}_c(k,l) - \overline{\mathbf{R}}_c(k,l))}{\sqrt{\sum_{k,l} (\mathbf{W}(k,l) - \overline{\mathbf{W}}(k,l))^2} \sqrt{\sum_{k,l} (\mathbf{R}_c(k,l) - \overline{\mathbf{R}}_c(k,l))^2}}, \tag{12.9}$$

where the mean value is denoted with a bar, and $|| \cdot ||$ is the $L2$ norm. The test image is deemed to be taken by the camera c^* with the maximal NCC value that is greater than a predefined threshold τ:

$$c^* = \underset{c \in \mathscr{C}}{\mathrm{argmax}}\{\rho(\mathbf{R}_c, \mathbf{W})\}, \rho(\mathbf{R}_{c^*}, \mathbf{W}) > \tau, \tag{12.10}$$

where τ is usually determined by Neyman–Pearson criterion [46]. Although more advanced detection statistics such as the peak-to-correlation energy [47] and the correlation over circular cross-correlation norm [48] have been proposed to improve the identification performance, NCC is still the most widely adopted SPN similarity measurement probably because of its simplicity.

SPN has demonstrated great promise in discriminating individual devices. Large-scale tests on millions of images spanning 6,896 individual cameras covering 150 models show a very high detection rate 97.6% at a false positive rate as low as

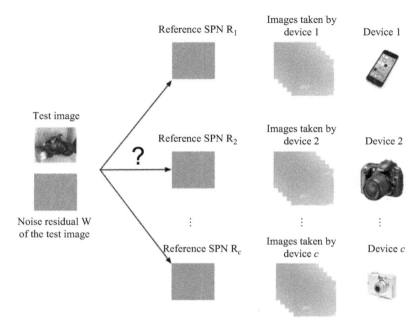

Figure 12.6   Source device identification based on SPN

2.4×10^{-5} [49]. The great potential of SPN has attracted much attention from researchers, and many efforts have been devoted to improving the performance of SPN-based source device identification. A feasible direction of improvement is to adopt more advanced denoising filters because the performance of the denoising filter $F(\cdot)$ has a direct impact on the quality of the noise residual. The basic and probably the most prevailing denoising filter for estimating the SPN is based on the Mihcak filter [50]. It works by calculating the fourth-level wavelet decomposition of the image and applying the Wiener filter in the high-frequency subbands in each of the four levels. Chierchia *et al.* [51] proposed to use a nonlocal denoising filter, block-matching and 3D (BM3D) filtering [52], which works by grouping 2D similar image patches found across the entire image into 3D arrays and collectively filtering the grouped image blocks. The sparseness of the representation due to the similarity between the grouped blocks makes it capable of better separating the true signal and noise. The results in [51] show that BM3D better prevents the image scene from propagating to the noise residual than the Michak filter. Another denoising filter, edge adaptive SPN predictor based on context adaptive interpolation (PCAI) [53,54], was proposed to suppress the effect of scene edges. It first predicts the value of a pixel from its neighboring pixels, then a Wiener filter is applied to the difference between the predicted image and the original image to obtain the noise residual. Because the prediction of pixel values is edge aware, the noise residual obtained with PCAI is expected to have less scene details than that obtained with the Michak filter.

Another line of research is dedicated to selecting or weighting the components in the noise residual $\mathbf{W}$ aiming to strengthen the PRNU signal $\mathbf{IK}$ and suppress the undesired signal Ξ in (12.6). Li [55] proposed five models to attenuate scene details by assigning less significant weighting factors to the strong components of SPN in the wavelet domain. The underlying rationale is that the stronger a component in $\mathbf{W}$ is, the more likely it is associated with strong scene details, and thus the less trustworthy the component should be. Lin and Li [56] further improved the quality of $\mathbf{W}$ by abandoning the components that have been severely contaminated by denoising errors. As mentioned in the last subsection, SPN is better preserved in images with high intensity and low textured scenes. For this reason, McCloskey [57] suggested giving a smaller weight to the pixels with a larger local gradient. A more sophisticated weighting scheme in [58] predicts the correlations between the blocks in noise residual $\mathbf{W}$ and the corresponding blocks in the RSPN $\mathbf{R}$ using image intensity and texture features. A block with a larger predicted correlation is expected to contain SPN of higher quality, so a larger weight is assigned to the center pixel of the block. While all the aforementioned weighting schemes deal with the noise residual $\mathbf{W}$ of the test image, some other works shifted the focus to the RSPN $\mathbf{R}$. Hu *et al.* [59] assumed that the larger components of $\mathbf{R}$ are more reliable while the smaller components are more sensitive to random noise. So they proposed to involve only a certain percent (e.g., 10%) of largest components of $\mathbf{R}$ into the calculation of correlation. Li and Li [60] proposed an estimator to construct a reliable RSPN from a limited number of images. Specifically, each image $\mathbf{I}_k$ and the corresponding noise residual $\mathbf{W}_k$ are segmented into nonoverlapping blocks. The quality of each block is then measured and sorted based on the entropy and average intensity of the block. The block with a higher ranking (i.e., higher quality) is assigned a larger weight. Finally, the RSPN in different block locations is estimated as the weighted average of the noise residuals in the same block location. A similar RSPN estimator was proposed in [61], where the equal weighting factor $1/N$ in (12.7) is replaced with a new weighting factor related with the variances of the undesirable noise in the noise residual $\mathbf{W}_k$.

Interestingly, while some of the processing components in the image acquisition pipeline introduce specific patterns or characteristics that are useful for identifying the source device, they may become the *interference sources* for the accurate estimation of SPN. For this reason, some works have been proposed to alleviate the influence of the "interferences" introduced during the image acquisition process. For example, the artificially interpolated color samples obtained through demosaicing are not physically captured by the sensor, thus the SPN components extracted from the artificial samples are expected to be less reliable than those extracted from the physical samples. Based on this assumption, Li and Li [62] proposed a couple-decoupled PRNU (CD-PRNU) extraction method to prevent the interpolation noise from propagating into the PRNU noise extracted from physical components. They first decomposed each color channel into four subimages and extracted the noise residual from each subimage. Finally, they assembled the noise residuals of the subimages to obtain the CD-PRNU. Another source of interference is the in-device lens-distortion correction, which allows users to take high-quality photos at a wide range of zoom. The lens-distortion correction desynchronizes the pixel-to-pixel correspondence between images taken at two different focal lengths and thus leads to a low accuracy for SPN-based source device identification. To reestablish synchronization between an image and the RSPN, Goljan and Fridrich [63] adopted the barrel distortion model in [18] and searched for its parameter to maximize the detection statistic between the noise residual and the RSPN. In [64], they extended their method to make it work for single image (i.e., without the RSPN) by searching for a maximum energy of the linear pattern [46] introduced into the image prior to lens distortion correction.

The processing components in the image acquisition pipeline not only inflict distortion but also introduce nonunique artifacts (NUAs) in the noise residual. These NUAs are shared among the devices with the same or similar in-camera processing procedures. The unwanted artifacts including the demosaicing artifacts, JPGE block artifacts, and the diagonal artifacts reported in [65] may give rise to false positives[1] and thus should be suppressed for improving the reliability for SPN-based device identification. Chen *et al.* [46] proposed two preprocessing operations to suppress the NUAs in RSPN. One operation is zero-meaning operation which removes the linear pattern in RSPN by subtracting the column average from each pixel in the column and subtracting the row average from every pixel in the row. The other operation is Wiener filtering in the frequency domain, which attenuates the periodic artifacts in RSPN. Kang *et al.* [48] suggested only keeping the phase components of the noise residual when constructing the RSPN. The underlying rationale is that the SPN is usually modeled as an additive white Gaussian noise in its estimation process, so it is reasonable to assume that the RSPN is a white noise signal with flat frequency spectrum to facilitate the removal of the contamination in the frequency domain [48]. Only keeping the phase components whitens the noise residual in the frequency domain and helps to remove the periodic artifacts. In view of the fact that the periodic artifacts manifest themselves as peaks in the DFT spectrum, Lin and Li [66] proposed a spectrum equalization algorithm to detect and suppress the peaks in the magnitude spectrum of RSPN.

12.5.3 Device linking

Another important application of SPN is device linking. As the name suggests, it is about linking the images acquired by the same device. But in the scenario of device linking, the source device or any other image from it is not available. In a typical case, we would like to know whether or not two given images came from the same camera, as shown in Figure 12.7. Device linking is particularly useful in the analysis of digital evidence in law enforcement when the source device is unavailable to the forensic investigators. One such example is the forensic investigation of online child abuse, where the criminals record moments of the ongoing crime by taking videos or images and share them over the Internet. These criminal recordings (not necessarily taken by the same device) are often accessible to the forensic investigators. By matching the recordings to those posted in social networks accounts that belong to suspected persons, the forensic investigators are able to find out the criminals [67]. Note that

---

[1]The SPN signals estimated from two devices may be slightly correlated due to the presence of NUAs.

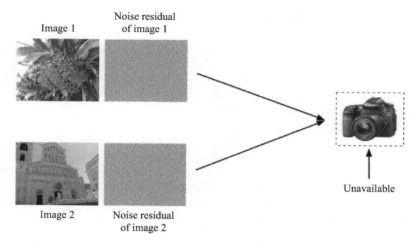

Image 1 — Noise residual of image 1

Image 2 — Noise residual of image 2

Unavailable

Figure 12.7   Device linking based on SPN

because the absence of the source device and the images taken by it prohibits the acquisition of a reliable RSPN, device linking can only be carried out based on the noise residual from each image, which may have been severely contaminated by other SPN-irrelevant interferences. Therefore, SPN-based device linking is a more challenging problem than the SPN-based source device identification.

The goal of device linking can be achieved by simply calculating the similarity (e.g., NCC) between each pair of the noise residuals extracted from the images under investigation and comparing it with a predefined threshold. But the images under investigation may differ in size, e.g., when one or several of them have been cropped. In view of this problem, Goljan *et al.* [68] recommended padding the images of different sizes with zeros and calculating the normalized circular cross-correlation [47], rather than the NCC, between each pair of the noise residuals of the images. If the ratio of the primary peak to the secondary peak of the normalized circular cross-correlation is higher than a threshold determined by Neyman–Pearson criterion, the images are believed to be from the same device. Unlike the abundant research in enhancing the performance of SPN-based source device identification, there have been few studies on SPN-based device linking in spite of its many potential applications. As far as we know, among the methods aiming to enhance the performance of source device identification, only Li's enhancer [55] has been applied to boost the performance of device linking. This is partially because that the absence of RSPN invalidates the enhancing methods that attempt to improve the quality of RSPN. Further studies are still needed to verify the effectiveness of the enhancing methods in Section 12.5.2 for device linking.

12.5.4   Source-oriented image clustering

There are circumstances where forensic investigators want to cluster a set of images taken by an unknown number of devices into a number of groups, such that the images in each group are acquired by the same device. Taking the aforementioned online child abuse as an example, if the forensic investigators can cluster a set of criminal images into groups, each including the images taken by the same device, they are able to link different crime scenes together and may obtain extra information from the grouped images (e.g., the images appearing in different social network accounts are associated to the same criminal). We refer to this task as the source-oriented image clustering. Since SPN is considered as the unique fingerprint of a device, source-oriented image clustering can be accomplished by extracting SPN from each image and then clustering the images based on the similarities between corresponding SPNs. Similar to SPN-based device linking, we do not have the access to the source devices or the RSPNs for source-oriented image clustering, so only the SPNs (i.e., noise residuals) extracted from single images are available. Source-oriented image clustering is seemingly similar to but actually differs from device linking. Device linking checks whether a limited number of (typically two) images are taken by the same device, so it involves only one device though the device itself is not available. While for source-oriented image clustering, both the number of devices and the number of images taken by each device are unknown. It may involve a large set of images, which makes the pairwise comparison in device linking computationally prohibitive for source-oriented image clustering. Moreover, to obtain accurate clustering, the dimension of SPN has to be very large, e.g., 512×512 pixels or above. The high dimension of SPN will impose a heavy burden on computation. All these difficulties make source-oriented image clustering much more challenging than device linking.

Bloy [69] presented a heuristic algorithm for clustering images iteratively based on SPN (i.e., noise residual), with the aim of forming one cluster in each iteration. To form a cluster, the algorithm randomly selects pairs of images until a pair is found to have an SPN correlation (i.e., NCC) higher than a threshold. The average SPN of the image pair, which serves as the cluster centroid, is correlated with the SPN of each remaining image. If one correlation exceeds a threshold that adaptively increases with the number of SPNs (images) in the cluster, the corresponding image is assigned to the cluster, and the SPN of the image is averaged into the cluster centroid. When the number of images in the cluster reaches 50, the algorithm stops updating the centroid but continues to add more similar images to the cluster until the entire dataset has been exhausted. Once a cluster is formed, the algorithm starts another iteration to form a new cluster until no further clustering is possible. The cluster centroid actually plays the same role as the RSPN in (12.7) and becomes more reliable as more SPNs are averaged into it. Note that the threshold used for determining whether or not one image belongs to the cluster should be able to well characterize the change of correlation after updating the centroid. However, the adaptive threshold in [69] was obtained by fitting a quadratic threshold curve based on the SPN correlations calculated from images taken by four cameras. It does not generalize well across different cameras and results in unsatisfactory clustering results. Moreover, one image (or its SPN if all the SPNs have been extracted beforehand) will be repeatedly loaded into the RAM until it has been clustered, which incurs extra I/O cost and makes the algorithm computationally infeasible for large-scale image databases.

Li [70] proposed to cluster a subset of images (*training set*) randomly chosen from the entire database and use the clustering results of the training set to classify the remaining images. Prior to the actual clustering, SPNs of the training set are extracted for constructing a pairwise similarity matrix, with the element at index (i,j) being the NCC between SPNs W_i and W_j. Based on the pairwise similarity matrix, a reference similarity and a membership committee are set up for each image to estimate the likelihood probability of assigning each class label to the corresponding image. The class label of each image is updated as the one with the highest likelihood probability in its membership committee. The clustering process terminates when there are no label changes in two consecutive iterations. Finally, the remaining images are attributed to their closest clusters identified in the training set. In spite of the good performance (an overall error rate of 1.444% using SPNs of 512×512 pixels), this clustering algorithm is very slow because the calculation of the likelihood probability involves all the members and their class labels in the membership committee. The time complexity is nearly $\mathcal{O}(N^3)$ in the first iteration, where N is the number of images in the training set. For large-scale image databases, the size of the training set has to be sufficiently large to well represent the entire database, so the algorithm becomes computationally prohibitive for large-scale image databases.

Liu *et al.* [71] formulated the source-oriented image clustering as a weighted undirected graph partitioning problem, where each image is considered as a vertex in the graph and the weight of an edge is the SPN similarity (i.e., NCC) between the two images linked by the edge. Instead of a fully connected graph, a sparse k-nearest graph is constructed to avoid calculating the similarity of every pair image. An m-class spectral clustering algorithm [72] is then employed on the k-nearest graph to partition the vertices (images) into m clusters. The m-class spectral clustering algorithm has a time complexity of $\mathcal{O}(N^{\frac{3}{2}}m + Nm^2)$, so it is more efficient than Li's algorithm [55] when $N \gg m$. But the spectral clustering algorithm requires an input of the cluster number m, which is unknown to the user. To determine the optimal cluster number, the same spectral clustering algorithm needs to be repeated for different value of m until the smallest size of the resultant clusters equals 1, i.e., one singleton cluster is generated. However, it is easy to form singleton clusters because some SPNs may have been severely contaminated by interferences, such as scene details [55] and CFA interpolation artifacts [62]. So the feasibility of such manner of determining the optimal cluster number is still an issue for source-oriented image clustering based on SPN.

Caldelli [73] proposed a hierarchical clustering algorithm for source-oriented image clustering. Similar to [70], only a random subset (training set) of the whole dataset is used for clustering, followed by a classification stage for the remaining images. Initially considering each image as a cluster, the algorithm first calculates the pairwise similarity matrix of the SPNs in the training set. It then merges the two most similar clusters into one and updates the similarity matrix by replacing the corresponding two rows and columns with the similarities between the merged cluster and all the other clusters. After the update, a silhouette coefficient, which measures the separation among clusters and the cohesion within each cluster, is calculated for each

SPN. The silhouette coefficients are averaged to give a global measure of the aptness of the current partition. This procedure repeats until all the images have been merged into one cluster. Upon completion of the clustering, the partition corresponding to the highest aptness is taken as the optimal partition. Villalba *et al.* [74] proposed a similar algorithm for smartphone image clustering. Its difference from [73] is that the calculation of the silhouette coefficient is performed for each cluster rather than for each fingerprint, and only the separation to the nearest neighboring cluster is measured. As reported in [73], with comparable accuracy, the hierarchical clustering-based algorithm is faster than [70]. But the time complexity $\mathcal{O}(N^2 \log N)$ of the hierarchical clustering is still too high for large-scale image databases.

It can be seen that the large-scale source-oriented image clustering problem cannot be well resolved by the above algorithms due to the large-scale number of images and the high dimension of SPNs. To alleviate the problem, the algorithms in [55] and [73] first cluster a training set randomly sampled from the entire database and classify the remaining images based on the clustering results of the training set. They work well if the training set can sufficiently represent the entire database, i.e., the training set includes a portion of images taken by all or most of the devices appearing in the entire database. However, sometimes the number of classes (i.e., the number of devices) is much higher than the average size of class (i.e., the number of images acquired by each device), which was referred to as the $NC \gg SC$ problem in [75]. The $NC \gg SC$ problem makes it difficult, if not impossible, to form a training set at random that can sufficiently represent the entire population.

To overcome these challenges, Lin and Li [75] proposed a clustering framework capable of handling large-scale image databases. By taking advantage of dimension reduction and the inherent sparseness of the pairwise similarity matrix, the algorithm first roughly but efficiently partitions the entire database into small subsets, with larger classes having a higher chance to be partitioned into the same subset. It then clusters each subset using the Markov cluster algorithm [76] to produce many small but highly pure subclusters, with each of them represented by an SPN centroid, the cluster size, and a cluster quality coefficient (calculated from the pairwise correlations of SPNs within the subcluster). If the similarity between the SPN centroids of two subclusters is higher than an adaptive threshold, the two subclusters will be merged and the SPN centroid of the merged cluster will be updated at the same time. It is worth mentioning that the adaptive threshold in [75] takes both the size and the quality of clusters into consideration and thus is more accurate than the threshold in [69], which only considers the cluster size. The centroids of the merged clusters will be used to attract the remaining images in the database, but unlike the classification stage in [70] and [73], an adaptive threshold is used to reduce the false attributions,[2] and the centroid and the quality of the clusters will be updated accordingly after attracting a certain number of images. The above procedures are repeated until no more notable clusters can be discovered. Because the algorithm allows larger classes to be clustered preferentially, the majority of images can be clustered in the first

---

[2]False attribution happens when one image is attributed to the cluster with the highest similarity, but actually it does not belong to the cluster and their similarity is still very low.

few iterations. The results on the 15,840 images in the Dresden image database [77] show that the algorithm is much more efficient than the algorithms in [55,71,73] and delivers a high level of clustering quality using SPNs of 1,024 × 1,024 pixels, with a precision rate of 99% and an F1 measure of 68%. It also demonstrates a high capability of solving the $NC \gg SC$ problem. On synthetic datasets consisting of 50,000 images, about 92% of classes are discovered when $NC = 1,250$ and $SC = 40$, and more than 76% of classes are discovered when $NC = 2,500$ and $SC = 20$.

12.5.5 Image forgery detection

Detecting image forgeries is an interesting but very challenging task due to the variety of image manipulations a user can perform with increasingly powerful image editing software. SPN exists in every *original* image taken by the source device, while the image forgery may damage or remove the SPN signal that is supposed to present in the forged regions. Therefore, when the RSPN of the source device is available, image forgeries can be exposed by detecting the absence of the SPN in suspect regions. Since SPN is the intrinsic fingerprint of the source device and not associated with any type of image forgeries applied after the image acquisition, techniques based on SPN can detect the image forgeries irrespective of the specific type of forgery. In addition, SPN is robust to some common image processing operations, such as JPEG compression, filtering, or gamma correction [45,46]. These characteristics make SPN a promising tool for detecting image forgeries.

Lukáš *et al.* [78] proposed two approaches, one for detecting the forgeries in a selected region of interest (ROI) and the other for automatically identifying the forged areas in an image **I**. In the first approach, to calculate the statistical evidence that a suspect region Ω in **I** has been tampered with, a large set of image regions $\mathbf{Q}_k, k = 1, \ldots, N$, of the same size and shape as Ω is collected either from the images taken by the same device (but from regions different from Ω) or from the images taken by other devices. These image regions are considered as "tampered" regions because the SPN presents in them are different from that presents in region Ω of the RSPN. The correlations $\rho(\mathbf{R}_\Omega, \mathbf{W}_k)$ are supposed to be subject to a generalized Gaussian distribution, where $\mathbf{R}_\Omega$ is the RSPN in the same region as Ω, and $\mathbf{W}_k$ is the SPN (i.e., noise residual) extracted from $\mathbf{Q}_k$. The smaller the correlation between the RSPN and the noise residual in Ω, i.e., $\rho(\mathbf{R}_\Omega, \mathbf{W}_\Omega)$, the more likely Ω has been tampered with. By fitting the generalized Gaussian distribution using the correlations calculated from the "tampered" regions, the probability that Ω has been forged can be calculated as

$$p = 1 - \Phi(\rho(\mathbf{R}_\Omega, \mathbf{W}_\Omega)), \tag{12.11}$$

where $\Phi(\cdot)$ is the cumulative distribution function of the estimated generalized Gaussian distribution. Ω is forged if $p > \alpha(= 10^{-3})$, and not forged otherwise.

The second approach is capable of automatically identifying the forged area. To detect forgeries of different shapes, 12 detection blocks of different shapes and sizes are prepared, as illustrated in Figure 12.8. Each detection block $i \in \{1, \ldots, 12\}$ is moved across the image under investigation and the RSPN of its source device

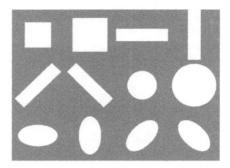

Figure 12.8   Window shapes used for automatic ROI detection in [78]

(overlapping approximately 50%–75%), and the correlation between the RSPN and the noise residual within the region covered by the detection block is calculated. For each block i, m regions with the smallest correlations, i.e., the m most likely forged regions, are selected (m was set to 8 in [78]). So there will be total of $m \times 12$ regions $\mathfrak{B}_k$ and their union $\mathfrak{B} = \bigcup_{k=1}^{m \times 12} \mathfrak{B}_k$ are initially identified as the forged regions. Then, the algorithm tries to refine the initial result: for each pixel $q \in \mathfrak{B}$, if the number of selected regions covering q, i.e., $t(q) = |\{\mathfrak{B}_k | q \in \mathfrak{B}_k\}|$, is no higher than the median value of $t(q)$ across the initially detected regions $\mathfrak{B}$, i.e., $q \in \mathfrak{B}$, pixel q is corrected as nonforged.

The work in [78] was improved by Chen *et al.* in [46]. They modeled the SPN detection problem as a binary hypothesis testing problem:

$$\begin{cases} H_0 : \mathbf{W} = \Xi, \\ H_1 : \mathbf{W} = \mathbf{R} + \Xi, \end{cases} \tag{12.12}$$

where $\mathbf{W}$ is the noise residual extracted from the image region in question, $\mathbf{R}$ is the RSPN of the source device c, and Ξ is the combination of other independent interferences. The forgery detection at each pixel q is formulated as a hypothesis testing problem applied to a sliding block surrounding q. As illustrated in Figure 12.9, a detection block[3] is sliding across the image, and the test statistic $\rho_q = \rho(\mathbf{R}_q, \mathbf{W}_q)$ within the block is calculated, where $\mathbf{R}_q$ and $\mathbf{W}_q$ are the RSPN and the noise residual in the detection block centered at pixel q, respectively. This produces a correlation map ρ, with the value at pixel q being the correlation ρ_q. Note that because SPN is pixel location sensitive, even if the forged region comes from the image taken by the same device c, it is still able to detect the forgery as long as the forged region does not exactly lie in the same position as in the image it comes from. To facilitate the decision-making, both the correlation distribution under hypothesis H_0, $p(x|H_0)$ and the correlation distribution under hypothesis H_1, $p(x|H_1)$ need to be estimated.

---

[3]The size of the detection was set to 128×128 pixels in [46].

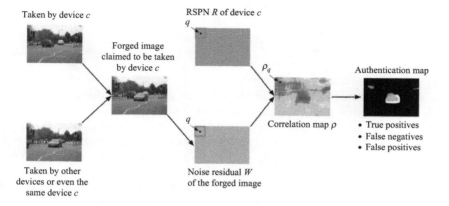

Taken by device c

Forged image claimed to be taken by device c

Taken by other devices or even the same device c

RSPN R of device c

q

ρ_q

q

Noise residual W of the forged image

Correlation map ρ

Authentication map

- True positives
- False negatives
- False positives

Figure 12.9   Image forgery detection based on SPN

$p(x|H_0)$ can be easily estimated from the images taken by other devices, while the estimation of $p(x|H_1)$ is difficult, because the correlation is heavily affected by the image content (e.g., the correlation between SPNs tends to be higher for the images with brighter and smoother scenes) and is most likely to be overfitting to the available images [46]. Therefore, instead of directly estimating $p(x|H_1)$ from correlations, the authors constructed a correlation predictor that maps the image features to the correlation value. Specifically, K image blocks of 128×128 pixels are cropped from several images taken by the source device. Four image features that affect the quality of SPN are extracted from each of the K image blocks: image intensity feature f_I, texture feature f_T, signal flattening feature f_S, and texture-intensity feature f_E. Let ρ be the correlation between the noise residuals of the K image blocks and the RSPN in the corresponding positions, and f_I, f_T, f_S, and f_E be the corresponding K-dimensional feature vectors. ρ is modeled as a linear combination of the features and their second-order terms, i.e., $\rho = \mathbf{H}\theta + \mathbf{\Psi}$, where $\mathbf{\Psi}$ is the modeling noise, $\mathbf{H}$ is a $K \times 15$ matrix containing the features and their second-order terms, and θ is the modeling coefficient to be determined. By applying the least square estimator (LSE), the estimated coefficients $\hat{\theta} = (\mathbf{H}^T\mathbf{H})^{-1}\mathbf{H}^T\rho$ are obtained. So the expected correlation $\hat{\rho}$ of an unseen image block can be predicted based on the image features extracted from it:

$$\hat{\rho} = [1, f_I, f_T, f_S, f_E, \ldots, f_E f_E]\hat{\theta}. \tag{12.13}$$

With the predicted correlation, the actual correlation ρ is modeled as a random variable following a generalized Gaussian distribution $G(\hat{\rho}, \sigma_1, \alpha_1)$, where the predicted correlation $\hat{\rho}$ is the mean, while the scale parameter σ_1 and the shape parameter α_1 can be estimated from the difference between the actual and predicted correlations of the K images blocks, i.e., $\rho - \mathbf{H}\hat{\theta}$. Then, the decision is made for each pixel independently: if $\rho_q < t$, pixel q is labeled as forged. Here, the threshold t is related with a constant false acceptance rate (CFAR) $\alpha(= 10^{-5})$:

$$\int_t^{\infty} p(x|H_0)\mathrm{d}x = \alpha. \tag{12.14}$$

Like in [79], we refer to this method as the CFAR method in this chapter. However, for a highly textured, black or saturated block, even if it is authentic, its correlation still tends to be low due to the attenuation of SPN. So to reduce the false positives (i.e., labeling nonforged pixels as forged), a pixel q will be labeled as nonforged if $\int_{-\infty}^t p(x|H_1)\mathrm{d}x > \beta$, where β was set to 0.01 in [46]. The resulting binary map $\hat{\mathbf{u}} \in \{0, 1\}^{M \times N}$ signifying the forged pixels (1 for forgery and 0 for genuine pixel) will be further dilated with a square 20×20 kernel to obtain the final result.

The CFAR method does not take into account the spatial dependencies exhibited by natural images but makes decisions independently for each pixel, which may generate inconsistent and fragmented binary map. To penalize the isolated points or the small disjoint regions and produce a smooth output, Chierchia *et al.* [79] adopted the Bayesian approach and Markov random field (MRF) model. This Bayesian-MRF method is based on the CFAR method but differs in both formulation and solution to the problem. It formulates the forgery detection as an optimization problem of finding the label map $\hat{\mathbf{u}} \in \{0, 1\}^{M \times N}$ that has the maximum posterior probability given the prior information:

$$\hat{\mathbf{u}} = \underset{\mathbf{u} \in \{0,1\}^{M \times N}}{\mathrm{argmax}}\ p(\boldsymbol{\rho}|\mathbf{u}, \hat{\boldsymbol{\rho}})p(\mathbf{u}), \tag{12.15}$$

where $M \times N$ is the image size, $\boldsymbol{\rho}$ is the actual correlations calculated in a block-wise manner (i.e., the correlation map in Figure 12.9), and $\hat{\boldsymbol{\rho}}$ is the predicted (or expected) correlations given by the correlation predictor in (12.13). In the above equation, $p(\boldsymbol{\rho}|\mathbf{u}, \hat{\boldsymbol{\rho}})$ is the conditional likelihood of observing $\boldsymbol{\rho}$, and $p(\mathbf{u})$ is the prior probability that takes into account the spatial dependencies of the pixels, which is modeled by the MRF model:

$$p(\mathbf{u}) = \frac{1}{Z}e^{-\sum_{c \in \mathscr{C}} V_c(\mathbf{u})}, \tag{12.16}$$

where Z is a normalizing constant, and $V_c(\mathbf{u})$ is the potential defined on cliques c (i.e., small groups of neighboring pixels). Only the single-site cliques and 4-connected two-site cliques are considered in [79]. By assuming the likelihood probability to be Gaussian under both hypotheses, with zero mean and variance σ_0^2 under hypothesis H_0, and mean $\hat{\rho}_i$ and variance σ_1^2 under hypothesis H_1 (obtained using the abovementioned correlation predictor [46]), (12.15) is formulated as

$$\hat{\mathbf{u}} = \underset{\mathbf{u} \in \{0,1\}^{M \times N}}{\mathrm{argmin}} \left\{ \sum_{i=1}^{M \times N} u_i \left[\frac{(\rho_i - \hat{\rho}_i)^2}{2\sigma_1^2} - \frac{\rho_i^2}{2\sigma_0^2} - \log \frac{\sigma_0}{\sigma_1} - \log \frac{p_1}{p_0} \right] + \beta R(\mathbf{u}) \right\}, \tag{12.17}$$

where p_0 and p_1 are the prior probability of forged and nonforged, respectively, and β is the edge-penalty parameter indicating how strong the interaction between pixels, and the regularization term $R(\mathbf{u}) = \sum_{i=1}^{M \times N} \sum_{j \in \mathcal{N}_i} |u_j - u_i|$, with $\mathcal{N}_i$, the set of 4-connected neighbors of pixel i, is the sum of all class transitions over all 4-connected cliques of the image. By resorting to the convex-optimization algorithm proposed in [80], the $\hat{\mathbf{u}}$ that gives the maximal probability can be obtained. This method incorporates the prior information and spatial dependencies between pixels and therefore produces a more consistent and smooth binary map.

As can be observed in the detection results presented in [46] as well as the authentication map in Figure 12.9, the falsely identified areas are largely located along the boundary of the forged area. The reason is that, when the detection block falls near the boundary between two different regions (i.e., forged and nonforged regions), the decision statistic ρ is a weighted average of two different contributions and more likely to exceed the decision threshold. As a result, missing detection occurs along the boundary between forged and nonforged regions.

Chierchia *et al.* [81] alleviated this problem by first segmenting the image under investigation and then calculating the decision statistic on the intersection of the detection block and the segmented objects. However, this method heavily depends on the performance of image segmentation, which itself is an ill-posed problem. In view of this, Chierchia *et al.* [82] proposed an algorithm based on the guided filtering [83] to avoid the unreliable image segmentation. The basic idea is to postprocess the calculated correlation map ρ by resorting to a pilot image, which can be a combination of the color bands of the original image or its denoised version, or any suitable field of features extracted from images [82]. The pilot image bears some valuable information, such as geometrical structures, of the image content and can be viewed as the soft-segmented version of the original image. By incorporating the structure information from the pilot image, the guided filtering is aware of the object boundaries and thus facilitates the decision-making process near boundaries. However, both the segmentation-based method [81] and the soft-segmentation-based method [82] will fail when objects in the original scene are hidden by placing a homogeneous background on them, e.g., an airplane is covered by a patch of blue sky, or objects are removed by image inpainting or texture synthesis. One such example is shown in Figure 12.10, where the paraglider and the pilot are removed by inpainting without leaving any visible traces. The segmentation-based methods are unable to detect the forgeries in this case because no structure information is available in the forged regions.

In view of the limitations of the segmentation-based detection algorithms, Lin and Li [84] proposed an algorithm to alleviate the missing detection problem along the boundary between forged and nonforged regions. They first applied the CFAR method [46] with two thresholds α and β to obtain an initial detection result Ω. Although the CFAR method suffers from the missing detection problem, it provides an indication that the nearby forged regions of the boundary of Ω may have been missed. So they modeled how the distribution of decision statistics changes as the detection block moves across the boundary of Ω and adjusted the threshold t in (12.14) for each pixel q:

$$\int_{t'(q)}^{\infty} p_{\Omega}(x, q) \mathrm{d}x = \alpha, \tag{12.18}$$

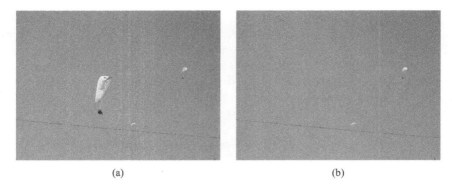

(a)   (b)

Figure 12.10   Object removal by image inpainting. The segmentation-based
methods are unable to detect the forgeries in this case. (a) Authentic
image. (b) Forged image

where $t'(q)$ is the adjusted threshold for pixel q, and $p_\Omega(x, q)$ is the distribution of decision statistics depending on the initially detected forged region Ω and how far pixel q is from Ω. With the adjusted threshold, a pixel q is labeled as forged if the decision statistic $\rho_q < t'(q)$. Similar to [46], to reduce the false positives, a forged pixel will be labeled as nonforged if $\int_{-\infty}^{t} p(x|H_1)dx > \beta$. The algorithm does not require to segment the image but makes use of the detection result of the CFAR method to identify the forged pixels that have been missed.

12.6 Summary and outlook

We have introduced different intrinsic device fingerprints and their applications in image provenance inference. Although with varying levels of accuracy, the device fingerprints arising from optical aberration, CFA interpolation, CRF, and in-device image compression are effective in differentiating devices of different brands or models. Although they cannot uniquely identify the source device of an image, they do provide useful information about the image provenance and are effective at narrowing down the image source to a smaller set of possible devices. More than half of the chapter was spent on SPN, which is the only fingerprint that distinguishes devices of the same model. Because of its merits, such as the uniqueness to individual device and the robustness against common image operations, it has attracted much attention from researches and been successfully used for source device identification, device linking, source-oriented image clustering, and image forgery detection. In spite of the effectiveness of SPN, it is by nature a very weak signal and may have been contaminated by image content and other interferences. Its successful application requires jointly processing a large number of pixels, which results in very high dimensionality of SPN. This may bring huge difficulties in practice, e.g., in large-scale source-oriented image clustering based on SPN, so it is essential to conduct research on the compact representation of SPN for fast search and clustering.

With the development of Internet and the rise of Big Data, the amount of data generated in different knowledge areas has explosively increased. Big Data opens new opportunities in identifying potential evidence from massive information, but the large scale size of digital images also presents new challenges for image provenance inference. Taking the source-oriented image clustering for example, the large scale size of image database impose a heavy burden on computation. One feasible solution would be combining the information from different fingerprints of an image to reduce the computational cost. For example, if we make use of the information from optical aberration, CFA interpolation, or even metadata of an image, and first partition the images of "similar" provenance into the same group, the computational complexity of the source-oriented image clustering algorithm in [75] can be significantly reduced.

Another line of research is the information integration of different fingerprints. Although attempts have been made to jointly use different fingerprints for image provenance inference, such as the work in [11], a universal and effective tool that allows the forensic investigators to synergically exploit these fingerprints and finally reach a decision based on their output is still lacking. This is by no means an easy task because it requires to carefully investigate the performance of each fingerprint under different application scenarios and employ a decision fusion engine to reach a comprehensive and informative conclusion. Further research will be required to integrate the information from different device fingerprints.

References

[1]   Mintzer F, Braudaway GW, and Yeung MM. 'Effective and ineffective digital watermarks'. *Proceedings of International Conference on Image Processing.* Vol. 3. IEEE; 1997. pp. 9–12.

[2]   Yeung MM, and Mintzer FC. 'Invisible watermarking for image verification'. *Journal of Electronic Imaging.* 1998;7(3):578–591.

[3]   Lin CY, and Chang SF. 'Semifragile watermarking for authenticating JPEG visual content'. *Proceedings of Electronic Imaging.* International Society for Optics and Photonics; 2000. pp. 140–151.

[4]   Wong P, and Memon N. 'Secret and public key image watermarking schemes for image authentication and ownership verification'. *IEEE Transactions on Image Processing.* 2001;10(10):1593–1601.

[5]   Li CT, and Yang FM. 'One-dimensional neighborhood forming strategy for fragile watermarking'. *Journal of Electronic Imaging.* 2003;12(2):284–291.

[6]   Li CT. 'Digital fragile watermarking scheme for authentication of JPEG images'. *IEE Proceedings – Vision, Image and Signal Processing.* 2004;151(6): 460–466.

[7]   Li CT, and Yuan Y. 'Digital watermarking scheme exploiting nondeterministic dependence for image authentication'. *Optical Engineering.* 2006;45(12): 127001-1–127001-6.

[8]   Zhu X, Ho AT, and Marziliano P. 'A new semi-fragile image watermarking with robust tampering restoration using irregular sampling'. *Signal Processing: Image Communication.* 2007;22(5):515–528.

[9]   Zhao X, Ho AT, Treharne H, Pankajakshan V, Culnane C, and Jiang W. 'A novel semi-fragile image watermarking, authentication and self-restoration technique using the slant transform'. *Proceedings of International Conference*

on Intelligent Information Hiding and Multimedia Signal Processing. Vol. 1. IEEE; 2007. pp. 283–286.

[10]   Alvarez P. 'Using extended file information (EXIF) file headers in digital evidence analysis'. *International Journal of Digital Evidence*. 2004;2(3):1–5.

[11]   Kee E, Johnson MK, and Farid H. 'Digital image authentication from JPEG headers'. *IEEE Transactions on Information Forensics and Security*. 2011;6(3):1066–1075.

[12]   Phil H. ExifTool. Kingston, Ontario, Canada; 2016. http://owl.phy.queensu.ca/phil/exiftool/.

[13]   Mahajan VN. *Optical imaging and aberrations: part I: ray geometrical optics*. Bellingham: SPIE-The International Society for Optical Engineering; 1998.

[14]   Johnson MK, and Farid H. 'Exposing digital forgeries through chromatic aberration'. *Proceedings of the 8th Workshop on Multimedia and security*. ACM; 2006. pp. 48–55.

[15]   Van LT, Emmanuel S, and Kankanhalli MS. 'Identifying source cell phone using chromatic aberration'. *Proceedings of IEEE International Conference on Multimedia and Expo*. IEEE; 2007. pp. 883–886.

[16]   San Choi K, Lam EY, and Wong KK. 'Source camera identification using footprints from lens aberration'. *Electronic Imaging*. 2006;6069. pp. 172–179.

[17]   San Choi K, Lam EY, and Wong KK. 'Automatic source camera identification using the intrinsic lens radial distortion'. *Optics Express*. 2006;14(24): 11551–11565.

[18]   Devernay F, and Faugeras OD. 'Automatic calibration and removal of distortion from scenes of structured environments'. *Proceedings of SPIE's 1995 International Symposium on Optical Science, Engineering, and Instrumentation*. International Society for Optics and Photonics; 1995. pp. 62–72.

[19]   Fischer A, and Gloe T. 'Forensic analysis of interdependencies between vignetting and radial lens distortion'. *Proceedings of IS&T/SPIE Electronic Imaging*. International Society for Optics and Photonics; 2013. Vol. 8665. pp. 86650D-1–86650D-15.

[20]   Yu J, Craver S, and Li E. 'Toward the identification of DSLR lenses by chromatic aberration'. *Proceedings of IS&T/SPIE Electronic Imaging*. International Society for Optics and Photonics; 2011. Vol. 7880: pp. 788010-1–788010-9.

[21]   Popescu AC, and Farid H. 'Exposing digital forgeries by detecting traces of resampling'. *IEEE Transactions on Signal Processing*. 2005;53(2):758–767.

[22]   Bayram S, Sencar H, Memon N, and Avcibas I. 'Source camera identification based on CFA interpolation'. *Proceedings of IEEE International Conference Image Processing*. Vol. 3; 2005. pp. 69–72.

[23]   Chang CC, and Lin CJ. 'LIBSVM: a library for support vector machines'. *ACM Transactions on Intelligent Systems and Technology*. 2011;2(3):1–27.

[24]   Pudil P, Ferri FJ, Novovicova J, and Kittler J. 'Floating search methods for feature selection with nonmonotonic criterion functions'. *Proceedings of the 12th IAPR International Conference on Pattern Recognition*. Vol. 2; 1994. pp. 279–283.

[25] Bayram S, Sencar HT, Memon N, and Avcibas I. 'Improvements on source camera-model identification based on CFA interpolation'. *Proceedings of International Federation for Information Processing Working Group 11.9 International Conference on Digital Forensics.* Orlando, FL, 2006. pp. 24–27.

[26] Long Y, and Huang Y. 'Image based source camera identification using demosaicking'. *Proceedings of IEEE Workshop on Multimedia Signal Processing*; 2006. pp. 419–424.

[27] Wold S, Esbensen K, and Geladi P. 'Principal component analysis'. *Chemometrics and Intelligent Laboratory Systems.* 1987;2(1–3):37–52.

[28] Swaminathan A, Wu M, and Liu KR. 'Non-intrusive forensic analysis of visual sensors using output images'. *Proceedings of IEEE International Conference on Acoustics Speech and Signal Processing Proceedings.* Vol. 5. IEEE; 2006. pp. 401–404.

[29] Swaminathan A, Wu M, and Liu KJ. 'Nonintrusive component forensics of visual sensors using output images'. *IEEE Transactions on Information Forensics and Security.* 2007;2(1):91–106.

[30] Cao H, and Kot AC. 'Accurate detection of demosaicing regularity for digital image forensics'. *IEEE Transactions on Information Forensics and Security.* 2009;4(4):899–910.

[31] Cao H, and Kot AC. 'Mobile camera identification using demosaicing features'. *Proceedings of IEEE International Symposium on Circuits and Systems.* IEEE; 2010. pp. 1683–1686.

[32] Lin S, Gu J, Yamazaki S, and Shum HY. 'Radiometric calibration from a single image'. *Proceedings of IEEE Conference on Computer Vision and Pattern Recognition.* Vol. 2. IEEE; 2004. pp. II–938.

[33] Lin Z, Wang R, Tang X, and Shum HY. 'Detecting doctored images using camera response normality and consistency'. *Proceedings of IEEE Computer Society Conference on Computer Vision and Pattern Recognition.* Vol. 1. IEEE; 2005. pp. 1087–1092.

[34] Grossberg MD, and Nayar SK. 'What is the space of camera response functions?'. *Proceedings of IEEE Computer Society Conference on Computer Vision and Pattern Recognition.* Vol. 2. IEEE; 2003. pp. II–602.

[35] Hsu YF, and Chang SF. 'Detecting image splicing using geometry invariants and camera characteristics consistency'. *IEEE International Conference on Multimedia and Expo*; 2006. pp. 549–552.

[36] Hsu YF, and Chang SF. 'Image splicing detection using camera response function consistency and automatic segmentation'. *2007 IEEE International Conference on Multimedia and Expo.* IEEE; 2007. pp. 28–31.

[37] Hsu YF, and Chang SF. 'Camera response functions for image forensics: an automatic algorithm for splicing detection'. *IEEE Transactions on Information Forensics and Security.* 2010;5(4):816–825.

[38] Ng TT, Chang SF, and Tsui MP. 'Using geometry invariants for camera response function estimation'. *Proceedings of IEEE Conference on Computer Vision and Pattern Recognition.* IEEE; 2007. pp. 1–8.

[39]   Ng TT, and Tsui MP. 'Camera response function signature for digital forensics –
        Part I: Theory and data selection'. *Proceedings of 1st IEEE International
        Workshop on Information Forensics and Security*; 2009. pp. 156–160.
[40]   Ng TT. 'Camera response function signature for digital forensics – Part
        II: Signature extraction'. *Proceedings of IEEE International Workshop on
        Information Forensics and Security*. IEEE; 2009. pp. 161–165.
[41]   Farid H. *Digital image ballistics from JPEG quantization*; Department of
        Computer Science, Dartmouth College, Technical Report TR2006-583. 2006.
[42]   Farid H. *Digital image ballistics from JPEG quantization: A followup study*;
        Department of Computer Science, Dartmouth College, Technical Report
        TR2006-583. 2008.
[43]   Sorell MJ. 'Digital camera source identification through JPEG quantisation'.
        Multimedia Forensics and Security. Hershey, NY, USA: Information Science
        Reference (IGI Global). 2008. pp. 291–313.
[44]   Kee E, and Farid H. 'Digital image authentication from thumbnails'.
        IS&T/SPIE Electronic Imaging. International Society for Optics and
        Photonics; 2010. Vol. 7541. pp. 75410E-1–75410E-8.
[45]   Lukas J, Fridrich J, and Goljan M. 'Digital camera identification from sensor
        pattern noise'. *IEEE Transactions on Information Forensics and Security*.
        2006;1(2):205–214.
[46]   Chen M, Fridrich J, Goljan M, and Lukás J. 'Determining image origin and
        integrity using sensor noise'. *IEEE Transactions on Information Forensics
        and Security*. 2008;3(1):74–90.
[47]   Goljan M. Digital camera identification from images – estimating false
        acceptance probability. *Digital Watermarking*. 2009;5450:454–468.
[48]   Kang X, Li Y, Qu Z, and Huang J. 'Enhancing source camera identification
        performance with a camera reference phase sensor pattern noise'. *IEEE
        Transactions on Information Forensics and Security*. 2012;7(2):393–402.
[49]   Goljan M, Fridrich J, and Filler T. 'Large scale test of sensor fingerprint
        camera identification'. *IS&T/SPIE Electronic Imaging*; 2009. Vol. 7254.
        pp. 72540I-1–72540I-12.
[50]   Mhak MK, Kozintsev I, and Ramchandran K. 'Spatially adaptive statistical
        modeling of wavelet image coefficients and its application to denoising'.
        IEEE International Conference on Acoustics, Speech, and Signal Processing.
        1999;6:3253–3256.
[51]   Chierchia G, Parrilli S, Poggi G, Sansone C, and Verdoliva L. 'On the Influence
        of Denoising in PRNU Based Forgery Detection'. *ACM Workshop on Multi-
        media in Forensics, Security and Intelligence*. NY, USA; 2010. pp. 117–122.
[52]   Dabov K, Foi A, Katkovnik V, Egiazarian K. 'Image denoising by sparse
        3-D transform-domain collaborative filtering'. *IEEE Transactions on Image
        Processing*. 2007 August;16(8):2080–2095.
[53]   Wu G, Kang X, and Liu KR. 'A context adaptive predictor of sensor pattern
        noise for camera source identification'. *IEEE International Conference on
        Image Processing*; 2012. pp. 237–240.

[54]   Kang X, Chen J, Lin K, and Anjie P. 'A context-adaptive SPN predictor for trustworthy source camera identification'. *EURASIP Journal on Image and Video Processing*. 2014;2014(1):1–11.

[55]   Li CT. 'Source camera identification using enhanced sensor pattern noise'. *IEEE Transactions on Information Forensics and Security*. 2010;5(2): 280–287.

[56]   Lin X, and Li CT. 'Enhancing sensor pattern noise via filtering distortion removal'. *IEEE Signal Processing Letters*. 2016 March;23(3):381–385.

[57]   McCloskey S. 'Confidence weighting for sensor fingerprinting'. *IEEE Computer Society Conference on Computer Vision and Pattern Recognition Workshops*; 2008. pp. 1–6.

[58]   Chan LH, Law NF, and Siu WC. 'A confidence map and pixel-based weighted correlation for PRNU-based camera identification'. *Digital Investigation*. 2013;10(3):215–225.

[59]   Hu Y, Yu B, and Jian C. 'Source camera identification using large components of sensor pattern noise'. *International Conference on Computer Science and Its Applications*; 2009. pp. 291–294.

[60]   Li R, Li CT, and Guan Y. 'A reference estimator based on composite sensor pattern noise for source device identification'. *Proceedings of IS&T/SPIE Electronic Imaging*. International Society for Optics and Photonics; 2014. Vol. 9028. pp. 90280O-1–90280O-7.

[61]   Lawgaly A, Khelifi F, and Bouridane A. 'Weighted averaging-based sensor pattern noise estimation for source camera identification'. *IEEE International Conference Image Processing*; 2014. pp. 5357–5361.

[62]   Li CT, and Li Y. 'Color-decoupled photo response non-uniformity for digital image forensics'. *IEEE Transactions on Circuits and Systems for Video Technology*. 2012;22(2):260–271.

[63]   Goljan M, and Fridrich J. 'Sensor-fingerprint based identification of images corrected for lens distortion'. *Proceedings of IS&T/SPIE Electronic Imaging*. International Society for Optics and Photonics; 2012. Vol. 8303. pp. 83030H-1–83030H-13.

[64]   Goljan M, and Fridrich J. 'Estimation of lens distortion correction from single images'. *Proceedings of IS&T/SPIE Electronic Imaging*. International Society for Optics and Photonics; 2014. Vol. 9028. pp. 90280N-1–90280N-13.

[65]   Gloe T, Pfennig S, and Kirchner M. 'Unexpected artefacts in PRNU-based camera identification: A 'Dresden Image Database' Case-Study'. *ACM Workshop on Multimedia and Security*; 2012. pp. 109–114.

[66]   Lin X, and Li CT. 'Preprocessing reference sensor pattern noise via spectrum equalization'. *IEEE Transactions Information Forensics and Security*. 2016;11(1):126–140.

[67]   Satta R, and Stirparo P. 'On the usage of sensor pattern noise for picture-to-identity linking through social network accounts'. *Proceedings of International Conference on Computer Vision Theory and Applications*. Vol. 3. IEEE; 2014. pp. 5–11.

[68]   Goljan M, Chen M, and Fridrich J. 'Identifying common source digital camera from image pairs'. *Proceedings of International Conference on Image Processing*; 2007. pp. 125–128.

[69]   Bloy GJ. 'Blind camera fingerprinting and image clustering'. *IEEE Transactions Pattern Analysis Machine Intelligence*. 2007;30(3):532–534.

[70]   Li CT. 'Unsupervised classification of digital images using enhanced sensor pattern noise'. *IEEE International Symposium on Circuits and Systems*; 2010. pp. 3429–3432.

[71]   Liu BB, Lee HK, Hu Y, and Choi CH. 'On classification of source cameras: a graph based approach'. *IEEE International Workshop on Information Forensics and Security*; 2010. pp. 1–5.

[72]   Yu SX, and Shi J. 'Multiclass spectral clustering'. *Proceedings of the 9th IEEE International Conference Computer Vision*; 2003. pp. 313–319.

[73]   Caldelli R, Amerini I, Picchioni F, and Innocenti M. 'Fast image clustering of unknown source images'. *IEEE International Workshop on Information Forensics and Security*; 2010. pp. 1–5.

[74]   Villalba LJG, Orozco ALS, and Corripio JR. 'Smartphone image clustering'. *Expert System with Applications*. 2015;42(4):1927–1940.

[75]   Lin X, and Li CT. 'Large-scale image clustering based on camera fingerprints'. *IEEE Transactions on Information Forensics and Security*. 2017 April;12(4): 793–808.

[76]   Van Dongen SM. *Graph clustering by flow simulation*. Netherlands: University of Utrecht; 2000.

[77]   Gloe T, and Bhme R. 'The "Dresden Image Database" for benchmarking digital image forensics'. *Journal of Digital Forensic Practice*. 2010;3(2–4):150–159.

[78]   Lukáš J, Fridrich J, and Goljan M. 'Detecting digital image forgeries using sensor pattern noise'. *SPIE*; 2006. pp. 362–372.

[79]   Chierchia G, Poggi G, Sansone C, and Verdoliva L. 'A Bayesian-MRF approach for PRNU-based image forgery detection'. *IEEE Transactions on Information Forensics and Security*. 2014;9(4):554–567.

[80]   Combettes PL, and Pesquet JC. 'Primal-dual splitting algorithm for solving inclusions with mixtures of composite, Lipschitzian, and parallel-sum type monotone operators'. *Set-Valued and Variational Analysis*. 2012;20(2):307–330.

[81]   Chierchia G, Parrilli S, Poggi G, Verdoliva L, and Sansone C. 'PRNU-based detection of small-size image forgeries'. *IEEE International Conference on Digital Signal Processing*; 2011. pp. 1–6.

[82]   Chierchia G, Cozzolino D, Poggi G, Sansone C, and Verdoliva L. 'Guided filtering for PRNU-based localization of small-size image forgeries'. *IEEE International Conference Acoustics, Speech, Signal Processing*; 2014. pp. 6231–6235.

[83]   He K, Sun J, and Tang X. 'Guided image filtering'. *Proceedings of European Conference Computer Vision*. Springer; 2010. pp. 1–14.

[84]   Lin X, and Li CT. 'Refining PRNU-based detection of image forgeries'. *Proceedings of Digital Media Industry Academic Forum*; 2016. pp. 222–226.

Chapter 13

EEG-based biometrics for person identification and continuous authentication

Min Wang[1], Hussein A. Abbass[1], and Jiankun Hu[1]

Establishing and confirming human identity is becoming critical in the vastly inter-connected society. The need for reliable user authentication techniques has increased in the wake of heightened concerns about security and rapid development in technologies. Biometrics is the science of recognizing an individual based on his or her physiological or behavioural traits, and it has become a legitimate method for identity determination.

Recent research reveals that electroencephalogram (EEG) is a promising feasible biometric that can be used for authentication. With its unique properties, EEG biometrics potentially has many advantages over current conventional biometrics such as fingerprints and retinal scans.

In this chapter, we will provide an overview of EEG biometrics and discuss some of the salient research issues that need to be addressed for making EEG biometric an effective tool for providing information security. We introduce brain signals, especially EEG signals and its analysis methods, before we discuss brainwave biometrics from four aspects, namely the criteria, the elicitation protocols, the feature extraction methods and the classification algorithms. The chapter is then concluded with discussions on how to integrate EEG biometrics with other biometric modalities for continuous authentication, followed by open research questions on the design of EEG-based biometric systems.

13.1 Brain and brainwaves

Brain signals have been investigated for decades within the medical field to study brain diseases like Alzheimer's [1], Parkinson's [2] and epilepsy [3]. In recent years, brain signals are also successfully applied in brain–computer interface (BCI) systems as the information medium between humans and computers [4]. Until now, BCI techniques have gained extensive attention and promising success in clinical applications such as

[1] School of Engineering and Information Technology, University of New South Wales, Australia

assistance and rehabilitation systems [5], as well as in public applications such as mental workload assessment [6,7], fatigue detection [8], emotion recognition systems [9] and neuro-feedback training [10,11]. These BCI systems have broad prospects in the medical field [5], consumer electronics and entertainment field [12,13] and others fields where a form of human–computer interaction takes place. Despite the sound development in the above-mentioned applications, scientific investigation on brain signals for authentication purpose as a biometric characteristic has just begun. In this section, we will give a brief introduction of the brain signals, especially for EEG or simply known as 'brainwave', and the EEG recording devices and analysis methods.

13.1.1   The human brain

As the main organ of the human central nervous systems, human brain comprises four basic components [14]: (1) **the brain stem** controlling unconscious automatic body process such as heartbeat and breathing; (2) **the limbic system** which is located deep within the brain and often referred to as the emotional brain; (3) **the cerebellum** or 'little brain' which has a symmetrical folded structure and is responsible for control of movement and equilibrium and (4) **the cerebrum** or cortex which occupies largest part of the human brain. The structure of cerebral cortex can be divided, by the longitudinal fissure, into two symmetrical hemispheres which are indirectly connected through thalamus and other cerebellar structures. The surface of cerebral cortex has a highly convoluted topography of sulci (furrows) and gyri (ridges), providing a much larger surface area in the limited volume of the cranial cavity. Cerebral cortex is generally associated with higher brain functions such as perception, awareness, memory, consciousness, thought, language, cognition and decision-making. An illustration of the above-mentioned brain components is given in Figure 13.1 using Brainstorm [15].

The cerebral cortex is further divided into four sections, the frontal lobe, parietal lobe, occipital lobe and temporal lobe [16], illustrated in Figure 13.2 using Brainstorm [15]. Each lobe has its counterpart over the two hemispheres. **Frontal lobe** is the region taking in charge of making most of our conscious thoughts and decisions, as well as controlling voluntary limb and eye movements. This region contains most of the dopamine-delicate neurons [17] which comprise a dopamine

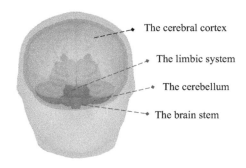

The cerebral cortex

The limbic system

The cerebellum

The brain stem

Figure 13.1   Main components of human brain

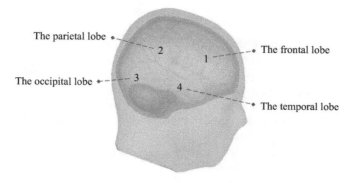

Figure 13.2   Side view of human cerebral cortex

system, being responsible for cognitive processing associated with reward, attention, short-term memory, planning and motivation. Frontal cortex is highly relevant to our personality [18]. **Parietal lobe** is responsible for integrating sensory information from external and internal feedback systems (such as skin, eyes, limbs, muscles) into a coherent representation of spatial relationships among things in the environment and our body [19]. It has been found that this region is important in spatial sense, navigation, motor behaviour and object-oriented actions [20]. **Occipital lobe** contains most area of the visual cortex, therefore is the visual processing centre of the human brain [21]. Functions of this region include low-level visuo-spatial processing (such as orientation), colour recognition and motion perception [22]. **Temporal lobe** involves in processing sensory input into derived, or higher, meanings for proper retention of visual memories, linguistic and emotional association [23]. This region is responsible for long-term memory and language comprehension, processing and production [24]. There are about 100 billion neurons heavily inter-connected in the human brain. Information is propagated across neurons or inhibited from one neuron to the next by synapses, an essential component at the end of each neuron for information transmission. Synaptic transmission generates subtle electrical fields, which is the post-synaptic potentials. The firing of collections of pyramidal neurons of the cortex generates electric fluctuations on the scalp surface.

13.1.2   Brain activity recording techniques

There are mainly two ways for recording brain activities. One is based on measuring the blood flow in the brain due to the fact that cerebral blood flow and neuronal activation are coupled that the activation of a brain region is accompanied by an increase of blood flow to that region [25]. The following techniques belong to this category of blood-flow-associated measurement:

Functional magnetic resonance imaging (fMRI) is a functional neuroimaging procedure using MRI technology to measure brain activity by detecting changes of the concentration of oxygenated and deoxygenated haemoglobin in response to strong magnetic fields. fMRI has good spatial resolution but relatively low time resolution on the order of seconds.

Near-infrared spectroscopy (NIRS) is a spectroscopic method based on the near-infrared spectrum region. It uses brain cortex reflection of infrared light through the skull to measure the concentration of oxygenated and deoxygenated haemoglobin in blood flow as an indicator of brain activity.

Positron emission tomography (PET) is an invasive nuclear imaging technique, which measures neuron metabolism by detecting gamma radiation of a decay inserted into the body of the respondent.

While the other category relies on measuring the neurons' electrical activity, this category includes following approaches:

Magnetoencephalography (MEG) maps brain activity by recording magnetic fields produced by electrical currents occurring in the brain. It is a functional neuroimaging technique relying on sensitive magnetometers.

Electroencephalograph (EEG) is an electrophysiological method that records the electrical pulses resulting from ironic current within the neurons of the brain by placing sensors on the scalp surface. There are several reasons why EEG is an exceptional tool for studying the brain activity and the underlying neurocognitive processes:

1. EEG has high temporal resolution, on the order of milliseconds, which allows continuous observation of brain activity and dynamic study of the underlying mechanisms by computational methods. The common sampling rates of EEG in clinical and research setting are in the range of 128–2,048 Hz; however, modern EEG collection (e.g. Neuroscan SynAmps) systems support sampling rates beyond 20,000 Hz if desired. With this high time resolution, EEG can capture the biological changes underlying the cognitive processes much better than other brain imaging techniques such as fMRI or PET.
2. EEG directly measures neural activity. EEG reflects correlated synaptic activity caused by post-synaptic potentials of cortical neurons. Our brain is constantly generating subtle but detectable electrical signals. EEG sensors directly collect these electrical signals generated by brain from scalp surface. It provides a relatively direct and clear way for looking at brain activity unlike other techniques, for example the fMRI which uses an indirect measuring method and requires a much deeper understanding of the relationship between what is measured and how it relates to cognitive processing.
3. Low costs. Hardware requirements and costs of EEG are significantly lower than other techniques such as fMRI, NIRS, PET and MEG which require bulky and expensive equipment and professional operations. For example, MEG requires equipment consisting of liquid helium-cooled detectors that can be used only in magnetically shielded rooms, altogether costing at least several million dollars.
4. Lightweight, portable, non-invasive and harmless. It's simply not possible to run a real-world study with an fMRI scanner. In contrast, EEG systems are lightweight, portable and therefore allow for more flexible data collection in real-world environments. Besides, it is non-invasive and harmless to subjects,

involving no exposure to high-intensity magnetic fields which is required by fMRI and MEG.

In a nutshell, EEG is a strong tool for investigating brain activity, and it is currently the only applicable cognitive neuroscience technique for utilizing brain signals in real-world applications beyond laboratory [26].

13.1.3   EEG sensors and distribution

EEG systems use electrodes attachable to the scalp to obtain electric potentials generated by the brain. There are two categories for EEG electrodes, wet and dry ones. For wet EEG electrodes, the small metal sensor disks connect to the skin via conductive gel, typically based on saline. It is important to make a proper combination of sensor metal and conductive paste in order to get good data and protect the metal from corroding too fast. Alternatively, there are dry EEG sensors, which directly contact to the scalp without any paste. Generally speaking, dry sensors are faster to apply, however more prone to motion effects in contrast with wet electrodes. For electrode arrays and placement, there are several common systems for defining electrode locations along the scalp. The international 10–20 system, illustrated in Figure 13.3, is a standard EEG electrode placement system, provided by the American Encephalographic Society in 1994. The numbers '10' and '20' refer to the percentage of points where electrodes are placed along lines of longitude and latitude. Each name of the electrodes begins with letter(s) indicating the general brain region where the electrode is deployed, and ends with a number or letter indicating the distance to the midline. An extension of the 10-20 system to higher density settings includes 10-10 and 10-5 systems, allowing for more than 300 electrode positions. However, typical surface-based research can

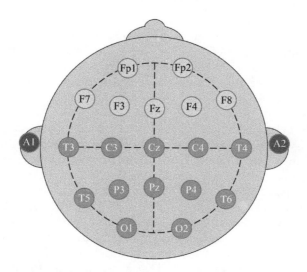

Figure 13.3   EEG electrode placement (10–20 system)

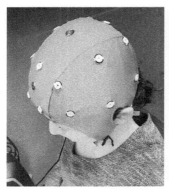

*Figure 13.4   EEG recording devices. Left: MindMedia NeXus-32; Right: Emotive
Epoc+*

work well with 32 channels or less. It is unwise to spend extra time on analysing EEG
arrays with 100 or more channels if 20 would have been sufficient.

There are currently around 15 companies designing EEG hardware and systems
all over the world. Figure 13.4 presents some examples of the EEG hardware, including
multi-channel cap with wet sensors such as the EGI's geodesic EEG system and
MindMedia NeXus-32 QEEG system, as well as portable headsets with dry sensors
such as the Emotiv Epoc and the single channel headset NeuroSky MindWave which
provide a wireless, mobile and quick access to brain activity.

13.1.4   EEG rhythms and oscillations

The synchronization of hundreds of thousands of similarly oriented neurons generates
measurable electrical field from the scalp. For a healthy and normal human subject
in awake state, the amplitude of his surface EEG is in the range of 10–200 mV [27],
and the frequency range of the brain's own intrinsic rhythms is in 0.5–40 Hz. The
recorded EEG signal is always a mixture of several underlying base frequency bands,
divided according to certain cognitive functions and psychophysiological states. The
basic EEG rhythms are presented in Figure 13.5.

Delta (0.5–4 Hz) rhythm is the predominant oscillation in EEG during deep sleep,
or we say slow-wave sleep. It shows relatively high amplitudes (75–200 mV) and a
strong coherence over the whole scalp. Delta band plays an essential role in the development and internal processing of memory, skills and acquired information. **Theta
(4–8 Hz)** band is generally correlated to brain processes associated with mental workload or working memory, especially in frontal region. An augmented theta oscillation
can be observed with increasing task difficulty, particularly when meeting higher
memory demands. This phenomenon is called theta-band power synchronization.
Alpha (8–14 Hz) oscillatory activity is the dominant rhythm in normal human and
is usually generated from posterior cortical area. A clear alpha peak can be observed
in frequency spectrum from raw EEG traces recorded in specific mental conditions.

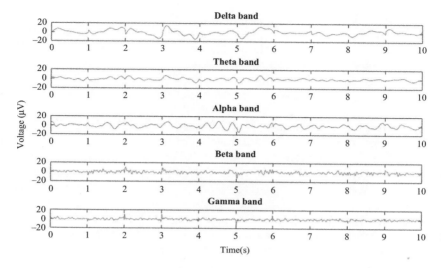

Figure 13.5   Basic EEG rhythms

Alpha waves have critical relations with sensory, motor and memory functions. It shows negative correlation between power and mental/physical workload, which is known as alpha suppression. **Beta (14–30 Hz)** waves commonly reflect the states of alertness, active concentration and focused attention. This frequency band is generated from both frontal and posterior sites. A 'mirror neuron system' that mimicking limb movements in our brain is also proved to be relevant to beta waves. **Gamma (above 30 Hz)** rhythmic activity is considered to be a carrier for transient functional integration of various sensory impressions across brain regions, while the underlying processing mechanism is still a black hole. In general, it can be interpreted as the low frequency rhythms are dominant during inactive states, while the high frequency waves are typically related to information processing.

13.1.5   EEG analysis

According to whether there exists specific stimulation for EEG elicitation in signal acquisition paradigm, EEG signals can be categorized into two types, the ongoing EEG and event-related potential (ERP). The human **ongoing EEG** is a continuous inner 'default activity' (ongoing thoughts or cognitive states) that can be collected in the absence of any particular stimulation; while **ERP** is a stimulus-averaged signal time-locked to the presentation of some event of interest. In general, ongoing EEG is convenient to collect, however, heavily relies on computational methods to extract useful information since the absence of stimulation makes the subjects' mental states under weak experimental control. Two users superficially undertaking the same biometric authentication procedure might actually be in very different cognitive states from acquisition stage, putting forward higher requirements on the classification methods. ERP, in contrast, are obtained by averaging multiple trials of a particular type of event, as a result enhancing brain activity related to the event of interest while meanwhile reducing irrelevant brain activity and noise. However, this stimulus repetition procedure also limits its application in many areas. ERPs have been identified thought all sensory channels, such as visual, auditory, tactile and olfactory stimuli. We can describe ERPs by the morphological characteristics, latency, number, amplitudes, components (positive and negative peaks such as P100, P300, N150) and topography (voltage distribution).

Since Fourier transform being first applied for EEG feature extraction in 1931, many classical methods have been introduced in the field of brainwave analysis, including frequency domain analysis, time domain analysis and time-frequency analysis. In recent years, a flexible combination of different methods (such as wavelet analysis, non-linear dynamics analysis, neural network (NN) analysis, chaos analysis, statistical methods and even deep learning methods) has been developed for EEG analysis, giving an impetus to research in this field. Besides, an integration of temporal, spectral and spatial information has also developed into an effective way for EEG analysis. Figure 13.6 illustrates the categories of current EEG signal analysis methods.

Time domain analysis appears first in signal processing domain since it provides a direct and intuitive way for extracting wave features from signal time series with clear physical meaning. Common methods include peak detection, waveform parameter analysis, coherent average, waveform recognition and analysis of zero-crossing point, histogram, variance and correlation. In addition, parametric models (such as the AR model) are also extensively used for extracting EEG features, which can be used for further classification. However, there is still no particularly effective waveform analysis method due to the complexity of EEG waves.

Frequency domain analysis. Spectrum analysis plays a critical role in EEG signal processing since many significant features of EEG signals are reflected in

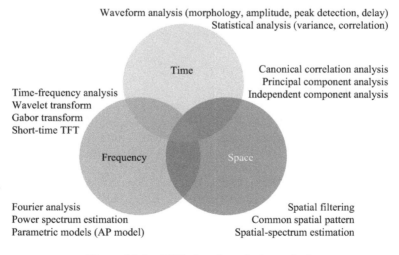

Figure 13.6   EEG signal analysis methods

the frequency domain where power spectrum estimation is an important analysis method. Spectrum analysis transforms EEG time series (where voltage varies with time) into EEG spectrum (where power varies with frequency), providing a clear view of the distribution and changes of signals' frequencies. Classical spectral estimation is directly based on definition, which is a periodic method using Fourier transform on finite length data. However, the variance characteristic of estimation using this kind of methods is poor and the estimated power fluctuates intensively along the frequency axis. In order to improve estimation resolution, techniques based on parametric models have been proposed and developed into a set of modern estimation methods. Frequency analyses are particularly useful in studies of cognitive-affective states where EEG is measured during specific tasks. However, power spectral estimation cannot reflect the time-varying characteristic of the EEG spectrum (EEG is a time-varying non-stationary process), therefore spectrum analysis only in frequency domain will lose time-varying information of the signal.

Time-frequency analysis is a technique which simultaneously analyses signal in both time and frequency domain using linear transformation or non-linear transformation. The linear transformation methods include short-time Fourier transform, Gabor transform and wavelet transform, while the non-linear transformation is mainly based on Wigner–Ville distribution and Cohen's class distribution. The main idea of time-frequency analysis is to transform signal time series into a function of two independent variables (time and frequency). That is to expand time-domain signal on a time-frequency plane, where we can clearly see the signal frequency components at each time point and how it changes. Compared with traditional Fourier analysis, time-frequency analysis is more conducive to present the characteristics, especially the transient characteristics, of non-stationary signals and time-varying signals. Currently, the most widely used time-frequency analysis method is based on wavelet transform theory, where the width of the window is automatically adjusted with different frequencies (shorter windows are applied at higher frequencies). This window-varying approach provides a potential way for real-time signal analysis and it fully embodies the idea of relative bandwidth analysis and adaptive resolution adjustment.

Time-space analysis. Considering the spatial distribution of EEG on the scalp, spatiotemporal analysis is able to reveal and enhance hidden features of EEG signals by integrating temporal information and spatial information from multi-channel EEG data. For instance, brain activity related to movement, perception and cognition presents significant difference in cortex distribution, therefore the fusion of spatial information with existing knowledge is more likely to dig out EEG patterns and features in-depth. Many techniques have been developed for time-frequency analysis, such as spatial spectrum estimation, classical statistical methods (canonical correlation analysis), spatial filtering and so on, where spatial filtering techniques combining with multi-dimensional statistical have been successfully applied in EEG signal processing. Typical techniques include principal component analysis (PCA), independent component analysis (ICA), common spatial pattern (CSP) and block term decomposition, and a lot of improved algorithm variants have been proposed based on the basic idea of these techniques. To be more specific, PCA is a statistical procedure that applies orthogonal transformation to convert a set of observations of possibly correlated variables into a set of values of linearly uncorrelated variables (principal components). Based on singular value decomposition of multi-channel EEG signal, it finds the principal components which can be used in feature extraction and EEG artefacts removal. ICA is based on higher order statistics, representing the current development trend of modern statistical analysis theory in signal processing. ICA is very suitable for multi-channel EEG signal analysis and processing, and it has achieved good performance in EEG artefacts removal, noise removal and feature extraction. CSP is another effective algorithm for EEG signal feature extraction by detecting the event-related desynchronization with spatial filtering. It has been extensively used in BCI systems to retrieve the component signal which best transduce the cerebral activity for a specific task (e.g. hand movement).

The overall development trend of EEG signal analysis is to integrating information from multiple aspects instead of analysing within only one domain. It is because EEG is complicated or even mysterious data source until now that losing any useful information may result in an incomplete understanding of the signal and its underlying mechanism. In recent years, deep learning methods (e.g. the convolution NNs which have been proved to be superior in solving image-related classification problems) have also been introduced in EEG analysis field. Taking advantage of deep learning algorithms' powerful learning capacity, some researches have designed and trained specialized deep NNs for automatic EEG feature extraction and classification with various forms of EEG inputs (such as EEG time series, specific features, spectral topography maps, heat maps, etc.).

13.2 EEG as biometric identifiers

EEG has been extensively studied in academic and commercial research as an effective tool for investigating cortical processes underlying cognitive-affective metrics such as fatigue, attention, engagement, emotion and mental workload. These cognitive-affective metrics can be regarded as psycho-physiological markers of mental states. Continuous monitoring of psycho-physiological markers from ongoing brain activity in operational environments is particularly useful in scenarios where wrong decision or operation could potentially result in hazardous consequences. For example, continuous assessment of the cognitive workload, fatigue and engagement in air-traffic controllers could provide useful information on how the brain responds to commonly monotonous environments and how the brain adapts to occasional emergency or serious situations. This information allows the design of closed-loop system, where the system can adjust itself to keep the user's mental state within a safe threshold or initiate counteraction based on the feedback on cognitive, affective and fatigue states. Besides, we can also use the information to optimize the system and improve the environments to achieve higher safety and productivity.

The rapid development of EEG-related research in biomedical engineering (especially the BCI techniques), consumer neuroscience (for instance on engagement, motivation, attention and vigilance) and marketing area has promoted a further

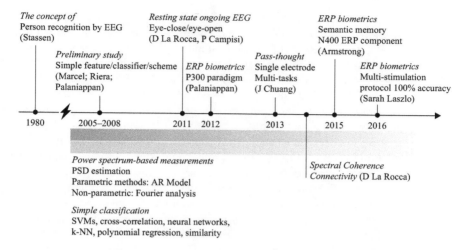

The concept of
Person recognition by EEG
(Stassen)

Resting state ongoing EEG
Eye-close/eye-open
(D La Rocca, P Campisi)

ERP biometrics
Semantic memory
N400 ERP component
(Armstrong)

Preliminary study
Simple feature/classifier/scheme
(Marcel; Riera;
Palaniappan)

ERP biometrics
P300 paradigm
(Palaniappan)

Pass-thought
Single electrode
Multi-tasks
(J Chuang)

ERP biometrics
Multi-stimulation
protocol 100% accuracy
(Sarah Laszlo)

1980   2005–2008   2011 2012   2013   2015   2016

Power spectrum-based measurements
PSD estimation
Parametric methods: AR Model
Non-parametric: Fourier analysis

Spectral Coherence
Connectivity (D La Rocca)

Simple classification
SVMs, cross-correlation, neural networks,
k-NN, polynomial regression, similarity

Figure 13.7   The development of studies on EEG biometrics

investigation on EEG in information security domain, to be specific, as a biometrics. The idea of using brainwaves for automatic user recognition was first proposed in 1980 [28], but not attracting much attention during the following decade. In the early stage, the research mainly focused on extracting simple features from EEG using frequency analysis or parametric models (e.g. the AR model) and applying traditional binary or multi-class classifiers for user verification and identification. Despite having some interesting preliminary findings which opened up a skylight for EEG biometrics, research in early stage have limitations in signal recording protocols, underlying psychophysiological evidences, and EEG analysis, feature extraction and classification methods. In the recent decade, brainwave biometrics has begun to attract attentions from both academic research and commercial areas. Many researchers have carried out experiments under different signal recording conditions and with well-designed protocols taking into consideration of the evidences from neuroscience and psychophysiology. The signal-analysis methods are more diversified and many popular techniques including deep learning have also been introduced for EEG feature extraction and classification. Figure 13.7 shows the development of studies on EEG biometrics and EEG-based authentication systems.

13.2.1   Criteria

Biometrics refers to automatic recognition of individuals through their unique physiological or behavioural attributes. Compared with passwords and tokens, biometrics is more convenient and safer by being as inherent factor of the individual. Our brain is a complicated system producing rich information. Anatomical studies of human brain have revealed a significant inter-individual variability of brain characteristics, indicating that human brain is a unique system that exist subtle individual distinctions in some attributes. Besides, the brain activity elicited by certain stimuli is highly individual. For example, people produce different mental responses to images of foods due to individual food preference and previous experiences. So the surface brainwaves, as direct reflections of the cortical activity generated by our brain, can be regarded as a unique physiological, psychological as well as behavioural attribute. The following is an analysis of the biometric criteria with respect to EEG identifier.

Universality: The attribute should be possessed by all humans. Brainwaves possess high level of universality that normal healthy people with no pathological effects on brain can use brainwave biometrics.

Permanence: The attribute should exhibit invariance over a period of time. The reliability of brainwave biometrics across different acquisition sessions, namely the intra-individual stability, is a critical issue under serious concern. In [29], the reliability of resting state EEG was investigated by comparing signals acquired from two sessions with a time interval of 15 months. Signal amplitude and frequency of the alpha-peak as well as the shape of the power spectrum of signal recorded at three median recording sites were extracted as features. Results confirmed a high re-test reliability of the extracted features across time. Beyond resting state, reliability of EEG was also analysed under cognitive tasks, for example a working memory task [30] and a psychomotor vigilance task [31]. The results indicated a higher reliability of task-related EEG within and across sessions compared to resting EEG. The later work (with 20 subjects and re-test intervals of 1,240 months) also confirmed that the intra-individual stability is higher compared to the inter-individual variation, which means we can differentiate EEG from different individuals. In addition to ongoing EEG, researchers also investigated the repeatability issue of ERP biometrics [32,33]. In [32], the researchers proposed an ERP biometric based on the variability of individuals' semantic network and resultant N400 components. A total of 45 subjects were asked to respond to a stream of text designed to be distinctively familiar to individuals to elicit the biomarker. Results showed that this biomarker presents robust identifiable features for individual verification with accuracy reliably above chance (82%–97%), more importantly, these features are stable after a lag of up to 6 months.

Distinctiveness: The attribute should be unique and discriminative amongst the population. While permanence is a matter of intra-individual difference over time, distinctiveness can be considered as an issue of inter-individual variance, which is mainly related to two facets including the innate variants from heritability and the postnatal variants resulting from individual personalities and personal experiences.

1. **Heritability factors.** Results from a twin study [34], which targets estimating the genetic contribution to individual differences, confirmed that EEG power spectrum presents highly heritable characteristics. These heritable characteristics, which are called common genetic factors, result in basic structural features as skull thickness and common neural properties, and they influence the whole spectrum in both hemispheres. Genetic contribution to individual differences has also been investigated in cognitive functions such as memory, workload and attention beyond resting state. Results from an ERP research [35], which elicits P300 using a delayed response working memory task, revealed a significant influence of genetic factors on variation of P300 amplitude and latency at frontal, central

and parietal regions. An fMRI twin study [36] investigated individual differences in NNs subserving cognition function and found a significant genetic influence on brain activation in NNs supporting digit working memory tasks. Results showed that subjects activating frontal–parietal networks responded faster than those relying on language-related brain networks (which were proved to be partly attributed to genetic influences), indicating that differences in cognition might be related to brain activation patterns that differ qualitatively among individuals. Evidences from relevant research lead to a conclusion that in addition to the influence of psychophysiological and cognitive factors, genetic and environmental factors also contribute to provide some individual-specific features of the brainwave signals.

2. **Personality correlates.** Substantial variability among individuals in characteristic patterns of thinking, feeling and behaving introduces a rich diversity of culture and lifestyle into our society. In the neuroscience of human behaviour and cognition, personality is considered as a result of combining individual's emotional, attitudinal and cognitive traits, thus defines an individual profile of each person. Research focusing on identifying relationships between brain activity and personality profiles has achieved promising results. A study [37] on associating EEG indicators with extroversion based on emotional imagery revealed that extroverts tend to present more rhythmic low-arousal EEG activity than introverts. Moreover, a correlation between personality variables (related to extroversion and neuroticism) and individual values of the antero-posterior spectral power gradient was observed in all frequency bands [38]. Besides, frontal asymmetry of cortical activation has also been proved to have association with affective disposition linked to extroversion and neuroticism, and alpha asymmetry in the right posterior region was observed to correlate with positivity personality trait [39]. A recent MRI study in human brain [40] even provided a structural basis of inter-individual differences in human behaviour and cognition.

In addition to the inherent influence of Heritability and personality factors, the level of uniqueness of brainwaves is also dependent on the signal acquisition protocols, feature extraction methods and classification algorithms. Such issues are discussed in the following sub-sections.

Collectability: The attribute should be easily collectable in terms of acquisition and digitalization, and measurable with practical devices. Collectability of brainwaves is mainly depending on the acquisition equipment and the elicitation protocol. Factors such as the number of electrodes, the complexity of the acquisition protocol and the time needed for extracting adequate information will limit the application of EEG biometrics. In fact, the rapid development of sensor technology and signal processing techniques has made EEG recording easy and user-friendly. With the embedding of EEG sensors in wireless headsets and other consumer electronics, quick collection of EEG is no longer a problem. So further investigation is needed to identify significant regions, frequencies and patterns in order to enhance efficiency, reduce the recording time and the number of electrodes needed, as well as simplify the acquisition protocols. Preliminary works have achieved promising performance with limited number of electrodes and simple protocols, which make signal collection user-convenient. For example, Professor Chuang and his group from UC Berkeley proposed a 'passthoughts' system [41] for user verification with brainwaves using a single-channel dry-contact wireless EEG headset.

Acceptability: People should be willing, or at least not against to have that attribute being collected and measured. There has been no specific investigation on public's acceptability and attitudes towards brainwave biometrics yet. Some people may have slight concerns about the potentiality of leaking privacy, such as emotions and thoughts. However, these side-effects can be largely avoided by proper design and control. While from another perspective, containing rich information is exactly an advantage of EEG biometrics over other techniques by allowing continuous authentication and assessment of the user's cognitive-affective states at the same time. This characteristic makes brainwaves very suitable for continuous authentication in closed-loop system of human–machine interaction, where EEG is a common assisted measurement for user's mental states assessment.

Circumvention: the attribute should be robust to imitation or counterfeit in case of intrusion and attacks. Exposed attribute like face and fingerprint are inferior in terms of anti-circumvention capacity as fingerprints can be easily left on objects and both of fingerprints and face images can be captured by high-resolution photography. In contract, brain signals are internal traits that cannot be captured without the user's awareness, thus are less prone to spoofing attacks.

Compared with current popular biometric techniques, such as fingerprints, face recognition and retina scans, brainwaves have intrinsic advantages.

1. **Brainwave biometrics have high security level.** Brain activity cannot be measured without a person's knowledge with current technology, therefore are least likely to be duplicated or counterfeited. While image-based techniques are vulnerable to some extent since images (such as fingerprints and faces) can be captured via high-resolution camera or film without the user's consciousness.
2. **Brainwaves provide a reliable biometrics for security.** A person cannot divulge any content of the brain biometrics voluntarily or under compulsion as the brainwave signatures are basically non-volitional that they are not under control of the person.
3. **Brainwaves are 'alive' biometrics [33].** The person must be alive in order to provide brain measurements as the lack of active brain activity is a clinical indicator of human brain death. This characteristic makes brainwaves a mutual safe biometrics, which not only protect the system but the user of that system as well.
4. **Brainwaves are natural continuous data sources.** One of the future trends of identity and access management is continuous authentication, which is very different from conventional one-time verification. Brainwaves offer a unique capacity for continuous identification and prove a valuable addition to the existing security apparatus.

It is certainly an unusual form of identification, but such intangible biometric technologies are increasingly being explored. For example, behavioural biometric systems based on particular movement patterns are being implemented into many multi-modal biometric systems. Brainwave authentication might sound like esoteric right now, but it is clearly a feasible means of authentication and brings potential prospective effects on design of the next generation biometric systems – the cognitive biometric systems.

13.2.2 Elicitation of brain response and the protocols

Collecting ongoing EEG under resting state is the simplest data acquisition protocol, which does not involve any mental or cognitive task. In most cases, it is a baseline procedure for signal calibration before performing cognitive tasks. However, EEG elicited by stimulation during a mental task may contain more information for brain biometrics as it is a reflection of people cognitive ability and attitude (including affective and emotional response) which are considered to be highly individual and even unique. Practical application requirements also drive the investigation on cognitive EEG biometrics beyond resting state. Existing evidences indicated that appropriate mental tasks may elicit brainwaves that are more intrinsically able to highlight individuals' distinctive traits; therefore, the design of proper and effective signal elicitation protocol is critical in brainwave biometric studies by directly affecting the potentials of the recorded signals.

Resting state EEG protocol: During the signal recording session, subjects will be asked to sit in a comfortable chair in a dimly lit room with body and mind relaxed. The environment of the room should be under control to minimize the internal/external noise and provide comfortable temperature in order to favour the attention and the relaxed state of the subjects. When the recording session starts, subjects will be simply asked to perform a few minutes of resting state with eyes closed or with eyes opened. There have been several studies on investigating resting state EEG for brainwave biometrics. An unobtrusive biometric system was proposed in [42] based on closed eyes resting EEG recorded at forehead sites (FP1 and FP2). Two sets of features were extracted, namely the single channel features from auto-regression (AR) and Fourier transform and the inter-channel features based on mutual information, coherence and cross-correlation. Through classical Fisher's DA, the proposed verification system achieved an EER of 3.4%, that is a GAR of 96.6%, with 51 users and 36 intruders. Brain ongoing activity under eyes closed resting condition was investigated in [43] for user identification. Signals were recorded from 48 subjects with an EEG cap of 56 electrodes. Features vectors were consisted of the reflection coefficients of a six-order AR model of the signals from selected electrodes. An analysis on suitable electrode configurations was also conducted by testing difference sets of symmetrically placed electrodes, and a maximum GAR of 96.08% was obtained by combining electrodes T7, Cz and T8. A comparison between two resting state conditions (eyes closed and eyes opened) was carried out in [44], which indicated that eyes closed condition generally performs better than eyes opened condition for user recognition with same features and electrode configurations. Meanwhile, the analysis on the longitudinal recordings indicated a high repeatability of the extracted EEG features, which is a significant issue for practical brainwave biometric systems. In another study [45], spectral coherence-based connectivity between brain regions were extracted as a possible brain biometric feature for user identification under resting conditions. Results showed that a combination of the functional connectivity features with power-spectrum measurements could allow 100% recognition accuracy on a test involving 108 subjects under eyes closed and eyes opened resting conditions.

ERP biometric protocol: In contrast with ongoing resting EEG, ERP is a stimulus-averaged signal time-locked to the presentation of event of interest. (For detailed information on ERP, refer to [46].) Being time-locked to the stimulation allows us to tightly control the subject's cognitive state being reflected in the resultant brainwaves. Furthermore, ERP is obtained by averaging over many trials of a particular type of event, this procedure helps emphasize the brain activity related to the event of interest and meanwhile helps reduce the effects from unrelated activity. During ERP collection session, subjects will be exposed to repeated stimulation (e.g. visual stimulus like food images). The subjects will be asked to respond to the stimuli or not to, depending on the investigation purpose and the type of EEG component we want to elicit. For example, experiments on P300 which is elicited by oddball stimuli (rare and unanticipated target stimulus embedded in a sequence of common stimuli) usually requires a response from subjects (e.g. with a button press when they detect the oddball stimulus). An example of the stimulation procedure is illustrated in Figure 13.8, where each stimulus is preceded and followed by a fixation interval aiming at reducing ocular artefacts and each trial is ended with a larger interval for relaxation.

A wide variety of stimulation has been investigated for ERP biometrics [33]:

(1)   Image of sine gratings. Sine gratings can elicit visual potentials over the posterior area and the primary visual cortex is known to be individual in its topographical pattern of folds [47].

(2)   Low frequency words. Psychophysiological evidences pointed out that ERP responses to low frequency words that within an individual's scope of knowledge differ from the responses to unknown words [48]. Individuals exhibit substantial variation in their knowledge of words.

(3)   Food images. Results from [49] indicated that structures in the ventral midbrain exhibit activation profiles in response to images of food, where food preference is considered to be highly individual.

(4)   Celebrity face images. Face stimuli elicit an occipital negativity peaking around 170 ms in the ERP. People's attitudes towards celebrities can be completely opposite. Results from [50] also indicated that structures in the orbitofrontal cortex exhibit activation profiles in response to images of faces, where people's judgment of attractiveness on these face is individual.

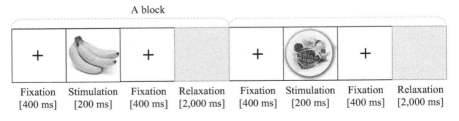

Figure 13.8   Example of the trial structure in ERP elicitation protocol

(5) Oddball targets. A large, positive deflection in voltage with a latency of roughly 300 ms, known as P300, is elicited when subjects are asked to respond to an oddball (rare and unanticipated) target stimulus embedded in a sequence of common stimuli.

The morphology and delay of the P300 is demonstrated to be correlated with human general intelligence and varying from person to person. P300 paradigm has been exploited for cognitive biometrics in several works [51,52], to be specific, a spatially varying oddball paradigm based on the common rapid serial visual paradigm was proposed in [51] and a colour varying oddball paradigm was designed in [52]. Other categories of stimulation for ERP biometrics are also worth investigating. The basic criteria for selecting a stimulation category is that this stimuli should be able to robustly elicit detectable ERP, and people's responses to the stimuli should be individually distinct.

By allowing precise control of the users' cognitive states through specific modes of simulation that likely to produce distinctive responses across subjects, ERP biometric protocol would be able to achieve higher identification performance. Additionally, a combination of multiple modes of stimulation can further boost the performance and improve robustness [33]. However, ERP is an active identification manner and requires repeated stimulation, limiting its applications in real-life scenario somewhat, especially for continuous authentication where active and repeated stimulation will interrupt the users from normal work. This is why we also need to investigate the ongoing EEG during cognitive tasks, in addition to resting state EEG and ERP, in order to design passive EEG biometric system which derives its outputs from arbitrary brain activities without the purpose of voluntary control.

Some classical mental tasks have been investigated for brain biometrics, including motion imagination, object recognition and counting, mental calculation, mental recitation, working memory task and free pass-thought task. In [53], EEG recorded during imagination of repetitive left- and right-hand movements and word generation with a random letter was studied for individual authentication. Results showed that imagination of hand movements performs better than word generation in identification accuracy and permanence, which indicated that some mental tasks are more appropriate for individual identification than others. A visual evoked potential (VEP)-based biometrics is proposed in [54], where the VEP signals were recorded from the subjects being shown black and white images of common objects. The mental task was to recognize and remember the picture being showed. EEG signals were filtered within 25–56 Hz to retain only gamma rhythm, which is considered to contain the dominant effects of perception and memory of visual stimuli. By spatial averaging to reduce the intra-class variance and extracting spectral power features from gamma band, a high GAR of 98% was achieved on the large dataset of 102 subjects. The good performance of VEP protocol can be explained by the evidence from neuroscience [55] that brain functions underlying VEP generation are influenced by genetic factors that result in different levels of perception and memory among individuals. Math calculation, geometric figure rotation, mental letter composing and visual counting tasks were investigated in [56] for person recognition since brain functions underlying these mental tasks can be reflected by the hemispheric brain wave asymmetry, which is considered to be distinct among individuals. The final HTER ranged from 0% to 1.5% for the mental tasks with a total of five subjects. A 'pass-thought' protocol proposed in [41] even allows subjects choosing their own mental thoughts as brain passwords. In this protocol, subjects were asked to choose a mental thought and focus on the pass-thought for 10 s. With customized thresholds to each subjects, 99% verification accuracy was achieved using single electrode at FP1 with a total of 15 individuals. They also conducted a usability survey of different mental tasks to see people's attitudes towards these tasks. Questions like '"was the task difficult?", "boring?", "would you like to repeat?", "are you able to recall?"' were asked, and the results indicated that people have no difficulty in recalling their chosen secret, especially the secret they come up with themselves, and the task preference is highly individual. Some of them prefer using their secret information such as a chosen colour or sport, while others prefer tasks involving no secret information such as responding to external stimuli or imagination of moving up right hand.

It is worth mentioning that designing brain biometric protocols is not an isolated process. The performance of brain biometrics is also dependent on signal processing, feature extraction and classification methods.

13.2.3   Feature extraction

Extraction of significant, representative and stable features from the collected biometric data is a key step in establishing effective authentication systems. Feature extraction has been performed in temporal, spectral and spatial domain, as well as a combination of multiple domains such as time-frequency analysis and time-space analysis. Furthermore, the algorithms for feature extraction are also varied. Extensively used methods include power spectrum density (PSD) function, autoregressive (AR) stochastic modelling, energy of the signal, auto-correlation function, morphological analysis, latency and area of characteristic peaks. A discussion of the commonly used algorithms for EEG feature extraction will be given in this sub-section, and based on which we will also introduce some novel ideas for identifying distinguished features for EEG biometrics.

Our brain is a continuous oscillator that generates rhythmic activity; therefore, features from frequency domain are more suitable for describing its characteristics. Here, we introduce two of the most widely used features in frequency domain, coefficients from AR stochastic modelling and PSD.

1. **Autoregressive (AR) model.** A stochastic process $u(n)$ is known as generalized stationary process if the average power of the process exists, the mean of the process is constant and its auto-correlation function is independent with the starting point, as follows:

$$E(|u(n)|^2) < \infty \tag{13.1}$$

$$\mu(n) = \mu \tag{13.2}$$

$$r(k,l) = r(k-l) = r(m) \tag{13.3}$$

Most stationary stochastic processes can be generated by a linear time-invariant system with white noise excitation, whereas linear time-invariant systems can be described by linear differential equations. This linear differential model is AR moving average (ARMA) model, which is defined as follows:

$$x(n) + \sum_{i=1}^{p} a_i x(n - i) = c + y(n) + \sum_{j=1}^{q} b_j y(n - j), \quad n = 0, \pm 1, \pm 2, \ldots$$

$$(13.4)$$

where xn is a discrete stochastic process that meets the requirements of the above ARMA process, yn is discrete white noise, $a_1, \ldots, a_n$ and $b_1, \ldots, b_n$ are coefficients of AR model and moving average, respectively, p and q are the order of AR and MA model, respectively. An ARMA process is usually denoted as ARMA(p, q) that can be expressed as follows:

$$A(z)x(n) = B(z)y(n), \quad n = 0, \pm 1, \pm 2, \ldots \tag{13.5}$$

where $A(z)$ and $B(z)$ are known as AR polynomial and MA polynomial,

$$A(z) = 1 + a_1 z^{-1} + \cdots + a_p z^{-p} \tag{13.6}$$

$$B(z) = 1 + b_1 z^{-1} + \cdots + b_q z^{-q} \tag{13.7}$$

where the backward shift operator is defined as $x(n - j)$. The transfer function of the linear time invariant system defined by the AR model is

$$H(z) = \frac{B(z)}{A(z)} = \sum_{i=-\infty}^{\infty} h_i z^{-i} \tag{13.8}$$

where h_i is the coefficients of impact response. Obviously, when $B(z) = 1$, the ARMA(p, q) degenerates into AR(p), namely the pth order AR model:

$$x(n) + a_1 x(n - 1) + \cdots + a_p x(n - p) = y(n) \tag{13.9}$$

The AR model can be regarded as a basic all-pole infinite impulse response filter. In fact, any ARMA process with finite variance can be uniquely represented as an AR process with a sufficiently large order. Therefore, in practical applications, we only need to estimate the AR coefficients, without having to estimate the MA parameters.

EEG signal from each channel can be assumed to be the output of an unique AR system driven by white noise with unique parameters. Therefore, the parameters of AR model are significant features of EEG signals. There are mainly two ways for fitting an AR model to the input signal, namely the Yule–Walker method and Burg method.

Yule–Walker method, also known as the auto-correlation method. Assume that the input signal and the output signal of the AR model, AR(p), are stationary complex stochastic signals. $y(n)$ is a white noise with mean of zero and variance of σ^2. Then, $x(n)$ and $y(n)$ satisfy the following difference equation:

$$x(n) = -\sum_{k=1}^{p} a_k x(n-k) + y(n) \tag{13.10}$$

Multiply both sides of the above equation by $x^*(n-m)$, $m \geq 0$, then operate mathematical expectation, there is,

$$E(x(n)x^*(n-m)) = E([-\sum_{k=1}^{p} a_k x(n-k) + y(n)]x^*(n-m))$$

$$= -\sum_{k=1}^{p} a_k E(x(n-k)x^*(n-m)) + E(y(n)x^*(n-m)) \tag{13.11}$$

By the definition of auto-correlation function and cross-correlation function, the above equation can be expressed as:

$$r_x(m) = r_{xy}(m) - \sum_{k-1}^{p} a_k r_x(m-k) \tag{13.12}$$

Since the AR model is a causal system, its output signal $x(n-m)$ is statistically independent of the input signal $y(n)$, which is white noise with mean of zero and variance of σ^2, there is,

$$r_{xy}(m) = E(y(n)x^*(n-m)) = E[y(n)]E[x^*(n-m)] = 0 \tag{13.13}$$

When $m = 0$, there is,

$$r_{xy}(0) = E(y(n)x^*(n)) = E\left(y(n) - \left[\sum_{k=1}^{p} a_k^* x^*(n-k) + y*(n)\right]\right)$$

$$= -\sum_{k=1}^{p} a_k^* E[y(n)x^*(n-k)] + E[y(n)y^*(n)] = \delta^2 \tag{13.14}$$

In summary,

$$r_x(m) = \begin{cases} -\sum_{k=1}^{p} a_k r_k(m-k) & m > 0 \\ -\sum_{k=1}^{p} a_k r_k(-k) + \delta^2 & m = 0 \end{cases} \tag{13.15}$$

For $m = 0, 1, \ldots, p$, there are linear equations:

$$
\begin{bmatrix} r_x(0) & \cdots & r_x(-p) \\ \vdots & \ddots & \vdots \\ r_x(p) & \cdots & r_x(0) \end{bmatrix} \begin{bmatrix} 1 \\ \vdots \\ a_p \end{bmatrix} = \begin{bmatrix} \delta^2 \\ \vdots \\ 0 \end{bmatrix} \tag{13.16}
$$

The above linear equations can also be expressed as a vector form:

$$
\widetilde{R}_{p+1} \begin{bmatrix} 1 \\ \theta_p \end{bmatrix} = \begin{bmatrix} 1 \\ \theta_p \end{bmatrix} \tag{13.17}
$$

where

$$
\theta_p = [a_1, a_2, \ldots, a_p]^T \tag{13.18}
$$

$$
\widetilde{R}_{p+1} = \begin{bmatrix} r_x(0) & \cdots & r_x(-p) \\ \vdots & \ddots & \vdots \\ r_x(p) & \cdots & r_x(0) \end{bmatrix} = E[\mu_{p+1}^*(n)\mu_{p+1}^T(n)] = R_{p+1}^* \tag{13.19}
$$

The above equations is known as Yule–Walker equation. The coefficients of the AR model, $a_1, \ldots, a_n$, can be obtained by solving this linear equations.

Burg method. In the Yule–Walker algorithm, calculation of the AR coefficients requires computing the matrix inversion. Besides, Yule–Walker equations of different orders need to be solved for AR models with different orders. In order to simplify the calculation procedure, Levinson proposed a recursive method, which can recursively obtain the AR parameters of mth order by the AR parameters of $(m-1)$th order. Define the kth coefficient of a mth order AR model as $a_k(m), k = 1, 2, \ldots, m; m = 1, 2, \ldots, p$, K_m is reflection coefficient, then $a_m(i|1 \leq i \leq m-1) = a(m-1)(i) + K_m a(m-1) * (m-i)$, $a_m(m) = K_m$. However, in practical applications, how to solve the reflection coefficient of the Levinson recursive algorithm is a problem. To solve this problem, Burg proposed a method to estimate the coefficients of AR model by minimizing the average power of the forward and backward prediction error based on the Levinson recursive algorithm.

Initially, set $m = 1$. Set the initial value of the power of the prediction error, and the forward and backward prediction errors as following:

$$
P_0 = \frac{1}{N} \sum_{n=1}^{N} |x(n)|^2, \quad f_0(n) = g_0(n) = x(n) \tag{13.20}
$$

Then calculate the reflection coefficient K_m by the following equation:

$$
K_m = \frac{-\sum_{n=m+1}^{N} f_{m-1}(n)g_{m-1}^*(n-1)}{\frac{1}{2}\sum_{n=m+1}^{N} [|f_{m-1}(n)|^2 + |g_{m-1}(n-1)|^2]} \tag{13.21}
$$

and calculate P_m, the power of prediction error:

$$P_m = \frac{1}{2}\sum_{n=m}^{N}[|f_m(n)|^2 + |g_m(n)|^2]$$ (13.22)

Then, the forward and backward prediction errors of the AR model can be achieved:

$$f_m(n) = \sum_{i=0}^{m} a_m(i)x(n-i) = f_{(m-1)}(n) + K_m g_{(m-1)}(n-1)$$ (13.23)

$$g_m(n) = \sum_{i=0}^{m} a_m^*(m-i)x(n-i) = g_{(m-1)}(n-1) + K_m^* f_{m-1}(n)$$ (13.24)

Let $m \leftarrow m + 1$, repeat the above steps until P_m converges. Then, the coefficients of AR model can be calculated by bringing the K_m obtained when P_m converges into the Levinson recursive equations.

2. **Power spectrum estimation.** In order to extract appropriate spectral features from the signal, we care about its distribution characteristics in the frequency domain, that is, the power spectral density of the discrete time random process. Power spectrum estimation is the process of estimating power spectral density of a random signal from a sequence of time samples. Depending on processing domains, estimation techniques can be categorized into non-parametric approaches and parametric approaches. Classic estimation methods based on Fourier analysis is the most commonly used non-parametric techniques, including the standard periodogram method, Bartlett's method and an improved Welch's method. A common parametric technique involves fitting the observations to an AR model.

    PSD estimation by Fourier analysis. From Parseval's theorem, we know that the energy of signal in frequency domain equals to its energy in time domain, which accords to the following equation:

$$\sum_{n=-\infty}^{+\infty}|f(n)|^2 = \frac{1}{2\pi}\int_0^{2\pi}|F(w)|^2 dw$$ (13.25)

where $f(n)$ is the signal in time domain and $|F(w)|$ is the corresponding Fourier transform. So, for the N point observations, $x_N(n)$, of stochastic process $x(n)$, its PSD can be estimated as:

$$\hat{S}_p(\omega) = \frac{1}{N}|(X_N(\omega)|^2$$ (13.26)

$$X_N(\omega) = \sum_{n=0}^{N-1} x_N(n)e^{-i\omega n}$$ (13.27)

For practical operation of PSD estimation based on Fourier analysis, the first step is converting signals from time domain into frequency domain. The most commonly used method to convert EEG signals into frequency domain is Fourier transform. The discrete Fourier transform (DFT), with expression:

$$X(k) = \sum_{n=0}^{N-1} x(n)\Omega_N^{nk} \tag{13.28}$$

where $\omega_N = e^{-2\pi i/N}$ is the Nth root of unit, is usually used to compute the coefficient of each frequency component, which is the amplitude of signal at different frequencies. Here, N is the length of the signal segment being calculated. In practice, fast Fourier transform (FFT) algorithm is widely used to compute the DFT of a sequence, or its inverse, since FFT significantly accelerates the calculation speed by reducing the computation complexity. After converting signals into frequency domain, we can estimate the PSD, which describe the distribution of power into frequency components composing the signal, by standard periodogram method or by more sophisticated methods such as Bartlett's method and Welch's method.

Standard periodogram method: Suppose $x(n)$ of length N is the EEG time series to be analysed. To estimate the PSD of the EEG segment, we first convert the signal into frequency domain by N point FFT and then compute the squared magnitude of the result within effective EEG band (0.5–42 Hz). Bartlett's method provides a way to reduce the variance of the estimated PSD in exchange for a reduction of resolution, compared to the standard periodogram method. A final estimate of the spectrum at a given frequency is obtained by averaging the estimates from the spectrums derived from non-overlapping segments of the original series. In detail, the original N point data series is split up into K non-overlapping data segments with each of length M. For each segment, the periodogram is obtained by computing the squared magnitude of the result of DFT or FFT and then dividing this by M. The final estimated PSD of $x(n)$ is an average of the periodograms for the K data segments. Welch's method is also based on the concept of applying periodogram spectrum estimates; however, it's an improvement on Bartlett's method, in that it reduces noise in the estimated power spectra in exchange for a reduction of resolution. Compared with Bartlett's method, Welch's method splits the original signal time series into L overlapping segments of length M, with D point overlapped and then applies a window function on these segments before calculating periodograms.

PSD estimation by AR model. From the linear system theory, we know that relationship between output $y(n)$ and input $x(n)$ of a discrete time stationary stochastic process through linear time-invariant discrete time systems can be expressed as a linear difference equation:

$$y(n) = h(n) * x(n) = \sum_{k=-\infty}^{+\infty} h(k)x(n-k) \tag{13.29}$$

The auto-correlation of response $y(n)$ can be expressed as:

$$r_y(m) = E[y(n)y^*(n-m)] = h^*(-m) * h(m) * r_x(m) \qquad (13.30)$$

Perform Fourier transform to both sides of the above equation, there is,

$$S_y(\omega) = H^*(\omega)H(\omega)S_x(\omega) = |H(\omega)|^2 S_x(\omega) \qquad (13.31)$$

From the above discussion, we know that EEG signal can be regarded as the response of a white noise excitation of zeros mean and a variance of δ^2 through linear time-invariant system, namely the AR model. The transfer function of AR model is,

$$H(z) = \frac{1}{A(z)} = \frac{1}{1 + \sum_{k=1}^{p} a_k z^{(-k)}} \qquad (13.32)$$

The PSD of the input white noise of the AR model is δ^2. After calculating the parameters a_k of the AR model, the power spectrum of the output signal can be obtained,

$$S_A R(\omega) = \frac{\delta^2}{1 + \sum_{k=1}^{p} a_k z^{(-k)}} \qquad (13.33)$$

For calculating the coefficients of AR model, the Yule–Walker method and Burg method can be used.

Coefficients from AR stochastic modelling are employed as features in most of the works on EEG biometrics. Some of the works rely on resting state EEG. In [43,57], the Burg's method was employed to extract the reflection coefficients for an AR model of 6th order and 12th order, respectively. Feature vectors were obtained by concatenating the coefficients extracted from different sets of electrodes. In [42], AR coefficients of a 100-order model were calculated by Yule–Walker method as features, which were then merged with other features such as mutual information, spectral coherence and cross-correlation at decision level for user authentication. There are also works on cognitive EEG. In [58], EEG data related to motion in a virtual environment were analysed through ICA and AR modelling. Signals from the whole scalp were divided into five groups, where ICA was performed for each group to select the most energetic component. An AR model of seventh order was then performed on the selected components for feature extraction. In [56], six AR coefficients were extracted by Burg's method from cognitive EEG during thought activity for user recognition.

Features can also be extracted from the characteristics of the estimated EEG spectrum. In [53], EEG was recorded when subjects were performing a motor imagery task and a words generation task. The estimated PSD values within 8–30 Hz from eight electrodes were extracted as features, where the electrodes and frequency bands were chosen based on results from research on matching relevant brain signal information with different mental processes. PSD was estimated every 62.5 ms with a window of 1 s using Welch's method. In [54], a multiple signal classification (MUSIC) algorithm was proposed to estimate dominant frequency and power content. Unique features were obtained by performing the MUSIC based spectral analysis of the VEP signals in gamma band. Other features from frequency domain include power of a specific band, the power ratio of two bands (e.g. the theta–beta ratio) and so on [52].

The above feature extraction methods based on AR modelling, PSD estimation or power in specific frequency band have been extensively applied in EEG biometrics. However, EEG dynamics associated with significant features for individual description can be distributed across multiple frequency bands, and informative EEG power in a specific band might very over time. Hence, the traditional temporal and spectral methods may result in great information loss. Time-frequency analysis provides a possible way for looking at this problem. Common methods for performing time-frequency analysis are short time Fourier transformation and wavelet transformation, the advantage of the latter one is the use of a flexible window that can automatically adjust its width with different frequencies.

Besides, evidences from neuroscience showed that regions in the human brain collaborate with each other to accomplish a task, forming a connective network among them, known as functional connectivity, which is considered to be unique among individuals. In general, functional connectivity captures deviations from statistical independence between distributed and spatially separated regions. The independence can be estimated by cross-correlation, mutual information, spectral coherence and phase synchronization measures as the phase locking value.

13.2.4 Classification algorithms

A proper classification algorithm is vital for achieving acceptable identification performance. The efficiency of the classification algorithms employed for EEG biometrics authentication systems greatly depends on the specific distribution of vectors of each class in feature space. It is important to use or design a suitable classifier fitting the scattering distributions generated by different classes. Different machine learning algorithms present specific capabilities in approximating different boundary surfaces among the actual decision regions in the feature space.

NNs are the most commonly used classification algorithms, which are suitable for classifying samples that are not linearly separable. Several algorithms based on NNs have been proposed for EEG classification, with different network architectures, configurations and training functions. The architectures being studied include divergent autoencoder network [32] and feedforward perceptron [59], the training functions include scaled-conjugate training function [60], the back propagation algorithm [54] and the Kohonen's Liner Vector Quantizer [61], and a pairwise comparison NN approach was proposed in [59]. Another direction of NNs is deep learning, which has achieved extensive attention since its emergence in machine learning community in 2006. Deep belief network were trained with differential entropy features extracted from multichannel EEG data in [9]. Deep recurrent-convolutional NNs were proposed in [62] for learning representations from the spectral topography maps of EEG time series. Convolutional NNs were proposed in [63] to detect the P300 from single-trial raw EEG data for BCI systems.

Cross-correlation is also widely used in EEG biometrics identification systems, especially for ERP biometrics [33] and calculating matching scores, which is the similarity between a reference template and a challenge sample [52]. The k-nearest neighbour classifiers were employed in [54,64] based on different distance measure techniques. Discriminant analysis (DA) based on different linear and non-linear discriminant functions was used for EEG biometrics user recognition in [42]. In [65], support vector machine with a linear kernel was applied to identify subjects with EEG features extracted from AR scholastic modelling. In [53], maximum a posteriori training was employed to adapt a generic model to a client-dependent model. In [56], the Manhattan distances between feature vectors from training and from validation datasets were computed, in order to implement a two-stage biometric authentication method. Polynomial regression was employed in [43,57] with different expansion degree values. A linear classifier, aiming at minimizing the mean square error was applied in [44]. A naive Bayes approach was adopted in [58] to model the calculated feature vectors using probability theory by assuming Gaussian distribution and statistical independence of elements from the generated feature vector.

13.3 EEG biometrics for continuous authentication

Conventional authentication systems do not require users to re-authenticate themselves for continuous access to the protected resources. In such systems, the protected resources are instantly made available to the users until the end of their access. This one-time authentication strategy may be appropriate for conventional applications where the security requirement is low, but can lead to breach problems in which the intruder targets a post-authenticated session. This type of authentication is insufficient for high-security environments as in the case of most trusted autonomous systems, where the access needs to be continuously monitored. In order to reduce the window of vulnerability, continuous authentication is needed. In continuous authentication, user verification is repeated in a loop throughout the active session to continuously monitor the presence and identity of the user, instead of merely authenticating once at the initial log-in stage or a few discrete times during a session.

EEG, as natural continuous data source, is a potential solution for continuous authentication, especially in the cognation-related autonomous systems, where EEG is usually collected as an assistant measure. Such systems all characterize the interaction among intelligent artificial entities and humans where safe and effective communication plays a significant role in the interaction. Continuous authentication of the human's identity is a necessary endeavour, which lays the foundations for safe and effective human–machine interaction, and towards machine trust, a concept proposed in [66].

13.3.1 Authentication systems

Authentication is the basic function of a security system to identify an individual and verify if the individual is who he/she claims to be. A reliable authentication

Table 13.1   Authentication methods

Categories	Something you have	Something you know	Something you are
Essences	Possessions	Knowledge	Uniqueness
Methods	Token	Passwords	Biometrics
Security defence	Closely held	Secretly kept	Forge-resistant
Examples	ID card	Login passwords	Fingerprint; signature
Advantages	Simple	Simple	High security; convenience
Disadvantages	Lost/stolen	Less secret with use; forgot/guessed	Device required

system requires high accuracy and stability, minimum risk of being faked or information disclosure, non-intrusive and having different credentials for different levels of security.

In general, the implementation methods of authentication can be classified into three categories, password based, token based and biometric based, as showed in Table 13.1. A password or token is something the individual knows or possesses and it can be vulnerable because it may be guessed, stolen or duplicated. In order to provide higher security, modern applications and systems usually require users to create longer and more complex passwords with combination of upper and lower case letter and numbers, which can easily be forgotten and causes extra inconvenience. Biometrics provide an effective way for realizing continuous authentication. It refers to automatic recognition of individuals through their unique physiological or behavioural attributes. Compared with knowledge or possession-based method like passwords and tokens, biometrics offer a more convenient and safer way by being as inherent factors of the individual [67]. Therefore, biometrics has become an important method for long in regard of computer and cyber security.

The process involved in using a biometric system is presented in Figure 13.9. In the enrolment stage, a biometric template is extracted and enrolled in the system after capturing and processing the chosen biometric, and then stored in a local repository or a central repository. Then in the verification stage, the chosen biometric is live-scanned again. The biometric template is extracted as in the first stage after processing the biometrics, and then being matched against stored templates to provide a matching score to application. At last, a secure audit trail is recorded with respect to system use. For continuous authentication systems, the above verification procedure should be repeated continuously without interrupting the user from normal operations.

13.3.2   Multi-modal biometrics

Robust authentication systems require multiple data resources, this is especially true regarding continuous authentication. A single biometric modality can be inadequate either because of noise in the recorded data or because of the absence of data during

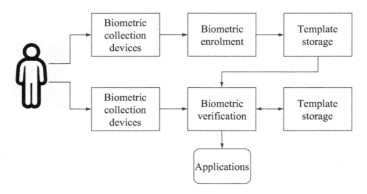

Figure 13.9   The process of biometric systems

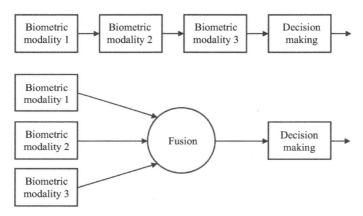

Figure 13.10   Illustration of the multi-modal system. Above: cascaded architecture; Below: parallel architecture

a time window. For example, it is unrealistic to assume that the user will speak non-stop to maintain voice-based signatures. Biometric systems based on single modality cannot guarantee extremely high accuracy all the time due to several factors, which are noisy data, intra-class variations, lack of distinctiveness and universality and spoof attacks. While multi-modal systems break the bottleneck by offering more robustness in terms of recognition accuracy as well as handling the poor quality of biometric samples. It has been demonstrated that multi-modal biometric systems are effective in increasing system's reliability and reducing vulnerability.

An illustration of the multi-modal systems is presented in Figure 13.10. For cascaded mode, the acquired multiple modalities are processed one after another. The output of one modality serves as an input to the processing of next modality. Within the frame of this scheme, the first modality is normally used as an index to narrow down the search space before the next modality is processed which in turn results in the reduction of recognition time. In comparison, parallel mode is more widely used, where multiple modalities are processed simultaneously and the obtained results are combined together to make a final decision. The output of the system will affirm the user identity continuously in real time by making decisions based on an integration of information from multiple biometric modalities. This has led to the investigation of different fusion strategies and the implementation of individual biometric modalities.

13.3.3 Fusion schemes

The multiple biometric observations acquired from different sources can be integrated at different levels. (1) **Sensor level:** the raw data from different sensors is integrated to form a new dataset which is used for feature extraction. (2) **Feature level:** the feature sets of different modalities are fused together to form a new feature set, provided that the feature sets must be independent and lie within the same measuring scale. (3) **Matching score level:** the feature vectors from different modalities are processed independently and matched with templates through different classifiers. The matching scores from individual modalities are then fused together to generate a composite matching score, based on which the decision module accepts or rejects the claimed identity. (4) **Decision level:** multiple matchers match the feature vectors with the templates and their decisions are fused together to reach the final decision by employing different techniques such as majority voting.

Information fusion at matching score level usually outperforms the others in terms of real time decisions and accuracy. Fusion at feature level provides good accuracy, however, requires complex classifiers and efficient dimension reduction techniques to reduce the computational overhead. Sensor level fusion reserves information from individual modalities but depends heavily on the operational conditions of the sensors. Fusion at decision level provides free selections of modalities, however, loses a lot of information and fails to meet the real time constraints. Fusion at matching score level is the most common approach due to its easy in accessing and consolidating the scores generated by individual identifiers. Consolidation of scores obtained from each biometric modality is usually divided into two methods. One method is to consider it as a classification problem where matching scores from individual modalities are put together to form a feature vector for a dual-class classifier: True (genuine user) or False (imposter). The other is combination method where scores from individual modalities are combined to generate a single score for the final decision. Since the matching score output by various modalities are heterogeneous, score normalization is needed to transform scores into a common domain before integrating them. The essence of classification method is to learn a decision boundary based on the matching score feature vector regardless of how the vector is generated, therefore the scores from different modalities can be heterogeneous and no pre-processing is needed for the feature vector before classification. While the combination method allows multiple options of combination schemes and rules.

A multi-modal system using face, ear and gait biometrics with fusion at matching score level is proposed in [68]. Multi-fusion structures are also being proposed to take advantages from both methods in recent research. The sum, product, minimum, median, maximum and majority vote rules are popular for fusion problems and combining classifiers in general pattern classification problems and have been extensively studied in the literature [69]. Three criteria for continuous verification based on multi-modal biometric is proposed in [70], which are (1) the different reliability of the different modalities must be accounted for, (2) older observations must be discounted to reflect the increasing uncertainty of continued presence of the legitimate user and (3) it must be possible to determine authentication certainty at any point in time. Regarding to the performance evaluation metrics, the authors argued that FAR and FRR are no longer adequate for continuous verification because time is not taken into account. By using a Hidden Markov Model in a Bayesian framework, they presented a holistic fusion method combining face and fingerprint across modalities and time simultaneously according to the criteria. Behavioural analysis-based biometrics, such as voice, keystroke dynamics, mouse movement and gait, present a good solution to continuous authentication. A survey on behavioural biometrics is made in [71,72]. Such systems offer better accuracy and show robustness against environment changes, sensor operating conditions and improper contact with the sensors. However, effective dimensionality reduction techniques over multi-modal biometric features is a problem need to solve.

13.3.4　EEG-based multi-modal continuous authentication

In [52], the authors proposed a multi-modal authentication system that continuously verifies the human user based on EEG and face images. The EEG modality is based on calculating cross-correlation of the elicited P300 potential, while the face modality is based on calculating the image distance of the dominant eigenfaces' coefficients. After score normalization, information is fused at matching score level by three fusion schemes (sum, max and min). Results showed that the fusion system with sum scheme outperform individual modalities, indicating that EEG biometrics can be integrated with other biometric modality and the integrated system can effectively reduce the system vulnerability and improve performance. This is the only work in current for combination of brainwaves with other biometrics. Research in this area needs to be continued.

Deep learning provides a promising solution for combing EEG with other biometrics in sensor level and feature level with its powerful learning capacity of extracting significant representations from the inputs. Multi-modal continuous authentication system based on deep learning is a potential research direction.

13.4　Research directions and challenges

In summary, there are huge research opportunities and challenges to be addressed to design a reliable, usable and secure EEG biometrics for user identification and continuous authentication. (1) A deeper understanding of the basic mechanisms underlying the psychophysiological process of brain signal generation and the acquisition protocols is needed in order to decide the frequency and region of interest as well as design proper protocols. (2) EEG signals detected on the scalp are very sensitive to endogenous and exogenous noise, therefore advanced artefacts removal techniques are needed. (3) The permanence and uniqueness of EEG biometrics need a further investigation. Unlike other biometrics, EEG biometrics are based on target brain responses elicited by specific protocols, ranging from resting states to cognitive states such as motion imagination and memory tasks. Therefore, permanence and uniqueness need to be analysed with respect to the protocol employed and also the extracted features. This procedure involves the elicitation protocols, the selection of recording sites and frequencies of interest, and the feature extraction methods. (4) There are many pieces of work on EEG biometrics under resting states, while the investigation on ongoing EEG during cognitive task is relatively scarce. (5) The major obstacle towards practical application of EEG biometrics is related to the inconvenient acquisition setup for users, consisting of a number of electrodes placed on the scalp and usually employed with conductive gel to reduce skin impedance. Therefore, minimizing the number of employed electrodes as well as applying consumer-grade dry sensors is an important issue to make EEG biometrics more user-friendly. (6) Public databases, collecting data from a large group of people using different acquisition protocols, are strongly needed. (7) Functional connectivity, which has been studied for decoding EEG in cognitive tasks, as well as deep learning algorithms, which are known for their powerful capacity in learning representations from input signals, are promising methods for EEG feature extraction and classification that should be considered for EEG biometrics.

References

[1] Penttilä M, Partanen JV, Soininen H, and Riekkinen P. Quantitative analysis of occipital EEG in different stages of Alzheimer's disease. Electroencephalography and Clinical Neurophysiology. 1985;60(1):1–6.

[2] Swann N, Poizner H, Houser M, *et al.* Deep brain stimulation of the subthalamic nucleus alters the cortical profile of response inhibition in the beta frequency band: a scalp EEG study in Parkinson's disease. Journal of Neuroscience. 2011;31(15):5721–5729.

[3] Adeli H, Ghosh-Dastidar S, and Dadmehr N. A wavelet-chaos methodology for analysis of EEGs and EEG subbands to detect seizure and epilepsy. IEEE Transactions on Biomedical Engineering. 2007;54(2):205–211.

[4] Curran EA, and Stokes MJ. Learning to control brain activity: a review of the production and control of EEG components for driving brain–computer interface (BCI) systems. Brain and Cognition. 2003;51(3):326–336.

[5] Ang KK, Chua KSG, Phua KS, *et al.* A randomized controlled trial of EEG-based motor imagery brain–computer interface robotic rehabilitation for stroke. Clinical EEG and Neuroscience. 2015;46(4):310–320.

[6] Dimitriadis SI, Sun Y, Kwok K, Laskaris NA, Thakor N, and Bezerianos A. Cognitive workload assessment based on the tensorial treatment of EEG estimates of cross-frequency phase interactions. Annals of Biomedical Engineering. 2015;43(4):977–989.

[7]   Wang S, Gwizdka J, and Chaovalitwongse WA. Using wireless EEG signals to assess memory workload in the n-back task. IEEE Transactions on Human-Machine Systems. 2016;46(3):424–435.

[8]   Trejo LJ, Kubitz K, Rosipal R, Kochavi RL, and Montgomery LD. EEG-based estimation and classification of mental fatigue. Psychology. 2015;6(05): 572.

[9]   Zheng WL, and Lu BL. Investigating critical frequency bands and channels for EEG-based emotion recognition with deep neural networks. IEEE Transactions on Autonomous Mental Development. 2015;7(3):162–175.

[10]   Kus R, Valbuena D, Zygierewicz J, Malechka T, Graeser A, and Durka P. Asynchronous BCI based on motor imagery with automated calibration and neurofeedback training. IEEE Transactions on Neural Systems and Rehabilitation Engineering. 2012;20(6):823–835.

[11]   Borghini G, Aricò P, Graziani I, *et al.* Quantitative assessment of the training improvement in a motor-cognitive task by using EEG, ECG and EOG signals. Brain topography. 2016;29(1):149–161.

[12]   Mugler EM, Ruf CA, Halder S, Bensch M, and Kubler A. Design and implementation of a P300-based brain–computer interface for controlling an internet browser. IEEE Transactions on Neural Systems and Rehabilitation Engineering. 2010;18(6):599–609.

[13]   Royer AS, Doud AJ, Rose ML, and He B. EEG control of a virtual helicopter in 3-dimensional space using intelligent control strategies. IEEE Transactions on Neural Systems and Rehabilitation Engineering. 2010;18(6):581–589.

[14]   Woolsey TA, Hanaway J, and Gado MH. The brain atlas: a visual guide to the human central nervous system. John Wiley and Sons; 2013.

[15]   Tadel F, Baillet S, Mosher JC, Pantazis D, and Leahy RM. Brainstorm: a user-friendly application for MEG/EEG analysis. Computational Intelligence and Neuroscience. 2011;2011:8.

[16]   Ribas GC. The cerebral sulci and gyri. Neurosurgical Focus. 2010;28(2):E2.

[17]   Seeman P. Brain dopamine receptors. Pharmacological Reviews. 1980;32(3): 229–313.

[18]   Miyake A, Friedman NP, Emerson MJ, Witzki AH, Howerter A, and Wager TD. The unity and diversity of executive functions and their contributions to complex "frontal lobe" tasks: a latent variable analysis. Cognitive Psychology. 2000;41(1):49–100.

[19]   Wagner AD, Shannon BJ, Kahn I, and Buckner RL. Parietal lobe contributions to episodic memory retrieval. Trends in Cognitive Sciences. 2005;9(9): 445–453.

[20]   Karnath HO, Ferber S, and Himmelbach M. Spatial awareness is a function of the temporal not the posterior parietal lobe. Nature. 2001;411(6840):950–953.

[21]   Zeki S, Watson J, Lueck C, Friston KJ, Kennard C, and Frackowiak R. A direct demonstration of functional specialization in human visual cortex. Journal of Neuroscience. 1991;11(3):641–649.

[22]   Posner MI, and Petersen SE. The attention system of the human brain. Annual Review of Neuroscience. 1990;13(1):25–42.

[23] Zatorre RJ. Pitch perception of complex tones and human temporal-lobe function. The Journal of the Acoustical Society of America. 1988;84(2):566–572.

[24] Corsi PM, and Michael P. Human memory and the medial temporal region of the brain. vol. 34. McGill University Montreal; 1972.

[25] Logothetis NK, Pauls J, Augath M, Trinath T, and Oeltermann A. Neurophysiological investigation of the basis of the fMRI signal. Nature. 2001;412(6843): 150–157.

[26] Wolpaw JR, Birbaumer N, Heetderks WJ, *et al.* Brain–computer interface technology: a review of the first international meeting. IEEE Transactions on Rehabilitation Engineering. 2000;8(2):164–173.

[27] Aurlien H, Gjerde I, Aarseth J, *et al.* EEG background activity described by a large computerized database. Clinical Neurophysiology. 2004;115(3): 665–673.

[28] Stassen H. Computerized recognition of persons by EEG spectral patterns. Electroencephalography and Clinical Neurophysiology. 1980;49(1):190–194.

[29] Näpflin M, Wildi M, and Sarnthein J. Test–retest reliability of resting EEG spectra validates a statistical signature of persons. Clinical Neurophysiology. 2007;118(11):2519–2524.

[30] Näpflin M, Wildi M, and Sarnthein J. Test–retest reliability of EEG spectra during a working memory task. Neuroimage. 2008;43(4):687–693.

[31] McEvoy L, Smith M, and Gevins A. Test–retest reliability of cognitive EEG. Clinical Neurophysiology. 2000;111(3):457–463.

[32] Armstrong BC, Ruiz-Blondet MV, Khalifian N, Kurtz KJ, Jin Z, and Laszlo S. Brainprint: assessing the uniqueness, collectability, and permanence of a novel method for ERP biometrics. Neurocomputing. 2015;166:59–67.

[33] Ruiz-Blondet MV, Jin Z, and Laszlo S. CEREBRE: a novel method for very high accuracy event-related potential biometric identification. IEEE Transactions on Information Forensics and Security. 2016;11(7):1618–1629.

[34] Zietsch BP, Hansen JL, Hansell NK, Geffen GM, Martin NG, and Wright MJ. Common and specific genetic influences on EEG power bands delta, theta, alpha, and beta. Biological Psychology. 2007;75(2):154–164.

[35] Wright MJ, Hansell NK, Geffen GM, Geffen LB, Smith GA, and Martin NG. Genetic influence on the variance in P3 amplitude and latency. Behavior Genetics. 2001;31(6):555–565.

[36] Koten JW, Wood G, Hagoort P, *et al.* Genetic contribution to variation in cognitive function: an fMRI study in twins. Science. 2009;323(5922): 1737–1740.

[37] Stenberg G. Personality and the EEG: arousal and emotional arousability. Personality and Individual Differences. 1992;13(10):1097–1113.

[38] Knyazev GG. Antero-posterior EEG spectral power gradient as a correlate of extraversion and behavioral inhibition. The Open Neuroimaging Journal. 2010;4(1):114–120.

[39] Alessandri G, Caprara GV, and De Pascalis V. Relations among EEG-alpha asymmetry and positivity personality trait. Brain and Cognition. 2015;97: 10–21.

[40]   Kanai R, and Rees G. The structural basis of inter-individual differences in human behaviour and cognition. Nature Reviews Neuroscience. 2011;12(4): 231–242.

[41]   Chuang J, Nguyen H, Wang C, and Johnson B. I think, therefore I am: usability and security of authentication using brainwaves. In: International Conference on Financial Cryptography and Data Security. Springer; 2013. p. 1–16.

[42]   Riera A, Soria-Frisch A, Caparrini M, Grau C, and Ruffini G. Unobtrusive biometric system based on electroencephalogram analysis. EURASIP Journal on Advances in Signal Processing. 2008;2008:18.

[43]   Campisi P, Scarano G, Babiloni F, *et al.* Brain waves based user recognition using the "eyes closed resting conditions" protocol. In: Information Forensics and Security (WIFS), 2011 IEEE International Workshop on. IEEE; 2011. p. 1–6.

[44]   La Rocca D, Campisi P, and Scarano G. On the repeatability of EEG features in a biometric recognition framework using a resting state protocol. In: BIOSIGNALS; 2013. p. 419–428.

[45]   La Rocca D, Campisi P, Vegso B, *et al.* Human brain distinctiveness based on EEG spectral coherence connectivity. IEEE Transactions on Biomedical Engineering. 2014;61(9):2406–2412.

[46]   Luck SJ, and Kappenman ES. The Oxford handbook of event-related potential components. Oxford University Press; 2011.

[47]   Bridge H, Clare S, Jenkinson M, Jezzard P, Parker AJ, and Matthews PM. Independent anatomical and functional measures of the V1/V2 boundary in human visual cortex. Journal of Vision. 2005;5(2):93–102.

[48]   Laszlo S, and Federmeier KD. Better the DVL you know: acronyms reveal the contribution of familiarity to single-word reading. Psychological Science. 2007;18(2):122–126.

[49]   O'Doherty JP, Buchanan TW, Seymour B, and Dolan RJ. Predictive neural coding of reward preference involves dissociable responses in human ventral midbrain and ventral striatum. Neuron. 2006;49(1):157–166.

[50]   Ishai A. Sex, beauty and the orbitofrontal cortex. International Journal of Psychophysiology. 2007;63(2):181–185.

[51]   Gupta CN, Palaniappan R, and Paramesran R. Exploiting the P300 paradigm for cognitive biometrics. International Journal of Cognitive Biometrics. 2012;1(1):26–38.

[52]   Wang M, Abbass HA, and Hu J. Continuous authentication using EEG and face images for trusted autonomous systems. In: Privacy, Security and Trust (PST), 2016 14th Annual Conference on. IEEE; 2016. p. 368–375.

[53]   Marcel S, and Millán JdR. Person authentication using brainwaves (EEG) and maximum a posteriori model adaptation. IEEE Transactions on Pattern Analysis and Machine Intelligence. 2007;29(4):743–748.

[54]   Palaniappan R, and Mandic DP. Biometrics from brain electrical activity: a machine learning approach. IEEE Transactions on Pattern Analysis and Machine Intelligence. 2007;29(4):738–742.

[55] O'donoghue T, Morris DW, Fahey C, *et al.* A NOS1 variant implicated in cognitive performance influences evoked neural responses during a high density EEG study of early visual perception. Human Brain Mapping. 2012;33(5): 1202–1211.

[56] Palaniappan R. Two-stage biometric authentication method using thought activity brain waves. International Journal of Neural Systems. 2008;18(01): 59–66.

[57] La Rocca D, Campisi P, and Scarano G. EEG biometrics for individual recognition in resting state with closed eyes. In: Biometrics Special Interest Group (BIOSIG), 2012 BIOSIG-Proceedings of the International Conference of the. IEEE; 2012. p. 1–12.

[58] He C, and Wang J. An independent component analysis (ICA) based approach for EEG person authentication. In: Bioinformatics and Biomedical Engineering, 2009. ICBBE 2009. 3rd International Conference on. IEEE; 2009. p. 1–4.

[59] Wang M, Abbass HA, Hu J, and Merrick K. Detecting rare visual and auditory events from EEG using pairwise-comparison neural networks. In: Advances in Brain Inspired Cognitive Systems: 8th International Conference, BICS 2016, Beijing, China, November 28–30, 2016, Proceedings 8. Springer; 2016. p. 90–101.

[60] Abdullah MK, Subari KS, Loong JLC, and Ahmad NN. Analysis of effective channel placement for an EEG-based biometric system. In: Biomedical Engineering and Sciences (IECBES), 2010 IEEE EMBS Conference on. IEEE; 2010. p. 303–306.

[61] Poulos M, Rangoussi M, and Alexandris N. Neural network based person identification using EEG features. In: Acoustics, Speech, and Signal Processing, 1999. Proceedings., 1999 IEEE International Conference on. vol. 2. IEEE; 1999. p. 1117–1120.

[62] Bashivan P, Rish I, Yeasin M, and Codella N. Learning representations from EEG with deep recurrent-convolutional neural networks. arXiv preprint arXiv:151106448. 2015.

[63] Cecotti H, and Graser A. Convolutional neural networks for P300 detection with application to brain–computer interfaces. IEEE Transactions on Pattern Analysis and Machine Intelligence. 2011;33(3):433–445.

[64] Su F, Zhou H, Feng Z, and Ma J. A biometric-based covert warning system using EEG. In: Biometrics (ICB), 2012 5th IAPR International Conference on. IEEE; 2012. p. 342–347.

[65] Brigham K, and Kumar BV. Subject identification from electroencephalogram (EEG) signals during imagined speech. In: Biometrics: Theory Applications and Systems (BTAS), 2010 Fourth IEEE International Conference on. IEEE; 2010. p. 1–8.

[66] Abbass HA, Petraki E, Merrick K, Harvey J, and Barlow M. Trusted autonomy and cognitive cyber symbiosis: open challenges. Cognitive Computation. 2016;8(3):385–408.

[67] Unar J, Seng WC, and Abbasi A. A review of biometric technology along with trends and prospects. Pattern Recognition. 2014;47(8):2673–2688.

[68] Yazdanpanah AP, Faez K, and Amirfattahi R. Multimodal biometric system using face, ear and gait biometrics. In: Information Sciences Signal Processing and their Applications (ISSPA), 2010 10th International Conference on. IEEE; 2010. p. 251–254.

[69] Kuncheva LI. A theoretical study on six classifier fusion strategies. IEEE Transactions on Pattern Analysis and Machine Intelligence. 2002;24(2): 281–286.

[70] Sim T, Zhang S, Janakiraman R, and Kumar S. Continuous verification using multimodal biometrics. IEEE Transactions on Pattern Analysis and Machine Intelligence. 2007;29(4):687–700.

[71] Bailey KO, Okolica JS, and Peterson GL. User identification and authentication using multi-modal behavioral biometrics. Computers and Security. 2014;43: 77–89.

[72] Pahuja G, and Nagabhushan T. Biometric authentication and identification through behavioral biometrics: a survey. In: Cognitive Computing and Information Processing (CCIP), 2015 International Conference on. IEEE; 2015. p. 1–7.

Chapter 14

Data security and privacy in the Internet-of-Things

Delphine Reinhardt[1,2] and Damien Sauveron[3]

According to current estimations, 200 billion devices will be connected until 2020 and will contribute to the realization of the vision of the *Internet-of-Things* (IoT) [1]. These devices can be, e.g., things, appliances, sensors, or actuators, referred to as *things* as illustrated in Figure 14.1. Examples of currently available devices include connected toothbrushes, fitness bracelets, and smart bulbs. However, the range of possibilities is almost infinite, and new connected devices are launched on a daily basis. Building on this first layer, the IoT architecture includes another layer called *communication technologies*, allowing these things to communicate and interact. They can be directly connected to the Internet or via a gateway, such as mobile phones or tablets, to enable new solutions for the third and last layer named *services and applications*.

The recent technological advancement in new *things* opens the doors to a myriad of novel applications, which can contribute to optimize resources as well as our life quality. For example, users' health can be better monitored using fitness bracelets or dedicated medical sensors connected to their personal devices. Load of an electricity grid can be better balanced by considering the electricity consumption of households reported by smart meters. Smart parking solutions can reduce the time required to find a free parking slot. Homes and offices can be equipped with, e.g., smart thermostats and bulbs allowing users to remotely monitor and control the heating and ambient light using their personal devices as depicted in Figure 14.2.

In this example of a connected home, each room is equipped with a connected temperature sensor, which can report the collected data to the smart air conditioning system. Based on the reported temperature in the rooms and the weather forecast fetched from the weather service in the cloud, the air conditioning system can automatically adapt to the current and future conditions based on machine-to-machine communication. User *A* can dim the smart light using his smartphone or tablet from any location in the house, before switching his smart TV on. The content of the film he wants to watch is retrieved from the streaming service located in the cloud. Similarly, when user *B* is away from home, she can remotely access the pictures taken by

[1]Institute of Computer Science 4, University of Bonn, Germany
[2]Privacy and Security in Ubiquitous Computing, Fraunhofer FKIE, Germany
[3]XLIM (UMR CNRS 7252/Université de Limoges), Faculté des Sciences et Techniques, France

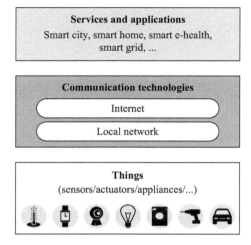

Figure 14.1   General IoT architecture

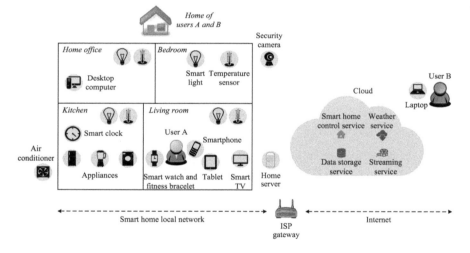

Figure 14.2   Example of IoT architecture: a smart home scenario

the connected security cameras through the smart home control service. She can also remotely switch on the lights using her laptop to give the impression that somebody is at home. As a result, the things can locally communicate with each other to report information about their conditions or execute different tasks within the *Smart Home Local Network*. Depending on the scenarios, additional services located in the cloud can be accessed through the *Internet Service Provider* (ISP) gateway. A home server can serve as an intermediary between the local network and the cloud if additional computational and storage capabilities are required to execute resource-intensive tasks efficiently.

Simultaneously to offer unprecedented opportunities for the society as a whole, the realization of the IoT vision also introduces potential risks that we highlight in Section 14.1. Section 14.2 gives an overview of the challenges of IoT followed by solutions proposed to address these risks in Section 14.3. We finally emphasize the importance of considering human factors in data security and privacy protection in Section 14.4.

14.1 Risks of IoT

In the absence of security and privacy-preserving mechanisms, the introduction of connected devices in our environment may represents a risk to the society. It may endanger both our security and privacy. In this context, security not only includes data security but also involves users' physical security and safety. Similarly, privacy not only is limited to the collection of personal data but may also extend to physical definitions of privacy. Note that the privacy risks may be either a direct consequence of the absence of appropriate protection mechanisms or the consequences of security threats. In the following sections, we detail selected examples of security and privacy threats encountered with current IoT products.

14.1.1 Examples of threats to security and privacy

In the past years, various attack scenarios highlighted the risks associated to the deployment of IoT devices. Within the scope of this section, we focus on four examples: (1) smart lighting systems, (2) smart TVs, (3) webcams, and (4) smart meters. These examples are, however, not exhaustive.

To attack smart light bulbs, multiple attack vectors have been exploited as detailed in [2]. For example, implementation weaknesses and a self-developed malware were leveraged to switch off Philips Hue lamps in [3]. The firmware of the LIFX bulbs was extracted and reverse-engineered to gain access to encrypted communication and reuse its content to take control over the bulbs as shown in [4]. Osram Lightify bulbs also open the doors to new attacks, as demonstrated in [5] that both Wi-Fi credentials can be accessed and communication between different devices is not sufficiently protected. The feasibility of attacks from far distance was also shown in [6], where a drone was used to take control over Philips Hue smart lamps located inside a building. The attackers could not only make these lights blink "SOS" in Morse, but also contaminate nearby lamps, which spread the attack across larger areas by replacing the firmware of these lamps on the fly.

As a result, different lighting systems have been shown to be vulnerable to attacks with different degrees of severity. Controlling a light bulb and switching it on and off may appear relatively harmless at first glance. However, it presents a danger to the society as it may lead to accidents, e.g., in households and offices, or blackout within entire areas as shown in [6]. Depending on the frequency at which the targeted bulbs are activated/deactivated, flickering effects may have direct consequences on users' health, including confusion, dizziness, nausea, or epileptic seizures. From a technical perspective, controlled light bulbs can be exploited for different purposes [7].

For example, they can be used as jammer to block Wi-Fi communication in their surroundings, as seeds for further attacks like botnets and worms, or even be fully controlled, i.e., no new firmware updates can be installed anymore [7]. Assuming a large scale attack, the stability of the electric grid can also be endangered when all bulbs would be simultaneously switched on and off. Moreover, smart lighting systems are foreseen to provide Internet access using the Li-Fi technology in a close future. Therefore, they must especially be secured to avoid potential new attacks.

The range of targeted devices is not limited to light bulbs, but also includes smarter devices like smart TVs. For example, it has been demonstrated in [8] that four different available smart TVs are vulnerable to attacks conducted under different settings. Even without specific knowledge about the devices' firmware, the authors were able to tamper them and open a remote connection to some of the tested devices. By extracting and analyzing the firmware, additional vulnerabilities have been explored, showing that smart TVs can be a target of more complex and potentially more dangerous attacks. As a result, smart TVs can be manipulated and data about the users can be gathered without their knowledge. By exploiting security vulnerabilities, personal information about the users can be collected, thus endangering their information privacy.

In the case of webcams and IP-cams, security vulnerabilities may directly endanger users' "physical" privacy, as attackers can access the collected video streams. For example, it has been shown in [9] that local and remote communications are unencrypted. The unencrypted storage of the data on the devices and a UART access allow local attackers to gain access to the collected video streams and manipulate the devices. Remote attackers can also easily access the associated accounts since these are often protected by weak passwords only. Additionally, they can also target the remote shell access. Consequently, both local and remote attackers can access and manipulate both collected data and devices. In case of an attack, this can mean that attackers can start, stop, and direct the controlled cameras to monitor the users and their environments as they wish, thereby putting users' privacy at stake.

Threats to users' privacy may not only result from security weaknesses, but also from the data collected by genuine devices and applications. For instance, connected fitness bracelets help users in monitoring and keeping track of their sports activities, but may also reveal insights about their lifestyle, their physical conditions, and the paths they follow during, e.g., their bicycling tours, including their home addresses. Similarly, smart lamps can reveal when users are home, when they wake up and go to bed, and in which room they currently are. When considering data collected by smart meters, it is possible to recognize the utilization pattern of household appliances based on their energy consumption. This means that the moment at which a device is switched on and off as well as its type can be recognized. Depending on the granularity at which the power traces are collected, it is even possible to recognize which film is currently running on a TV as shown in [10]. In usual household scenarios, multiple appliances may work simultaneously. As a result, their individual traces are aggregated and identification of each running device becomes more difficult. However, research efforts are currently made to be able to disaggregate the overall energy consumption, and hence recognize the individual contributing devices.

Things do not need to be complex and collect rich information about users, like the aforementioned examples, to put their privacy at stake. Indeed, binary sensors are sufficient to be able to identify which user is located in a particular room as demonstrated in [11].

As a result, deployment of things in users' environment provides information to the application developers and any parties having access to the collected data on their lifestyle. For example, the time at which users wake up, when they come home, when and where they drive their cars, and which devices they use and when. These inferences can in return be used to profile users and provide (or deny) them corresponding services and/or predict their behaviors.

In summary, with these different real-world examples we have highlighted that existing things may not be resistant to a variety of security attacks. In fact, they open the doors to further attacks on a wider scale. These security weaknesses may also endanger users' privacy by enabling unauthorized parties to get access to sensitive data about the users. Even without these security threats, things often monitor the users and their environment allowing the establishment of a fine-granular portrait of the users' habits. Consequently, things often present a risk for users' security and privacy. Interested readers may want to check the online search engine showing currently vulnerable things available in [12] to get an overview of the current state or check their own devices. Therefore, building secure and privacy-aware IoT products and applications is mandatory.

14.2 IoT challenges

As compared to previous computing systems, building secure and privacy-aware applications is especially made difficult by the following challenges.

14.2.1 Resource constraints

IoT devices are usually constrained in terms of computing and storage resources. Moreover, they are often running on a limited energy budget, e.g., powered by batteries. Their size is also often optimized to be better integrated in the users' environment, allowing a ubiquitous deployment.

14.2.2 Device heterogeneity

Usual IoT deployments are composed of heterogeneous devices in terms of resources and communication standards. Moreover, there is wide range of communication technologies used by different things of the IoT. Figure 14.3 presents a simplified view of the stack, which is restricted to more widely used wireless communication technologies. It can be noted that things can also be connected with wire via Ethernet or *Power-line communication* (PLC) technologies. From this perspective, data security and privacy must be addressed at each level of the communication stack as well as at both ends, i.e., at the thing side as well as at the service and application side.

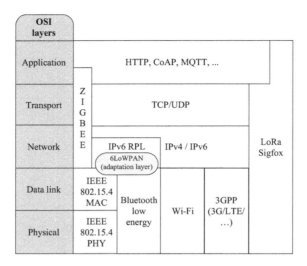

Figure 14.3   A simplified stack of protocols used in IoT communication

14.2.3   Mobility

The devices involved in IoT are often mobile and hence need to establish dynamic connections. This results in spontaneous and brief interactions. Consequently, well-established methods to protect both security and privacy are not applicable in this context. The multiplicity and interconnection of IoT devices thus build a surface for attacks, making them vulnerable both locally and remotely.

14.2.4   Heterogeneity of access levels

Some devices might require end-users to authenticate themselves to authorize some operations like setting up configuration or accessing data. Others might provide a partial or a full open access to any user. Essentially, this is an access to the collected data in the operational phase. However, it might also be an access for configuration purposes by only connecting to some insecure physical connectors or logical ports.

14.2.5   Remote features

For instance, remote update feature might be very useful to enable the devices to be updated when security issues have been detected and an update is provided by the manufacturer. Without such features, the security vulnerability will likely be present for the lifetime of the devices since most users are not security experts. However, this update process must be secure enough to prevent an attacker from updating devices with malicious code. Generally speaking, remote features, like access, should always be allowed only for the authentified users. Obviously, as any device connected to a network, especially Internet, things have to be secure for any communication technologies they use since data are exchanged in this way.

14.2.6 Deployment environment

Devices can be deployed in either adverse or friendly environments. For example, a smart meter installed in the home of a malicious user who wants to reduce his bill is considered to be deployed in an adverse environment. In contrast, a fridge located in a kitchen, whose user has no interest to attack it, is deployed in a friendly environment. Different threat models exist depending on the environments they are deployed in. For example, unattended devices are more likely to be physically attacked in adverse environments. On the other hand, devices deployed in friendly environments are more likely to be attacked through communication inputs. It must be noted that the classification of the devices' environments as *friendly* and *adverse* depends on the perspective adopted. For example, referring to Figure 14.2, an end-user would consider that his temperature sensors are deployed in a friendly environment, whereas his security cameras would be considered in an adverse environment. From the point of view of manufacturers of these devices who are willing to remotely update firmware (for security reasons or because there are new features to deploy) and who do not want to disclose the firmware binary, both devices operate in an adverse environment.

14.2.7 Transparent deployment and lack of interfaces

As highlighted in Section 14.1, users' privacy can be endangered by the data collected by the IoT devices under normal conditions as well as the result of conducted security attacks. In a genuine IoT deployment, users' privacy protection is already challenging as most of the devices are integrated in the users' environment, and may not be noticed. Users may therefore not be aware that data are collected about them when entering, e.g., a public space. Most of IoT devices do not have interfaces allowing users to consult the collected data. Moreover, the nature of these data, such as binary information or sensing readings, may seem harmless at first glance. The integration of IoT devices in the users' homes, however, blurs the boundary between online and physical privacy, while the boundary between privacy and public data tends to disappear when IoT devices are deployed in public spaces. This raises the yet unresolved question of data ownership.

In summary, the development of secure and privacy-preserving applications is made challenging by the resources constraints, heterogeneity of devices and access levels, mobility of devices, necessity to have remote features, transparent deployment, as well as the lack of interfaces.

14.3 Security and privacy solutions for IoT

Within the scope of this section, we provide an overview of solutions that have been developed to address the risks of IoT detailed in Section 14.1. To this end, we categorize them according to their positions in architecture presented in Figure 14.1.

14.3.1   Solutions for the IoT layer

As highlighted in Section 14.2.6, things can operate in adverse environments, i.e., not directly controllable and/or in the presence of potential attackers, depending on the adopted perspective. From the perspective of *end-users*, their concerns are often related to confidentiality, privacy, and integrity of the data [13]. A first method to address these issues and protect the data is to securely store them in order to prevent attackers from accessing them. However, a secure memory is often not enough to ensure a sufficient protection. Indeed, not only the stored data, but also the cryptographic keys used to cipher them have to be protected. Despite encrypting the data, unattended devices are susceptible to be attacked by local adversaries. These adversaries may try to access the JTAG port [14,15] or an unprotected UART port [16]. Moreover, physical attacks like side-channel attacks [17–21], fault injection [22–27], and probing and circuit modification [27,28] are shown to be possible. To protect the things against these attacks, a secure hardware execution environment for the sensitive operations can be introduced as proposed in [29].

From the perspective of *manufacturers*, a sufficient level of trust in the devices to be updated needs to be guaranteed to ensure that they are genuine and not rogue. Authentication partially contributes to the solution, but it does not provide any guarantees that the cryptographic materials required in the authentication have not been extracted from a genuine device to build a rogue one. It is especially true if symmetric cryptography is used with keys shared by several devices. With asymmetric cryptography, each device would have its own key pair, which might help to set up a blacklist in case the device is considered as likely to be compromised. However, even if solutions to set up and manage keys exist [30], maintaining such blacklists is not a simple task. Consequently, it might only be a partial solution if the notion of trust needs to be extended to additional users. For instance, the additional users can be end-users, who need to trust a remote device they do not own. For remote access to a thing, applying an authentication mechanism is often not sufficient and trust might be required through an attestation mechanism. Attestation is an interactive process between a prover and a verifier, through which the latter ascertains the current state and/or behavior of the former. Remote attestation mechanisms [31] can be software-or hardware-based or even hybrid. A survey of the attestation techniques dedicated to IoT is proposed in [32]. For instance, a secure and trusted channel protocol to establish a secure communication channel between sensing devices is proposed in [33]. The fact that each end is in a trusted state for the trust establishment is especially useful in sensitive context like when things are left unattended. In this case, the mutual remote attestation of the devices is performed in the *Trusted Execution Environment* embedded on the devices.

In order to automatically identify weaknesses and assess the security of IoT devices, the testbed presented in [34] using penetration-testing methodologies can be leveraged. Additionally, the authors of [35] propose a scanner called *IoTScanner*, which includes a range of radios to locally recognize the existing wireless infrastructure as well as participating devices. As a result, the surrounding devices can not only be identified but also be classified allowing the corresponding privacy threats to be inferred.

14.3.2 Solutions for the IoT communication layer

In addition to protect the things against local security threats, communication between the things within the local network as well as the Internet needs to be protected. As illustrated in Figure 14.3, wireless communication plays a key role in the IoT protocol stack, as they allow things to be easily deployed and support their mobility. However, there are often paths for adversaries to access data exchanged between things. In this case, access is to understand not only as read, but also as modify or block. Moreover, both attended and unattended things can be targeted by such attacks. Additionally, it potentially allows adversaries to remotely update the things' firmware or install a malware, if the things support such features [8,36] and in absence of authentication mechanisms. Note that we introduce suitable IoT authentication solutions in Section 14.3.3.

14.3.2.1 Application layer

To ensure data protection at the application layer, some standard security solutions exist such as *Internet Protocol Security* (IPSec) and *Datagram Transport Layer Security* (DTLS). IPSec provides secure end-to-end communication among remote things in 6LoWPAN. It is based on the *Encapsulating Security Payload* [37] and the *Authentication Header* [38]. The former guarantees confidentiality, integrity, and data authentication, while the latter ensures the integrity of the entire IPv6 datagram, i.e., both the application data as payload and IPv6 headers. DTLS is used to provide an end-to-end security between two communicating things in *Constrained Application Protocol* [39].

14.3.2.2 Data link layer

At the link layer, each technology applies different built-in security mechanism standards:

Bluetooth Low Energy (BLE) standard
The *Cipher Block Chaining-Message Authentication Code* (CCM) algorithm and a 128-bit AES block cipher provide encryption and authentication.

IEEE 802.11 standard (Wi-Fi)
WPA2 ensures authentication and encryption using the *Counter Mode Cipher Block Chaining Message Authentication Code Protocol* (CCMP) [40].

IEEE 802.15.4 standard
A 128-bit AES block cipher is used to cipher the payload and to compute the *Message Authentication Code* (MAC) appended to the message, ensuring the integrity of the MAC header and the attached payload data. Additionally, there is an *Access Control List* (ACL) to maintain a list of valid nodes.

LoRa standard
The payload data are encrypted using AES128 in *Counter Mode* (CTR). Messages are signed by a 4-byte *Message Integrity Code* (MIC) taken from an AES128 CMAC computation [41].

14.3.2.3 Network layer

As compared to both application and data link layers, there are no dedicated security standards that can be applied at network layer for routing operations. However, its protection is necessary, as multiple routing attacks can be launched including wormhole, blackhole, sinkhole, selective forwarding, and hello flooding. The scope of these attacks has been extensively studied in [42–48]. Secure routing protocols and *Intrusion Detection Systems* (IDSs) can be leveraged to secure this layer.

Secure routing protocols
Numerous secure routing protocols have been proposed in the context of IoT [42]. For example, a *Secure Multi-hop Routing Protocol* (SMRP) is introduced in [49]. In this scheme, the security is guaranteed by a preauthentication of the things at the time of creation of the network and before joining it. The authentication is based on a list of authorized things identified by their network and data-link addresses and multilayer parameters including *User-Controllable Identification* [50].

An alternative to SMRP is proposed in [51]. Instead of relying on preauthentication, this scheme relies on the establishment of a unique key for all the things belonging to the same path. As a result, it provides a secure end-to-end routing based on an authentication scheme with a complexity of $\mathcal{O}(n)$ which is computationally efficient since the protocol is polynomial-based.

Beside, *SecTrust* proposed in [52] is a lightweight secure trust–based routing framework for sensor nodes in IoT. It builds upon an estimation of the trustworthiness of the neighboring things. Their trust level is estimated based on, e.g., past interactions and observed behavior. By doing so, untrusted things can be identified and isolated to prevent common routing attacks.

Intrusion detection systems
The application of the aforementioned secure routing protocols can prevent attackers from launching successful routing attacks. They can further be complemented by *IDSs*, which aim at detecting both malicious behaviors and network disruptions by analyzing the activities in the network [53]. To discover these anomalies, the authors of [53] take into account particular features of IoT like IPv6 to protect the network against malicious activities.

Another IDS architecture based on Raspberry Pi platforms is proposed in [54]. This solution could be easily integrated into an IoT environment and would provide a system, which is portable, easy to configure and use.

As an alternative, the characteristics of wireless radio communications are leveraged in [55] to protect connected areas like smart homes and smart factories. Using neural networks, potential anomalies are detected based on variations of monitored wireless signals.

14.3.3 Solutions for IoT services and applications layer

After having highlighted different solutions dedicated to the protection of the things and communication layers in the IoT architecture introduced in Figure 14.1, we present solutions for the last architecture layer, namely the *services and applications* layer. At this layer, different security schemes need to be applied to provide authentication, confidentiality, integrity, privacy, and trust. Note that authentication plays an important role in this context, as most security mechanisms at this layer rely on it as premise to any additional security rules. In what follows, we present different mechanisms targeting these goals.

14.3.3.1 Authentication

Authentication is usually a building block to provide security and privacy-protecting solutions. Due to the resource constraints of the things detailed in Section 14.2, the proposed protocols for authentication and key establishment follow the same goal and aim to be especially lightweight. Different strategies can be adopted to reach this common goal as illustrated by the following solutions.

Lightweight authentication protocols based on elliptic curve cryptography
Traditional asymmetric cryptosystems like RSA are expensive to support and are energy-consuming. As a result, they cannot be directly integrated into the IoT. As an alternative, ongoing researches often promote solutions based on *Elliptic Curve Cryptography* (ECC). Depending on the nature of the devices to authenticate, different schemes can be used.

For *thing-to-thing* authentication, an *efficient Certificateless Signcryption Tag Key Encapsulation Mechanism* (eCLSC-TKEM) is proposed in [56]. It is initiated with elliptic curves to establish a shared key between a drone and a smart object. It especially minimizes the computational overhead incurred at the smart object.

For *thing-to-server* authentication, solutions dedicated to RFIDs and based on ECC are introduced in [57,58]. In [58] an *Elliptic Curve Diffie–Hellman* key agreement protocol is leveraged to generate a temporary shared key used to later encrypt transmitted messages. An ECC-based authentication protocol relying on more lightweight operations like XOR is presented in [57].

Proxy-based authentication protocols
An alternative to authenticate entities contributing to IoT using ECC is to use proxies for both thing-to-thing authentication [59] and thing-to-cloud authentication [60]. In a nutshell, resourceful devices, e.g., smartphones, laptops, and gateway routers, referred to as *proxies* support resource-constrained things in the process of authentication as depicted in Figure 14.4 [59,61]. By doing, no heavy asymmetric key cryptography is required at thing side and an authentication to things potentially belonging to a remote network is possible.

In detail, we assume two resource-constrained connected objects A and B, respectively, located in Networks 1 and 2 as illustrated in Figure 14.4. According to the scheme proposed in [59], A can use the proxies $P_{1,1}$, $P_{1,2}$, and $P_{1,3}$ to authenticate and establish keys with B. Simultaneously, B uses its own set of proxies, i.e., $P_{2,1}$, $P_{2,2}$, and $P_{2,3}$ located in its own network. As a result, the resource-intensive cryptographic operations are conducted by the proxies on behalf of A and B. The communication between the proxies is secured using well-established techniques, such as IPSec or *Transport Layer Security* (TLS). In contrast, the resource-constrained things, e.g., A

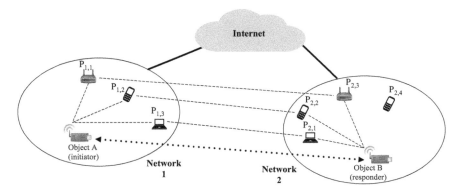

Figure 14.4   A thing-to-thing proxy-based authentication protocol

and *B*, have a list of neighboring proxies in their network and own the corresponding pre-shared key to authenticate and secure their communication. After having applied the protocol, the two resource-constrained devices *A* and *B* share a Diffie–Hellman key reconstructed through the Lagrange polynomial interpolation [62]. This key is only known to *A* and *B*, i.e., the proxies cannot collaborate to derive it.

A variation of the aforementioned protocol introduced in [59] is detailed in [61]. Instead of relying on a list of proxies known by the resource-constrained devices as in the former scheme, suitable proxies are selected based on their respective trust level estimated by a dedicated trust model.

Instead of authenticating two devices located in different networks, different IoT scenarios may require to authenticate a remote host located in the cloud to authenticate an object, e.g., object *C* in Figure 14.5. While the nature of the parties to authenticate is different, the same proxy-based principle can be applied as presented in [60]. Again, the protocol ends by the creation of a shared key between the remote host in the cloud and the thing. Consequently, this lightweight solution enables to safeguard sensitive data generated by the resource-constrained devices.

In addition, proxy-based authentication can also be applied between two devices having heterogeneous capabilities. As compared to previous proposal, it can be used when a highly resource-constrained thing wants to authenticate a more powerful server. In [63], an ephemeral pair of private and public keys is assigned by a *Trusted Third Party* to each proxy. Each proxy is then able to sign messages for the server on behalf of the resource-constrained device using the lightweight one-time signature scheme of Lamport [64]. To be protected against misbehaving proxies and/or against unreachable server issues due to unreliable communication between the server and the proxies, the authors rely on a Reed–Solomon code [65].

Proxy reencryption-based authentication protocols
Using these protocols, a thing can securely delegate its rights or digital signature to another thing with the help of a proxy. If proxy reencryption schemes based on asymmetric and/or symmetric ciphers have been explored in several contexts, the first

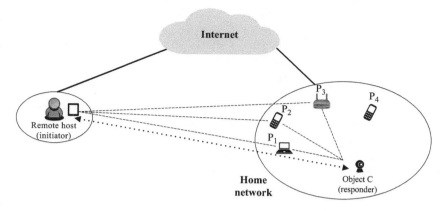

Figure 14.5 A cloud-to-thing proxy-based authentication protocol

work targeting highly resource-constrained devices in IoT is [66]. Its authors proposed an authenticated key agreement protocol based on lightweight proxy reencryption using a symmetric scheme to encrypt data. Unfortunately, this proposal was broken recently by the authors of [67], who discussed some possible alternatives to the original protocol.

14.3.3.2 Data access control

After authentication, access control solutions are usually applied to ensure both confidentiality and integrity in the concerned systems. In the context of IoT, access control can be bidirectional, i.e., things may need to access data stored on the cloud from anywhere at any anytime and vice versa. In both cases, access control mechanisms ensure that only authorized parties can access the given data, thus guaranteeing confidentiality and data privacy according to their owners' requirements. Moreover, only certain parties can be authorized to execute operations like computations or deletions on the accessed data, therefore catering for integrity. Assuming a medical scenario, the owner of a smart healthcare device may control the access to her collected data by retaining privacy sensitive data for herself, while allowing other information to be shared only with medical staff and the remaining might be publicly available. Like for authentication, the design of access control mechanisms should take into account the resource constraints imposed by the things.

Access control to data of things

In this first category, we focus on access control solutions for data collected and stored by the things. An operating system service called *Beetle* is introduced in [68]. It mediates access between things and applications using the *Generic Attribute Profile* of the application-level of the *Bluetooth Low Energy* (BLE) standard. Additionally, the things are virtualized at the application layer. By doing so, different programs can safely access the things' data independent of the underlying hardware functionalities. Moreover, a fine-grained and transparent access control to connected things is supported. With a demonstrator [69], the authors show how applications can get access to resources stored on things over *Local Area Network* with Beetle serving as intermediary and enforcing access control.

Apart from authorization systems enforcing access control, several solutions based on *Attribute-Based Encryption* (ABE) and tailored to the IoT constraints are proposed to control the data access based on different attributes. In this case, the value of the attributes determines whether an access to the data can be granted according to the associated access control policies. For example, a lightweight *Ciphertext-Policy ABE* (CP-ABE) solution is introduced in [70]. By leveraging pre-computation techniques, it efficiently grants access to data stored on things to users showing the required attributes. Furthermore, the authors propose an access control scheme based on *certificateless signcryption* in [71]. In addition to controlling access, it protects the privacy of the queries.

Data access control from things to cloud

The second category of access control solutions targets the access of data stored on the cloud by things. In this case, CP-ABE solutions are also proposed. For example, a *Lightweight Data Sharing Scheme* [72] ensures access control over ciphertext data stored on the cloud to things. To reduce the computation overhead, proxy servers are used to conduct the computationally intensive ABE decryption operations. Alter-natively, a solution based on both functional encryption and CP-ABE is proposed in [73]. A central server running a *Functional Virtual Machine* (FVM) can execute different functions on encrypted data coming from different sources. The FVM sup-ports fine-grained access control by providing ciphertexts, which could be accessible only by authorized users. This function might be useful for resource-constrained things willing to perform data processing operations.

14.3.3.3   Confidentiality

To ensure data confidentiality, a well-established solution is to encrypt data before transmission and storage. As explained in Section 14.3.2.2, each communication tech-nology has often already built-in mechanisms to secure communication. Additional symmetric encryption mechanisms are often chosen among the 13 lightweight block ciphers tested in [74]. It includes *AES, Fantomas, HIGHT, LBlock, LED, Piccolo, PRESENT, PRINCE, RC5, Robin, Simon, Speck,* and *TWINE*. The authors of [74] have designed a benchmarking framework allowing their evaluation with regards to different metrics and processors, while taking into account the specific constraints and requirements of the things. At the time of writing, none of the tested ciphers has won the competition though. It is however worth noting that symmetric cryptographic systems in IoT require to tackle the not so simple issue of key management.

Several ABE schemes presented for access control can also be adapted to achieve confidentiality. As an example, a lightweight no-pairing ABE scheme based on the *Elliptic Curve Decisional Diffie–Hellman* assumption instead of bilinear Diffie–Hellman assumption introduced in [75] can be used to secure transmission and storage as well as access control for things. The authors of [76] demonstrate for the first time that *Identity-Based Encryption* (IBE) has become practical for things even pop-ulated with low-cost ARM Cortex-M microcontrollers or reconfigurable hardware components. The adopted IBE scheme is the one proposed in [77] and based on the *Ring Learning with Errors* problem.

In addition to the aforementioned schemes, post-quantum cryptographic schemes for IoT are also an alternative to ensure confidentiality. Interested readers can refer to [78] for more details.

14.3.3.4 Anonymity and privacy

Confidentiality is the basis for privacy protection. By ensuring confidentiality, only given parties should get access to the collected or exchanged data. In this case, security mechanisms also contribute to both confidentiality and privacy by, e.g., securing the storage of data on things. However, privacy goes beyond confidentiality, as honest-but-curious authorized parties may still be interested in inferring insights about IoT users based on the collected data and interactions between the things. This is especially the case of IoT products and application providers, who may be interested in profiling their users to send them targeted advertisement based on the users' observed behaviors. Like security, privacy may play a role in users' decision to adopt or not a product or an application as shown by the abandon of the Google Glass project [79]. Within IoT, the threats to privacy are multiple. The data collected by things can be analyzed in isolation or combination within an application or even merge between applications provided by the same company. In this section, we first consider methods applied to protect users' privacy when considering honest-but-curious service providers centrally having access to the data collected by their users. We then consider distributed scenarios, in which multiple devices contribute data, before considering user-centered privacy protection.

Identity, location, and behavior

Assuming an IoT scenario, three key information can be inferred about the users, namely their identity, location, and current behavior. The granularity of the different information may however vary with the leveraged sensor modalities, their combination, and their own collection of granularity degrees. For example, the location of an user can be determined at room-level in a smart home scenario, while it may be determined at building-level in a smart city scenario. Inferring users' current location can also provide additional information about their identity and behavior.

In order to protect users' location privacy, different schemes have been proposed for location-based services and mobile crowdsensing systems, which are foreseen to contribute to the realization of IoT. For example, mobile crowdsensing leverages the users' personal devices, such as mobile phones and tablets, to collect sensor readings. Since most applications annotate the collected sensor readings with spatiotemporal information, the users' privacy can be endangered. As illustrated in [80,81], the proposed solutions can be first distinguished based on the key principles they rely on, i.e., *pseudonyms, k-anonymity, cryptography*, and/or *differential privacy*. A finer classification leads to the identification of the following categories: *anonymity, pseudonymity, spatial cloaking, data perturbation*, and *data aggregation*.

When the users' location is recorded by worn devices, the concepts of *mix networks* and *mix zones* can be applied to ensure *anonymity* by unlinking their identities from the reported locations. Alternatively, users can use *pseudonyms* to report their collected data or apply *spatial cloaking*, i.e., reporting their location with a coarser degree of granularity. Spatial cloaking can also be combined with *k-anonymity*, so that the resulting coarser location is shared with at least $k - 1$ other users. Using *data perturbation*, the individual sensor readings remain hidden, while the application can still compute statistical results over their complete set. Finally, the sensor readings from different users/sensors can be merged together to build aggregates and therefore become indistinguishable.

The underlying concepts applied in the case of location privacy can also be leveraged for different sensor modalities and data collected within IoT scenarios. For example, the concept of data aggregation can be used when *fog computing* is leveraged at the edge of the IoT network to provide more resources to the resource-constrained devices. In contrast to the case of mobile crowdsensing, the collected data are not directly processed by the applications, but are pushed to intermediaries for further processing. In this case, it is necessary to protect the data while still allowing certain operations. Among others, one solution proposed in [82] is called *Lightweight Privacy-Preserving Data Aggregation*. It combines cryptographic solutions, namely homomorphic Paillier encryption, the Chinese Remainder Theorem, and one-way hash chains, with differential privacy to provide a secure and privacy-preserving solution.

The concept of *spatial cloaking* can also be extended to different preprocessing steps to reduce the granularity of the collected data and/or remove particular elements of sensor streams. For example, the impact of different local preprocessing techniques on power data is investigated in [83,84]. The effects of temporal down-sampling, temporal averaging, noise addition, linear value quantization, and adaptive cluster-based quantization on the recognition of running appliances based on their energy consumption captured by smart metering data are measured and the trade-off between privacy protection and accurate and timely reporting is quantified. Besides, a solution called *RTFace* [85] blurs given faces from video streams, thus supporting selective privacy for video-based IoT.

Data and context privacy

In addition to threats coming from honest-but-curious and malicious applications, both things and external attackers may threaten users' privacy. As we have high-lighted in Section 14.1, things may be the target of security attacks and be controlled by attackers, thus becoming an internal threat. In contrast, external attackers may observe the interactions of things without being part of the network. Since wireless sensor networks are key components of the IoT, privacy-preserving solutions proposed in this area can also be applied in the context of IoT due to common topologies, communication technologies, and resource constraints. As a result, a distinction between solutions dedicated to *data privacy* and *context privacy* can be made as proposed in [86]. The former aims at providing protection against internal attackers, while the latter focuses on external ones.

One solution to ensure *data privacy* is to apply data aggregation between the things. In this case, the goal is not only to hide individual contributions to the central data collection point, but also to protect the collected data against honest-but-curious and malicious things with which data may need to be exchanged to, e.g., complete a common task or forward data to their destination. Note that the protection is also needed, when things are encrypting their communication using respective private keys. For example, a technique described in [86] and originally introduced in [87] is to slice the original data to be sent into pieces, mix these pieces between neighboring nodes, and aggregate them. By doing so, the degree of trust in neighboring devices is lowered as they get only partial data sets.

In contrast, the protection of *context privacy* is based on modifying the routing of messages between sensor nodes or things [86]. Such modifications prevent external attackers from inferring information based on the things' interaction patterns. Again, solutions originally designed for wireless sensor networks can be applied in the IoT. A tradeoff between privacy protection vs. additional resource-consumption and latency is necessary. Among the solutions studied in [86], different flooding schemes can be leveraged to hide the original paths followed by messages. Alternatively, dummy packets can be injected or fake data sources can be introduced to confuse external attackers.

In addition to protect the content of exchanged data and their routing, it can also be important to provide anonymity-preserving security schemes, so that things or users are not traceable. For example, existing RFID-based authentication schemes aim at preventing attackers from data stored on the tags using lightweight cryptography, but usually generate computation overheads and latency [88]. In addition to addressing these issues, a new RFID-based authentication architecture introduced in [88] ensures anonymity, untraceability, secure location, and forward secrecy. Hence, it not only supports functional requirements, but also protects anonymity and privacy during its execution.

User-centered privacy protection

As compared to other security goals, privacy and its protection are centered on the users. One reason behind this is that users have different privacy conceptions based on their age, gender, experience, or culture as shown in orthogonal areas. Multiple studies have been conducted to understand how potential users consider the risks associated to their privacy as well as the rewards associated to privacy losses. Most of these studies have been done for, e.g., coupons, mobile permissions, online social networks, or online shopping. Past studies, hence, mainly focus on the consequences of one device, service, or action on users' privacy. Due to the transparent integration of things into users' environments, the lack of interface, the collection of rich sensor data (see Section 14.2), and users' privacy conceptions need to be especially investigated in this context. Recent studies conducted in [89,90] follow this goal, but more research efforts are required to allow to refine the portrait of users' conceptions and understanding. For example, with respect to their privacy the reactions of 200 participants to 2,800 hypothetical IoT scenarios is analyzed in [89] and confirm that contextual parameters impact the users' acceptance of IoT data collection as shown in other areas. Similarly, a study involving 1,007 participants and 380 scenarios has been conducted in [90]. Each participant tested different scenarios, which differed in terms of, e.g., collected sensor modalities and collection purposes. Again, the results confirm that users' privacy preferences are context dependent. Based on users' answers, it is shown that private locations and collection of biometrics raise more privacy concerns than public locations and environmental data, respectively. Moreover, the participants seem to have consistent privacy preferences, as they could be predicted with a reasonable accuracy. The aforementioned studies are not only important to understand the privacy conceptions of potential users, but also to gain insights about their requirements in terms of privacy protection and hence contribute to provide usable solutions adapted to their needs as discussed in more detail in Section 14.4. For example, using the solution proposed in [91], users can control their privacy by defining privacy policies for each collected sensor data stream. The defined policies are then enforced by a so-called *privacy mediator* implemented at the edge of the network in the form of a cloudlet.

14.4   Human factors in IoT security and privacy

The aforementioned works aim at securing the IoT and protecting privacy by taking into account the existing resource constraints and the IoT characteristics. However, the proposed solutions should not only be usable from a technical perspective, but also take into consideration the human factors. This starts with *developers* of IoT solutions, who need to secure their applications and protect the privacy of their users under an increasing ready-to-market pressure, but may not have sufficient background knowledge in security and privacy [92]. This issue is not specific to IoT, but the devices' multiplicity, their heterogeneity, their interactions, and their mobility in IoT increase the resulting complexity for developers of IoT products and applications. In the absence of knowledge in this area, developers may search for security and privacy solutions available publicly in forums or repositories. By doing so, the same weaknesses can be introduced in many products and applications based on the same source. For example, a weak or hard-coded password in a source code may not be changed during the integration phase, thus easing its guess by attackers and opening the doors to other attacks. Additionally, weaknesses can be introduced not only by the choice of inappropriate solutions, but also by flawed implementations that can have severe consequences. Moreover, selecting each security and privacy solution individually increases the risk of introducing new threats, which can only be addressed by adopting a holistic perspective. While the same challenges already exist in orthogonal areas, the IoT and its characteristics introduce new threats, which have not been addressed yet, and sharpen the need for appropriate solutions. Providing developers with guidelines, tools and methods, as well as plug and play solutions can contribute in helping them making better design decisions and hence improve the security and privacy of their products and applications. This is not only for the sake of the underlying business, but also to be compliant with the *General Data Protection Regulation*, which will be enforced in 2018.

Helping developers is a first step to foster the development of secure and privacy-preserving applications. However, *end users* may also play a role in this ecosystem at different levels. End users can be involved in security-related mechanisms by, e.g., choosing passwords to control the access to the deployed devices and corresponding mobile apps, or updating IoT components to the latest version. However, security and privacy protection is not the primary task of end users in the IoT context. This means that they may not apply protecting mechanisms like downloading updates or apply them in a correct way, as their design has not been determined in an user-friendly way from the beginning. Like the developers, they are not experts and may not be aware of the following consequences, when using easy to remember passwords, e.g., 1234, for example. As a result, end users may believe to be protected, even if it is not or only partially the case. Nevertheless, the end users are not to be blamed, but the design of the underlying solutions. When only considering desktop- and mobile-based applications, users already show difficulties in creating and remembering strong passwords. Assuming that IoT devices also require a password-based authentication, it will not scale and thus may lower the overall protection level as weak passwords, and the same passwords will be used. It is therefore necessary to reduce the overheads for end users to allow a better security protection of IoT applications.

In recent years, research in usable security and privacy has mostly focused on domains based on one-device-to-one-user relationships. With the emergence of IoT, the equation becomes more complex. From these one-to-one relationships, we are moving not only from one-to-many devices, but also from one-to-many users, thus leading to *many-devices-to-many-users* relationships. Indeed, the IoT is composed on many things, which collect data about their surrounding environment and available users. Assuming a smart home scenario, each deployed thing, e.g., the smart light switches and the smart door locks, gathers information about the behavior of the house's habitants. By deploying sensors in smart offices and cities, the number of the monitored persons may be extended from few to millions. The collection of data by multiple things about multiple users can make it more difficult to infer individual behaviors but not impossible. In this more complex setting, users should, however, still be able to consent, understand, audit, and delete information collected about them. Solutions tailored to one-device-to-one-user relationships are still not yet optimal. Therefore, new concepts and paradigms taking into account the IoT challenges detailed in Section 14.2 are necessary to cater for privacy protection in IoT.

In summary, human factors should not be ignored in the design of security and privacy solutions. Otherwise, the overall security and privacy protection levels may be lowered. While it is an additional factor to include in the already complicated equation, it is a sine qua non condition to minimize the potential risks associated to IoT discussed in Section 14.1 and develop solutions accepted by potential users.

14.5 Summary

IoT is an example of the interplay of *security and privacy* and *society*. The concept of IoT opens doors to new applications, which can contribute to the citizens' security and safety. Simultaneously, it presents a risk for the society as a whole if no dedicated efficient solutions are proposed. In this chapter, we have highlighted the potential risks of IoT by addressing different threats to privacy and security incurred by currently available devices. Note that our selection is by no means exhaustive and additional risks may be brought to light in future. Providing security and privacy in this context is therefore mandatory, but is made difficult by different challenges, especially the resource constraints when working in the IoT context. We have classified and presented a selection of different solutions, which can be applied at different layers of the IoT architecture, namely things, communication, and services and application layers. For example, it includes methods proposed for, e.g., authentication, data access control, confidentiality, and anonymity and privacy. We have finally highlighted the importance of the human factors in IoT privacy and security, which should not be ignored in the design of future solutions to prevent voiding their effects due to their inappropriateness to be applied or used by people.

References

[1]   A Guide to the Internet of Things: How Billions of Online Objects Are Making the World Wiser. Online: https://www.intel.com/content/www/us/en/internet-of-things/infographics/guide-to-iot.html (accessed in 06.2017).

[2]   Morgner P, Mattejat S, and Benenson Z. All Your Bulbs Are Belong to Us: Investigating the Current State of Security in Connected Lighting Systems; 2016. Online: https://arxiv.org/pdf/1608.03732.pdf (accessed in 06.2017).

[3]   Dhanjani N. Hacking Lightbulbs: Security Evaluation of the Philips Hue Personal Wireless Lighting System; 2013. Online: http://www.dhanjani.com/blog/2013/08/hacking-lightbulbs.html (accessed in 06.2017).

[4]   Chapman A. Hacking into Internet Connected Light Bulbs; 2014. Online: https://www.contextis.com/resources/blog/hacking-internet-connected-light-bulbs/ (accessed in 06.2017).

[5]   R7-2016-10: Multiple Osram Sylvania Osram Lightify Vulnerabilities (CVE-2016-5051 through 5059); 2016. Online: https://community.rapid7.com/community/infosec/blog/2016/07/26/r7-2016-10-multiple-osram-sylvania-osram-lightify-vulnerabilities-cve-2016-5051-through-5059 (accessed in 06.2017).

[6]   Ronen E, O'Flynn C, Shamir A, and Weingarten AO. IoT Goes Nuclear: Creating a ZigBee Chain Reaction; 2016. Online: https://eprint.iacr.org/2016/1047.pdf (accessed in 06.2017).

[7]   Ronen E, O'Flynn C, Shamir A, and Weingarten AO. IoT Goes Nuclear: Creating a ZigBee Chain Reaction; 2016. Online: http://iotworm.eyalro.net (accessed in 06.2017).

[8]   Bachy Y, Basse F, Nicomette V, *et al.* 'Smart-TV Security Analysis: Practical Experiments'. *Proceedings of the 45th Annual IEEE/IFIP International Conference on Dependable Systems and Networks (DSN)*; 2015. pp. 497–504.

[9]   Stanislav M, and Beardsley T. Hacking IoT: A Case Study on Baby Monitor Exposures and Vulnerabilities; 2015. Online: https://www.rapid7.com/docs/Hacking-IoT-A-Case-Study-on-Baby-Monitor-Exposures-and-Vulnerabilities.pdf (accessed in 06.2017).

[10]   Greveler U, Glösekötterz P, Justusy B, and Loehr D. 'Multimedia Content Identification through Smart Meter Power Usage Profiles'. *Proceedings of the International Conference on Information and Knowledge Engineering (IKE)*; 2012. pp. 1–8.

[11]   Wilson D, and Atkeson C. 'Simultaneous Tracking and Activity Recognition (STAR) Using Many Anonymous, Binary Sensors'. *Proceedings of the 3rd International Conference on Pervasive Computing (Pervasive)*; 2005. pp. 62–79.

[12]   Shodan Is the World's First Search Engine for Internet-Connected Devices. Online: https://www.shodan.io/ (accessed in 08.2017).

[13]   Arias O, Wurm J, Hoang K, and Jin Y. 'Privacy and Security in Internet of Things and Wearable Devices'. *IEEE Transactions on Multi-Scale Computing Systems*. 2015;1(2):99–109.

[14]   Fabien M, Bossuet L, and Gonzalvo B. 'JTAG Combined Attack'. *Proceedings of the 8th IFIP International Conference on New Technologies, Mobility & Security (NTMS)*; 2016. pp. 1–5. Available from: https://hal.archives-ouvertes.fr/hal-01382957.

[15]   Tellez M, El-Tawab S, and Heydari MH. 'IoT Security Attacks Using Reverse Engineering Methods on WSN Applications'. *Proceedings of the IEEE 3rd World Forum on Internet of Things (WF-IoT)*; 2016. pp. 182–187.

[16]   Wurm J, Hoang K, Arias O, Sadeghi AR, and Jin Y. 'Security Analysis on Consumer and Industrial IoT Devices'. *Proceedings of the 21st IEEE Asia and South Pacific Design Automation Conference (ASP-DAC)*; 2016. pp. 519–524.

[17]   Aly H, and ElGayyar M. Attacking AES Using Bernstein's Attack on Modern Processors. Progress in Cryptology – AFRICACRYPT 2013. Vol. 7918 of Lecture Notes in Computer Science; 2013. pp. 127–139. Available from: http://dx.doi.org/10.1007/978-3-642-38553-7_7.

[18]   Bernstein DJ. Cache-Timing Attacks on AES. The University of Illinois at Chicago; 2005.

[19]   Coron JS, Kocher P, and Naccache D. Statistics and Secret Leakage. Financial Cryptography. Vol. 1962 of Lecture Notes in Computer Science; 2001. pp. 157–173. Available from: http://dx.doi.org/10.1007/3-540-45472-1_12.

[20]   Muir JA. *Techniques of Side Channel Cryptanalysis*. University of Waterloo, Ontario, Canada; 2001. Master's thesis, Master of Mathematics in Combinatorics and Optimization, University of Waterloo, Ontario, Canada.

[21]   Percival C. 'Cache Missing for Fun and Profit'. *Proceedings of BSDCan*; 2005. pp. 1–12.

[22]   Bar-El H, Choukri H, Naccache D, Tunstall M, and Whelan C. 'The Sorcerer's Apprentice Guide to Fault Attacks'. *Proceedings of the IEEE*. 2006;94(2):370–382.

[23]   Boneh D, DeMillo RA, and Lipton R. On the Importance of Checking Cryptographic Protocols for Faults. Advances in Cryptology—EUROCRYPT '97. Vol. 1233 of Lecture Notes in Computer Science; 1997. pp. 37–51. Available from: http://dx.doi.org/10.1007/3-540-69053-0_4.

[24]   Giraud C, and Thiebeauld H. A Survey on Fault Attacks. Smart Card Research and Advanced Applications VI. Vol. 153 of IFIP International Federation for Information Processing; 2004. pp. 159–176. Available from: http://dx.doi.org/10.1007/1-4020-8147-2_11.

[25]   Govindavajhala S, and Appel AW. 'Using Memory Errors to Attack a Virtual Machine'. *Proceedings of the IEEE Symposium on Security and Privacy (S&P)*; 2003. pp. 154–165.

[26]   Skorobogatov SP, and Anderson RJ. Optical Fault Induction Attacks. Cryptographic Hardware and Embedded Systems (CHES). Vol. 2523 of Lecture Notes in Computer Science; 2003. pp. 2–12. Available from: http://dx.doi.org/10.1007/3-540-36400-5_2.

[27]   Kömmerling O, and Kuhn MG. 'Design Principles for Tamper-Resistant Smartcard Processors'. *Proceedings of the USENIX Workshop on Smartcard Technology (WOST)*; 1999. pp. 9–20.

[28]   Skorobogatov S. Tamper Resistance and Hardware Security; 2014. Online: http://www.cl.cam.ac.uk/šps32/ PartII_030214.pdf (accessed in 08.2017).

[29]   Shepherd C, Arfaoui G, Gurulian I, *et al.* 'Secure and Trusted Execution: Past, Present, and Future – A Critical Review in the Context of the Internet of Things and Cyber-Physical Systems'. *EEE Trustcom/BigDataSE/ISPA*; 2016. pp. 168–177.

[30]   Garcia-Morchon O, Rietman R, Sharma S, Tolhuizen L, and Torre-Arce JL. 'A Comprehensive and Lightweight Security Architecture to Secure the IoT Throughout the Lifecycle of a Device Based on HIMMO'. *Proceedings of the 1st International Symposium on Algorithms and Experiments for Wireless Sensor Networks (ALGOSENSORS)*; 2015. pp. 112–128. Available from: http://dx.doi.org/10.1007/978-3-319-28472-9_9.

[31]   Steiner RV, and Lupu E. 'Attestation in Wireless Sensor Networks: A Survey'. *ACM Computing Surveys*. 2016;49(3):51:1–51:31. Available from: http://doi.acm.org/10.1145/2988546.

[32]   Abera T, Asokan N, Davi L, *et al.* 'Invited – Things, Trouble, Trust: On Building Trust in IoT Systems'. *Proceedings of the 53rd ACM Annual Design Automation Conference (DAC)*; 2016. pp. 121:1–121:6. Available from: http://doi.acm.org/10.1145/2897937.2905020.

[33]   Shepherd C, Akram RN, and Markantonakis K. 'Establishing Mutually Trusted Channels for Remote Sensing Devices with Trusted Execution Environments'. *Proceedings of the 12th International Conference on Availability, Reliability and Security (ARES)*; 2017.

[34]   Sachidananda V, Siboni S, Shabtai A, Toh J, Bhairav S, and Elovici Y. 'Let the Cat Out of the Bag: A Holistic Approach towards Security Analysis of the Internet of Things'. *Proceedings of the 3rd ACM International Workshop on IoT Privacy, Trust, and Security (IoTPTS)*; 2017. pp. 3–10. Available from: http://doi.acm.org.insis.bib.cnrs.fr/10.1145/3055245.3055251.

[35]   Siby S, Maiti RR, and Tippenhauer NO. 'IoTScanner: Detecting Privacy Threats in IoT Neighborhoods'. *Proceedings of the 3rd ACM International*

Workshop on IoT Privacy, Trust, and Security (IoTPTS); 2017. pp. 23–30. Available from: http://doi.acm.org/10.1145/3055245.3055253.

[36] Costin A, Zaddach J, Francillon A, and Balzarotti D. 'A Large-Scale Analysis of the Security of Embedded Firmwares'. *Proceedings of the 23rd USENIX Security Symposium (USENIX Security)*; 2014. pp. 95–110. Available from: https://www.usenix.org/conference/usenixsecurity14/technical-sessions/presentation/costin.

[37] Kent S. IP Encapsulating Security Payload (ESP); 2005. Online: https://tools.ietf.org/html/rfc4303 (accessed in 08.2017). Available from: http://www.ietf.org/rfc/rfc4303.txt.

[38] Kent S. IP Authentication Header; 2005. Online: http://www.ietf.org/rfc/rfc4302.txt (accessed in 08.2017).

[39] Shelby Z, Hartke K, and Bormann C. The Constrained Application Protocol (CoAP); 2014. Online: https://tools.ietf.org/html/rfc7252 (accessed in 08.2017).

[40] Jonsson J. 'On the Security of CTR + CBC-MAC'. *Proceedings of the 9th Annual International Workshop on Selected Areas in Cryptography (SAC)*; 2003. pp. 76–93.

[41] Miller R. LoRa Security, Building a Secure LoRa Solution; 2016. Online: https://labs.mwrinfosecurity.com/assets/BlogFiles/mwri-LoRa-security-guide-1.2-2016-03-22.pdf (accessed in 08.2017).

[42] Airehrour D, Gutierrez J, and Ray SK. 'Secure Routing for Internet of Things: A Survey'. *Journal of Network and Computer Applications*. 2016;66: 198–213. Available from: http://www.sciencedirect.com/science/article/pii/S1084804516300133.

[43] Baadache A, and Belmehdi A. 'Struggling against Simple and Cooperative Black Hole Attacks in Multi-Hop Wireless Ad Hoc Networks'. *Computer Networks*. 2014;73:173–184. Available from: http://www.sciencedirect.com/science/article/pii/S1389128614002801.

[44] Bonnefoi PF, Sauveron D, and Park JH. 'MANETS: An Exclusive Choice between Use and Security?' *Computing and Informatics*. 2008;27(5): 799–821.

[45] Di Pietro R, Guarino S, Verde NV, and Domingo-Ferrer J. 'Security in Wireless Ad-Hoc Networks—A Survey'. *Computer Communications*. 2014;51:1–20.

[46] Gagandeep G, and Aashima A. 'Study on Sinkhole Attacks in Wireless Ad Hoc Networks'. *International Journal on Computer Science and Engineering*. 2012;4(6):1078–1085.

[47] Islam N, and Shaikh ZA. Security Issues in Mobile Ad Hoc Network; 2013. pp. 49–80. Available from: https://doi.org/10.1007/978-3-642-36169-2_2.

[48] Wu B, Chen J, Wu J, and Cardei M. A Survey of Attacks and Countermeasures in Mobile Ad Hoc Networks; 2007. pp. 103–135. Available from: https://doi.org/10.1007/978-0-387-33112-6_5.

[49] Chze PLR, and Leong KS. 'A Secure Multi-Hop Routing for IoT Communication'. *Proceedings of the IEEE World Forum on Internet of Things (WF-IoT)*; 2014. pp. 428–432.

[50] Chze PLR, Yan WKW, and Leong KS. 'A User-Controllable Multi-Layer Secure Algorithm for MANET'. *Proceedings of the 8th International Wireless Communications and Mobile Computing Conference (IWCMC)*; 2012. pp. 1080–1084.

[51] Harn L, Hsu CF, Ruan O, and Zhang MY. 'Novel Design of Secure End-to-End Routing Protocol in Wireless Sensor Networks'. *IEEE Sensors Journal*. 2016;16(6):1779–1785.

[52] Airehrour D, Gutierrez J, and Ray SK. 'A Lightweight Trust Design for IoT Routing'. *Proceedings of the 14th IEEE Intl Conf on Dependable, Autonomic and Secure Computing, 14th Intl Conf on Pervasive Intelligence and Computing, 2nd Intl Conf on Big Data Intelligence and Computing and Cyber Science and Technology Congress (DASC/PiCom/DataCom/CyberSciTech)*; 2016. pp. 552–557.

[53] Wallgren L, Raza S, and Voigt T. 'Routing Attacks and Countermeasures in the RPL-Based Internet of Things'. *International Journal of Distributed Sensor Networks*. 2013;9(8):1–11. Available from: http://dx.doi.org/10.1155/2013/794326.

[54] Sforzin A, Mármol FG, Conti M, and Bohli JM. 'RPiDS: Raspberry Pi IDS – A Fruitful Intrusion Detection System for IoT'. *Proceedings of the IEEE Conferences on Ubiquitous Intelligence Computing, Advanced and Trusted Computing, Scalable Computing and Communications, Cloud and Big Data Computing, Internet of People, and Smart World Congress (UIC/ATC/ScalCom/CBDCom/IoP/SmartWorld)*; 2016. pp. 440–448.

[55] Roux J, Alata E, Auriol G, Nicomette V, and Kaâniche M. 'Toward an Intrusion Detection Approach for IoT Based on Radio Communications Profiling'. *Proceedings of 13th European Dependable Computing Conference (EDCC)*; 2017. pp. 1–4. Available from: https://hal.laas.fr/hal-01561710.

[56] Won J, Seo SH, and Bertino E. 'A Secure Communication Protocol for Drones and Smart Objects'. *Proceedings of the 10th ACM Symposium on Information, Computer and Communications Security (ASIACCS)*; 2015. pp. 249–260.

[57] Alamr AA, Kausar F, Kim J, and Seo C. 'A Secure ECC-based RFID Mutual Authentication Protocol for Internet of Things'. *The Journal of Supercomputing*; 2016. pp. 1–14. Available from: http://dx.doi.org/10.1007/s11227-016-1861-1.

[58] Jin C, Xu C, Zhang X, and Li F. 'A Secure ECC-Based RFID Mutual Authentication Protocol to Enhance Patient Medication Safety'. *Journal of Medical Systems*. 2015;40(1). Available from: http://dx.doi.org/10.1007/s10916-015-0362-8.

[59] Porambage P, Braeken A, Kumar P, Gurtov A, and Ylianttila M. 'Proxy-Based End-to-End Key Establishment Protocol for the Internet of Things'. *Proceedings of the IEEE International Conference on Communication Workshop (ICCW)*; 2015. pp. 2677–2682.

[60] Porambage P, Braeken A, Gurtov A, Ylianttila M, and Spinsante S. 'Secure End-to-End Communication for Constrained Devices in IoT-Enabled

Ambient Assisted Living Systems'. *Proceedings of the 2nd IEEE World Forum on Internet of Things (WF-IoT)*; 2015. pp. 711–714.

[61] Saied YB, Olivereau A, Zeghlache D, and Laurent M. 'Lightweight Collaborative Key Establishment Scheme for the Internet of Things'. *Computer Networks*. 2014;64:273–295. Available from: http://www.sciencedirect.com/science/article/pii/S1389128614000437.

[62] Shamir A. 'How to Share a Secret'. *Communications of the ACM*. 1979; 22(11): 612–613. Available from: http://doi.acm.org/10.1145/359168. 359176.

[63] Saied YB, Olivereau A, and Laurent M. 'A Distributed Approach for Secure M2M Communications'. *Proceedings of the 5th International Conference on New Technologies, Mobility and Security (NTMS)*; 2012. pp. 1–7.

[64] Lamport L. Constructing Digital Signatures from a One-Way Function. SRI International Computer Science Laboratory, Palo Alto; 1979.

[65] Sklar B. Reed–Solomon Codes; 2001. Online: http://www.facweb.iitkgp.ernet. in/~pallab/mob_com/art_sklar7_reed-solomon.pdf (accessed in 08.2017).

[66] Nguyen KT, Oualha N, and Laurent M. 'Authenticated Key Agreement Mediated by a Proxy Re-Encryptor for the Internet of Things'. *Askoxylakis I, Ioannidis S, Katsikas S, Meadows C, editors. Proceedings of the 21st European Symposium on Research in Computer Security (ESORICS)*; 2016. pp. 339–358. Available from: http://dx.doi.org/10.1007/978-3-319-45741-3_18.

[67] Nuñez D, Agudo I, and Lopez J. 'The Fallout of Key Compromise in a Proxy-Mediated Key Agreement Protocol'. *Livraga G, Zhu S, editors. Proceedings of the 31st Annual IFIP WG 11.3 Conference on Data and Applications Security and Privacy (DBSec)*; 2017. pp. 453–472. Available from: http://dx.doi.org/10.1007/978-3-319-61176-1_25.

[68] Levy AA, Hong J, Riliskis L, Levis P, and Winstein K. 'Beetle: Flexible Communication for Bluetooth Low Energy'. *Proceedings of the 14th ACM Annual International Conference on Mobile Systems, Applications, and Services (MobiSys)*; 2016. pp. 111–122.

[69] Hong J, Levy A, and Levis P. 'Demo: Building Comprehensible Access Control for the Internet of Things Using Beetle'. *Proceedings of the 14th Annual International Conference on Mobile Systems, Applications, and Services Companion (MobiSys)*; 2016. pp. 102. Available from: http://doi.acm.org/10.1145/2938559.2938578.

[70] Oualha N, and Nguyen KT. 'Lightweight Attribute-Based Encryption for the Internet of Things'. *Proceedings of the 25th International Conference on Computer Communication and Networks (ICCCN)*; 2016. pp. 1–6.

[71] Li F, Hong J, and Omala AA. 'Efficient Certificateless Access Control for Industrial Internet of Things'. *Future Generation Computer Systems*. 2017.

[72] Li R, Shen C, He H, Xu Z, and Xu CZ. 'A Lightweight Secure Data Sharing Scheme for Mobile Cloud Computing'. *IEEE Transactions on Cloud Computing*. 2017;PP(99):1.

[73] Sharma D, and Jinwala D. 'Functional Encryption in IoT E-Health Care System'. *Jajoda S, and Mazumdar C, editors. Proceedings of the 11th*

International Conference on Information Systems Security (ICISS); 2015. pp. 345–363. Available from: http://dx.doi.org/10.1007/978-3-319-26961-0_21.

[74]   Dinu D, Corre YL, Khovratovich D, Perrin L, Großschädl J, and Biryukov A. Triathlon of Lightweight Block Ciphers for the Internet of Things. IACR ePrint archive; 2015.

[75]   Yao X, Chen Z, and Tian Y. 'A Lightweight Attribute-Based Encryption Scheme for the Internet of Things'. *Future Generation Computer Systems*. 2015;49:104–112. Available from: http://www.sciencedirect.com/science/article/pii/S0167739X14002039.

[76]   Güneysu T, and Oder T. 'Towards Lightweight Identity-Based Encryption for the Post-Quantum-Secure Internet of Things'. *Proceedings of the 18th IEEE International Symposium on Quality Electronic Design (ISQED)*; 2017. pp. 319–324.

[77]   Ducas L, Lyubashevsky V, and Prest T. 'Efficient Identity-Based Encryption over NTRU Lattices'. *Proceedings of 20th International Conference on the Theory and Application of Cryptology and Information Security (ASIACRYPT)*; 2014. pp. 22–41. Available from: https://doi.org/10.1007/978-3-662-45608-8_2.

[78]   Cheng C, Lu R, Petzoldt A, and Takagi T. 'Securing the Internet of Things in a Quantum World'. *IEEE Communications Magazine*. 2017;55(2):116–120.

[79]   Turgut D, and Bölöni L. 'Value of Information and Cost of Privacy in the Internet of Things'. *IEEE Communications Magazine*. 2017;1:9–52.

[80]   Christin D. 'Privacy in Mobile Participatory Sensing: Current Trends and Future Challenges'. *Journal of Systems and Software (JSS)*. 2016;116:57–68.

[81]   Christin D, Reinhardt A, Kanhere SS, and Hollick M. 'A Survey on Privacy in Mobile Participatory Sensing Applications'. *Journal of Systems and Software (JSS)*. 2011;84(11):1928–1946.

[82]   Lu R, Heung K, Lashkari AH, and Ghorbani AA. 'A Lightweight Privacy-Preserving Data Aggregation Scheme for Fog Computing-Enhanced IoT'. *IEEE Access*. 2017;5:3302–3312.

[83]   Reinhardt A, Englert F, and Christin D. 'Enhancing User Privacy by Preprocessing Distributed Smart Meter Data'. *Proceedings of the 3rd IFIP Conference on Sustainable Internet and ICT for Sustainability (SustainIT)*; 2013. pp. 1–7.

[84]   Reinhardt A, Englert F, and Christin D. 'Averting the Privacy Risks of Smart Metering by Local Data Preprocessing'. *Pervasive and Mobile Computing (PMC)*. 2015;16(0):171–183.

[85]   Wang J, Amos B, Das A, Pillai P, Sadeh N, and Satyanarayanan M. 'A Scalable and Privacy-Aware IoT Service for Live Video Analytics'. *Proceedings of the 8th ACM Conference on Multimedia Systems (MMSys)*; 2017. pp. 38–49. Available from: http://doi.acm.org/10.1145/3083187.3083192.

[86]   Li N, Zhang N, Das SK, and Thuraisingham B. 'Privacy Preservation in Wireless Sensor Networks: A State-of-the-Art Survey'. *Ad Hoc Networks*. 2009;7(8):1501–1514. Available from: http://dx.doi.org/10.1016/j.adhoc.2009.04.009.

[87] He W, Liu X, Nguyen H, Nahrstedt K, and Abdelzaher T. 'PDA: Privacy-Preserving Data Aggregation in Wireless Sensor Networks'. *Proceedings of the 26th IEEE International Conference on Computer Communications (INFOCOM)*. IEEE; 2007. pp. 2045–2053.

[88] Gope P, Amin R, Islam SKH, Kumar N, and Bhalla VK. 'Lightweight and Privacy-Preserving RFID Authentication Scheme for Distributed IoT Infrastructure with Secure Localization Services for Smart City Environment'. *Future Generation Computer Systems*.

[89] Lee H, and Kobsa A. 'Understanding User Privacy in Internet of Things Environments'. *Proceedings of the 3rd IEEE World Forum on Internet of Things (WF-IoT)*; 2016. pp. 407–412.

[90] Naeini PE, Bhagavatula S, Habib H, *et al.* 'Privacy Expectations and Preferences in an IoT World'. *Proceedings of the 13th Symposium on Usable Privacy and Security (SOUPS)*; 2017. pp. 399–412. Available from: https://www.usenix.org/conference/soups2017/technical-sessions/presentation/naeini.

[91] Davies N, Taft N, Satyanarayanan M, Clinch S, and Amos B. 'Privacy Mediators: Helping IoT Cross the Chasm'. *Proceedings of the 17th International Workshop on Mobile Computing Systems and Applications (HotMobile)*; 2016. pp. 39–44. Available from: http://doi.acm.org/10.1145/2873587.2873600.

[92] Wurster G, and van Oorschot PC. 'The Developer Is the Enemy'. *Proceedings of the ACM New Security Paradigms Workshop (NSPW)*; 2008. pp. 89–97. Available from: http://doi.acm.org/10.1145/1595676.1595691.

Chapter 15

Information security algorithm on embedded hardware

Raul Sanchez-Reillo[1]

15.1 Introduction

Nowadays security is a parameter that shall be considered in any IT development. There are several reasons for it, ranging from the pure preservation of the Intellectual Property (IP) by avoiding reverse engineering by competitors to the protection of the privacy of the individuals related. Embedded hardware is not spared from this consideration, with the additional constraint of a potential limitation in the resources available to provide security.

Let us start by illustrating some of the most important requirements to be considered when designing and developing embedded hardware. As already mentioned, one of these requirements is to avoid reverse engineering. This covers not only protecting the source code of the solution, but also avoiding copies and discovery of its internal functionality and calculations. This is something that is directly in contradiction with the whole development process, where the developer shall be able to inspect all internal functionality. Therefore, the platform used for developing the embedded hardware shall be able to deny the access to internal resources once the development is finished. Again, this contradicts the possibility of requiring firmware updates or critical changes in configuration data.

From the hardware point of view, another potential item to protect is the possibility of some information leakage due to side channel signals, such as differences in power consumption or electromagnetic emissions. Protecting embedded hardware against these kinds of attacks is one of the most relevant fields of study nowadays.

Also, the information stored in the embedded hardware shall be protected. Access to such information should be controlled and, if personal data is included, also highly protected. This may need storing information in a ciphered way, as well as providing a set of access rules before allowing writing or reading such information.

But in most of the situations, an embedded hardware is of no use unless it is connected to the external world. In such cases connections shall be protected as to provide a reasonable level of security. In few words, the communication shall be designed in a way that the three major security requirements are fulfilled: confidentiality,

[1]Carlos III University of Madrid – Electronics Technology Department – University Group for Identification Technologies, Spain

authenticity of both ends, and integrity of the message. The first requirement is provided to avoid a potential attacker to discover the information exchanged by intercepting the data frame transmitted. The second, typically forgotten in many implementations, provides mechanisms so that the embedded hardware can trust the external world, and at the same time, the external world can check that the embedded hardware is also trustable. Last but not the least, third requirement shall be fulfilled to protect message transmitted from someone manipulating it to commit any kind of fraud (e.g., changing the amount of money to be debited from an account from 100 to 1000 USD).

This chapter will provide an overview to all these security requirements, applying them to different platforms used to implement embedded hardware. In order to provide a better understanding, Section 15.2 will cover a taxonomy of the technologies used to develop embedded systems. Then the security requirements and their mechanisms will be covered in Section 15.3 in order to provide the basis for the explanation of how to implement such security mechanisms discussed in Section 15.4, finishing with conclusion and future trends.

15.2   Classification of embedded systems

When studying embedded hardware, the first thing to consider is the wide variety of technologies that can be used for implementation. In a simple way, we can distinguish technologies such as developing your own integrated circuit, till using a general purpose programmable platform, such as a mobile device. As to illustrate the major differences and challenges, this section will cover the most significant cases in separate subsections.

15.2.1   Application specific integrated circuits

Developing embedded hardware as an Application Specific Integrated Circuit (ASIC) is one of the most costly alternatives both in money and development effort. On the other hand, it is the option where the designer has whole freedom in the implementation of all kinds of security mechanisms needed. This alternative is only recommended in those cases where performance has to be optimized as well as the number of units to be developed is high enough to justify the development cost.

These kinds of alternatives might be considered out of reach for most of the current applications as other technologies could offer a viable solution at much lower cost. But with a correct design of ASIC, power consumption could be masked, parallel activities can be executed in separate areas of the IC, as well as storage areas can be scrambled and spread across the IC surface, not allowing an attacker to be able to detect where a sensible piece of information can be located. Examples on the implementation of security modules using ASICs can be found in [1–3].

15.2.2   Field programmable gate arrays

If either development time or cost is not affordable to develop the embedded hardware as an ASIC, a close alternative can be found in Field Programmable Gate

Arrays (FPGAs). FPGAs are programmable ICs that can hold any digital electronics circuit, including microprocessor-based solutions. In fact, there are some commercial FPGAs that include built-in microprocessors [45], while others can implement microprocessors through programming of FPGA (i.e., using its generic logic cells).

This kind of device allows development using high-level description languages, such as VHSIC Hardware Description Language, which reduces the development cost of ASICs. Even though the development time could be high, it still allows the possibility of designing parallel computation, as well as an ad-hoc circuitry that will improve the performance. Also some masking mechanisms can be added in order to avoid information leakage, although their flexibility and performance may not reach the one in an ASIC development.

In addition, FPGA shall also provide the feature of being capable of locking any reprogramming, once the development has been finished. Security related to FPGA-based solutions has been deeply studied in the last decade, designing alternatives to overcome many security problems, as in [6], [7], or [8]

15.2.3 Microprocessor-based embedded systems

But the classical approach to build an embedded hardware is to use a general purpose microprocessor (or better to say a microcontroller) as the basis of the development. With current technology, as well as the huge variety of commercial products available, the designer can select low-cost, low-power microcontrollers with the combination of peripherals that better fit the final system requirements. Commercial products offer not only 8-bit (currently starting to be deprecated) but even 32-bit microprocessors, with internal units that can speed up many of the operations to be implemented. For example, ARM Cortex-M [9]-based microcontrollers [10] also contain multiplier and accumulation blocks that can ease the implementation of digital signal processing.

Also, the development of solutions based on last-generation microcontrollers can be done using high-level programming languages, such as C++. There are also high-end professional development environments capable of tracking variables and instruction results at execution time. These kinds of functionalities allow a very short time for development, as well as potentially a fully debugged solution.

The drawbacks of this solution appear with the limitation of the architecture to execute instructions sequentially, although by the use of interrupts and exceptions, a multiple thread implementation can be achieved. This may limit not only the performance achieved, but also the possibility of masking internal operations.

15.2.4 Single-board computers

The use of a microprocessor-based design may face another drawback. If the final solution is meant to be quite complex, having to handle many different devices, the programming may achieve a high level of complexity. Therefore, the larger the complexity, the higher the probability of including bugs in the development, and also leaving some security holes. In such a case it could be better to trust the low-level development to a platform with a reliable operating system, which handles that kind of services in a reliable way. If the low-level programming is already provided by the operating system, the developer shall only focus on the specifics of the application, easing the work and reducing the development time.

The perfect example of these kinds of solutions is the use of single-board computers (SBCs), which in other words is a PC running on operating system such as Windows or Linux. These SBCs are built in a single board of the size of a 3.5" drive (or even smaller) with most of the common connectors included (e.g. USB, VGA/HDMI, Ethernet, and WiFi) [11]. As they are regular computers, the development can be done using desktop computers and development platforms. Once developed, the solution can be downloaded into the SBC, which will behave the same way as it did at the desktop computer.

Unfortunately, by adding this new level of abstraction, we are also inheriting the potential security holes of both the platform and operating system. The possibility of masking internal operations may become less feasible than with a simple microprocessor-based design. Also, masking internal operations and data handling may not become possible as the designer loses most of the possibilities of performing a specific power and electromagnetic design.

15.2.5   General purpose mobile platforms

Following with the idea of implementing an embedded hardware using SBCS, a new alternative has appeared in the last years: the use of smartphones or tablets as the basis of the development. Smartphones, as well as any other kind of mobile devices, are currently very powerful pieces of hardware, containing not only a 32-bit (or even 64-bit) microprocessor, but also an operating system and a whole variety of peripherals embedded (e.g. touch screen as output and as input device, WiFi, Bluetooth, USB, 3G or even 4G, NFC, and smart card interface).

With this approach, development of an embedded system will be reduced to choosing the model (e.g., size and features), developing an app, and creating the appropriate casing for the target application. The drawbacks are the same ones of SBCs, with a probable additional inconvenience of the potential instability of the device and operating system, due to the extremely short time to market imposed by the mobile sector.

15.3   Security requirements and mechanisms

As stated in the introduction, independent of the technology used for developing the embedded hardware, it is necessary to include a set of security mechanisms to cover the requirements outlined earlier. This section will be based in explaining each requirement in detail and describing the most important mechanisms to fulfil them.

Many of these mechanisms are based on the use of cryptographic algorithms [12], based either on secret key (symmetric cryptography) or public key (asymmetric cryptography). For readability a very simple introduction will be given to both concepts.

Secret key cryptographic algorithms are those whose functionality is based on both ends of the communication sharing the same secret key, which is used to both cipher and decipher the message to exchange. The benefits of using this kind of cryptography are basically their simplicity and the low computational power needed, allowing processing close to real time. On the other hand, the inconveniences are derived from its lower robustness against attacks, as well as on the distribution and handling of those secret keys (i.e., each user has to use different keys for different receivers, and in all cases the user shall be able to provide the relevant key to the receiver). Typical examples of these kinds of algorithms are DES, 3-DES (also known as TDES or DES3), or the currently recommended AES, which could be implemented in different ways [13].

Public key cryptography is based on the idea of each user having only two related keys where the message ciphered with one of those keys can only be deciphered with the other key. Therefore, each user will keep one of those keys secret (named private key), while the other is publicly available (named public key, and which can be even posted in the yellow pages). With this mechanism, if user A wants to transmit a confidential message to user B, the message shall be ciphered with the public key of B. On the other hand, if user B needs to be sure that the message has been sent by user A, A should send the message ciphered with its own private key, so that the only way to decipher the message is by using the public key from A (i.e., everybody will know that the message has been sent by A). As it can be seen, public key cryptography intrinsically provides not only confidentiality but also authenticity of the sender of the communication. This is one of the benefits of this approach, in addition to the robustness against attacks and the trivial distribution of keys. Unfortunately, the computational power required by these algorithms is extremely high, not recommending its use with large messages. Typical examples of this kind of cryptography are RSA (the Rivest-Shamir-Adleman cryptosystem) and Elliptic Curve Cryptography (ECC).

Both approaches can be used nowadays, and there are even cryptographic schemes that use both of them, for example, ciphering a large message with AES using a randomly generated secret key, and then sending such key to the receiver by using RSA.

With these concepts known, the rest of this section will cover the security requirements and mechanisms. It will start by covering those mechanisms needed to ensure communication, to later handling storage and program integrity, and finally considering side channel attacks.

15.3.1 Information exchange

The basics of security in information exchange recommends that the following three services are guaranteed:

- Authenticity of both ends of the communication, so that each of the two actors can trust their counterparts, acknowledging that they belong to the same system.
- Confidentiality, so that only the receiver can understand the message sent.

- Integrity of the information exchanged, so that nobody can intercept the communication, change the message, and forward the modified message to the receiver, while receiver is not able to detect such a change.

The way these three requirements can be fulfilled in an embedded system is explained in the following subsections.

15.3.1.1   Authentication of both ends

Authentication of both ends of the communication can be achieved by using secret key cryptography. The process can be split into two different steps called *internal authentication* and *external authentication*, with possibility to merge both of them into one single transaction (typically known as *mutual authentication*). Internal authentication is the process with which the external world can check that the embedded hardware is trustworthy, while external authentication is the process by which the embedded hardware can acknowledge the trust of the external world. Figure 15.1 shows an example of how to implement both mechanisms, where "terminal" refers to the external device with which data is being exchanged.

As it can be seen, both mechanisms are identical except for which is the actor involved in generating the random number and taking the decision. The whole process is executed on both ends sharing the same secret key (K) and algorithm (which could be any of them, e.g., AES). The end taking the decision is the same one generating the random number (R). The implementation of a mutual authentication mechanism is based on both ends generating a random number (RA and RB), exchanging them, performing the same calculation at each end, and sharing the result. Then both ends can determine if their counterpart has obtained the same result. In order to avoid cryptanalysis, some implementations decide to exchange only some part of the results, being different from the part sent by the embedded hardware, than the one sent by the external world. For example, considering an 8-byte result, the embedded hardware sends only three least significant bytes, while the terminal sends only three most significant bytes, keeping two of the bytes out of any exchange.

Although this process achieves the authentication of both ends in the communication, it may suffer from a serious vulnerability: if K is the same for all devices deployed, then either the disclosure of K or its discovery through cryptanalysis will compromise the security of the whole system and the privacy of all users. Therefore it is necessary to have a different key for each deployed device. But it is not viable to have a random K for each one, as this will require keeping an accessible inventory of all the keys used, adding a new vulnerability to the system.

There is a simple way to overcome this limitation. All keys within an application can be different by deriving them from a common *seed* using a hashing algorithm and some unique identification for device (i.e., embedded hardware). This way K will be different for each one, minimizing the possibility of a cryptanalysis success, as it may not have enough data to obtain K from the results given by the device or the external world. This process is called *diversification*.

But going one step ahead, in order to further avoid the minimum possibility of having the diversified key of a single embedded device being discovered, it would be better to have a different key in each use of the system (i.e., in each session). This is

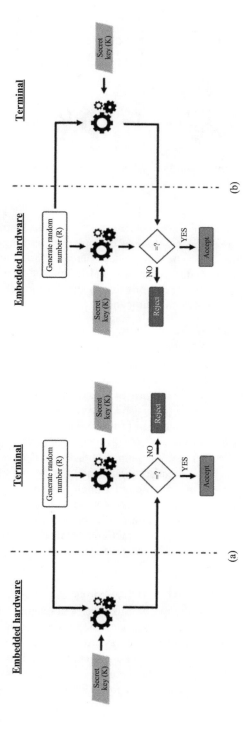

Figure 15.1 (a) Internal authentication; (b) external authentication

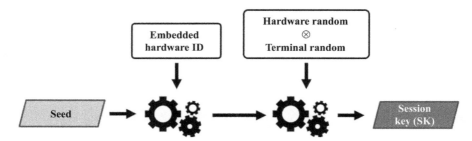

Figure 15.2   An implementation of the generation of a session key

typically known as using *session keys*, and the process to generate them is exemplified in Figure 15.2. The session key (SK) is obtained by applying a hashing algorithm (or a set of them) combining the seed, some unique identifier from the device, and random numbers generated by the embedded hardware and terminal. Once generated, SK will be used for all cryptographic operations during the session using the card, for example, for performing the mutual authentication.

15.3.1.2   Confidentiality of the message

The typical way of adding confidentiality to an information exchange is by ciphering the information using any kind of cryptographic algorithm. As long as the crypto-graphic algorithm is known by both parts of the communication, and the keys involved are also handled, this is preserved. In the case of a secret key approach, the algorithm can be publicly known, but the key is to be kept secret.

But with the considerations mentioned in the previous subsection, the use of a single static secret key is not recommendable. Brutal force attacks or cryptanalysis can be executed to obtain such a key, enabling an attacker to decipher all messages exchanged. Therefore, it is recommended to be done after having obtained an SK, and then using such SK for all ciphering within a single session.

As a consequence, the best practices recommend to create a *secure channel*, through which the exchange of information can be considered secure. One way of doing this is by following three basic steps in each communication session: (a) authen-ticating both ends of the communication; (b) generating an SK; and (c) ciphering the message exchanged using such SK.

15.3.1.3   Checking the integrity of the message

There are several ways to allow the receiver to check the integrity of the message. One of the simplest ways is to send, together with the message, a ciphered summary of the message being transmitted. In such a case, the message can even be trans-mitted unciphered, if only the integrity checking is demanded. This will reduce the computational cost, as ciphering will only be done with a summary of the message, instead of the whole message. Therefore, even public key cryptography could be used, if desired.

The importance is to know how to create such a summary. This should be done in a way that the following rules are preserved:

- The resulting summary shall be short and, if possible, of a predefined length (e.g. 64 bytes).
- The execution of the summary algorithm shall be fast, as the message to be processed may be huge.
- The modification of a single bit in the originating message shall result in a completely different summary.
- The process shall not be reversible, i.e., the originating message shall not be obtained from the summary.

These kinds of functions are provided by *hash algorithms*, and the well-known examples are MD5 (already deprecated) or SHA-3. Secret key cryptographic algorithms are also considered as hash algorithms, although their execution is slower than those of real hashing algorithms. Therefore sometimes the same secret key algorithm is used for hashing, but only if the size of the messages is within certain size limits.

15.3.1.4   Secure messaging

The most recommended option is to combine the above three mechanisms. This is already standardized in certain systems, such as smart cards (e.g. ISO/IEC 7816-4 [14]). In that case, just by using secret key cryptographic algorithm the three requirements are fulfilled. Figure 15.3 illustrates this process, called as secure messaging (SM).

As it can be seen, both the command and the data to be sent to the smart card (i.e., or any other embedded hardware) is processed with SK obtaining a hash result. Such result is appended to the data and ciphered using SK. Then, the message sent from the terminal to the card is the command plus the ciphered data, which contains also the result of the hash, which is the integrity check block. So the card can perform the reverse operation using SK, and finally obtain both the data and integrity check block. The card also calculates the integrity check block and if it matches the one in the message, the command will be executed. If SK is not the same as the one from the terminal, the integrity check block calculated by the card will not be the same as the one in the message, and therefore, the command won't be executed.

15.3.2   Storage security

Another important requirement is the protection of the information stored in the embedded hardware. Such information could be personal data, application data, and/or configuration data. It can even include cryptographic data such as the application seed. Therefore the protection shall be robust enough to avoid different kind of attacks.

Of course, from the software level, access to such information shall be controlled by a set of access conditions, including denying all kind of accesses, or establishing mechanisms for reading and/or writing (which can be different between them). A non-authorized access to that information is a very important security breach that qualifies the embedded hardware as a non-secured one.

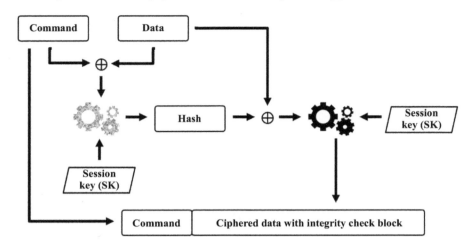

Figure 15.3   An implementation of secure messaging

The abovementioned access control methods can be implemented in many different ways, but most of the time they are implemented by presenting certain access codes (such as PINs or passwords) and perform certain security operations in a predetermined order. In case PINs or passwords are used, the system shall be able to control the amount of time each of them have been presented incorrectly. If a certain number of successive wrong presentations are reached, the access shall be blocked. This kind of mechanism is widely known as it is the one used by SIM cards in mobile devices, or by banking smart cards.

But even further protection shall be considered in order to avoid reverse engineering or even side-channel attacks. The latter will be further discussed at the end of this section, but the former can be avoided by using two main mechanisms.

The first one, available in most platforms, is to store all protected information ciphered with a device-dependent key. In such a case, if attacker is able to access the memory physically, such a key will be needed to understand the information stored. As the information will be protected only internally, there is no need to share that device-dependent key with anyone, so a significant level of assurance can be granted.

The second mechanism is based on storing the information (either in plain mode or ciphered) in pseudo-random memory addresses. In other words, instead of storing a certain piece of information in sequential memory cells, the device splits that information in pieces and stores each piece in a different location at the memory. Obviously this means to manipulate the addressing decoder, and this is typically only available in devices implemented using ASICs or FPGA, and only being emulated in microprocessor-based devices. In addition, in ASICs or FPGAs, the memory area can also be split into pieces and placed in different areas of the IC, making it more difficult for an attacker to be able to determine where the information is stored. This is definitely not possible in microprocessor-based approaches, as well as in SBCs or mobile platforms.

15.3.3   User- and service-related security

Two additional requirements shall be considered. The first one is who (or what) is allowed to use the embedded hardware. The second one is how to control the application integrity, particularly in those cases where firmware upgrades are allowed. The first of the requirements is similar to the access conditions defined earlier, but where users are the ones operating the device, also usability has to be considered. Users can be identified by the use of some knowledge (e.g., PIN or password), by the belonging of a certain token (e.g., a smart card), or by the recognition of a biometric characteristic (e.g., fingerprints). The particular application will provide further requirements as to be able to determine which is the most suitable way of granting access to the device, as it may be, or not, possible to ask the user to learn a complex and long character string to be used for identification.

Regarding the second requirement, some mechanisms shall be implemented to avoid hacking the whole system by overriding all its functionality. The first mechanism shall be a predefined security protocol as to be able to access the functionality of updating the current firmware or changing configuration settings. The second one is, once access has been granted, to first download the whole update, and then checking its authenticity and integrity before performing any update. A lack of integrity can lead to erroneous update and, therefore, to malfunction of the device. The lack of authentication may lead to the downloading of a Trojan Horse, which is able to inspect the operation and data of the device, with the intention of either performing a reverse engineering or commissioning any other kind of fraud.

15.3.4   Hardware vulnerabilities

Most of the requirements mentioned earlier can be covered in all development platforms with a relatively smaller amount of additional work. Unfortunately, even after following all these recommendations, further vulnerabilities can be present. The most significant examples of these vulnerabilities are the ones that we can call as hardware vulnerabilities, some of them being non-invasive, others partially invasive, while the rest being either invasive or even destructive. Let us illustrate some of them [15–17]:

- *Side channel attacks*: These kinds of attacks are non-invasive and try to obtain internal information by analysis of the behaviour of certain parameters of the embedded hardware. The most known are:
  - Timing attacks: The idea is to operate the device and calculate the time needed to obtain the result. By analysing different input data and timing obtained, some information (e.g., the keys used by a cryptographic algorithm) can be guessed.
  - Power analysis: In this case the idea is more or less the same one, but instead of analysing differences in execution time, the parameter to analyse is the power consumption. These kinds of attacks can be simple power analysis (SPA) or differential power analysis (DPA), DPA being much more powerful.

o   Electromagnetic analysis: Again, following the same ideas of SPA and DPA, the parameter to analyse is not the power consumption, but the electromagnetic signals originated by the currents flowing within the microelectronics of the embedded hardware.

- *Fault injection attacks*: The philosophy of these attacks is to provoke a certain hardware fault, which leads to a processing mistake that could provide valuable information to the attacker. Different mechanisms can be used to inject those faults, such as supplying noisy power, or noisy clock signal, excessive temperature, high-energy radiation, and laser injection. This kind of attack is typically considered as semi-invasive, as some tampering is performed with the device, but the device is still fully operative.
- *Physical tampering*: This includes removing all kinds of protective layers as to be able to access the internals of the IC. This is one of the kinds of attacks that was mentioned earlier, in the storage subsection. They typically require the use of very expensive equipment, including electronic microscopes.

Protection against these kinds of attacks requires a precise design of the hardware, addition of parallel processes that could mask the proper hardware operation [6], continuous control of any malfunctioning, and inclusion of collateral mechanisms that may detect some of the physical tampering attacks. Therefore a correct implementation to avoid these kinds of attacks is usually not affordable, except when using some predesigned *secure element* (SE) [18]. For example, some commercial microprocessors and microcontrollers are including a submodule internally that is considered to be an SE [1920]. Whenever possible, it is recommended that these kinds of SEs are used.

15.4   Implementation of security mechanisms in embedded systems

Once the main mechanisms and requirements have been described, it is time to consider how these can be implemented in embedded hardware. Starting from the simplest approach, we will consider how most of them could be implemented by programming, noting the limitations of such approach. After that, we may consider a more complex solution, such as developing them as a security coprocessor. Unfortunately, this approach may be too expensive in many practical applications, so an alternative will be described using commercially available components, such as smart cards.

15.4.1   Software-based implementations

Obviously, many of the security mechanisms described earlier can be implemented in software, and therefore available for all platforms. Information exchange, especially when using secret key cryptography, ciphering the information stored, establishing access control logic, introducing user authentication mechanisms, as well as integrity and authenticity in firmware updates are easily covered.

The problem arises in two main areas. The first one is related to hardware vulnerabilities, which in most cases cannot be solved only by programming, but will need ad-hoc hardware design. The second one is theoretically easy, but practically not found in many commercial products. The problem arises when an open general purpose platform is used. This kind of platform presents unintentionally many backdoors open. For example, a multiapplication platform may require that some applications share some data. Therefore a mechanism initially thought to provide further functionality and application cooperation can be exploited by a Trojan Horse to gather restricted information from other application or to, for example, impersonate the user in other applications.

Additionally, there is an indirect problem, which derives from the idea of implementing the security mechanisms every time a new product is being developed and/or probably by engineers that are not experts in security. This can lead to flaws in the design or implementation of some of the security mechanisms.

Finally, another drawback of a software-based solution is that the computational time is much higher than the hardware-based solutions. In the case of AES implementations, a software-based implementation may take 499 ms for a 16-byte payload, while the hardware-based can take only 052 ms [21]. For RSA it has also been shown that a hardware-based implementation can be 88 times faster than the software-based [22]. This is the price to pay for an easier and more flexible implementation.

15.4.2 The use of a security co-processor

Hardware vulnerabilities can be solved if all the security-related parts of the embedded hardware are implemented as a security co-processor, leaving the rest of the functionality to be done using a software-based platform. Unfortunately, the development of a security co-processor requires a high level of expertise as well as time and resources, so it is unaffordable in most of the embedded hardware deployments.

However, by using FPGAs some of the hardware-based implementation can be achieved following the work done by the scientific community. An optimized hardware implementation for AES can be found in [23]. A comparative analysis of different hardware implementation of AES can be observed in [24]. Even reconfigurable hardware has been used for implementing AES [25]. Reconfigurable hardware has also been used for ECC implementation [26]. Even to get the best of both worlds, hardware/software codesign has also been applied to ECC [27].

For the developer interested in implementing a hardware solution, the use of commercial IP cores is a possibility. For example, not only an AES implementation can be used [28], but also an RSA [29] or even combined with ECC [30]. Further protection should be placed to those IP cores, particularly those against hardware vulnerabilities.

A more recommended solution is to search in the market for already designed and developed security co-processors, or, as they are most known nowadays, as SE. In case these elements are available, most of the vulnerabilities could be resolved, as well as a major reduction in development time and cost can be achieved. However, using SE is not trivial, as its use by the final application shall be done properly.

Also, the application shall be developed in a way that it does not add any other vulnerability outside the use of the SE. For example, a point of service (i.e., a terminal that is designed to allow payments with credit cards) can be developed using all kinds of SEs, but it may happen that the casing of the terminal and its location may not allow the user to hide the typing of the PIN code, so any attacker can observe such PIN code, and impersonate the user in future payments. In that case, the embedded hardware has added a new vulnerability to the system. Similar to this example related to the user interaction, it can be extended to application development. In order to help the implementation of security in applications and embedded hardware, there is a new trend of trying to provide a trusted execution environment (TEE) [31]. The approaches and results are still not much stable, but most platforms are working on providing such functionality (e.g., Android OS [32]).

This approach being a solution that minimizes the development effort, it should consider some important questions when deciding the security provider. Is the co-processor designed and distributed from a reliable party? What will the SE or TEE do if an attack is detected? Can it be blocked? These are major questions that should be resolved before taking a decision. Nowadays, there are several microprocessor/microcontroller manufacturers that provide SE embedded in the IC. The only drawback of these solutions is the lack of possibility of changing the SE in case of an update or a vulnerability detected.

15.4.3   Smart cards and common criteria

Following the recommendations of the last subsection, the best approach to build a secure embedded hardware is to include an SE within the design and development. The important question is which SE to choose. Should it be an SE already included into my central processing unit or an external component? Should it be a removable component or a fixed one? These questions have are answered considering that detected attacks may completely block the embedded device. That will mean having to dispose the hardware and using a new one. If the SE is an external component that could be removed, then only the SE should be replaced, not the rest of the embedded hardware.

From the commercially available SEs, smart cards [33] show themselves as one of the best options. From the very beginning of their deployment (back in the 1980s), smart cards have been designed considering security as one of their major requirements. They have gradually included all kinds of security mechanisms: access control rules, protected execution operating system, secret key cryptography, SM, ciphered storage, public key cryptography, protection against side channel attacks, protection against fault injection, etc. From the software point of view smart cards operating system include, from the very beginning, the concept of a tamper-proof operating system [34].

Also, smart card industry is devoted to demonstrate the security of their products, in particular those considered of the best quality. In order to do so, smart card industry participates frequently in Common Criteria [35] evaluations. Their level of success is so high that in the list of common criteria certified products [36] the largest numbers are IC and smart card-related products (913 among the total of 2,029 certified products, in 2016). Also the level of assurance achieved by smart card products is extremely high, many of them are EAL5+, which means that they even go beyond the category of semi-formally designed and tested. Obviously an EAL5+ certification includes all tests and requirements defined for EAL1 till EAL5, and it has to be noted that the number of certified products with a higher EAL is extremely low.

15.5 Conclusion

Adding security to an embedded system is not a trivial task to perform. The possible mechanisms to be added, as well as the easiness in their development, depend on the technology used to build the embedded hardware. The most difficult mechanisms to be implemented are those dealing with hardware vulnerabilities. For most of the developments this can exceed both the available budget and time.

If the embedded system can be split into the security part and the rest of the application, the designer can count on using a commercial security co-processor such as a smart card, which has most of, if not all, those mechanisms embedded. However, using this kind of SE requires a certain level of knowledge and expertise as an inefficient use of them may lead to additional vulnerabilities that will destroy the initial benefits added. The industry is currently working on developing a reliable and accessible TEE that will ease all these tasks as well as the best way to use the functionalities offered.

References

[1] Chang-Soo Ha, Jong Hyoung Lee, Duck Soo Leem, Myoung-Soo Park, and Byeong-Yoon Choi. ASIC design of IPSec hardware accelerator for network security. In: Proceedings of 2004 IEEE Asia-Pacific Conference on Advanced System Integrated Circuits [Internet]. IEEE [cited 2017 Aug 6]. p. 168–71. Available from: http://ieeexplore.ieee.org/document/1349439/

[2] Rakers P, Connell L, Collins T, and Russell D. Secure contactless smart-card ASIC with DPA protection. IEEE J Solid-State Circuits [Internet]. 2001 Mar [cited 2017 Aug 6];36(3):559–65. Available from: http://ieeexplore.ieee.org/document/910496/

[3] Jin Park, Jeong-Tae Hwang, and Young-Chul Kim. FPGA and ASIC implementation of ECC processor for security on medical embedded system. In: Third International Conference on Information Technology and Applications (ICITA'05) [Internet]. IEEE [cited 2017 Aug 6]. p. 547–51. Available from: http://ieeexplore.ieee.org/document/1489020/

[4] Xilinx. All Programmable SoCs and MPSoCs [Internet] [cited 2017 Aug 6]. Available from: http://www.xilinx.com/products/silicon-devices/soc.html

[5] Altera. Stratix 10 – Overview [Internet] [cited 2017 Aug 6]. Available from: https://www.altera.com/products/fpga/stratix-series/stratix-10/overview.html

[6] Lumbiarres-Lopez R, Lopez-Garcia M, and Canto-Navarro E. Implementation on MicroBlaze of AES algorithm to reveal fake keys against side-channel

attacks. In: 2014 IEEE 23rd International Symposium on Industrial Electronics (ISIE) [Internet]. IEEE; 2014 [cited 2017 Aug 6]. p. 1882–7. Available from: http://ieeexplore.ieee.org/document/6864902/

[7]   Trimberger SM, and Moore JJ. FPGA security: motivations, features, and applications. Proc IEEE [Internet]. 2014 Aug [cited 2017 Aug 6];102(8):1248–65. Available from: http://ieeexplore.ieee.org/document/6849432/

[8]   Zhang J, and Qu G. A survey on security and trust of FPGA-based systems. In: 2014 International Conference on Field-Programmable Technology (FPT) [Internet]. IEEE; 2014 [cited 2017 Aug 6]. p. 147–52. Available from: http://ieeexplore.ieee.org/document/7082768/

[9]   ARM. Cortex-M Series processors [Internet] [cited 2017 Aug 6]. Available from: http://www.arm.com/products/processors/cortex-m

[10]   STMicroelectronics. STM32 ARM Cortex microcontrollers – 32-bit MCUs – STMicroelectronics [Internet] [cited 2017 Aug 6]. Available from: http://www.st.com/en/microcontrollers/stm32-32-bit-arm-cortex-mcus.html

[11]   Eetimes.com. Best single board computers 2016 [Internet] [cited 2016 Dec 4]. Available from: http://www.eetimes.com/document.asp?doc_id=1328716

[12]   Schneier B. Applied cryptography? Protocols, algorithms, and source code in C. John Wiley & Sons, Inc. New York, NY, USA, 1993.

[13]   Fathy A, Tarrad IF, Hamed HFA, and Awad AI. Advanced encryption standard algorithm: Issues and implementation aspects. In: Hassanien AE, Salem ABM, Ramadan R, Kim T. (eds) Advanced Machine Learning Technologies and Applications. AMLTA 2012. Communications in Computer and Information Science, vol 322. Springer, Berlin, Heidelberg. 2012. https://doi.org/10.1007/978-3-642-35326-0_51.

[14]   ISO/IEC 7816-4:2013 – Identification cards – integrated circuit cards – Part 4: Organization, security and commands for interchange [Internet]. 2013. Available from: https://www.iso.org/standard/54550.html

[15]   INFOSECInstitute. Hardware attacks, backdoors and electronic component qualification [Internet] [cited 2017 Aug 6]. Available from: http://resources.infosecinstitute.com/hardware-attacks-backdoors-and-electronic-component-qualification/

[16]   Berkes J. Hardware attacks on cryptographic devices implementation attacks on embedded systems and other portable hardware [cited 2017 Aug 6]; Available from: http://www.berkes.ca/archive/berkes_hardware_attacks.pdf

[17]   Tarnovsky C. DEF CON 20 - Attacking TPM Part 2 – Chris Tarnovsky – YouTube [Internet]. 2013-05-20. 2013 [cited 2017 Aug 6]. Available from: https://www.youtube.com/watch?v=h-hohCfo4LA

[18]   GlobalPlatform. GlobalPlatform made simple: Secure element [Internet] [cited 2017 Aug 6]. Available from: https://www.globalplatform.org/ mediaguideSE.asp

[19]   ARM. Security on Arm – TrustZone [Internet] [cited 2017 Aug 6]. Available from: https://www.arm.com/products/security-on-arm/trustzone

[20]   ARM. Processors SecurCore Series [Internet] [cited 2017 Aug 6]. Available from: http://www.arm.com/products/processors/securcore

[21]   Botta M, Simek M, and Mitton N. Comparison of hardware and software based encryption for secure communication in wireless sensor networks. 2013 [cited 2017 Aug 7]; Available from: https://hal.inria.fr/hal-00850899

[22]   Abdullah Said Alkalbani, Mantoro T, and Tap AOM. Comparison between RSA hardware and software implementation for WSNs security schemes. In: Proceeding of the 3rd International Conference on Information and Communication Technology for the Moslem World (ICT4M) 2010 [Internet]. IEEE; 2010 [cited 2017 Aug 7]. pp. E84–9. Available from: http://ieeexplore.ieee.org/document/5971920/

[23]   Abd Elfatah AF, Tarrad IF, Awad AI, and Hamed HFA. Optimized hardware implementation of the advanced encryption standard algorithm. In: 2013 8th International Conference on Computer Engineering & Systems (ICCES) [Internet]. IEEE; 2013 [cited 2017 Aug 7]. pp. 197–201. Available from: http://ieeexplore.ieee.org/document/6707202/

[24]   Farooq U, and Aslam MF. Comparative analysis of different AES implementation techniques for efficient resource usage and better performance of an FPGA. J King Saud Univ – Comput Inf Sci [Internet]. 2017 Jul [cited 2017 Aug 7]. 29(3):295–302. Available from: http://linkinghub.elsevier.com/retrieve/pii/S1319157816300143

[25]   Gaj K, and Chodowiec P. Comparison of the hardware performance of the AES candidates using reconfigurable hardware [cited 2017 Aug 7]. Available from: https://pdfs.semanticscholar.org/7503/97d262efd2195df929378006c4bb2de298e2.pdf

[26]   Lien E-J. Efficient implementation of elliptic curve cryptography in reconfigurable hardware. 2012 [cited 2017 Aug 7]; Available from: https://etd.ohiolink.edu/rws_etd/document/get/case1333761904/inline

[27]   Pontow L, and Paar C. Elliptic curve cryptography as a case study for hardware/software codesign. 2004 [cited 2017 Aug 7]. Available from: https://www.emsec.rub.de/media/crypto/attachments/files/2010/04/da_larspontow.pdf

[28]   IPcores. AES IP Core: ultra-compact advanced encryption standard (Rijndael) implementation [Internet] [cited 2017 Aug 8]. Available from: http://ipcores.com/aes_ip_core.htm

[29]   IPcores. RSA IP core [Internet] [cited 2017 Aug 7]. Available from: http://ipcores.com/rsa_ip_core.htm?gclid=CM3g_v_zxdUCFQEo0wod23cH9Q

[30]   IPcores. RSA/ECC IP core [Internet] [cited 2017 Aug 8]. Available from: http://ipcores.com/rsa5x_rsa_ecc_crypto_accelerator_ip_core.htm

[31]   GlobalPlatform. GlobalPlatform made simple guide: Trusted Execution Environment (TEE) guide [Internet] [cited 2017 Aug 6]. Available from: https://www.globalplatform.org/mediaguidetee.asp

[32]   Android.com. Trusty TEE [Internet] [cited 2017 Aug 6]. Available from: https://source.android.com/security/trusty/

[33]   Zoreda JL, and Otoìn JM. Smart cards. Artech House; 1994. p. 244.

[34]   Sanchez-Reillo R. Tamper-proof operating system. In: Encyclopedia of Biometrics [Internet]. Boston, MA: Springer US; 2014 [cited 2017 Aug 6]. pp. 1–8. Available from: http://link.springer.com/10.1007/978-3-642-27733-7_291-3

[35]   CommonCriteria. Common criteria [Internet] [cited 2017 Aug 6]. Available from: https://www.commoncriteriaportal.org/

[36]   CommonCriteria. Certified products [Internet] [cited 2017 Aug 6]. Available from: https://www.commoncriteriaportal.org/products/

Index